Thalia
Delighting in Song

ESSAYS ON ANCIENT GREEK POETRY

Emmet I. Robbins earned an international reputation as a scholar of ancient Greek poetry, possessing a broad cultural background and a command of many languages that allowed him to present sensitive and informed readings of poets from Homer to the tragedians. *Thalia Delighting in Song* assembles for the first time his work from 1975 through 1999, reflecting his close reading of the Greek texts and his firm grasp of their literary, historical, and mythological contexts.

Among the essays included in this volume are important reflections on the poetry of Homer, Alcman, Sappho, Pindar, and Aeschylus. Also featured are Robbins's writings that situate Greek texts in their wider contexts, comparing Greek poetry and modern opera for example, or assessing the enduring influence of myth in the Indo-European traditions, accounting for links between Greek literature and the poetry, sagas, and songs of several other cultures. *Thalia Delighting in Song* ensures that the next generation of classicists will continue to benefit from the insights of one of the foremost scholars in the field.

Emmet I. Robbins (1939–2011) was Chair of the Department of Classics at the University of Toronto.

Bonnie MacLachlan is an Associate Professor Emerita in the Department of Classical Studies at the University of Western Ontario.

PHOENIX

Journal of the Classical Association of Canada

Revue de la Société canadienne des études classiques

Supplementary Volume LIII

Tome supplémentaire LIII

EMMET I. ROBBINS
Thalia Delighting in Song

ESSAYS ON ANCIENT GREEK POETRY

UNA EST QUAE REPARET SEQUE IPSA RESEMINET ALES

edited by
BONNIE MACLACHLAN

UNIVERSITY OF TORONTO PRESS
Toronto   Buffalo   London

© University of Toronto Press 2013
Toronto   Buffalo   London
www.utppublishing.com

ISBN 978-1-4426-1343-0

Library and Archives Canada Cataloguing in Publication

Robbins, Emmet, 1939–2011
Thalia delighting in song : essays on ancient Greek poetry /
Emmet I. Robbins ; edited by Bonnie MacLachlan.

Includes bibliographical references and index.
ISBN 978-1-4426-1343-0

1. Greek poetry–History and criticism.   I. MacLachlan, Bonnie, 1944-   II. Title.

PA3092.R62 2013   881'.0109   C2013-901148-X

University of Toronto Press acknowledges the financial assistance to its publishing program of the Canada Council for the Arts and the Ontario Arts Council.

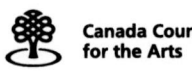

Canada Council   Conseil des Arts
for the Arts   du Canada

ONTARIO ARTS COUNCIL
CONSEIL DES ARTS DE L'ONTARIO
50 YEARS OF ONTARIO GOVERNMENT SUPPORT OF THE ARTS
50 ANS DE SOUTIEN DU GOUVERNEMENT DE L'ONTARIO AUX ARTS

University of Toronto Press acknowledges the financial support of the Government of Canada through the Canada Book Fund for its publishing activities.

For Jay Macpherson

1932–2012

Contents

FOREWORD	ix
PUBLICATIONS OF EMMET ROBBINS	xiii
PREFACE	xv
Public Poetry Alcman, Stesichorus, Simonides, Pindar, Bacchylides	1
The Education of Achilles	58
Achilles to Thetis: *Iliad* 1.365–412	72
Alcman's *Partheneion*: Legend and Choral Ceremony	88
'Every Time I Look at You ...': Sappho Thirty-One	101
Who's Dying in Sappho Fr. 94?	108
Sappho Fr. 94: A Further Note	119
Sappho, Aphrodite, and the Muses	121
Heracles, the Hyperboreans, and the Hind: Pindar, *Ol.* 3	145
Intimations of Immortality: Pindar, *Ol.* 3.34–5	157
The Broken Wall, The Burning Roof and Tower: Pindar, *Ol.* 8.31–46	167
The Gifts of the Gods: Pindar's Third *Pythian*	175
Jason and Cheiron: The Myth of Pindar's Fourth *Pythian*	192
Cyrene and Cheiron: The Myth of Pindar's Ninth *Pythian*	202

Pindar's *Oresteia* and the Tragedians 217

Nereids with Golden Distaffs: Pindar, *Nem.* 5 229

The Divine Twins in Early Greek Poetry 238

Famous Orpheus 254

To Be Redeemed from Fire by Fire: The Deaths of Heracles and Siegfried 275

BIBLIOGRAPHY 285

GENERAL INDEX 309

INDEX LOCORUM 318

Foreword

> *es zieht ein Mondenschatten*
> *als mein Gefährte mit*
> W. Müller

To perfect his bread he experimented for years with different recipes, at last arriving at an ideal wholegrain loaf that he baked every Saturday morning. To play Bach properly in his living room he built himself a (red) harpsichord there. To walk the road to Compostela, a traditional pilgrim's route traversing Spain from east to west, he taught himself Spanish and read every pilgrim's account or bit of lore available. To teach the ancient Greek poets he made himself a master of every aspect of classical philology – from metrics, papyrology, epigraphy to mythography and matters of taste. ER was a teacher of much more than ancient Greek. Not only to those of us fortunate enough to be his students but to everyone who knew him he taught what a difference it makes if you go at things with your whole heart. Whether the task was bread or Bach or pilgrimage or explaining the moral unity of a poem of Alcman, he held nothing back.

The field of facts that he navigates so calmly was and is as deep and diverse as that of any classicist alive. Yet to read, teach, and understand the ancient Greek poets requires more than a mastery of data and a zest for method. It takes tact. A kind of attunement: maybe the Greek word would be *harmonia*. Many a clever person can parse information and construct polished arguments. Far more rare is the capacity to tune one's own learning to the intention of the original text, to hear what it is saying from *its* side. There is a quotient of humility in this and a dazzle of intuition. ER's beautiful essay on 'Sappho, Aphrodite, and the Muses' is a good example. It begins by summarizing how scholars have puzzled over Sappho's relation to goddess and to cult, gradually sifting out ER's own very distinct picture of the intimate communion between Aphrodite and Sappho. 'The poetry burns with the sense of a woman who lives easily and confidently with her divinity at all times,' he says (129). It is not the usual view of Sappho. Unusual too is his emphasis on 'the shadow side' of Sappho's mentality and practice; he finds bittersweetness even in a poem conventionally read as joyous, the so-called epithalamium of Hector and Andromache (fr. 44), for he cannot help but see this brilliant couple's wedding day against the background of their fate. All of Sappho's eroticism strikes him so. 'My reading simply sees poetry of passion as poetry of suffering,' he says (131). He understands pain as the mechanism by which Sappho opens out a personal erotic moment onto the larger rhythms of human life. He prefers (with Rilke) to translate Alcaeus' epithet for her (*ioplok'*) as 'weaver of darkness' (131). His attunement to her sensibility is especially in evidence here, weighing the balance of darkness and light in the poet's attitude. No one else reads Sappho this way, no one else strikes through to the heart of her religiosity, its profound chiaroscuro.

ER's Sapphic essay culminates in a unique interpretation of fr. 2. He says this poem evokes no real garden, picnic, banquet, communal celebration, or sexual encounter but rather 'the imaginative garden where a devotee and her divinity meet' (135). It is a seasonless and uncanny location blended of religious and erotic enchantments, to which he compares the mystic orchard of Rumi and the garden where John of the Cross experiences his dark night of the soul – analogies that might seem remote or unconvincing until a third text is adduced, from Gregory of Nazianzus. It is a poem in which Gregory sits alone in a garden longing for God. The garden is so very like Sappho's that it contains the same unusual word as Sappho uses for the deep mood of religious attention that pours through both their souls as they wait (*koma*). Both poets, he argues, are talking about the same kind of soul's tension and release; both imagine it happening in an unearthly scenario of rustling trees and divine consolation. Both look to a divinity who will redeem the poor human moment with an hour of gold. 'What I most wish to emphasize (he concludes) is that the religion of Aphrodite is not only personal but that it foretokens, in its ability to instill peace or bliss, a world beyond death and pain' (139). The interpretation is passionate and particular, the argument limpid, the tact perfect. There is something almost debonair about the way he arrives at his end.

What exactly is it we learn from the teachers who change our lives? Facts and the respect for facts, method and its exactitudes, style and the restraint of style, are all part of it. But more than these, like Cheiron the centaur, ER taught a way of being. Pindar tells us that once when Apollo asked Cheiron a trick question the centaur laughed a clear little laugh and said, 'Well okay, if I have to measure myself against one who is wise, I'll answer you' (*Pythian* 9.50). It would be a bold thing, to laugh at Apollo. But deepminded Cheiron knew exactly whereof he spoke. There is something almost debonair in the way he holds his knowledge up to the light of the god.

ER and I had more than one conversation about the word 'debonair' on the road to Compostela in 1984 (I walked across Spain with him). It was one of his favourite words that summer. Etymologically *de bon air* means something like 'having the right atmosphere around one.' The right atmosphere might include sweetness, aptness, elegance. But also, he insisted, 'there must be an integrity of person that includes the knowledge of one's own real place.' How many of us know our own real place. Or can take the measure of things starting with ourself. When he said

FOREWORD

this I remember we were sitting by the side of the road outside a town called Najera, eating blood oranges. Blood oranges are quick to eat but tricky to peel. ER had two knives, for different sizes of oranges.

Anne Carson (2011)

Publications of Emmet Robbins

1968 The Concept of Inspiration in Greek Poetry from Homer to Pindar. (University of Toronto) PhD Thesis.
1975 Jason and Cheiron: The Myth of Pindar's Fourth Pythian. *Phoenix* 29 205–13
— Review: Roloff Beny in Italy. *University of Toronto Quarterly* 44.4 417–19
1977 Review: M.S. Silk, *Interaction in Poetic Imagery. Phoenix* 31 364–6
1978 Cyrene and Cheiron: The Myth of Pindar's Ninth Pythian. *Phoenix* 32 91–104
1980 'Every Time I Look at You …': Sappho Thirty-One. *TAPhA* 110 255–61
1982 Famous Orpheus. In: Warden, John (ed.), *Orpheus. The Metamorphosis of a Myth* (Toronto) 3–24
— Heracles, the Hyperboreans, and the Hind: Pindar *Ol.* 3. *Phoenix* 36 295–305
1983 Review: M. Gregor-Dellin, *Richard Wagner: His Life, His Work, His Century. Canadian Forum* December
1984 Intimations of Immortality: Pindar *Ol.* 3.34–9. In D.E. Gerber (ed.), *Greek Poetry and Philosophy: Studies in Honour of L.E. Woodbury* (Chico CA) 219–25
— Review: D.A. Campbell, *The Golden Lyre: The Themes of the Greek Lyric Poets. EMC/CV* 3.1 75–8
1985 Review: A.J. Podlecki, *The Early Greek Poets and Their Times. University of Toronto Quarterly* 54.4 75–8
1986 The Broken Wall, the Burning Roof and Tower: Pindar, *Ol.* 8.31–46. *CQ* 36 317–21
— Pindar's 'Oresteia' and the Tragedians. In Martin Cropp, Elaine Fantham, S.E. Scully (eds), *Greek Tragedy and Its Legacy: Essays Presented to D.J. Conacher* (Calgary) 1–12
1987 Nereids with Golden Distaffs: Pindar's Fifth *Nemean. QUCC* 25 25–33
1990 Achilles to Thetis. *EMC/CV* 9.1 1–16
— Sappho Fr. 94: A Further Note. *Phoenix* 44.4 381–2
— Who's Dying in Sappho Fr. 94? *Phoenix* 44.2 111–21
— The Gifts of the Gods: Pindar's Third *Pythian. CQ* 40.2 307–18

— To Be Redeemed from Fire by Fire: the Deaths of Heracles and Siegfried. In Hans de Groot and Alexander Leggatt (eds), *Craft and Tradition: Essays in Honour of William F. Blissett* (Calgary) 147–56
1991 Editor (with C. Brown, R. Fowler, P.M. Matheson Wallace): *Collected Writings of Leonard E. Woodbury* (Atlanta GA)
1992 Review: A. Gostoli, *Terpander*. CR 42.1 8–9
1993 The Education of Achilles. *QUCC* 45 7–20
— Review: Three Perspectives on Pindar CR 43.1 10–13
1994 Alcman's Partheneion: Legend and Choral Ceremony. CQ 44.1 7–16
— The Divine Twins in Early Greek Poetry. In Emmet I. Robbins and Stella Sandahl (eds), *Corolla Torontonensis: Studies in Honour of R.M Smith* (Toronto) 29–46
— Editor (with Stella Sandahl): *Corolla Torontonensis: Studies in Honour of Ronald Morton Smith* (Toronto)
1995 Sappho, Aphrodite, and the Muses. *AncW* 26.2 225–39
1996 Review: B. Gentili, *Pindaro: Le ditiche*. *Phoenix* 50.1 338–41
1997 Public Poetry: 5 chapters on Alcman, Stesichorus, Simonides, Pindar, Bacchylides. In Douglas E. Gerber (ed.), *A Companion of Greek Lyric Poetry* (Leiden) 223–87
1996–9. Over 50 encyclopaedia articles on Greek poetry and poets. In Hubert Cancik, Helmuth Schneider, August Friedrich von Pauly (eds), *Der neue Pauly: Enzyklopädie der Antike* (Stuttgart)

Preface

Emmet Robbins, former Chair of Classics at the University of Toronto, is acknowledged internationally as a major contributor to scholarship on Greek poetry. Also a musician and someone well-versed in several languages and literatures, Robbins's rich cultural background enabled him to bring a wide perspective to the Classical field, delving into comparisons between Greek poetry and later European literature and music, including opera.

Emmet Robbins's published work, from 1975–1999, reflects a close reading of ancient Greek poetic texts, together with a grasp of their literary, historical and mythological contexts. He has long been admired for his penetrating studies of the work of Pindar, perhaps the most difficult of the Greek poets. His work has enjoyed a reputation for being permanently fresh and informative: none of it has gone out of date, and several of the seminal ideas he was the first to venture have been confirmed by subsequent interpretations. That he became one of the foremost scholars in the field of Greek poetry is attested by the fact that he was asked to supply all the articles on Greek poets for *Der Neue Pauly* (the new version of the standard encyclopedia for Classics, the *Realencyclopädie der classischen Altertumswissenschaft*) and the chapter on publicly-performed poetry for *A Companion to the Greek Lyric Poets* (Brill 1997).

Emmet Robbins's writing displays a calm mastery of virtually all facets of the discipline of Classics. Securely grounded in philology, he turns to metrics, history, papyrology, epigraphy and mythography – all in the interest of offering an interpretation that both makes sense and taps into the depths of the poetry. With a particular sensitivity to the chiaroscuro nature of human existence he connects us to the elegiac moments in many of the poems he studies, and supplies parallels from some of the richest writers to succeed their classical forbears – a Sufi mystic, St John of the Cross, Rilke, Hofsmannsthal. Music, which conveyed Greek lyric in its first performances, is embedded in Robbins's interpretations, with figures such as Mozart's Countess Almaviva (*Marriage of Figaro*) or music that recalls Sappho such as Debussy's setting of the masterly artifice of Pierre Louÿs.

Robbins's work is penetrating and comprehensive, but for the most part confined to a reading of a single text, and has been appropriately disseminated in the form of articles, book chapters etc. It is now time to gather the work of Emmet Robbins into a single volume, for students and scholars to be to able consult his views on the major and minor questions that continue to present themselves in this field. I have chosen to present this material in chronological order (although arranging the Pindaric articles in the traditional order of the poet's work). Robbins' essays on Alcman, Stesichorus, Simonides, Pindar, and Bacchylides that appeared in the Brill handbook precede these.

Cheiron, the centaur-teacher of heroes, was a figure to whom Robbins returned on many occasions ('The Education of Achilles,' Cyrene and Cheiron,' 'Jason and Cheiron,' 'The Broken Wall,' and 'The Gifts of the Gods'). This figure, who has received scant attention from other scholars, was for Robbins as he was for Pindar an important figure – a healer, prophet and teacher who exemplified the civilizing arts along with the raw power of nature. Robbins had a deep respect for both dimensions of life, and conveyed this to his students.

In 'The Education of Achilles' Robbins traces the tradition of the Greek hero at Troy as both killer and healer back to his mentoring by the centaur – like Achilles a semi-feral creature. Robbins draws attention to Achilles' hands, which feature so strongly in the *Iliad* as instruments of both bloodshed and healing, and connects this with the etymology of Cheiron's name. In 'Cyrene and Cheiron: the Myth of Pindar's Ninth *Pythian*' Robbins examines the poetic account of Apollo's wooing of the eponymous nymph Cyrene. Hands figure here too, but in a gentler mode. The request of the god for advice about how to begin the courtship with the nymph is phrased as a question whether to place his hand on Cyrene. This elicits a smile from the centaur, and the exchange is characterized, as Robbins notes, by courtesy, affection, and intimacy. The centaur embodied something central to early Greek thinking, namely the inseparability of polarities, articulating the most significant features of human life. The offspring of the union of Cyrene and Apollo, Aristaeus, would embody this unity-in-polarity, as Pindar says. *Agreus* and *nomios*, he was engaged in both the wild and tame aspects of nature. (Here Robbins identifies a particularly fruitful link between νόμος [traditional belief and social behaviour] and νομός [the pastoral, solitary life]). The Ninth *Pythian* calls forth Robbins's musical sensibilities, and he describes it as being full of happy harmonies, like a sonata in a major key.

The form of Pindar's Fourth *Pythian* is not so tidy, and in 'Jason and Cheiron' Robbins appeals to Cheiron's *cheirourgia* to resolve a structural problem in the ode whose resolution has long eluded critics. Since antiquity readers have struggled to see the relevance of the lengthy mythical narration of Jason's quest for the Golden Fleece to the celebration of the victory of the king of Cyrene. Despite the poem's reputation for being unsurpassed in the Pindaric corpus for its length and brilliance, it is anomalous in making scant reference to the victory or victor. Robbins manages to read in the mythical narrative an implied message to the king, and Jason's acknowledgement of his debt to the centaur supplies a resolution for the long-standing dilemma. The veiled message would be rendered more effective by the extent and vividness of the narrative.

In 'The Broken Wall, the Burning Roof and Tower: Pindar, *Ol.* 8.31–46,' Robbins once again directs attention to Cheiron in order to clarify confusion brought about by the attempt to link the mythical account to praise of the victor. Critics have condemned Pindar for altering the Homeric account of the role of the Aeacids in both the construction and destruction of Troy. Robbins challenges the view of the poem as a curious amalgam of badly co-ordinated elements by shifting the focus to the motif of collaboration, in both the myth and the victory. Collaboration in fulfilling the will of the gods makes sense of the Aeacids' work at Troy as well as the victor's achievement, and Cheiron's mentorship of heroes serves as paradigmatic of a joint enterprise with divine sponsorship.

That Pindar attributed victory in the games to an athlete's φυά, his inherited talent and skill, is not a new observation, but to identify the importance of *mothers* in an ode feels un-Pindaric, where patronymics and the masculine world of the games are the usual backdrop for a victor's performance. In *Nemean* 5, three generations of Aeginetan victors are celebrated with a mythical account of Aeacid heroes, highlighting the excellence of the maternal family and praise for the island Aegina as the athletes' mother. In 'Nereids with Golden Distaffs: Pindar, *Nem.* 5,' Robbins follows the thread common to the Aeacids' and the victors' successes: in all cases the maternal inheritance is an essential component, but it will only issue in renown when the hero/athlete severs the umbilical cord.

The relationship between mother and son is the focus of 'Achilles to Thetis: *Iliad* 1.365–412.' The hero's extended outburst to Thetis after Agamemnon's decision to take his concubine for himself is in Robbins's view not, as readers like Kirk would have it, of little value. It both establishes Achilles' dependence on the one figure who will be a sympathetic advocate for him throughout the poem and provides important factual information, crucial for understanding the actions of some of the principal players in the battlefield drama.

The death of Agamemnon when he returned from Troy was the subject of the first play in Aeschylus' trilogy, the *Oresteia*. In the second and third plays it is the revenge killing of Clytemnestra by her son and its aftermath that occupies the stage. This narrative also appears in the mythical section of Pindar's Eleventh *Pythian*, and in 'Pindar's *Oresteia* and the Tragedians,' Robbins makes a compelling case for the Aeschylean trilogy having adapted elements from Pindar's Eleventh *Pythian*. Here Robbins is taking on Farnell and others who have argued that the influence was in the other direction. Another remarkable contribution in this piece is Robbins's demonstration of the relevance of a tale of revenge in a poem celebrating an athletic victory.

Violence lurks beneath the surface of heroic performance, and not just in battle. The exploits of Heracles are characterized by aggression in the service of good, and such violence can be explicit or merely hinted at, as in Pindar's Third *Olympian*. In 'Heracles, the Hyperboreans and the Hind: Pindar, *Ol*. 3' Robbins works with the different mythical traditions of Heracles' obtaining the olive tree for the Olympic games. He points out that Pindar's version of the story differs from other accounts in which the hero took the tree away from the Hyperboreans against their will. Heracles also obtained a hind with gilded horns from these utopian people, and vase-paintings appear to associate this with a violent wresting of the animal from a divinity. Robbins's essay focuses on ways in which the poet's treatment of both acquisitions suppresses the brutality that informed traditional accounts; in the Third *Olympian* the hero succeeded with πειθώ not βία.

Heracles' *vita* included another encounter with divinity, but after his *mors* – with his apotheosis from the funeral pyre at Oeta. Robbins looks at the final chapter of the hero's life in 'To Be Redeemed from Fire by Fire: The Deaths of Heracles and Siegfried.' By comparing *Götterdämmerung* and Sophocles' *Trachiniae* he focuses not only on the two protagonists but also on the two heroines, Brünnhilde and Deianira. This yields Robbins some striking insights. He challenges Jebb's characterization of Deianira as representative of the 'perfect type of gentle womanhood' by looking at the features she shares with her Wagnerian counterpart – also driven to killing her husband out of sexual jealousy. He makes sense of Deianira's name ('man-slayer') and builds a strong case for an affirmative answer to the vexed question, 'Did she know the true power of the love-potion?' As Brünnhilde casts light on Deianira, so does Siegfried on Heracles: their deaths are purifying, redeeming the earlier fires lit by the primal passions of jealousy and anger. But the redemption signifies two distinct world-views: whereas the audience of Wagner's drama could read Siegfried's death as signaling the end of a corrupt divine order, this is not so for the audience of the *Trachiniae*. They watched Heracles' funeral procession at the end of the play and heard Hyllus' comment on the abiding cruelty of the gods. Robbins reminds us that Nietzsche pointed out in *The Birth of Tragedy* that the Greeks could accept this as a fundamental, dark and unchanging truth of existence, one that gave heroism its validation.

Robbins's recognition of the Greek understanding that 'glory comes trailing clouds of pain' introduces his 'The Gifts of the Gods: Pindar's Third *Pythian*.' This is one of the poet's four poems for Hieron, the powerful tyrant of Syracuse. The mythical sections in all of these odes focus on sinners and their punishment. In his study of the Third *Pythian*, as elsewhere, Robbins takes on critics who have argued that the mythical narratives sit awkwardly or are at best irrelevant in an epinician. In this ode the poet refers to Coronis' punishment by immolation for her infidelity to Apollo, and to the thunderbolt that would kill her son Asclepius when he attempted to resurrect the dead. A second mythical section is no less dark, chronicling the unhappy fates of the children of Peleus and Cadmus. Cheiron cannot be called upon as a healer, for he too is dead. Robbins recognizes in these Pindaric accounts a re-working of the Homeric description of the dispensations of Zeus. Where the epic version describes these as coming from two urns, one distributing joys and the other pains, Pindar addresses Hieron with the ostensibly less comforting assertion that painful divine gifts outnumber the pleasurable ones by a ratio of 2:1. With myths that chronicle a movement from pain to joy then to more pain the poet touches on the mutability of human experience. Nonetheless, Robbins reads the ode as consolatory, and defends the relevance of the myths to the epinician experience. Hieron might in fact have lost an anticipated victory, and at a time when he was also suffering from ill-health, but the gift of the ode offers assurance to the tyrant that, since life is subject to shifting fortunes, he could anticipate a kinder fate in the future.

Robbins returns to the Third *Olympian* in 'Intimations of Immortality: Pindar, Ol. 3.34–9.' The ode was composed for an Olympic victory earned by Theron, like Hieron a Sicilian tyrant. It was performed at a major public Acragantine festival for the Dioscuri, which Robbins reads as having particular relevance for celebrating this victor. Unlike Hieron, who feuded with his brother Polyzelus, Theron was close to his brother Xenocrates. Both tyrants were likely present at this festival for the divine twins. In the mythical section of the ode we are given the story of Heracles' founding of the games at Olympia and his procuring the olive tree from the Hyperboreans, which would offer shade for the athletes and crowns for the victors. Robbins sees here an appropriate means of offering tribute to Theron: as victor he wears a crown with links to a land of the blessed, the place where Heracles got a foretaste of the unending beatitude he would enjoy on Olympus. Noting that Pindar in this ode both incorporates the story of Heracles' *parergon* and foregrounds the Dioscuri (mediators between mortality and immortality), Robbins reads the Third *Olympian* as offering Theron a glimpse of the eschatology promised to the truly fortunate, described by the poet in his companion song for the same victory, the Second *Olympian*.

The wealth of associations attached to the Dioscuri is further explored in 'The Divine Twins in Early Greek Poetry,' in Robbins's words 'two of the most appealing and memorable figures in Greek myth.' He traces some important features of the twins to their Vedic forbears, the Asvins, including their mutual attachment to each other in life and death, their solicitous attention to humankind, and their connection with horses and with light. The Tyndarid brothers' association with both horses and light can account for their presence in the (fragmentary) mythical section of Alcman's Louvre *Partheneion*, a poem that was performed at a celebration of the goddess of the light at dawn. As horsemen the twins were particularly appropriate for songs celebrating victors in equestrian events, and appear in Pindar's First and Fourth *Pythians*, as well as his Tenth *Nemean*. In the *Nemean* ode, possibly Pindar's last epinician, the poet describes the twins' final conflict on earth, their fight with the sons of Aphareus. Castor, the mortal brother, lies dying, and Polydeukes' appeal to his father Zeus results in the brothers' right to share mortality and immortality, a choice that Robbins reads as paradigmatic of dedication, suffering and transfiguration. Their role as divine mediators between life and death lies just beneath the surface of the poignant narrative that closes this ode, and may have – as in the Third *Olympian* – offered solace to the victor, but perhaps also to Pindar at the end of his career.

Another figure whom Robbins identifies as a mediator between this world and the next is Orpheus ('Famous Orpheus'). The title for the piece reflects the reputation of Orpheus not only among the Greeks but through the Middle Ages, the Renaissance and the Early Modern Period, where his powers ranged widely – a lover who braved the powers of darkness, a musician, prophet and priest, an avatar of Christ who harrowed hell, and a central figure on the operatic stage. Tracing Orpheus' roots to the Argonautic saga, Robbins links the role of this figure in the Greek tradition with that of the shaman-traveller who returned from a voyage to the other side with secret knowledge, being more closely connected with the Underworld and the Mother Goddess than with the Olympians. In a *tour de force* Robbins links Orpheus to Tamino, the musician who charms wild animals and quells the darker forces in Mozart's *Magic Flute*.

Among the melic poets Robbins displays a particular affinity for Alcman and Sappho. In 'Alcman's Partheneion: Legend and Choral Ceremony' he tackles the difficult question of the relation between the fragmentary mythical section describing a battle between the Dioscuri and the Hippocoontids and what follows, a performance song of young women for a festival of the Dawn Goddess. In his joining of the two halves he likens the song's structure to a Petrarchan sonnet. Electing to read the myth as a Laconian version of a battle in which the two fraternal pairs quarrel over women (not cattle), Robbins is able to make sense of the pivotal gnome at the end of the legendary section – that grace, not force, opens the gates of heaven. In the battle language of the second half of the diptych he sees the girls engaging in playful exaggeration that leads to a triumph of grace and beauty over violence.

Robbins's hermeneutics could develop an argument around a single personal pronoun. In "'Every Time I Look at You ...': Sappho Thirty-One" the pivotal neuter relative pronoun τό of v. 5 is crucial for understanding the poem – perhaps the most famous poem to have come down to us from Greek antiquity. Robbins navigates deftly through the mass of scholarship that claims to have produced a conclusive reading of the poem, all circulating around the vexed τον (there are 31 citations for this in his first footnote). What provoked Sappho's famous symptoms? The article makes a careful assessment of the evidence, grounding its conclusions in the poet's concern with her own mortality. That this was a central concern to Sappho has been confirmed by the discovery of a new Sapphic poem (*P. Köln* inv. 21351).

Recalling Lucretius' *surgit amari aliquid* in 'Sappho, Aphrodite and the Muses,' Robbins conveys the power of love poetry – Sappho's in particular but also love poetry that came later in the Western tradition – to merge feelings of passion with those of suffering. With his close reading of Sappho's fr. 2, informed by others in the Sapphic corpus, Robbins makes a profound contribution to scholarship on this poet. Sappho, he argues, treats erotic suffering not as leading to despair but as making possible a vision of the larger whole. He reminds us of Rilke's words describing the poet as 'weaver of darkness,' and sees the poet opening up a deeper universe in which human pain is but a part. This same perception he attributes to some of the deepest thinkers among the early Greek poets, but also to mystics in the later tradition such as Rumi, St John of the Cross, and Gregory of Nysa.

The same insight, as those who knew him will acknowledge, was possessed by Robbins himself.

Robbins's breadth of vision characterized his approach to writing book reviews. His rich cultural background informed assessments of books such as the collection of Italian photographs of Roloff Beny and the English translation of a biography of Wagner (in which he was drawn to find some essential features missing from the German original of 900 pages). His critical appraisals, while never glossing over shortcomings of substance, were always balanced by praise when warranted. In his reviews of books about Greek poetry his stance against jargon or superficiality is clear, but equally obvious is his ability to accept discordant views, when argued with critical acumen and solid scholarship. A case in point is his comparison of Mary Lefkowitz' *First-Person Fictions. Pindar's Poetic 'I'* and Leslie Kurke's *The Traffic in Praise: Pindar and the Poetics of Social Economy* (CR 43.1 [1993] 9–10). This review obliged Robbins to enter the vigorous debate in Pindaric scholarship that emerged in the last decade of the 20th century, over whether epinicians were monodic or choral songs. His review respected the strengths of each side, but he did not withhold his personal judgement that no song can be read as unambiguously choral, excluding a performance that reflected the poet's own voice. This stance immediately removes the need for positions to be hardened on either side of the debate. Robbins's ready facility with Greek metre is clear in a number of his reviews, permitting him to challenge the colometry claimed for a fragment of Terpander, in Antonia Gostoli's *Terpander: introduzione, testimonianze, testo critico, traduzione e commento* (CR 42.1 [1992] 8–9), or to clarify the differences in metrical terminology used by scholars in the Anglo-German tradition and the Italian practice followed in the Urbino school led by Bruno Gentili. His admiration for Glenn Most's *Measures of Praise* [*Phoenix* 44.3 (1990) 276–9] is anything but measured. Most's magisterial command of the philosophical and philological tools necessary to probe the integrity of a Pindaric text clearly struck a resonance in Robbins.

In his reviews, his articles, in the classroom, as Department Chair – in all aspects of his academic life – Robbins was a Cheiron, able to balance opposing forces and act as a gentle and wise mentor to students and colleagues.

At the suggestion of Emmet Robbins two of his close friends and academic colleagues were invited to share some thoughts about the personal and professional influence he had on their lives and work.

Recollections

Father Owen Lee is Emeritus Professor of Classics, St Michael's College, University of Toronto, and an author and music critic.

I have been asked to remember Emmet Robbins and 'the experiences we had together.' I certainly remember, in 1960, on my first day in front of a university lecture hall, completely miscasting an eager, smiling, bespectacled young man as the villainous Labrax ('The Shark') in our class traversal of Plautus' *Rudens* – and watching him tackle the tough assignment through the month to come humbly and with good humour. I remember, soon thereafter, recommending that he invest in the Flagstad/Furtwängler recording of *Tristan und Isolde* and the three-volume Lucretius by Cyril Bailey (then on sale) and seeing him explore their music and poetry to a degree far beyond my ken. I remember his impressive defence of his Ph.D. thesis ('The Concept of Inspiration in Greek Poetry') and also his Stoic sadness when, on the demise of the old Honour Course system at the University of Toronto, the four college departments of Classics clashed head-on; he was an expert teacher by then, and he had close friends on each campus – Leonard Woodbury at U.C., D.O. Robson at Victoria, Des Conacher at Trinity, and Father James Sheridan at St Michael's.

I remember happily making the rounds of the pavilions at Expo 67 with him, attending the productions sent to Montreal by the Stockholm Opera and the Wiener Staatsoper, and learning from his impeccable taste and lively enthusiasm. I remember the postcards he sent me from his travels in Europe: 'Germany is great!' 'Edinburgh is a jewel!' 'Goodness but I love Spain!' I remember running into him by chance at Bayreuth in the summer of 1969, and remaining there with him to see seven Wagner operas in the festival city. But it was in Italy that, for some time, he made his home, quietly working in a Vatican department.

Perhaps above all I remember staying with him for three days in his modest apartment on the Dorotheergasse in the heart of Vienna, occupying his bed while he slept on a couch, feasting with him on freshly bought ham and cheese, peppers, tomatoes and beer, and discovering new subtleties in Mozart with him at the keyboard of his harpsichord. Through his eyes I saw the baroque Vienna of Fischer von Erlach and Lukas von Hildebrandt, the wonders of the Ringstrasse, and the paintings of Vermeer and Velasquez in the Kunsthistorisches Museum. He also showed me things the tourist never sees – the Freihaustheater where Mozart conducted his *Magic Flute* (a landmark even then marked for extinction) and what he was sure was the Faninal Palace in *Der Rosenkavalier*. He served my Mass in the Stephansdom and again in the Kapuzinerkirche, got a little sentimental with me over new wine at a Heurige in Beethoven's Heiligenstadt, and took me to hear the latest Wunderkind, Alfred Brendel, play Schumann's *Kinderszenen* in the Palais Schwarzenberg. And through all this he helped me with an article I was writing on Horace and gave me a startling new insight into Aeschylus.

I am proudest of him among all the students I have taught. I was happiest with him among all the departmental chairmen I have served. And I learned more, and in gentler ways, from him than from any other of my friends. His kindness won for me a teaching award from the University of Toronto. And when, even after his heroic pilgrimage on foot to Santiago de Campostela, illness struck him, and he was unable to be at the conferral of the honorary doctorate that I owed to him, my first words to convocation were,

'I would like to thank Professor Emmet Robbins of the Department of Classics, who first recommended me for this honour. He cannot be here today, but he has been a blessing in my life, and it was from him that I learned that the best way to know God was to love many good things.'

Owen Lee (2010)

Margaret Visser is a well-known author and broadcaster, and also a classicist.

Emmet taught me ancient Greek, and he taught me a great deal more besides. He was one of the first Canadians I ever met socially. It happened after Greek class, in a University College corridor. He was wearing an academic gown – a defiant upholding of tradition in the year 1966 – and he fixed me with his intense brown eyes and started asking me questions. That very first meeting convinced me that this was a man who knew what he thought important, and was prepared to pursue his interests with every ounce of his intelligence and energy.

I was a mature student – married, the mother of a small child. I learned later that he thought I would never stay the academic course. I did, and it was in large measure because he showed me what application and what accuracy and discipline meant. These were things I thought I knew. He gave them dimensions I had never guessed.

He became a family friend, the godfather of our second child, and we travelled together in Europe and in Turkey; he visited our country house in France. Emmet has always been a witty and insightful companion. He loves the Greeks, Italy, painting, and music with all his heart – *sans partage* as the French say (and Emmet is very French Canadian) – but never *sans partager*. He mastered cooking as he mastered languages and everything else that interested him, and many are the excellent dinners I remember sharing with Emmet. He has always shared what he knows. And what he has taught me I shall never forget.

Margaret Visser (2010)

Acknowledgments

The idea of making Emmet Robbins's works more easily accessible for scholars and students by collecting them in one volume arose from conversations with him and a small group of his friends, which included John Traill, Philippa Matheson, and myself. I would like to thank my collaborators for collecting material, helping with editing and proofreading, and for much fruitful discussion. An important figure in all stages of this project, until her death in March 2012, was Jay Macpherson, a close friend and colleague of Emmet Robbins. It is to her that he dedicated the book. Several of the articles and book chapters were not available in an electronic version, and the composite bibliography needed to be drawn from footnotes. I owe a debt of thanks to Raquel Ricardez, a graduate student at the University of Western Ontario, for help in retrieving full citations for the bibliography, to Dugald Matheson for help in producing electronic versions of the articles, and to Emmet Robbins's student and long-term friend, Maggie Rogow, for help with the final proofreading.

Philippa Matheson undertook the major task of typesetting the book, and has done so with her usual high degree of professionalism. I also want to thank Suzanne Rancourt of the University of Toronto Press for assistance in the various stages of bringing this book to completion, and the Press readers for careful proofreading and a number of helpful suggestions.

The text is basically identical to the original publication of Robbins's work, with the addition of minor typographical changes, the continuous numbering of the notes in 'Public Poetry,' and the occasional editorial comment (e.g., on the new fragment of Sappho that corroborates Robbins's insights about this poet, below 144).

Emmet Robbins died on August 16, 2011.

Bonnie MacLachlan (2012)

PUBLIC POETRY

Alcman

The oldest of the choral lyric poets of whose work something survived, Alcman lived and wrote in Sparta of the 7th century.[1] Previous figures are no more than names. There are two lines of a Delian processional hymn (prosodion) for the Messenians by Eumelus of Corinth: it is our oldest fragment of choral lyric (*PMG* 696), possibly as early as the 8th century. Other names to survive from the early Archaic period are Thaletas (or Thales), who is said to have come from Crete to Sparta and composed paeans and hyporchemata, and Polymnestus of Colophon, who was mentioned by both Alcman (145 = 225 Calame) and Pindar (fr. 188) and is said to have worked in Sparta too, composing prosodia for pipe accompaniment.[2] Arion of Corinth, who was important in the history of the dithyramb (Her. 1.23), is said by the *Suda* to have been a pupil of Alcman, while Sacadas of Argos is said by Plutarch to have taught his chorus to sing a three-part nome using three different modes in turn.

From this it may be clearly seen that the earliest choral lyric poets are associated with the Peloponnese, and often with Sparta. Whereas the

---

First published in Douglas E. Gerber (ed.) *A Companion to the Greek Lyric Poets*. *Mnemosyne* Supplement 173. ISBN: 9004099441. Leiden/New York (1997) 223–87, under the heading 'Public Poetry.'

1 In addition to *PMG* (Page 1962) and *PMGF* (Davies 1991), Alcman has been edited with a full collection of testimonia by Calame (1983); see also Garzya 1954. Also crucial for understanding the long Louvre *Partheneion* are Page 1951a and Puelma 1977. For further bibliography see Gerber 1994.
2 The testimonia for these poets are collected and translated by Campbell 1982–1993: 2.286–335 and 3.202–7.

monodic poets used their own dialects, and the elegiac poets the international language of hexameter poetry, there seems to have been from early on a literary language with a more or less strongly marked Doric component that was available to the choral lyric poets. The most reasonable explanation of this impurity of the language is the existence of a literary *koine* in mainland Greece, parallel to the literary language of epic, and used by the choral lyrists, who all worked in Dorian cities. Alcman's language shows a strong influence of Laconian (a local Doric vernacular used at Sparta), but it contains some Aeolic forms, and some fragments even show forms that are found in Homer. In later time Stesichorus, Simonides, Bacchylides, and Pindar continued to use a literary language strongly marked by Doric elements, though in each case the influence of the dialect spoken in the place of their birth is evident too.[3]

What we find in Alcman is a side of Spartan society that complements the military picture found in Tyrtaeus. Alcman himself alludes to the importance of music at Sparta, saying that the playing of the lyre competes with martial pursuits (41 = 143 Calame), and Pindar echoes this (fr. 199). Alcman and Tyrtaeus were probably alive in the same Sparta. There has always been debate whether Alcman was born in Sparta or in Sardis. The former is more probable, the only piece of internal evidence we have to connect him with Sardis being fr. 16 (= 8 Calame), where the reference to Sardis is not necessarily a reference to Alcman himself. An unwillingness in later times to believe that the closed and militaristic society of Sparta could ever have produced poets will have abetted a tendency to believe that Tyrtaeus' birthplace was Athens and Alcman's Sardis. Alcman is placed in the reign of Ardys (c. 652–c. 619) by the *Suda*, which, however, places Ardys earlier in the century. Eusebius offers either 659 or 609. Alcman seems to have mentioned King Leotychidas (5 fr. 2 col. i.14 = 80 Calame), and his reign was late in the seventh century. It seems likely, then, that Alcman belongs to the second half of the century, and may have lived into the sixth.

Poetry

We are told in the *Suda* that Alcman's work comprised 'six books, lyric poetry and the Κολυμβῶσαι.' It is unclear what the 'Diving Women' was, and whether or not the designation describes something apart from the six books. He was especially famous for his partheneia but may well have composed other types of choral poetry too. Probably because of the parochial nature of his poetry he was considered a difficult poet, and this explains

---

3 See Calame 1983: xxxi–xxxii; Wilamowitz 1922: 101.

why he attracted considerable attention from scholars in antiquity. Perhaps for the same reason – he was not readily intelligible – time has dealt harshly with him, and no poem survives that is certainly complete. The remains show an extensive use of iambic, trochaic, and dactylic rhythms. Ancient metricians called the dactylic tetrameter the 'Alcmanic': fr. 27, three lines in this metre, is quoted by Hephaestion, who uses it as an example of a metre in which Alcman wrote entire strophes. It is the beginning of a poem, probably a partheneion, with an invocation and the actual mention (quite rare) of a chorus.

The only considerable piece of Alcman we have is the *Partheneion*, 101 lines in three papyrus-columns, discovered in 1855 by Mariette in Egypt and now in the Louvre (1 = 3 Calame). Of these three columns the first 34 lines (column i) are badly mutilated because of the disappearance of the left-hand side of the column, whereas lines 35–101 (columns ii and iii) may be restored with almost complete confidence. A coronis opposite the fifth line of column iii makes it clear that the poem ended only four lines after our text runs out. It is not known how much is missing at the beginning of the poem, but if one full column of 35 lines has been lost before our first column the whole would have consisted of 140 lines. The strophes are 14 lines long, with the metrical pattern abababab ccddef.[4] There are in addition two damaged sets of scholia for this poem, ΣA from the papyrus containing the poem and ΣB from Oxyrhynchus.

The first column contains the remains of a myth and moral reflection on the story told. The first surviving word is the name of Pollux (Polydeukes) and this is followed by a list of names given, apparently, in *praeteritio* (οὐκ ... ἀλέγω, 1; παρήσομες, 12). The names after Pollux are those of the dead sons of the Spartan King Hippocoon. They must have been killed either by the sons of Tyndareus, Castor and Pollux, or possibly by Heracles since the later versions of the story exist in which Heracles gained the throne of Sparta for Tyndareus after he had been exiled by his brother Hippocoon. But Heracles is not mentioned in our fragment. The gnomic passage immediately following the catalogue (13–21) suggests that the story told was one of erotic violence; if this was the case, it is very possible that it was the story, mentioned by Euphorion, that the Tyndaridae were erotic rivals (ἀντιμνηστῆρες) of the Hippocoontidae.[5]

---

4 The first eight lines may be seen as four couplets, but if they are viewed as two identical strophes abab and abab, the whole may be thought of as our earliest example of triadic structure, with the last six lines an epode.

5 Calame (1977b: 55–7) thinks that the rivalry between the sons of Hippocoon and the sons of Tyndareus had to do with Helen, sister of Castor and Pollux.

After this (22–34) there are no commonly accepted supplements for the text; there seems to be mythical narrative again, but the subject is unclear. It is thus uncertain whether the story told is a new one or whether it is a continuation of the previous story. There is mention of an arrow (30) and of a marble millstone (31), and of death and misconduct (27, 31). This seems best to correspond to what we know about the fight of the Dioscuri, or Tyndaridae, with the Apharetidae, Idas and Lynceus. This myth is in some versions a story of cattle-rustling, in others a story of erotic rivalry. The latter well fits the tenor of the passage as a whole.[6]

In the better-preserved part of the papyrus, the chorus of maidens is engaged in a ritual presentation to a goddess. Two figures, Agido and Hagesichora, stand out from the choir, and are clearly not members of the rank and file; it may be significant that both names are derived from words that mean 'lead.' The object presented is named as a φᾶρος (61). This would normally be understood to be a garment, but the scholiast tells us that one Sosiphanes, a commentator in antiquity, identified it as a plough; presumably he had some knowledge that made him say this. The goddess is identified as the Dawn-goddess (Ἀῶτις, 87) and this would correspond to the appellative Ὀρθρίαι of 61 if this word is a dative and not a feminine nominative plural referring to the chorus. Many candidates have been suggested for the goddess: Artemis (Orthia), Aphrodite, Helen, Eileithyia, and Phoebe.[7] Again, the relationship of Agido and Hagesichora is not clear. For those who follow Calame, the whole ceremony is a *rite de passage* that accompanies the transition from childhood to adulthood and Hagesichora is the leader supervising this ceremony. But Puelma has argued very persuasively for seeing Agido as the more important of two leaders in a religious ceremony. δευτέρα (58) is crucial to any understanding of the whole, but there are several candidates for second place and lack of agreement whether second place is opprobrious or complimentary: Agido is second to Hagesichora;[8] Hagesichora to Agido, but the comparison does not denigrate Hagesichora so much as set her in a class with her companion and apart from the rest of the choir;[9] 'second' is a reference to the rank and file, who cannot compete with either of the two who are singled out;[10] 'second' is not specific in its reference but applies to any maiden who might

---

6 See, e.g., Robbins 1994: 7–17 [reprinted in this volume 88–100] and Gendler 1995: 3–21.
7 Robbins 1994: 9 n13 [in this volume 91 n13].
8 Calame 1983: 270.
9 Puelma 1977: 29–31.
10 Page 1951a: 90.

be compared to the superior two and is a rhetorical way of emphasizing the beauty of both Agido and Hagesichora.[11]

Who in fact are the Peleiades or 'Doves' mentioned in line 60? Many, following Page,[12] think that they are a rival choir. Still others take them to be the celebrated star-cluster with a reference here to the time of the performance, when these stars are visible. But it is most likely that we have here a reference to Agido and Hagesichora. The priestesses at Dodona were called 'Doves,' and other animal names are found in cult in the Greek world: it is well known, for instance, that the devotees of Artemis at Brauron were called 'Bears.'

Is there in fact a competition and, if there is, what is the contest? Agonistic language is ubiquitous. For some it pits the maidens against the rival choir, while for Calame there is probably a footrace occurring, but within the group, not against a rival choir. It seems most likely, on balance, that the language of war is playful exaggeration, a sustained metaphor; the competition suits the self-deprecation of the singing chorus, who proclaim that their own charms cannot compete with those of Agido and Hagesichora.

There is another catalogue of names at lines 70–6 and some or all of these must be names of members of the choir. But not all are names of girls present – Aenesimbrota (73), for instance, appears to be absent. The numbers ten and eleven seem to be important for lines 98 and 99 (with δεκ- actually in the text and ἕνδεκα to be restored to the text from the scholia): these numbers must bear some relation to the names of the catalogue at 70–6. But solutions are very varied and no single suggestion has met with general approval.

One question that deserves to be asked is what relation there is between the mythical part of the poem and the occasion described in the less lacunose portion. Here we may hazard the conjecture that the myth or myths, since they probably told of erotic violence, were a foil to the playful competition and erotic language of the ceremony, where rivalry certainly exists but is not deadly. Further, such a contrast may have served to emphasize peaceful passage to sexual maturity as pubescent maidens were presented to the community as ripe for legitimate marriage. The contrast between force and persuasion (βία and πειθώ) is a common one in Greek, and it usually works to reinforce the superior efficacy of the latter. The poem may enact this truth, with force (in the myth) ceding to grace in the ceremony, the whole underscored by a theme of competition. It is

---

11 Pavese 1992: 66.
12 Cf. Campbell 1982–1993: 2.365.

of particular interest in any case to note that in our first substantial piece of choral lyric we find the elements that we see so clearly two centuries later in the epinician odes of Pindar: there is a myth told, with attendant moralizing and theological reflection, and there is much about the occasion and the performance.

Another papyrus-fragment (3 = 26 Calame), published in 1957, provides the much more fragmentary remains of another partheneion of Alcman. Here we appear to have had an original of 126 lines, 14 strophes of 9 lines each. The myth is entirely lost, as is the second column of 23 lines, but we are fortunate to have the beginning, with its invocation of the Muse. There are many elements familiar from the Louvre *Partheneion*. The choir seems to be performing in the early morning (7); it is carrying an offering, in this case a garland (65), though no divinity is mentioned, and it may be engaged in a competition, if ἀγών· (8) means 'contest' and not simply 'meeting-place,' as it well may (cf. Pindar, *Pyth.* 10.30). Further, the maidens pay lavish compliment to the beauty of their leader Astymeloisa and play upon the etymology of her name (74). In both poems there is the same affectionate gaiety and delicacy. Many have emphasized the homoeroticism of the poetry,[13] though it is perhaps dangerous to do so, for we must remember that these were public performances before the city and meant to present to the community nubile young women ready for marriage and motherhood: praise of beauty is to be expected but it serves an encomiastic purpose that is not principally homoerotic.[14]

Of the papyrus-finds, none has caused a greater flurry than fr. 5 col. iii (= 81 Calame), published in 1957. This is a commentary on Alcman, with short quotations from the text it is interpreting. The surprise was to discover apparent evidence that Alcman engaged in cosmogonic speculation, naming Thetis as a primal demiurge who organized matter out of formlessness. Alcman became an honorary Presocratic philosopher, despite the lack of any previous evidence that he belonged to this company.[15] But Most has shown that it was a mistake to see a cosmogonist in Alcman.[16] What we have in the papyrus is a commentary by a scholar of the second century AD who knew Aristotelian philosophy and was applying interpretative techniques practised in his own time, in particular that of allegory, to elicit what he believed were the hidden meanings of Alcman's text. What he no doubt had before him was a partheneion that mentioned Thetis and her changes

---

13 E.g., Calame 1983: 395.
14 Stehle 1996: 30–9 (esp. 31–3), 73–88.
15 See, e.g., Kirk, Raven, and Schofield 1983: 47–9.
16 Most 1987: 1–19.

of shape when she wrestled with Peleus and took different forms in her attempt to elude him (cf. Pindar, *Nem.* 4.62–5). He understood this to refer to the emergence of different elements through the agency of the goddess. Most's demonstration is entirely convincing and gives us, in place of the unknown Alcman, the familiar poet who used myths that were appropriate to the situation of the Spartan girls who were uttering them. In this lost poem too there must have been a story of erotic struggle, leading in this case to a celebrated wedding attended by the gods. The point here was in all likelihood not the condemnation of erotic violence but the demonstration of the inevitability of marriage, in this case of a fated union.

There is little else among the other fragments of Alcman long enough to invite anything but the most tentative comment on possible context or to give us a further idea of the contents of his poetry. He was said by the *Suda* to be ἐρωτικὸς πάνυ εὑρετὴς ... τῶν ἐρωτικῶν μελῶν. Fr. 58 (= 147 Calame) mentions the boy Eros (παῖς) who descends onto flowers and plays (παίσδει) there. Alcman may have been the first to introduce this figure, next found in Anacreon, into Greek poetry, and it has been suggested by Easterling that the venue here is the symposium, with the flowers those of garlands worn there and the passion alluded to the familiar male homoeroticism.[17] There are in some of the excerpts, certainly, sentiments remarkably like those we find in the monodists, and lines like the following resemble utterances in Archilochus (191), Sappho (47, 130), Anacreon (358, 413 *PMG*), and even Ibycus (287 *PMG*) – the emphasis on repeated onslaught (δηῦτε) is entirely typical:

    Ἔρως με δηῦτε Κύπριδος ϝέκατι
    γλυκὺς κατείβων καρδίαν ἰαίνει   (59[a] = 148 Calame)

But it is not impossible that this quotation comes from a maiden-song; statements such as that of the *Suda* about his erotic poetry may be based on nothing more than the erotic flavour that can be detected in the *partheneia*. Athenaeus, who quotes the above fragment (13.600f), introduces it with the testimony of two earlier scholars, Chamaeleon and Archytas, that Alcman was 'a leader in erotic songs, the first to publish a licentious song, being prone in his habits to the pursuit of women.' Athenaeus goes on to quote another passage (59[b] = 149 Calame) that is supposed to prove that Alcman fell wildly in love with one Megalostrata, a poetess, but the lines quoted refer only to Megalostrata's beauty and musical gifts and say nothing of

17 Easterling 1974: 34–41.

his passion for her. They are much like the utterances we are familiar with from the mouths of the maidens in the partheneia.

The well-known lines on the sleep of nature (89 = 159 Calame) have been much discussed. It is no longer fashionable to doubt their authenticity as once was the case,[18] but the abundance of apparently Homeric phrases is anomalous in our remains of Alcman and needs to be accounted for. Either we must believe that the paucity of our remains will not allow us to make accurate inferences about Alcman's language, or we must accept, with Calame, the idea that Alcman writes in an artificial poetic language that was never exactly coincident with his dialect and that would admit various admixtures of Doric, Aeolic, and Homeric phraseology. In fact there are no unquestionable Doric forms in the fragment as transmitted: editors commonly restore them (e.g., μελισσᾶν for μελισσῶν, 4) but they are not thoroughgoing, usually not changing the Ionic-Attic εὕδουσι (1, 6 – Doric would be εὕδοντι). Calame, for instance, writes σῆρες for the received θῆρες of line 4. Whether or not this is correct, it is a valuable reminder that the texts of all our lyric poetry date from a period when the dialects in which there were composed were no longer understood, and that modern editors, who have a better knowledge of the dialects than did Alexandrian scholars, often have difficult decisions to make, since the temptation to restore a 'correct' form in a passage may not take into account a deliberate use by a poet of a form that was available in a literary dialect.[19]

The poem on the sleep of nature is probably incomplete, though the ring-composition of the lines, framed by εὕδουσι in the first and last lines, suggests that the six lines form a unit. It is tempting to see in them a passage that contrasts the quiet of nature, describing all animate and inanimate nature asleep in a peaceful night (though night is not explicitly mentioned), with human restlessness. The opening of *Iliad* 2 foreshadows this contrast, and it becomes a commonplace in Hellenistic literature and Roman poetry;[20] some have even thought that the poem of Alcman must have been the archetype of the later passages. Moreover, the passage bears

---

18 E.g. Wilamowitz, Maas, Fränkel, and Latte: see Calame 1983: 574.
19 It is in fact ironic that the epigraphical evidence suggests that θῆρες, which is the Homeric form, is in fact the form that would be used in the Laconian of Alcman's day, the σ for θ being a convention that was established after the fourth century BC. But since our earliest evidence, the papyri, have σ for θ (cf. the Louvre *Partheneion passim*) and since all our citations must go back to the Alexandrian edition, there was never an attempt made to restore what must have been the earliest written form of the text.
20 Cf. Apoll. Rhod. 3.744 ff.; Theocr. 2.38 ff.; Virg. *Aen.* 4.522.

a similarity to Ibycus 286, where the quiet of a natural setting is juxtaposed with the turbulence in the poet's heart. The other explanation of the lines that is most often entertained is that they describe the hush of the landscape that precedes the appearance of a god; the parallel adduced is Eur. *Bacch.* 1084 ff. If the lines are part of the description of a ritual, including an epiphany, it may be in honour of Artemis[21] or, as in the passage from Euripides, Dionysus. Some substance is lent to the latter hypothesis by fr. 56 (= 125 Calame), where a habitual scene with female devotees on a mountain peak is described, with activities that seem to be Dionysiac.

Stesichorus

The notice in the *Suda* says that he was called Stesichorus 'because he was the first to establish a chorus of singers to the cithara' (πρῶτος κιθαρῳδίᾳ χορὸν ἔστησεν) and that his name was originally Tisias.[22] It is as a composer of choral poetry that he has traditionally been described in accounts of Greek literature. But with the coming to light in the past thirty years of papyrus fragments that give us a much better idea of the extent and nature of his poetry the emphasis has shifted: the number of those who think of him as a composer of choral song is diminishing and there is an increasing tendency now to place him in a citharodic tradition.[23] The model most frequently cited is Demodocus in *Odyssey* 8.256–60, who plays the *phorminx* while Phaeacian youths dance.[24] There remains the possibility that Stesichorus' career began with the composition of choral poetry and that he turned at a later point in life to citharodic narrative,[25] but there is no evidence in the remains for such a development and it is thus a very

---

21 See Calame 1983: 574.
22 In addition to Davies *PMGF* and Page *PMG* and *SLG*, see Vürtheim 1919. For the so-called Lille fragment, see Parsons 1977: 7–36, and Bremer 1987: 128–74. For further bibliography, see Gerber 1994: 50–89. [Note that fragments preceded by "S " are to be found in *SLG*.]
23 For instance, Gentili 1988: 125; Lerza 1982: 28–9; West 1971: 307–13. See the remarks of Davies 1988: 52–3.
24 *Iliad* 18.604–6 provides a similar scene, with singer playing the lyre while a chorus dances. The line mentioning the lyre-singer is not in the manuscripts because it was deleted by Aristarchus and so the case is not clear-cut. But if it is removed the dancers are left with no music at all and hence it should probably be retained.
25 Segal 1989: 146.

dubious hypothesis to posit that he composed different sorts of poetry at different stages in his career.[26]

The most famous name in early citharodic poetry is that of Terpander. Originally from Lesbos, he was active in Sparta of the early seventh century. Very few, if any, fragments of his work have survived.[27] He seems to have been an important innovator in music, for he is credited with having increased the number of strings of the lyre from four to seven and to have established musical nomes to which he sang poetry, Homer's, and perhaps his own. It is possible that he used metres that are forerunners of the dactylo-epitrite.[28] This metre, of such importance in the poetry of Pindar, is found, perhaps for the first time in Greek poetry, in Stesichorus.[29] It is a loose combination of dactylic units with units containing a single short (usually analyzed as cretics) to form lines that may vary in length and from each other. The so-called *asynarteta* of Archilochus (e.g., frr. 168–71, 191), with their individual combinations of dactylic and iambic or trochaic elements, show a similar fusion of cola with two shorts and one short.[30] This seems to have been an important and early development in early Greek verse: in Alcman, for instance, dactylic lines combine with trochaic. Thus from the very beginning we see poetry that combines trochees or iambs with dactyls (or anapaests) as well as the unmixed forms – the dactylic hexameter and the iambic trimeter.[31] The dactylo-epitrite lends itself especially well to narration, and the poetry of Stesichorus was classified in antiquity as ἔπη, for it was suited to epic themes. Stesichorus was, in Quintilian's famous phrase, *epici carminis onera lyra sustinentem* (*Inst. or.* 10.1.62). All this is consonant with his having been a citharode in the tradition of Terpander, an ἀοιδός of the sort we know of from Homer. He may well have instituted choruses as part of his presentations, but the choruses need not have sung his work. Burkert continues to maintain that he was a choral poet.[32] If he was, the remarkable prevalence of speeches

---

26 It was once fashionable to assume that there was such a development in the career of Ibycus (see Woodbury 1985: 195) with a Sicilian period of choral composition giving way to a Samian period of monody, but the theory is on the whole a curiosity now.
27 Page *PMG* (p. 362) says '*fragmenta melica exstant me iudice nulla*'; Gostoli (1990) accepts six as genuine.
28 Gostoli (preceding note) 129.
29 Haslam 1974: 51–3.
30 Kirkwood 1974: 43
31 The very first extant Greek inscription, the so-called Nestor's Cup from the island of Ischia dating from the late eighth century, shows a combination of dactylic and iambic lines. See Heubeck 1979: 109–16.
32 Burkert 1987: 43–62.

in the newly discovered fragments suggests that the individual parts were taken by members of the choir and in this case we would have an important fore-runner of tragedy. Stesichorus was universally credited in antiquity with having invented triadic structure;[33] this, Burkert believes, is the strongest argument in favour of choral composition. But it is questionable whether triadic structure implies a particular type of performance; it seems rather to be a principle of composition. There is a common tendency in early Greek poetry to employ what Fränkel calls 'Dreigliedrigkeit,' or articulation in units of three;[34] similarly, West analyzes both the Sapphic and Alcaic strophes as essentially triadic, with an identical line repeated (principle of strophe and antistrophe) and followed by a variation (principle of epode).[35] It is further to be observed that the poems of Stesichorus seem to say nothing whatsoever about occasion. In this they differ markedly from the choral lyric of Alcman or Pindar and, free of local markers, could have been performed anywhere in the Greek world. It is easier to imagine a travelling citharode performing them than to imagine, as Burkert does, travelling choirs, for which we lack clear evidence.

Stesichorus came from Magna Graecia. Tradition links him with both Sicily and south Italy (Mataurus). He was called 'the Himeraean,' which suggests links with the city of Himera on the north coast of Sicily, and he is reputed to have died in Catania. The dates in the *Suda* are c. 632 to c. 556 and while they are suspect as being based on synchronization with other poets – the first gives him a *floruit* of a conventional forty years after Alcman while the second puts his death in the year of the birth of Simonides[36] – they are generally accepted as not unlikely and would put his long working life almost within the sixth century. Though he attracted nothing like the learned commentary that Alcman did, it was observed (*Suda*) that he wrote in the Doric dialect. What we find in the new papyrus fragments is a language with the mixture of Homerisms, Doric, and literary Aeolic that is familiar as the poetic *koine* known in mainland Greece and exported to its colonies; this language was available to citharodic poets like Terpander as well as to choral poets like Alcman in early Sparta.

---

33 The *Suda*, s.v. τρία Στησιχόρου, says that it was proverbial to accuse an uneducated person of not knowing even 'the three of Stesichorus,' i.e. strophe, antistrophe, and epode. See Davies 1982: 206–10.
34 Fränkel 1975: 517 (= 1962: 591–2).
35 West 1971: 313. The short adonic of the Sapphic stanza is, on this attractive analysis, attached to the third Sapphic to make a longer third line; similarly the last two lines of the Alcaic strophe are joined to create a line that is longer (and metrically different) from the first two, which are identical.
36 Simonides mentions Stesichorus by name (564 *PMG*).

We find essentially the same language in Ibycus, a younger contemporary of Stesichorus; in fact there is disagreement about the attribution of some of the recently discovered papyri, the language not serving to distinguish the two poets.[37]

Poetry

The *Suda* also tells us that the works of Stesichorus were collected in 26 books. This is an unusually large number. Since he was cited by title rather than by book-number, it is likely that each book contained one poem. These works may have been very considerable indeed, for a sign on a papyrus-fragment (S 27) of the *Geryoneis* indicates line 1300 and this may have come well before the end of the poem. And his *Oresteia* was in two books. We have the following titles: *Funeral Games of Pelias, Geryoneis, Cerberus, Cycnus, Oresteia, Sack of Troy, Homecomings, Helen, Boar-Hunters, Eriphyle, Europia*, along with the titles of poems that are generally regarded as spurious – *Calyce, Daphnis,* and *Rhadine* (277–9). One feature of his poetry that attracted the notice of ancient commentators was his originality in matters of myth (193.17–18) and we are told, for instance, that he was the first to have Athena born fully armed from the head of Zeus (see 233), the first to portray Heracles in his garb of lion skin and carrying a club and a bow (229). It was once the fashion to attribute to the lost works a formative influence on the development of Greek myth, with the idiosyncratic versions that varied from the more traditional stories of Homer and Hesiod. But Philip Brize has subjected all the stories attributed to Stesichorus to a careful analysis and compared these versions to what is known through iconography.[38] His conclusions (Brize 1980: 28–9) are very sobering and suggest that Stesichorus and the vase-painters and other artists were legatees of a rich and varied oral tradition that they both inherited and exploited. In the case of the birth of Athena and the garb of Heracles, for instance, there is visual evidence that antedates Stesichorus; he may have introduced certain elements into his poetry but this does not mean that he made them up.[39]

Our most valuable find for purpose of getting some idea of the span and rhythm of a long poem of Stesichorus is the extensive but very

---

37 E.g. P. Oxy. 2735 (= Ibycus S 166–219) is ascribed by some scholars to Stesichorus. Identity of dialect has in some cases led to a difference of opinion in attribution in the case of Sappho and Alcaeus too.
38 Brize 1980.
39 Brize 1980: 24–5. Page speculates, for instance (*PMG* pp. 95–6), on the possible influence of the *Oresteia* of Stesichorus on the metopes from Heraeum at the mouth of the Sele river near Paestum. But Brize (19) shows that this is most unlikely.

damaged fragments belonging to the *Geryoneis*. It is the leisurely pace of the narrative, with so much of the poem evidently given over to speeches, that has made it difficult to continue to believe that such a poem can have been sung by a choir. Previous to the publication and ordering of the pieces by Page in 1973 (= S 7–87)[40] only three quotations have been known: one mentions the cup of the sun in which Heracles travelled (185); one describes the place on the Spanish mainland near the river Tartessus (modern Guadalquivir) where Eurytion, the herdsman of Geryon, was born (184); and one describes the cup which Pholus the centaur offered to Heracles (181). Since the papyrus-fragments have allowed the reconstitution of the metrical scheme of an entire triad, it has been possible to reprint the previously known fragments showing lacunae and inaccuracies in the quotations as well as the likely disposition of the metrical cola. It has also become possible to distinguish many of the actors in the drama. They include, in addition to Geryon and Eurytion, Callirhoe, the Oceanid mother of Geryon, Erythia, the Hesperid mother of Eurytion and the eponym of the island on which Geryon lives, and Menoetes, the herdsman of the kine of Hades and companion of Eurytion.[41] It is clear that the gods are active and given speaking roles too (S 14).

Fragments S 7 and S 8 describe the birth of Eurytion and his later arrival on the island where he was to tend the cattle. Heracles must have commandeered the cup of the sun for his passage from the continent to the island of Erythia and back again with the cattle after he had killed Geryon. The famous fragment may refer either to his arrival on Erythia or to his arrival back on the mainland, whereupon he returned the cup to the sun who then used it for his night voyage back to the land whence he would depart in his chariot on the morrow for his daily voyage. Menoetes seems to be the one who warns Geryon of the approach of Heracles, who has dispatched Eurytion and his dog Orthus upon arrival in Erythia.[42] It is not immediately apparent why there should be two herdsmen on the island Erythia, but Vürtheim, remembering that Stesichorus is credited by Aelian (279) with the invention of pastoral poetry, remarked that the supplying of Eurytion with a companion creates a situation well known from pastoral,

---

40 See Page 1973c: 138–54.
41 The attribution of the speeches is sometimes self-evident, sometimes helped by the brief account in Apollodorus (2.5.10) which may well be a résumé of the poem of Stesichorus.
42 Menoetes, if as is likely he is present in the poem, is probably spared. He will meet Heracles again when the latter descends to Hades for Cerberus (Apollodorus 2.5.12).

i.e., the possibility of amoebaean song between herdsmen.[43] Geryon's own name is cognate with γῆρυς and γηρύω. Vürtheim further speculates (20) that the poem must have dilated on the geography of the West, and, while not provable, this is highly plausible. In addition to the description of the Tartessus and of the island of Erythia we know that Stesichorus mentioned in the poem the island called Sarpedon in the stream of Ocean.[44] Just as the *Odyssey*, composed on the shore of Asia Minor, shows particular interest in the geography of the Black Sea and no doubt draws on sailors' stories, the *Geryoneis*, composed in Sicily, shows a parallel interest in the western sea.

When Menoetes begs Geryon to avoid confrontation with Heracles, Geryon answers with a speech (S 11) that has something in common with the famous statement of the heroic ideal in the *Iliad* (12.322 ff.) but is also invested with a memorable originality. Geryon will fight because he is mortal, and in this he is like Sarpedon. But his alternative to dying is to 'reach hateful old age' (age has the pejorative evaluation here that it does in Mimnermus but does not have in Homer);[45] and if he refuses to fight he leaves a legacy of reproach (ὀνείδε[, 22) to his family, reproach (ἐλέγχεα, 11–12) being a luxury which only gods can afford to incur. And so Geryon goes unflinching to the unequal combat. The duel is preceded by an appeal from his mother, who bears her breast to him like Hecuba of *Iliad* 22.83 ff., though she has much in common too with Thetis, another divine mother who laments her own lot in bearing a short-lived son (*Iliad* 1.414–16). It may be no simple coincidence that the new fragments of Stesichorus have given us another fraught scene, in the Lille Papyrus, where a mother tries to prevent her children from fighting.

The description of Geryon's death (S 15) must have been famous in antiquity; here and only here, there seems to be an instance where the literary description influenced the vase-painters.[46] Heracles shoots an arrow into one of the three heads, from which the helmet has been struck, and the arrow pierces the brow, causing the head to droop like a damaged flower. The description of the death of the monster makes the creature human and sympathetic.

43 Vürtheim 1919: 21.
44 The *Cypria* (fr. 24 Allen = 32 Bernabé = 26 Davies) says that the Gorgons lived on this island.
45 Old age in Homer is normally a time of fulfilment and honour and people do not fear it; it is unpleasant only if the external circumstances, like poverty or war or death of children, make it so.
46 See Brize 1980: 60–1.

The *Cerberus* and the *Cycnus* were poems about Heracles too.[47] Several of Stesichorus' poems – *Sack of Troy, Helen, Returns, Oresteia* – were concerned with myths of the Trojan Cycle. In addition to the several testimonia to the *Sack of Troy* (*Iliupersis*) that were previously known (196–205) there is now a collection of fragments from P.Oxy. 2619 (S 88–132). The two most substantial of these (S 88–9) are about the Trojan Horse; the other pieces are too fragmentary to give much sense of the drift, though S 104 appears to be a lament by Helen for her daughter Hermione.[48] Fragments S 133–47 are from another papyrus (P. Oxy. 2803) and contain a poem the title of which is given by the papyrus as the *Wooden Horse* (S 133b). This title was previously unknown. It is not clear whether or not what we have here is the same poem as the *Sack of Troy*, but attempts have been made to join the fragments from the two papyri (S 105). The *Trojan Horse* may have been either an alternative title for the poem or the name of one book of a longer work.[49] A Roman monument of the Augustan era has relief-illustrations of scenes from the 'Sack of Troy according to Stesichorus' on it (205). Since these include a central scene of the departure of Aeneas with Anchises, there has been much debate whether the inspiration can really be a poem of Stesichorus, with most scholars inclining to scepticism.[50]

Helen was clearly important in several poems – the *Sack of Troy*, the *Helen*, and the *Homecomings* (*Nostoi*) of which the only remaining fragment (209) describes her interpreting a portent to Telemachus. Most famous of all Stesichorus' poems in antiquity was the so-called Palinode, of which Plato in the *Phaedrus* quotes three lines (192), saying that Stesichorus, blinded for his slander of Helen, recognized the reason for his affliction and composed the recantation (= palinode) which caused his sight to be restored. The whole discussion of the poem was much complicated by the publication of a papyrus commentary on Stesichorus (193) that quotes the first lines of two palinodes, and other evidence has come to light, printed

---

[47] The *Scylla* (220) has a very shadowy existence. There may have been a poem with this name by Stesichorus and it may have been concerned with Heracles (Vürtheim 1919: 26–7).

[48] It may be a lament by Demeter for Persephone, who was called Hermione in Sicily: see Page 1973d: 56. But in any case we have (Lerza 1982: 49–50) a third instance of a mother concerned with the fate of her children. Unfortunately the tiny fragments of the *Boar-Hunters* do not allow us to see how Stesichorus treated Althaea.

[49] Page (1973d: 64–5) is not persuaded that the poems are the same or that they should be joined.

[50] See Campbell 1991: 3.107, Brize 1980: 20.

by Davies in his apparatus, that seems to corroborate that there *were* in fact two palinodes. What their relation to each other was, or in which poem the slander occurred, is still unclear. But it seems on the whole likely that the palinodes were separate poems from the original in which the poet spoke ill of Helen. The papyrus says that Stesichorus criticizes Homer in one palinode and Hesiod in the other for their accounts of Helen. What seems certain is that Stesichorus was concerned with correcting the version that sent Helen to Troy, for we know from a passage in Plato's *Republic* (9.586c) that Stesichorus maintained that the war at Troy was fought over a phantom. Somehow Stesichorus exculpated Helen, absenting her from Troy, and he criticized poets who promulgated the story of her actual presence at Troy and gave her responsibility for the city's destruction. His own final version was, apparently, that Helen spent the war-years with Proteus in Egypt (193.15–16). This version of the myth later became popular: we find it, for instance, in the *Helen* of Euripides but we do not know for certain whether it originated with Stesichorus.[51] The blindness referred to looks like an incident from literary history that has been turned into biography. Stesichorus may well have said in the emended version that he was blind to the truth when he composed in the manner of earlier poets: the idea of figurative blindness, or ignorance of truth, is deep-rooted in Greek, the best known instance being in the imagery of the *Oedipus Tyrannus* of Sophocles.

The *Oresteia*, in two books (210–19), was also famous. Influential in fifth-century Athens, it was quoted by Aristophanes in the *Peace* (211–12). Several motifs found in the tragedians may have been taken from Stesichorus, who in turn may have been the first to use them in literature: Iphigeneia summoned to Aulis on the pretext of marrying Achilles (217); the dream of Clytemnestra, which in Stesichorus as in Aeschylus is of a snake (219); the recognition of Orestes and Electra[52] at the tomb of Agamemnon, in Stesichorus as in Aeschylus facilitated by a lock of hair (217); Orestes protecting himself against the Furies with a bow given to him by Apollo (217), found again in the *Orestes* of Euripides. The main difference between the Stesichorean version and what we know from epic is the primary responsibility given to Clytemnestra for the death of Aga-

---

51 Herodotus has a story which he got from Egyptian priests (2.113–17) that Helen spent the years of the Trojan War in Egypt. Since he improbably maintains that Homer knew this version and suppressed it, both his testimony and the antiquity of the story are suspect. Hecataeus (*FGrHist* 1 F 307–9) and Hellanicus (*FGrHist* 4 F 153) both know the story of Helen in Egypt but do not specifically say that Stesichorus was the source.
52 Stesichorus is said to have had a predecessor Xanthus who composed an *Oresteia* that introduced Electra's name into the story (699–700 *PMG*).

memnon. Stesichorus may have been crucial in giving the story the new emphasis that it everywhere has in tragedy. But his *Oresteia* was set in Laconia, not Mycenae or Argos.

None of the papyrus-discoveries had, however, yielded more than a dozen lines of the unbroken text until 1977 when a long fragment, called the 'Lille Papyrus,' was published, with thirty-three virtually intact lines. The attribution, based on the dialect, metre, and the general similarity (e.g., importance of speeches) to what we had already learned about Stesichorus from the previous papyrus-discoveries, has strengthened the convictions of those who felt that the style was more citharodic than choral. The great surprise was to find a speech from the mother of Eteocles and Polynices, for there was no known title of Stesichorus from the Theban cycle, the closest being the *Eriphyle*, and there have not been lacking scholars who want to attribute the new discovery to the known poem.[53] Worthy of note perhaps is that the division of inheritance proposed between the brothers twice mentions the χρυσόν that Polynices will take to Argos (222, 229). This may well point to the golden necklace of Harmonia with which Eriphyle was later bribed to send Amphiaraus and which caused Alcmaeon to murder her (ΣPind. *Pyth.* 3.94).

The speaker of the lines, who is addressing Tiresias at the outset and who turns at 218 to her sons, is not named. Some have seen in her Jocasta; others, thinking that Stesichorus accepts the version of the *Odyssey* (11.271–80) where Jocasta (or Epicasta as she is called in Homer) seems not to have borne children to Oedipus and to have committed suicide upon discovery of the incest while Oedipus lived on after her death, call the speaker Euryganeia, the name given by the epic *Oedipodia* to a second and non-incestuous wife.[54] It is, again, uncertain whether Oedipus is dead, or alive in the palace and disinherited as the Queen speaks. Remarkable about the fragment is the way it, like the *Oresteia*, anticipates tragedy. Tiresias is, for the first time, present as adviser to the House of Labdacus, and seems to have just revealed the will of Apollo (209), who here, as in the *Oresteia*, is closely concerned with the fortunes of a tragic family: the alternatives expressed by the Queen at 216–17, who sees a disjunction between her family or the city surviving, recalls Aeschylus *Septem* 745–9, where Laius was faced with a similar dilemma. If the Queen is Jocasta, then Euripides

---

53 See Segal 1989: 156 n1; March 1987: 131–3. The metrical scheme of the Lille Papyrus does not correspond exactly to that of the fragments (S 148–50) tentatively assigned to the *Eriphyle*.

54 ἐπ' ἄλγεσι of the first surviving line may mean 'additional' woes and so point to the discovery of incest; but it may mean simply 'with accompanying woes.'

in the *Phoenissae* is drawing a precedent he knew from Stesichorus when he allows her to live after the discovery of incest and when he has her try to mediate between the quarrelling brothers. There is something that anticipates Sophocles' Jocasta too in this Queen who wishes to evade what the oracle has pronounced.

The better-preserved part of the papyrus makes it clear that Tiresias has revealed a prophecy of Apollo and that the Queen, hoping to escape the full horror of what she has heard, proposes a way out ot the fratricidal strife that is threatening. She suggests a division of the patrimony, with the drawing of lots to determine who will remain in Thebes and who will depart with the 'cattle and the gold.' Tiresias and the sons seem to concur just as the continuous text ends. In what follows enough can be read to make out that the casting of lots took place and that Polynices lost and left Thebes. Tiresias seems to prophesy the future marriage of Polynices to the daughter of Adrastus of Argos and to foretell that the strife will continue. This suggests that he has concurred only because he heard the Queen phrase her solution as a *postponement* of the fulfilment of the oracle (ἀμβάλλων 230); as a seer he must know that it is not possible to escape the fratricide, but he can accept the Queen's desperate expedient for the moment.

The long poems of Stesichorus, inasmuch as we can now catch a glimpse of how he composed, make us understand why he was often compared to Homer (e.g., *Anth. Pal.* 7.75; 9.184.3). If it is *prima facie* easier to think of these poems as sung by a bard rather than a chorus, it must be remembered that the longer poems of Pindar and of Bacchylides in particular[55] show the same fondness for dramatic confrontation and for speeches: in Bacchylides 5 the bulk of the poem is a series of exchanges between Meleager and Heracles and the narration of the hunt for the Calydonian boar is put into the mouth of Meleager, while in the Fourth *Pythian* there is an elaborate dialogue between Jason and Pelias. It will not be surprising to find that since there has come to be doubt about the choral nature of the poems of Stesichorus there has arisen at the same time questions whether the performance of epinician poetry was always, or even usually, choral.

Simonides

The date traditionally accepted for the birth of Simonides is the first of two possibilities given by the *Suda*; it is the 56th Olympiad (556/552 BC), which is the date the *Suda* gives for the death of Stesichorus; his death

---

[55] Segal (1989: 160) calls Bacchylides the successor of Stesichorus.

is placed in the 78th Olympiad (468/464) and it is specified that he lived for 89 years.[56] The *Suda* also reports that some authorities put the birth of Simonides a generation later, in the 62nd Olympiad (532–528 BC), and while this date has been strenuously defended[57] there has not on the whole been general acceptance of the lower chronology. The chief reason that the later dating has seemed attractive is that, of many associations reported for the poet in the course of his life, the most securely fixed poetry is from the time of the Persian Wars and there has been some reluctance to make the best attested activity in his life the period of his advanced age. We have a long life with few other episodes that can be precisely dated.

Poetry

Simonides was in the Alexandrian canon of the nine lyric poets, but he is the only one for whom no precise number of books can be ascertained. In addition, or perhaps as a consequence, it is difficult to assign the remaining fragments to specific genres in the majority of cases, and we see considerable discrepancy among ancient authorities in naming the types of composition. The *Suda* speaks of dirges (θρῆνοι), encomia, epigrams, paeans, tragedies, 'and other works.' There is no trace of tragedies by Simonides; scholars generally assume that he composed dramatic dithyrambs of a sort familiar to us from Bacchylides and that these were taken as tragedies, to which they bore some resemblance. We know in addition that Simonides was crucial in the development of the epinician ode, of which fragments survive, and that he composed hymns (e.g., 576, 589 *PMG*), a probable propempticon (580 *PMG*), 'prayers' or 'curses' (κατευχαί, 537, 538 *PMG*),[58] while among the 'convivalia' or elegies for performance at symposia (19–33 *IEG*) there may have been scolia. Mention of a category called 'Compound' or 'Miscellaneous' (σύμμικτα, 540 *PMG*) seems further to indicate Alexandrian confusion in the classification. The *Suda* gives in addition the titles of long works in elegiacs such as 'The Reign of Cambyses and Darius' and 'The Sea-Battle of Artemisium.' It also lists 'The Sea-Battle of Salamis' in lyric metres.

---

56 The lyric fragments of Simonides are collected by Page *PMG* and the remains of the elegy are edited by West *IEG*²; for the epigrams ascribed to the poet, see Page 1981: 186–302. Further bibliography is collected by Gerber 1994: 129–52. Volume 29.2 (1966) of *Arethusa* is devoted entirely to the new elegiac fragments of Simonides, but appeared too late to be taken into account here.
57 Stella 1946: 1–24. Molyneux (1992) argues in great detail for acceptance of the earlier dating.
58 Page *ad loc.* thinks that this was the title of a single poem, not of a book.

Simonides, so far as we can tell, was the first poet to write odes for victors in the crown games of Greece. Most interesting in the testimonia and the quotations of these poems (506–19 PMG)[59] is the frequent connection of the victors with the Dioscuri, Castor and Pollux. We are told by Pindar (Ol. 9.1–2) that an old refrain by Archilochus was sung for the victor at Olympia, and the scholiast on the passage in question quotes it. But aristocrats must have begun in the sixth century to demand more elaborate celebration than the chanting of simple refrains, and when games at Delphi, Nemea, and the Isthmus were added to those at Olympia poets were commissioned. Ὕμνοι were addressed directly to gods and since this is the word most often used by the epinician poets of their songs, it is tempting to see a hymn for the divinized Heracles as forerunner of the *epinikion* for mortals,[60] a partial secularization of the genre. The term Kastor- or Iolaos-song is used by Pindar (Pyth. 2.69, Isth. 1.16) and this too suggests a song for superhuman ἀθληταί. Καστόρειον (Castor-Song) has been called 'simply synonymous' with *epinikion*.[61] At Olympia Heracles and the Dioscuri attend and administer the games (Pindar, Ol. 3.34–7). It is accordingly interesting to note that Simonides says that not even Pollux (a boxer) or Heracles 'would have lifted hands' against Glaucus of Carystus (509 PMG). This extravagant praise suggests the extreme youth of the victor,[62] for such a compliment might appear hybristic if addressed to an older man, and it also suggests a certain humour in Simonides' style which we do not find in Pindar and Bacchylides.[63] A story which was common in antiquity was that Simonides in his epinician poetry was told by a patron to collect part of his fee from the Dioscuri since he had in his commissioned song spent so much time praising them (510 PMG). The poet was summoned to the door by two youths; when he had exited the hall collapsed on the assembly. Simonides is said to have been able to identify all the bodies because he remembered where all guests had been seated: the story is told as evidence of the poet's phenomenal memory, which was ascribed to his invention of an art of mnemonics, but it is equally

---

59 519 PMG is a collection of 166 papyrus-fragments, most very tiny, from epinician poetry and paeans.
60 Heracles is the archetypal ἀθλητής because of his performance of labours (ἄθλιοι).
61 Fränkel 1975: 435 n18 (= 1962: 494 n18).
62 The victory is thus put at 520 BC; see Molyneux 1992: 33–42.
63 507 PMG is a quotation from an epinikion that commenced with mention of how Crius, whose name means 'ram,' got 'sheared' when he went to Olympia. Some have seen a good-natured play on words here, but it is more likely that there is a cruel reference to his defeat and that the ode was for an Athenian enemy of the Aeginetan Crius: see Page 1951b: 140–2.

interesting because of what it seems to say about the traditional role of the Dioscuri in epinician poetry.[64]

With Simonides we see clearly that the poet is, to a much greater degree than before, outside the social group for which he composes. Several sources say that Simonides was the first to work for pay.[65] He was a paid professional moving from one venue to another and composing upon commissions from his patrons, who gave him his fee. Links are repeatedly mentioned with the great houses of Thessaly and Sicily, and with the Pisistratid court in Athens.[66] In being the first to compose *epinikia* and to praise the ἀρετή of the living, Simonides may have been the first to promote the link between possession of money and the celebration of success in poetry. This seems to have led to a rich anecdotal tradition about his venality and miserliness. Several sources mention his fondness for money, though the stories are stereotyped and not likely to reveal a biographical truth.[67] The most famous of the stories is told repeatedly.[68] Simonides maintained that he had two containers, one in which he kept the money he received for his poetry, in the other of which he kept the thanks (χάριτες) he received. This latter chest, he maintained was always empty – the money container was the only one of use. There may have been something in the poetry to give rise to this (623 *PMG* cites a word for 'chest,' for instance), but the stories most likely gained currency because of the new situation in which the poet found himself. The tradition also credited him with a particular σοφία. This too may be a result of his association with the ruling class of his time, for there is a long tradition of associating sages with rulers – one need only cite the traditional linking of Periander with Thales, Croesus with Solon, Pericles with Anaxagoras,

---

64 There is considerable debate as to how much truth there may have been in various parts of the story. But the point at issue here – that the Dioscuri were intimately associated with epinician poetry – is unconnected with the historicity of the event reported, for the story, even if untrue, undoubtedly arose because of mention of Castor and Pollux in odes for victors. Molyneux (1992: 54 n2) interprets the passage in Quintilian to mean that he knew at least four odes that praised the Dioscuri.

65 E.g., Callimachus fr. 222 Pf.; ΣPind. *Isth.* 2.9; ΣAr. *Pax* 698 (citing the criticism of Xenophanes); Chamaeleon *apud* Ath. 14.656d; Arist. *Eth. Nic.* 1121a6–7, *Rh* 1391a8.

66 The pseudo-Platonic *Hipparchus* 228B–C says that this son of Pisistratus brought Simonides and Anacreon to Athens, as does Aristotle, *Ath. Pol.* 18.1. The most famous story related about a sojourn of Simonides in Sicily is of his reconciling Hieron of Syracuse to Theron of Acragas and preventing war between them (Diod. Sic. 11.46; ΣPind. *Ol.* 2.15).

67 See Bell 1978: 29–86.

68 In addition to the scholiast on Aristophanes (above n65) the scholiast to the hypothesis of Theocritus 16 and Stobaeus (*Ecl* 3.10.38).

and in myth Tiresias with the rulers of Thebes. As someone who received a fee for his services, Simonides was inevitably seen as a proto-sophist at a time when the earliest paid teachers were becoming notorious in the Greek world. And in the case of the sophists democratic prejudice seems to have influenced the popular picture, which became in part a caricature, and so Simonides easily became a clever miser (κίμβιξ and σοφός).

The two longest citations of the poetry of Simonides (542 & 543 PMG), have both been reconstructed as poetry from the prose of the authors who quote them. 542 is in fact from a discussion by Socrates with the sophist Protagoras in Plato's dialogue *Protagoras*. The piece, addressed to Scopas, has a long history of being analyzed for its philosophic content and its importance in the history of Greek thought, since Simonides appears to be discussing what it means to be good and to be commending that man who of his own free will does nothing base. The heart of the piece is the apparent contradiction between an initial text that says approvingly that it is hard to be good, and a restatement of the same idea which attributes the maxim to the sage Pittacus, only to disapprove of it in the rephrasing. The extended discussion of such an issue, if it is in any way representative of much of the poetry that has been lost, makes it easy to understand why Simonides was assimilated to philosophers and sophists. But the recent tendency has not been to look for depth of philosophical doctrine or originality in the piece but to point to the strong emphasis on praise and blame in the poem.[69] This seems more helpful, for the doctrine expressed is not strikingly new, and it is constant with praise of the great: what is said is that no one is so perfect as to be blameless and that praise and love (ἐπαίνημι καὶ φιλέω [27], both words from the encomiastic repertoire) are merited by the person who does not do any more evil than ἀνάγκη obliges him to do. Read this way the lines may even be an apology for the regimes of the powerful. We see here our first extended excerpt from a praise-poem; the iambic poetry of blame is much older, for its practitioners did not rely on money to produce their work.[70]

A papyrus-fragment (541 PMG) which sets out much the same line of reasoning has been ascribed to Simonides because of the similarity of the

---

69 It is seen as belonging to an encomium and fitting easily into the genre by Most (1994: 127–52). Carson (1992: 110–30) finds it consonant with the epinician genre. Lesky (1963: 215 = 1966: 188–9) classifies the poem as a scolion.

70 The generally accepted view is that Simonides, who was allegedly in Athens during the time of the Pisistratids, left for Thessaly after the expulsion of Hippias in 511/510 BC. This cannot be proved but is not unlikely. If it is correct, poems for Scopas will probably antedate the turn of the century. Pindar's first surviving praise-poem, *Pyth.* 10, is also for a Thessalian and is dated to 498 BC.

ideas expressed to those in the poem for Scopas. It is said here that the desire for pleasure, ambition, or profit often militates against the desire for goodness and makes virtue difficult. Sentiments like this are not uncommon in the surviving snippets of the poetry of Simonides, but they are on the whole commonplace rather than original, even if Simonides' expression of them is especially fine. 579 *PMG* states that Virtue is enthroned in lonely and almost inaccessible isolation on a rocky crag; this is an adaptation of Hesiod, *Works and Days* 289 ff. The idea that man is ἀμήχανος and at the mercy of the gods is powerfully put forward in 526 and 527 *PMG*, but this was also given memorable expression in Archilochus. Fr. 584, which asks whether life is desirable without pleasure, is reminiscent of Mimnermus.[71] Fr. 531 is a brief quotation that seems to say that reputation is important because it survives us and 'is last to sink beneath the earth.' Again, it is not *per se* new, for the idea that fame lives on is as old as Greek poetry and was a sentiment particularly appropriate to epitaph and dirge. Especially noteworthy is how the emphasis on human fragility, something we see repeatedly in the citations from poetry, became transformed in the tradition into an emphasis on money-making as the only human activity that had durable value. The Hibeh Papyrus 17 (c. 250 BC) attributes to Simonides the dictum that 'all things grow old except money-making, and kind actions grow old most quickly of all.' Since this is alleged to have been addressed to Hieron's wife, it provides a good example of how the new situation in which the poets received money from patrons was understood to mean in the case of Simonides that he valued money more than the traditional goods of human life, especially when he had continued to emphasize, in the archaic manner, the ephemerality of human accomplishment (cf. 520, 521 *PMG*), and the horror of death, which is likened to the whirlpool of Charybdis (521 *PMG*). 520–7 *PMG*, that speak so eloquently of human vulnerability, are assigned to dirges, though not all these fragments are certainly attributable to this genre. A remarkable stylistic feature of these pieces is the poet's strong tendency to express himself in negative statements.

The second of the two long citations of Simonides we possess (543 *PMG*) is quoted by Dionysius of Halicarnassus for no other purpose than to show that a piece of poetry, allegedly from triadic composition, reads like prose if the colometry is not known. It has been notoriously difficult, in fact, to restore it to anything that resembles triadic composition, for the

---

71 The publication of new papyri (19–20 *IEG*²) has in fact led to the definite attribution to Simonides of a piece that, because of its similarity to Mimnermus 2, was formerly frequently ascribed to Semonides, who antedated Simonides by more than a century.

responsions are all almost undetectable. The generally accepted presentation of the text now is that of Page,[72] and it seems to show that Dionysius chose his text in such a way as deliberately to hide the metrical correspondences: the first three lines of Page's printed text, part of the end of an antistrophe (1–7), seem to correspond to the last two and one-half lines (ἔπος ... μοι) from the beginning of the strophe (21–7); the full epode intervenes (8–20), and so the quotation, with its minimal overlap, fools us and easily makes Dionysius' point. The piece is rightly admired as one of the treasures of Greek lyric. It is a description of Danae adrift with the infant Perseus on a menacing sea by night, speaking to her sleeping child and praying to Zeus, who she probably does not know is the father of her child.

We have no idea from what sort of poem this fragment comes. Because of its dramatic nature and mythical subject-matter it is often thought to be from a dithyramb; in its pathos and tenderness and its emphasis on emotion it seems to anticipate Euripides. There is considerable evidence for the treatment of mythological subjects in Simonides: we hear, among others, of a dithyramb on Memnon (539 *PMG*), a poem called Europa (562 *PMG*),[73] and there are references to the Theseus-story (550, 551 *PMG*), and the Argonautic Saga (540, 544–8, 567? *PMG*). It is hard to imagine that the Danae-fragment could come from the myth of an epinician ode since the subject is not heroic, and we do not in any case have the evidence that would allow us to say whether Simonides used myth extensively, as Pindar and Bacchylides do, in his odes for victors. Bergk thought that the Europa-poem, with its long soliloquy by the abducted Europa, influenced Horace, *Odes* 3.27,[74] and indeed Simonides had considerable influence on the Roman poets. His pathetic effects were admired by Catullus, who speaks of something as *maestius lacrimis Simonideis* (38.8). The Danae-fragment resembles the Europa-poem we see in Horace: in both poems a maiden loved by Zeus is carried over the sea and in desperation appeals to heaven, there being a certain irony in the fact that the as yet unknown lover is Zeus himself. If there were several poems like this it may have given rise to the strange title κατευχαί.[75]

---

72 See Page 1951b: 133–40.
73 The scholiast on Homer says that Bacchylides and Hesiod told the Europa-story. It is usual to attribute this to the dithyrambs of Bacchylides (fr. 10), though it is not indicated by the source that the story was told in a dithyramb.
74 See Oates 1932.
75 The story given by the Homeric scholiast as from the mysterious κατευχαί (537 *PMG*) is one known from Ovid, who is thought to have got it from Simonides. Here too we have a story of maidens carried off and praying to a divinity who brings unexpected succour (*Met.* 13.669 ff.).

Simonides was especially famous for his poetry connected with the Persian Wars. The famous lyric encomium of those who fell at Thermopylae (531 *PMG*) speaks of 'this precinct of noble men' (ἀνδρῶν ἀγαθῶν ὅδε σηκός, 6) and may refer to a shrine at Sparta for Leonidas and the Three Hundred, or to a sanctuary at Thermopylae itself in honour of all those who died in engagements at the famous pass.[76] There are references to a lyric poem for the battle of Artemisium (532–4 *PMG*), possibly for performance at Athens at the shrine of the wind-god Boreas or at the Panathenaea; Boreas had given the Athenians help in the battle (Her. 7.188 ff.). The *Suda* mentions an elegy for Artemisium and a lyric poem for Salamis, but because the few quotations relating to Artemisium were lyric it had been believed that the *Suda* had reversed the genres and the battles. New evidence has, however, enlarged our knowledge of Simonides' poetry for the Persian Wars and it has become clear from the papyri that there was in fact an elegy for Salamis (5–9 *IEG*²). The Suda states that Simonides composed in the Doric dialect. The lyric fragments do show strong influence of Doric while the elegiac poems, as to be expected, are in an Ionic-Homeric language.

One of the most startling papyrus publications of recent years has been extensive fragments of an elegy for Plataea by Simonides (10–14 *IEG*²).[77] The proemium (10 *IEG*²) may be an invocation of Achilles, and the poem continues with a compendious description of his death and burial with Patroclus and mention of the fall of Troy. The poet goes on to introduce Homer and his rôle in giving deathless glory to the warriors who fought at Troy and he then (19) takes leave of Achilles to summon the Muse to assist him in celebrating those who fought for Greece at Plataea. There is considerable detail discernible about the battle: mention of Pausanias and the Spartans, the Megarians, and the arrival of the Peloponnesian troops at the Isthmus. Many of the supplements are made possible by reference to the account in Herodotus and considerable space seems to be devoted to the prophecy of Tisamenes given in Herodotus (9.36) before the papyrus runs out. The appearance of this poem strongly supports the theory that elegy was performed publicly.[78] It has been suggested that the occasion may have been the Festival of the Eleutheria at Plataea, and that poets like Simonides may have entered competitions with elegies as they did with

---

76 See Molyneux 1992: 186–7.
77 The reconstituted long fragment (11 *IEG*²), which allows West to offer about thirty lines of quite continuous text – now our longest piece of Simonides, is the result of a combination of fragment 2327, known to E. Lobel and published in 1954 in volume 22 of *The Oxyrhynchus Papyri*, with fragment 3965, published by P. Parsons in 1993 in volume 59.
78 Bowie 1986a: 13–35.

their tragedies at other festivals. This would give new meaning to the old story that Aeschylus left Athens because he was defeated by Simonides in a competition to compose an elegy for Marathon (*Vita Aeschyli* 8).[79]

There is no area in which Simonides held such undisputed pre-eminence as in the composition of elegy. Ironically, it is just this pre-eminence that has rendered it almost impossible to isolate with certainty the compositions that are his. For throughout antiquity, from the time Simonides was alive to the time the Palatine Anthology was put together, epigrams and elegiac couplets were ascribed to him almost indiscriminately. There is only one epigram that all authorities are agreed is unquestionably his; it is the one quoted by Herodotus (7.228) who says it was inscribed by Simonides as an epitaph for his friend the seer Megistias who died at Thermopylae. Even the words used by Herodotus do not put the matter beyond all doubt, for he says that Simonides was the one ἐπιγράψας, which technically means only that he provided and paid for the inscription, but almost all authorities are willing to believe that Herodotus means us to understand that Simonides composed it as well. The other two epigrams quoted in the same place, including the most famous of all Greek couplets, with the dead addressing the passerby and telling him to bring the news of their death back to the Spartans whose behests they followed, command much less agreement. They are frequently cited as Simonidean but there are scholars who vigorously contest the attribution.[80] After Herodotus there is no ancient author before Aristotle who ascribes an epigram to Simonides. This compounds the problem, because poetic couplets do not contain the name or *sphragis* of the author: this means that many undoubtedly genuine works that were inscribed became anonymous to later generations while conversely many were attributed to Simonides by people who had little solid reason for the attribution. It is reasonably certain that when Meleager put together his *Garland*, a precursor of the *Greek Anthology*, c. 100 BC he drew on an earlier collection of epigrams ascribed to Simonides, probably made in the late fourth century BC. The epigrams that found their way into the *Anthology* are generally known as the 'Simonidea' and they form a large group of both epigrams meant for inscription (and in some cases known to have been inscribed) and purely literary elegies. A few of them are very likely to be authentic, while some are patently late literary exercises. But we have absolutely no certain way of separating true from false. Some ninety 'Simonidean' epigrams, ranging in length from two to twelve lines, are divided by Page into several categories: 1) on

---

79 Boedeker 1995: 217–29.
80 E.g., Page 1981: 232.

events before the Persian Wars and ascribed to Simonides; 2) on events before the Persian Wars and anonymous but possibly Simonidean; 3) and 4), like 1) and 2) but on events of the Persian Wars; 5) on events and people contemporary with Simonides and ascribed to him; 6) on events and people contemporary with Simonides and anonymous but possibly Simonidean; 7) miscellaneous ascriptions; 8) anachronistic ascriptions; 9) spurious and clearly falsely attributed.[81] The likelihood that surviving epigrams for rival states or families are by Simonides suggests his stature throughout Greece. He was employed by patrons of all sorts and his poetry is not proof of his politics or personal loyalties.

Pindar

Pindar's poetic career seems, from what we know, to have been entirely in the fifth century.[82] The ancient *Vita* of Pindar in the Ambrosian manuscript quotes the first-person utterance of someone who maintains that he was born in the year of a Pythian festival (fr. 193), and this has usually been taken as spoken in the poet's voice. The favoured years are 522 and 518, with the later date preferred since it corresponds to the notice in the *Suda* that Pindar was born in the 65th Olympiad. If 518 is correct he may be an exact contemporary of Bacchylides; he was a slightly younger contemporary of Aeschylus, who was born in 525. His birthplace was near Cynoscephalae near Thebes; his father's name is variously given as Daiphantus, Pagondas, or Scopelinus, his mother's as Cleodice. *Pyth.* 5.75–6, discussed below, speaks of the clan of the Aegeidae as ἐμοὶ πατέρες. If this first-person utterance applies to the poet and not just to the chorus of the poem, Pindar was a member of an aristocratic family prominent in Thebes and in Sparta. P. Oxy. 2438 records a dithyrambic victory of Pindar in Athens in 497/6 or 496/5. The first definitely datable epinician ode is *Pyth.* 10 from 498. The name of Pindar's wife is given in the Ambrosian *Vita* as Megacleia, that of his son as Daiphantus, and those of his daughters as Protomache and Eumetis. Fr. 94c is apparently a *daphnephorikon* (a type of partheneion) written in honour of his son, with his daughters in the maiden-chorus. Many of the epinician odes are

---

81 See Page 1975: vii–viii.
82 The standard text of the epinician odes is by Snell and Maehler (1987) and that of the fragments by Maehler (1989); also important for its full account of the MSS tradition is the edition by Turyn (1952). For further bibliography, see Gerber 1969, and Gerber 1989 and 1990. My thanks are due to Maggie Rogow for helpful advice and criticism.

definitely datable, with *Pyth.* 8, the last, from 446. If Pindar died at age 80, as some ancient sources state, the probable year was 438. There are many anecdotes told about his life, most of them in the ancient lives.[83] The recent tendency has been to view these anecdotes with considerable scepticism.

Poetry

According to the Ambrosian *Vita* Pindar's works were collected in seventeen books in the library at Alexandria. These comprised eight types of poetry: hymns (1); paeans (1); dithyrambs (2); prosodia (2); partheneia (3); hyporchemata (2); encomia (1); threnoi (1); epinician odes (4). Only the last survived as a book-text. Some idea of the other works may be gleaned from fragments, either in citation in prose authors or from papyrus fragments. The most substantial fragments are from *Paeans* 2, 4, and 6; these come from volume 5 of *The Oxyrhynchus Papyri*, published in 1908, which contained portions of *Paeans* 1–10.[84] The epinician odes were arranged according to venue, for victors at Olympia, Delphi (*Pythians*), the Isthmus, and Nemea, in order of prestige and antiquity of the games. The last three odes at the end of the collection of *Nemeans* are not for victors at Nemea, and the final poem is in fact for an athlete entering upon a magistracy. These anomalous poems were appended to the *Nemeans* for the sake of convenience at a time when the *Nemeans* were the final book of the collection; the order of the last two books became reversed in the manuscripts with the result that the *Nemeans* now precede the *Isthmians*, a book that is mutilated at the end and thus incomplete. There are 45 complete poems, plus one fragmentary final *Isthmian*.[85] Because we have a book-text we have – what we do not possess in the case of the other lyric poets – substantial scholia, going back in large measure to Didymus in the first century BC but doubtless preserving many comments of the first Alexandrian commentators. These are indispensable for our understanding of the poet since the ancient commentators, even if they were living a few centuries subsequent to Pindar, possessed a feeling for the Greek language which we cannot hope to equal and many works now lost to us on which to base their judgements.[86] The existence

---

83 These may be found in Lefkowitz 1981: 57–66.
84 There are altogether fragments of 22 paeans.
85 There has been some doubt whether *Isth.* 3 and 4 should be classed as a single poem or as two.
86 The scholia have been edited in three volumes by Drachmann (1903, 1910, and 1927).
   There is a marked recent tendency to view the scholiasts with caution since it is felt

of victor-lists often enabled the scholiasts to date the poems accurately. Partial lists have reached us, either on papyrus, in inscriptions or as compilations.

Within the individual books the odes are grouped according to the importance attached to the athletic events, with the equestrian victories placed first, followed by victories in gymnastic contests (pancration, wrestling, boxing, pentathlon, and foot-races, in this order). The victory with the four-horse chariot carried the greatest prestige and was placed first, followed by the victories with the single courser and with the mule-chariot. Both the *Olympians* and the *Pythians* show anomalies, however. The First *Olympian*, for a victory with the single horse, precedes odes for chariot-victors; it was given pride of place because of its famous opening praising the Olympic games. And neither *Pythians* 2 nor 3 is clearly for a chariot-victory at Delphi: 2 does not name the venue and 3 seems to be neither for a victory nor for a chariot. But both poems are for Hieron of Syracuse and were placed with *Pyth.* 1, which is for a chariot victory of Hieron, because of the importance of the addressee. The book of *Pythians* has as its final poem an ode in honour of a victor with the pipe.

Pindar's language is the literary language found in Alcman, Ibycus, Stesichorus, and Bacchylides, with a stronger Doric flavour than is found in the Ionian Bacchylides, but fewer local peculiarities than in the Laconic of Alcman, though Pindar will on occasion use a Boeotian word.[87] There is an admixture of other dialects, in particular Aeolic, and epic forms are also present. The epinician odes fall roughly into two categories metrically. About half are in dactylo-epitrites, a metre found first in Stesichorus (above 10) and also used by Simonides and Bacchylides, with the other half in 'Aeolic' metres, based on iambs and choriambs.[88] Only one ode (*Ol.* 13) combines both metres. The great majority of the odes are triadic, but seven (*Ol.* 14; *Pyth.* 6, 12; *Nem.* 2, 4, 9; *Isth.* 8) are monostrophic. Most of the triadic odes have three to five triads, approximately 100 lines; the Fourth *Pythian* with thirteen triads and 299 lines is a remarkable exception.

There is no external evidence for the performance of the epinician odes and the indications given in the poems themselves lead critics to different

---

that in many cases their interpretations are based on mere guess-work. In particular, the scholiasts are more eager than are most contemporary scholars to find biographical elements in the poems.

87 E.g., αἱμακουρίαις at *Ol.* 1.90.

88 For a straightforward explanation of the metre and of the colometry of modern editions, see Nisetich 1980: 35–9.

conclusions. Most of the poems we have were undoubtedly sung in the presence of the victor at his home, but some shorter ones were probably performed at the place of victory. An impromptu song doubtless greeted the victor immediately upon his triumph, and we have seen (20 above) that this might incorporate a traditional refrain of Archilochus. In several instances we have pairs of odes from Pindar for the same victory (*Ol.* 2 and 3, 4 and 5, 10 and 11; *Pyth.* 4 and 5). The reasons for there being two poems seem not always to be the same: it may be that one celebration was private, the other public (*Ol.* 2 and 3?), that one was commissioned by the victor, the other unofficially (*Pyth.* 5 and 4), that the two were performed at different times in the festivity (*Ol.* 4 and 5), or that one was performed immediately at the place of victory and the other, longer poem later at the home of the victor (*Ol.* 11 and 10). In one instance, Hieron's victory with the chariot at Delphi in 470, we have a short and perfunctory poem of Bacchylides (4) that was clearly performed at Delphi, and a magnificent poem from Pindar, *Pyth.* 1, that was the officially commissioned ode. And wealthy patrons might commission two odes for the same victory, as Hieron did in 476 (Bacchylides 5 and Pindar *Ol.* 1).

It has regularly been assumed since antiquity that the epinician odes were all performed chorally. But this assumption no longer seems as certain as it once did, and it has been challenged, most notably by Lefkowitz.[89] Triadic composition is itself no proof of choral performance as we have seen (above 11), and both the long poems of Stesichorus and the triadic poem of Ibycus to Polycrates are now widely held to be citharodic or for solo performance. At the heart of the problem is the use of the first-person pronoun in Pindar. Some scholars insist that it is primarily the voice of a chorus referring to itself (as it undoubtedly is in the non-epinician poetry of Pindar), some say that it is always the poet and does not presuppose a chorus, and some take the position that the reference may fluctuate, being sometimes the poet and sometimes a chorus. Even those who continue to believe that the odes were for the most part performed chorally are now willing to believe that this is not necessarily true for all of them. The most reasonable conclusion is that whatever the circumstances of performance – and they may have varied – the first-person utterance must always include the poet. Pindar may on occasion have travelled with his poems to the places where they were performed: the first-person indications of his presence

---

89 Davies 1988: 52–64; Lefkowitz 1991. The debate has continued: see Heath and Lefkowitz 1991: 173–91 (an exhaustive presentation and discussion of the evidence), followed (*ibid.*) by Carey 1991: 192–200; Morgan 1993: 1–15; D'Alessio 1994: 117–39; Lefkowitz 1995: 139–50.

(e.g., ἦλθον, κατέβην) are variously taken as indicating his actual presence or as a convention used figuratively of the presence of the poem (or of a chorus in performance).

Pindar's patrons are the rich and powerful of the entire Hellenic world, especially ruling princes who entered the equestrian events in the major games as a way of displaying their wealth and acquiring pan-Hellenic glory. The addressees of his epinician odes range from Sicily in the west to Rhodes in the east (*Ol.* 7), and from Thessaly in the north (*Pyth.* 10) to Cyrene in the south (*Pyth.* 4 and 5). Somewhat surprisingly, there are no odes for victors from Sparta. Less surprisingly, Athens does not figure largely, for it was aristocrats, not democrats, who were Pindar's patrons: and of the two short odes for victors from Attica (*Pyth.* 7, *Nem.* 2), the first is for an Alcmaeonid, Megacles. Pindar's own city of Thebes, enemy of Athens throughout the fifth century, is well represented (*Pyth.* 11; *Isth.* 1, 3, 4, 7). Despite the fact that Thebes had sided with the Persians when they invaded Greece and had actually fought against the Athenians at Plataea (it was later punished for its apostasy), Pindar's official position as a poet of all Greece has him proudly proclaim the repulse of the barbarians that threatened Hellas: in the First *Pythian* he salutes the Athenian rôle at Salamis, the Spartan rôle at Plataea, and the successes gained by the rulers of Syracuse against Etruscans and Carthaginians in the waters off Sicily and Italy (70–9); in *Isth.* 8, for a victor from Aegina, Pindar mentions the 'rock of Tantalus' that had been averted from Greece by a god (10). Since Aeginetans had won special distinction in the battle of Salamis they could take this as praise of their island. Like Thebes, Aegina was throughout the period during which Pindar composed a rival and enemy of Athens. Though there is little or no sense in Pindar that his privileged aristocrats are a threatened species, it is true that he lived to see the overthrow of the ruling houses of Syracuse, Acragas, and Cyrene for which he composed his greatest poems. His regular stance is that the glory of victory not only redounds to the credit of the individual who achieved it but is a boon for the entire polis and wider community (τό γ' ἐν ξυνῷ πεπονᾱμένον εὖ, *Pyth.* 9.93).[90] But it would be wrong to think that the victor-ode was primarily for a civic celebration as was Athenian tragedy. Even if the victor's polis is named and is understood to bask in the reflected glory of the victory of a native son, the ode was primarily commissioned by a wealthy individual whose achievements and generosity are the *raison d'être* of the song. It was once fashionable to think that Pindar was uncomfortable in his task of praising athletic victory and sought to alleviate the necessity

---

90 This matter is discussed by Kurke 1991.

of enumerating all the individual's feats; but there is no reason to attribute this distaste, if it is felt by moderns, either to the Greek poet or to a Greek audience.[91] Greek literature is from the beginning filled with admonitions to excel;[92] the foundation of Greek humanism is the belief in the possibility of outstanding accomplishment in a brief and precarious human existence.[93] Pindar's *gnomai* remind us how fully he proclaims this creed: life without toil and risk is not worth living (θανεῖν δ'οἷσιν ἀνάγκα, τά κέ τις ἀνώνυμον / γῆρας ἐν σκότῳ καθήμενος ἕψοι μάταν, / ἁπάντων καλῶν ἄμμορος; Ol. 1.82–4). Sport is a form of competition that provides an obvious theatre for display of merit. And Pindar's language is replete with expressions for excellence (ἄριστος, ἀρετά, κορυφαί, ἄωτος, ἄεθλον). The poet's task is to immortalize this excellence in poetry, the only sure form of continuing life after death. A secondary task is to proclaim it in the face of detractors, for no accomplishment that sets man apart from his peers is unattended by the envy (φθόνος) of the small-minded.[94]

Among Pindar's poems are two groups that stand out, those for Sicilian and those for Aeginetan patrons. Together they account for over half the odes. The fourteen Sicilian poems are mostly to be found among the *Olympians* and *Pythians*[95] and bespeak the concern of the ruling families there to win in the events that conferred the greatest prestige at the most important sites and to commission the most important poet to celebrate their success. Nine of the eleven complete Aeginetan odes are among the *Nemeans* and *Isthmians*:[96] these odes are mostly for youthful victors in less spectacular events.

Of the Sicilian odes four (*Ol.* 1; *Pyth.* 1–3) are for Hieron of Syracuse, while two are for his relative-by-marriage and general Chromius (*Nem.* 1 and 9), and four are for the royal house of Acragas, also allied to Hieron by marriage.[97] Two of the poems for Hieron's victories can be dated: *Ol.* 1 is for 476 with the horse Pherenicus, and *Pyth.* 1 is for his chariot

---

91 See Heath 1986: 85–98, esp. 92–4.
92 The best known formulation is αἰὲν ἀριστεύειν καὶ ὑπείροχον ἔμμεναι ἄλλων (Homer, *Il.* 6.208).
93 The most memorable statement of this idea is Glaucus' speech to Sarpedon at Homer, *Il.* 12.310–28.
94 See Kirkwood 1984: 169–84.
95 With the exception of *Nem.* 1 and 9; *Isth.* 2.
96 The exceptions are *Ol.* 8, *Pyth.* 8. The fragmentary *Isth.* 9 is for an Aeginetan.
97 Hieron was married to the daughter of Xenocrates (addressee of *Pyth.* 6 and *Isth.* 2); Theron (addressee of *Ol.* 2 and 3), brother of Xenocrates, was father of Demarete, wife of Gelon; Gelon was brother of Hieron and founder of the Syracusan dynasty from whom Hieron inherited the throne. After Gelon's death Demarete became wife of another of Hieron's brothers, Polyzelus, whose own daughter was married to Theron.

victory at Delphi in 470, though this victory pales in insignificance in a poem which celebrates far more the military victories of Hieron and his founding of the new city at Aetna on the slopes of the mountain to reward his veterans. The Third *Pythian*, among the poems which strain belief that the epinicians were performed chorally, appears to be a consolation to an ailing Hieron and to mention past but not present victories,[98] while *Pyth.* 2 is not definitely datable.[99] Pindar is generally taken to have visited the Sicilian courts in 476, the year of the first three *Olympian* odes. The Second *Olympian* is remarkable for the great eschatological passage it contains outlining a doctrine of judgment and reincarnation. This doctrine is so unlike the normal theology of the epinician poems, which do not deal with survival after death except inasmuch as it is conferred as poetic immortality, that it is quite reasonably thought to show Sicilian religious influence, perhaps doctrine that was important to Theron of Acragas, the addressee.[100] We shall see (below 53) that the dual verb of line 88 of this poem has been thought to refer in uncomplimentary fashion to Simonides and Bacchylides, and this possibility is not to be discounted, despite general reluctance today to find evidence for personal quarrels in the poetry of Pindar.

Whether or not the common enmity of Thebes and Aegina with Athens provided a bond between Pindar and his patrons on Aegina,[101] Pindar, as a Theban, boasts a personal link with the island: at Isth. 8.16–30 he explains that it is especially fitting that he give praise since Thebe and Aegina were sisters, both daughters of the river Asopus. Aegina provides an unparalleled source of heroic myth, for through her son by Zeus, Aeacus, Aegina was the source of the great heroes of saga, Peleus and Telamon and their sons Achilles and Ajax. Like Bacchylides (below 50) Pindar exploits the rich fund of Aeginetan myth in his Aeginetan poems.

Pindar's connection with the city of Cyrene also deserves mention. Three of the Pythian odes are Cyrenean. The Ninth *Pythian* from 474, for Telesikrates of Cyrene, is the most popular of Pindar's poems because of its central myth, which tells of Apollo's union with the Thessalian nymph Cyrene and of her translation to North Africa where she became the eponym of a Greek colony. The erotic theme of the myth is clearly

---

98 On *Pyth*. 3 and the equestrian victories of Hieron, see Robbins 1990: 307–18 [reprinted in this volume 175–91]
99 The possibilities are discussed by Most 1985: 60–8, who plausibly dates it early, to 477 BC. Some scholars have seen in this poem an offering for Hieron's victory with the chariot at Olympia in 468, when Bacchylides composed ode 3.
100 Lloyd-Jones 1985: 245–84.
101 It is remarkable that the Aeginetan boy-victors more than once have an Athenian trainer: Melesias in *Ol*. 8 and *Nem*. 4, 6; Menander, *Nem*. 5.

linked to the treatment of the victory, for the victor is also seen as one who brings back a bride (= victory) from mainland Greece to adorn his city.[102] *Pythians* 4 and 5 are for King Arcesilaus, the eighth and last in the line of rulers descended from Battus, founder of the colony.[103] The Fourth *Pythian* is Pindar's most ambitious poem and was commissioned in 462, to honour the victory by the king in the chariot-race at Delphi, by a political refugee, Demophilus, who had spent his exile in Thebes and hoped by the magnificent offering to win his recall to his native city. The extended myth of the poem is the story of Jason and the Argonauts and is apposite because the king claimed descent from one of the Argonauts, Euphemus, who had on the return voyage of the Argo received at the site of Cyrene a pledge that his descendants would colonize the area.[104] The accompanying Fifth *Pythian*, the king's own commission, does not contain mythical narrative, but shows a remarkably detailed knowledge of the topography of the city, one unparalleled in the other works of Pindar.

The Pindaric ode appears to be made up of a number of disparate elements that are hard for us to reconcile into a whole of which all the parts are clearly related. In a developed ode (i.e., one of the poems with the normal length of five triads) we can consistently count on finding five components.[105] There must be, first of all, the essential information about the victor: his name, the name of his father and, in many cases, of his clan, the name of his city and of the victory which he won. If the victor has won at other times and in other places there will be a catalogue of these victories. It is likely that other victories were won by other members of the family in previous generations, and since Pindar likes to emphasize inheritance (which he usually calls φυά) he will probably mention these victories too. This indispensable material constitutes the objective 'programme' of the ode;[106] it relates specifically to the occasion and was doubtless expected by the patron, who provided the necessary information. Second, the poet speaks self-consciously of his own poetry and of his own song. Pindar is in fact the first Greek poet in whom we find repeated and ubiquitous reflection on the nature of his rôle as poet and on his art. He regularly talks of and to his Muse, he mentions

---

102 See Köhnken 1985.
103 Herodotus in Book 4.145–67 tells the story of the first six kings, named alternately Battus (the name of the founder) and Arcesilaus.
104 On the possible further relevance of the myth, see Robbins 1975: 205–13 [reprinted in this volume 192–201].
105 See Fränkel 1975: 440 (= 1962: 500).
106 The term 'Programm' is that of Schadewaldt 1928.

principles of selection (καιρός) and the rules or constraint that govern his utterance, he mentions the poet's obligation to praise (χρέος) and tender what is the legitimate reward (ἄποινα) of the victor, and he comments on the relationship of inborn ability to acquired skill in poetry, generally privileging the native ability of the σοφός.[107] Third, there are γνῶμαι or aphorisms that encapsulate the traditional wisdom that the σοφός teaches. These often form bridge-passages that articulate the sections of the ode. There is a long tradition of such didactic utterance in Greek poetry, and there were entire collections of ὑποθῆκαι or sayings; one of these collections was attributed to the sage and mentor Cheiron, an important presence in Pindar's poetry.[108] The moralizing *gnomai*, by offering ethical reflection on the events commemorated in the poem, lift the occasional to the level of the universal. Fourth, there are ubiquitous hymnal elements (Pindar calls his own epinician odes ὕμνοι), prayers and addresses to gods, and other theological reflection. No poet is more insistent that all achievement and all glory, in fact all elements of human life both good and bad, are the disposition of divinity. In addition to the major Olympians, many lesser divinities, some little more than divinized abstractions, are present in the odes: examples are Τύχη (*Ol.* 12), the Χάριτες (*Ol.* 14), Ἡσυχία (*Pyth.* 8), and Ὥρα (*Nem.* 8). And finally, most odes of any length have a mythical narrative. Like the *gnomai*, the myths place the actual in a wider context and provide material that somehow illuminates the occasion. The myths very frequently draw on material that is particular to the family or city of the addressee. This part of the Pindaric ode is the one that makes the most immediate appeal to the modern reader, for he tells the stories with incomparable brilliance. Compression is the key-note: the narrative emphasizes carefully chosen scenes from a larger whole that is likely to be well known to the audience. Pindar is concerned, however, to emphasize that he is giving a true account of past events. He may criticize his predecessors for their versions and substitute a different story. On occasion he appears to be choosing the preferred version from among many that were current; on occasion he appears to be making up a new version in good faith as more in keeping with his canons of appropriate behaviour – the

---

107 The poet is thus in many respects like the victor in that he requires inborn talent that is developed by training. The idea is memorably expressed in the contrast between the σοφός ὁ πολλὰ εἰδὼς φυᾷ and the μαθόντες at *Ol.* 2.86. There are good remarks on this in Hubbard 1985: 107–24.
108 He occurs in *Pyth.* 3, 4, 6, 9; *Nem.* 3; *Isth.* 8, usually in the rôle of mentor and guide to the heroes of myth (Achilles, Jason, Asclepius), who are themselves paradigms.

Muse who inspires him is in every case the guarantor of the truth of his account.[109]

Criticism

Pindar's epinician poems possess these various elements in such apparently random order and with such abrupt and difficult transitions that it is not surprising that criticism in the modern period has been obsessed with a search for what gives individual poems their unity. In an important and often-cited article Young traced nineteenth-century solutions to the unity-problem to what he considered their *fons et origo malorum* in the editions of Boeckh (1811–21) and Dissen (1830). Working in conjunction they developed the notion that each poem could be reduced to a *summa sententia* or *Grundgedanke*, a short thematic statement informing in each case the various parts of the poem.[110] This approach necessarily privileged the gnomic utterances, for by their very nature they provided just the short encapsulating maxims that might serve such a purpose. Recently it has been shown that this approach is not so new as Young posited and that earlier critics from the Renaissance onwards had offered similar solutions to the problem of unity. Young's own solution, which provides a '*Grund* on which the *Gedanken* of the poem are built,' is found to be in effect not very different from the views he criticizes.[111] Other critics have found the *vinculum* that binds the parts elsewhere, frequently in the idea of a repeated word or image. Boeckh also posited the influential idea of historical allegory in the poems of Pindar, i.e., that much in the poems referred to events in the victor's own life or to politics of the time. Myths were particularly susceptible to being read for covert historical references. It is undeniable that the nineteenth century had a penchant for biography that is unpalatable to contemporary Pindaric criticism: this trend culminates in Wilamowitz's great book on Pindar, which is biographical throughout.[112]

The reaction against historicist criticism found its apogee in the influential work of Bundy.[113] This was in effect an extension of Schadewaldt's

---

109 The most famous instance of Pindar correcting his predecessors is his account of Pelops' ivory shoulder in *Ol.* 1. In some instances we have an existing literary version of the account that Pindar sets straight, e.g., *Ol.* 7.20–34 and Homer, *Il.* 2.653–70.
110 Young 1964.
111 Heath 1986: 97–8.
112 Wilamowitz 1922. The conjectural dates given in the Teubner text for poems that are not securely datable by external evidence are Wilamowitz's dates.
113 Bundy 1962a and 1962b.

earlier insistence on the programme and concentrated exclusively on the rhetoric of praise. For Bundy Pindaric odes served 'the single purpose of eulogizing men and communities' and did not indulge in recondite allusiveness that contained 'personal, religious, political, philosophical and historical references that might interest the poet but do nothing to enhance the glory of a given patron' (Bundy 1962b: 35). The great advance of this approach was that it made poems and passages that had previously been mysterious and inaccessible much more comprehensible, for they could be seen upon analysis to be variations of a limited number of commonplaces.[114] The poems were virtuosic displays of the poet's skill in manipulating *topoi*, which were 'foil' for the climax or 'cap' of direct victor-praise. The disadvantage of the approach was that the poet became less interesting: his thought was jejune or non-existent and his technique the only thing worth studying. In this sense Bundy continued an established tradition of devaluing Pindar as a thinker.[115] And Bundy's work led to a downplaying of the political and historical setting of the odes, though this may also have been caused in part by hostility to historical allegory.[116] Reaction has come from a number of quarters, in particular from those who have taken Pindar's intelligence seriously.[117] The very idea of 'unity' has been challenged as a post-Pindaric notion inappropriate to the study of a Pindaric ode, for it involves, no matter where it is found, a reductionist and centripetal tendency that does scant justice to the manifold diversity of the poetry. Now we have come full circle and a critic can say again, 'Pindar in fact could use his odes as springboards for advancing personal interests which were only indirectly connected with the objective epinician program'[118] or 'digression was no crime until Pindar's licence to digress was revoked and that (...) was a relatively recent development.'[119]

A detailed analysis of one of Pindar's odes will serve to add substance to the points made above. The rubrics are intended to point to issues raised in the foregoing discussion.

114 See Lloyd-Jones 1973: 109–37.
115 Norwood's famous phrase (1945: 184) that Pindar could 'think like a child and sing like an archangel' is an example.
116 E.g., Carey 1981: 4 'Recent research into the conventions of Pindaric poetry has rendered speculation on the historical ambiance of individual odes largely unnecessary ...'
117 Hubbard 1985: 107–24.
118 Hubbard 1992: 78.
119 Heath 1986: 98.

The Eighth *Pythian*

The poem is dated by the scholiast to 446 BC and this date is generally accepted. It is the last datable poem of Pindar.

1 The Political Background

Since this is of importance for understanding the poem it must be sketched.[120]

After the Athenian victory over the Boeotians at Oenophyta in 457, Aegina was forced to become a member of the Delian League and to pay tribute. The tribute imposed was higher than that of any of the other allies. In 447, however, an Athenian force was defeated in Boeotia at Coronea (Thuc. 1.113) and Boeotia was evacuated. The following year, the year of our poem, Athens had to contend with revolts in Euboea and Megara, and a Peloponnesian force under the Spartan king Pleistoanax advanced into Attica as far as Eleusis but mysteriously withdrew (Thuc. 1.114). Negotiations began which led to the Thirty Years Peace, concluded between Athens and Sparta probably early in 445.

It is likely, but not certain, that the Pythian victory of Aristomenes, won in August/September of 446, was celebrated after the invasion and withdrawal but before the negotiated peace. For some recent critics the events of 446 are unimportant for the poem: one flatly states that by the time of the athletic victory 'it had become clear that the Spartans would do nothing for the Aeginetans.'[121] This has the advantage of hindsight – it is true that the Thirty Years Peace did not relieve the position of Aegina, but unlikely that the conditions of it were published in 446,[122] when Aeginetans might still have entertained hope because of the recent Athenian reversals and willingness to negotiate. Another recent treatment ignores events of 446 too, but in a diametrically opposed way.[123] It advances the unusual view that the Athenian Empire crumbled at Coronea and the Aeginetan aristocrats could regard their city as free again since 447. The references to Typhoeus and Porphyrion at the beginning of the poem are to a vanquished monster and the words ἐλευθέρῳ στόλῳ (98) are to a voyage of freedom already under way. We have a clear instance of historical allegory in the

---

120 Some commentators, nonetheless, discuss the poem without any consideration of the political events of the period: cf. Carne-Ross 1985: 169–84 (a good example of treatment of a poem in terms of dominant or recurring images).
121 Figueira 1991: 90.
122 Brown 1951: 1–6 sets out the details of the question well.
123 Pfeijffer 1995: 156–65. Pfeijffer's interpretation is anticipated by Boeckh, who thought that the reference to freedom required a date before 457 for the poem, despite the scholiast (Boeckh 1821: 308). See also L.R. Farnell 1930–2: 2.192.

poem, with the defeated monsters symbols of a defeated Athens. The poem becomes triumphalist and so loses the wistfulness regularly found in it.

Apart from the fact that this reading ignores the central myth as a possible source of understanding of the overall tone of the poem, it attaches mistaken emphasis to the tense (or aspect) of the imperative κόμιζε in the final prayer. It is maintained that 'the polis is already "on a voyage of freedom" at the moment the ode is being sung' since it has already liberated itself from the yoke of foreign domination. But Aegina was *not* free in 446. To call her free is wishful thinking (the province of prayer). In a prayer the thing prayed for does not usually exist yet – it is called into being by the invocation if the patronage solicited is granted. The prayer to Hesychia with which the poem opens contains the present imperative δέκευ (5), for instance. This means not that Hesychia has already received Aristomenes but that the reception is coincident with the invocation to a beneficial power that will not refuse it.[124] Aegina's course of freedom will come into being with the special protection of the goddess addressed. Prayer is prolepsis, not performance utterance.[125]

For another scholar, on the other hand, the events of 446 are important, but since it is impossible to decide whether the poem was written before or after the invasion of Attica two rival readings must be entertained. If the composition is *before* the invasion of Attica the addressee is being warned, through the invocation of Hesychia, not to be rash but to think twice before running off to ally himself with the invading forces; if the composition is *after* the invasion, the invocation of Hesychia is an apology for inactivity, directed at those who felt that intervention might have produced more conclusive results.[126] Apart from the unsatisfactory nature of the explanation that is meant to work in two different circumstances (only one of which can have obtained), the reading fails to satisfy because it views Hesychia as pacifism with regard to an external foe. The reference of ἡσυχία is, as we would expect, to the internal politics of Aegina.[127]

---

124 There is a parallel at the end of the Sixth *Olympian*. Poseidon is asked to grant a voyage καμάτων / ἐκτὸς ἐόντα to Syracuse and to swell the power of the poet's song (δίδοι, 104, and ἄεξε, 105). The trouble-free voyage will be the result of the prayer if it is granted. It makes a difference whether a present imperative is directed to a god in a prayer or to a mortal in an injunction: the imperatives addressed to Hieron at the end of the First *Pythian* (85 ff.) pretend that the qualities he is encouraged to manifest already exist. They may in actual fact *not* exist but the poet tactfully suggests that they do.
125 The present and aorist imperatives are equivalent in such phrases: see Hummel 1993: 326.
126 Cole 1992: 101–11.
127 Pfeijffer 1995: 156–65.

It makes pre-eminent sense to believe that in the year 446 there were on Aegina opposing groups, aristocrats of long-standing hostility to Athenians on the one hand and powerful families sympathetic to Athens on the other.[128] Pindar appeals for civic concord at a time of high tension: the strain so near the surface will have existed even before the battle of Coronea and would continue even after the Peace. These difficulties have a special interest for the Eighth *Pythian* since it is the only poem of Pindar's for an Aeginetan victor that can be securely dated to the period after the subjugation of the city in 457. The city is asked to avoid fratricidal strife and join in unison in celebrating the victory of one of its native sons.[129] Pindar's sympathies will naturally have been with the aristocrats, his patrons: he had in all likelihood composed earlier for the Meidylidae, the clan of Aristomenes (cf. fr. 190). He allows the possibility (59–60) that he had on his voyage to Delphi had a prediction of Aristomenes' victory, and this would suggest that he knew beforehand that Aristomenes was competing. Perhaps he had already been approached to write an ode if Aristomenes should win. Aeginetan aristocrats had some reason for hope since Coronea; but to proclaim or even imply that Athens had been defeated was premature in 446 (and was belied by the terms of the Peace when they were actually promulgated). The ray of hope, and it was no more, could still be extinguished by civil strife, and the aristocratic faction would hear a covert reminder that peace at home was the prelude to and precondition of eventual discomfiture of an external enemy, represented by the monsters of the opening triad. Athens could not be openly mentioned, for Athens was as yet far from defeated. 'In contrast to the Pythian victory, this victory (i.e., the reacquisition of freedom) had not yet been won.' [130]

2 Voice

The Eighth *Pythian* provides two passages (55–60 and 98–100) that are central to the whole discussion of first-person reference.

---

128 For the likely existence of an Athenian ἀποικία on the island see Figueira 1991 *passim*.
129 This is a more attractive explanation than to posit that Pindar is by an invocation of Ἡσυχία merely trying to defuse the φθόνος that regularly attends the victor at the time of his reintegration into the polis (Kurke 1991: 210 n30).
130 Krischer 1985: 123. Krischer's demonstration of the ways in which the Eighth *Pythian* consciously recalls the First is very persuasive evidence that there is a political background to the Eighth. No one will deny that in the First the actual victory at Delphi pales beside the political events celebrated, Hieron's founding of Aetna and his defeat of the Carthaginians and Etruscans. In an environment where Pindar is not free to speak as openly as he was in 476, he can do so most effectively by allusion to his own poetry.

In the first of the two passages cited the speaker maintains that he had a prophecy on the road to Delphi. One scholiast took the passage starting at 55 (τοιαῦτα μὲν) to be spoken by the chorus *in persona victoris*.[131] The 'I' is thus Aristomenes, who would have received from Alcmeon a prophecy of victory as he set out from Aegina to compete in the games. This solution has found few adherents, though it was attractive to Bundy, who was eager to eliminate anything personal on the part of the poet from his poetry.[132] It may be that the scholiast, in making this unusual claim for the reference of the pronoun, is privy to information lacking to us, but in the absence of any external information and of certain parallels,[133] and without an indicator in the poem that there is an assumed voice, we would do best to abandon this proposal.

A variation of this idea is that the words are spoken by members of a group, perhaps a theoric group, from Aegina to Delphi.[134] There is a problem of who actually received the prophecy if the singular conceals a group: there must be a bit of fudging, for the impression is of spontaneous prophecy, perhaps even a vision, and this is hardly likely to have happened to a group.[135] So in this case too the experience is really the victor's and a chorus, which overlaps to some degree with the theoric group that accompanied Aristomenes, is in effect speaking *in persona victoris*. The fundamental question at issue here is whether the 'I' excludes the poet.

There is no incontrovertible instance of a choral 'I' that must exclude the poet. The instance that is often supposed probative, *Nem.* 7.85,[136] is an unresolved crux.[137] Two others are disputed: *Pyth.* 5.76 and line 98 of the same Eighth *Pythian*. In the former case, mentioned above, it is maintained that ἐμοὶ πατέρες cannot refer to Pindar, since even if there were *Theban* Aegeidae, as we know there were (*Isth.* 7.15), we do not know that Pindar's own ancestors came to Cyrene. But to refuse to grant the poet's licence to capitalize on a link between himself and the city of the addressee by naming as a link the Aegeids, who were certainly emigrants

---

131 Σ78a, 82, 83, Drachmann *Scholia* 2.214. It is not clear where the scholiast thinks the chorus abandons the voice of the victor and returns to his own persona.
132 Bundy 1962b: 69–70. So too Floyd 1965: 187–200.
133 The scholiast on *Pyth.* 9.91 (= Σ161, Drachmann *Scholia* 2.236) takes the passage in question there as spoken by the victor: see also P. Giannini in Gentili *et al.* 1995: 612.
134 Slater 1979: 68–70.
135 As observed by Giannini in Gentili *et al.* 1995: 576, *ad* 56–60.
136 Carey 1981: 16.
137 D'Alessio 1994: 133–5. D'Alessio disposes of the supposed problem of *Pyth.* 3.78 and of those who think that the utterance there excludes the poet.

via Sparta and Thera from Pindar's own πάτρα, is impossibly restrictive.[138] And, in any case, those who believe that a chorus excludes the poet in *Pyth.* 5 face an exaggeration at least as problematic, for Pindar would then use poetic licence in allowing a Cyrenean chorus that will hardly have consisted entirely of Aegeidae to act as though they were all descendants of this clan (for the entire chorus will say ἐμοὶ πατέρες). On balance, then, it is best to assume that Pindar introduces the mention of the Aegeid clan because it is Theban and he wants to establish a link between himself and the city of the addressee; he may in addition have been an Aegeid. Equally, it would be amusingly literal-minded to insist that the speaker who calls Aegina 'mother' at the end of the Eighth *Pythian* cannot be Pindar, since Aegina is technically his aunt,[139] but mother only to native Aeginetans. Here too Pindar pushes the link beyond the literal.

And so it is most likely that the person speaking is the one who at 29 ff. maintains that he cannot dilate on the glories of Aegina. It is the poet who received the prophecy on the road to Delphi. If so we have an astonishing intrusion of personal voice into a public poem, for the poet is allegedly presenting a biographical detail. Why does he do it?

There are two questions to answer here: who gave the prophecy and what was its content? The second must be guessed at, for Pindar, significantly, is silent about what was revealed to him. It may be that he was told the name of the victor. This would almost force us to believe that he had been commissioned in advance to write a poem for Aristomenes if he should win. This is possible, for, as suggested above, Pindar probably knew the family, and, knowing as little as we do about how he received his commissions, we cannot exclude the possibility that he was approached before the crown games by aristocrats who intended to retain him in the event of a victory.[140] Viewed in purely mercenary terms, this would lend some substance to Pindar's puzzling statement that the γείτων who delivered the prophecy was a guardian of his material benefit (κτεάνων φύλαξ ἐμῶν, 58), for he was offering the virtual assurance of a commission.[141] It might even be the case that Pindar had prayed for the success of Aristomenes and the

---

138 Pindar likes to forge a link between himself and the addressee: cf. *Ol.* 6.82 ff., which establishes a link between Thebes and Stymphalos (here too it is the relationship of the cities, not a blood relationship, that is paramount).
139 The nymph Metope (*Ol.* 6.85) is mother by Asopus of both Thebe and Aegina.
140 See Robbins 1990: 312–13 [in this volume 182] for the suggestion that Pindar was commissioned in advance by Hieron for a victory that he did not, as it turned out, win.
141 On Pindar's advertisement of the fact that his is a well-paid Muse, see Woodbury 1968: 527–42.

prophecy was the result of petition or inquiry rather than a spontaneous apparition. We have no way of knowing.[142]

But Pindar's lack of explicitness does suggest that he is implying something, or at least allowing his Aeginetan audience to fill the silence. It lends an attractiveness to the idea that the prophecy was something that he can only hint at and that this was that the days of Athenian hegemony were numbered.[143]

To the question 'who gave the prophecy?' there must be a definite answer, though there is not universal agreement. Since the time of the scholiast there has been a division of opinion. The scholium mentioned above as saying that the prophecy was given to Aristomenes (whose voice is assumed by the chorus) says that Alcmeon was the prophet and so contradicts another notice that says that it was Amphiaraus (this notice, incidentally, does not name Aristomenes as the recipient, suggesting that this scholiast may well have made the more traditional assumption that the recipient was Pindar).[144] The vast majority of critics until recently have assumed that the subject of ὑπάντασεν and ἐφάψατο (59, 60) is Alcmeon, because he is mentioned in the principal clause of the same sentence. Hubbard has argued powerfully for the understanding of the scholiast who believes that Amphiaraus gave the prophecy,[145] and has found followers.[146] The strength of the argument is that he has shown that syntactically the sentence does not require Alcmeon to be understood as subject of the subordinate clause just because he has been named in the main clause, and that there is strong evidence for an oracle of Amphiaraus at Thebes whereas there is none for a cult of Alcmeon. The passage is viewed as the patriotic outburst of a Pindar who is eager to advertise the importance of a Theban shrine. Considerations of 'unity' are irrelevant; Pindar is simply using the poem as a springboard for an interest that is not connected with the programme.

That Pindar has something to say in this poem that is more than the praise of Aristomenes seems clear, but this wider concern is consistent with

---

[142] Krischer's statement (1985: 123) that Pindar would in this case have received in a dream the name of the future victor and that this is unparalleled is a bit extreme, for it seems to imply that Pindar would thus have received out of the blue an unknown name. He may in fact have been receiving confirmation; if this is so the practice is less extraordinary.

[143] Krischer, *loc. cit.*; Hubbard (1993: 203) says the same thing: 'it may have foretold a general reversal in Aegina's political fortune.'

[144] Amphiaraus, Σ78b; Alcmeon, Σ78a.

[145] Hubbard 1993.

[146] E.g., D'Alessio 1994: 135 n60.

the whole, and it regards Aegina rather than Thebes. It is not crucial to this argument to establish who gave the prophecy, but despite Hubbard's powerful argument Alcmeon still makes better sense, and this gives the poem greater unity.

It should be noted that whether the prophecy was given by Amphiaraus or Alcmeon it is exceptional. Amphiaraus' oracle was forbidden to native Thebans (Her. 8.134); hence Pindar's encounter with the hero would be most unusual and could not have been regular divination. There is no tradition of any oracle of Alcmeon at Thebes, Aegina, or Argos,[147] and so a prophecy of Alcmeon is exceptional too.[148] Either way we are faced with something unusual that Pindar is reporting. But Alcmeon is the subject of a myth that begins with the words φυᾷ τὸ γενναῖον ἐπιπρέπει / ἐκ πατέρων παισὶ λῆμα (44–5), and the oracle is reported to have been delivered by someone who prophesied συγγόνοισι τέχναις (60, in emphatic position at the end of sentence and triad).[149] Now, Amphiaraus was a hereditary prophet, but there is little point in emphasizing this here, whereas there is an important point underlined if Alcmeon, who is seen as reproducing his father's excellence as a fighter, is also seen to be showing his father's prophetic skill: Amphiaraus was proverbially known for two things – he was ἀμφότερον μάντιν τ' ἀγαθὸν καὶ δουρὶ μάρνασθαι (Ol. 6.17).[150] The applicability of the myth to the occasion is precisely the emphasis on inherited excellence: Aristomenes is displaying the φυά of his family, seen previously in his maternal uncles Theognetus and Cleitomachus, and so honouring his πάτρα (36–8). The point is considerably weakened if Amphiaraus is the speaker, but the words themselves explain and justify the otherwise unparalleled prophetic powers of Alcmeon.

Further, the sentence that begins at line 55, χαίρων δὲ καὶ αὐτός ... makes little sense if Amphiaraus is the subject of the subordinate clause.

---

147 Wilamowitz (1922: 441) thought that Pindar might have been living at Argos, where he is reputed to have died, when he composed this, his last poem. A shrine of Alcmeon would at least make sense there, for he was an Argive hero.

148 At *Anth. Pal.* 2.393 ff. Christodorus describes a statue of Alcmeon the seer in the baths of Zeuxippus in Constantinople. This evidence is very late (6th century AD), but it does show that Christodorus knew of a tradition that gave the son of Amphiaraus prophetic powers. Christodorus thinks that the statue in question is of the poet Alcman; but he talks nonetheless of the 'famous seer' (μάντις ... ὁ βοώμενος). Or is Christodorus' statement based simply on his understanding of this passage in Pindar?

149 Cf. *Pyth.* 10.12: τὸ δὲ συγγενὲς ἐμβέβακεν ἴχνεσιν πατρός.

150 It has often been noted that if μάχεσθαι is substituted for μάρνασθαι this is a hexameter line. Pindar is thought to be quoting from an epic source here, probably the lost *Thebais*. See Huxley 1969: 45.

Why should Pindar 'rejoice too and praise Alcmeon' because *Amphiaraus* delivered a prophecy? He has good reason to rejoice and praise Alcmeon too (i.e., in addition to Alcmeon's father's praise in the first prophecy, 44–5) if Alcmeon did something for him, i.e., made a special revelation. χαίρων probably points to reciprocal χάρις, the poet's praise for the favour received.[151] Hubbard maintains that if we recognize Amphiaraus as the one who delivered the prophecy to Pindar we have an exact symmetry, with two *laudatores*, Pindar and Amphiaraus (in the myth), and two *laudandi*, Aristomenes and Alcmeon (in the myth), a balance which is destroyed on the traditional interpretation. But the symmetry is in any case imperfect, for Pindar *does* praise Alcmeon, the *laudandus* of the myth, giving the prophecy as reason for this praise.

3 The Myth
This is the only poem for an Aeginetan victor in which Pindar draws on a myth that is not that of the Aeacids. This, in itself remarkable, becomes even more surprising when we consider that the myth told is in fact that of the destruction of Pindar's own native city of Thebes (at a time when Boeotia had recently been liberated!). It is an unusually dark choice, for normally it is Thebe that Pindar addresses as his mother (*Isth.* 1.1): the eclipse of Thebes in the poem seems to prompt him to address Aegina as mother. In fact all the victories celebrated in this poem have a dark underside that is either explicitly or implicitly present. It has been thought that the choice of the story of two attacks on Thebes, the first unsuccessful and the second successful, may hint at the fact that Xenarces, the father of Aristomenes, was unsuccessful in the games.[152] This seems unlikely, for the fact that no victory of the father is mentioned makes this ode not unlike others in which there is no mention of the father's success. We can assume that he never scored an athletic triumph, but we need not believe that he ever competed unsuccessfully. It would be a rather tactless choice of mythical material on Pindar's part if this were the case.[153] In a memorable passage Pindar imagines Aristomenes' defeated enemies and their lack of joyous return to their mothers.[154] It is impossible not to

---

151 On this point, see Most 1985: 101 with n32.
152 Wilamowitz 1922: 441.
153 Krischer 1985: 123.
154 Cf. *Ol.* 8.68–9. The comparison of these two passages is instructive: both describe the return of the defeated athletes, but the passage in *Ol.* 8 does mention a return to the mother.

remember here that Alcmeon too had a return not without shadow, for he either returned to murder his own mother Eriphyle or, if he murdered her before his departure with the Epigoni, had no mother to return to.[155] Most remarkable of all, perhaps, is that the prophecy of Amphiaraus, who witnesses the victory of the second army sent against Thebes, details the cost of the victory: Adrastus, more successful on the second expedition than on the first, will nonetheless have a *nostos* to Argos with the body of his son. The light in this poem is light with attendant darkness.

4 The Ending

If this is the case, the traditional reading of lines 95–7, perhaps the most famous in all Pindar, is surely correct. They are generally seen as elegiac, often as the supreme statement in Greek poetry of the human condition, where pain is prevalent but redeemed by flashes of joy. Here as elsewhere Pindar uses metaphors of vicissitude. Lines 92–4 with their image of increase and fall remind one of similar sentiments elsewhere – the prosperity that is swung aloft at *Ol.* 2.21–2, 37, the winds of fortune at the end of the Seventh *Olympian*. The *gnōmē* in this case ends with fortune in the dust. The reflection on the lot of man follows immediately.

A recent article proposes a new reading of these lines.[156] They are not a reflection on human fortunes but a reworking of a common epinician *topos*: life without victory is equivalent to death, man is dead (a shade) without victory but given life by achievement. Thus read, the words are a compliment to Aristomenes. The sadness is gone and something more encouraging is put in its place. This provides a more upbeat ending to the poem, though the transition to the last lines is difficult unless we remove from the final prayer the note of apprehension usually found there and read it as a notice that Aegina's freedom has already been won.

The new interpretation is not, however, convincing. σκιᾶς ὄναρ is supposed to mean 'the dream felt by the shade' (a subjective genitive, not an objective genitive as it is usually construed). But parallels are lacking for dreaming dead, and the very concept seems dubious. More important, a text adduced as probative points rather to the greatest difficulty in the reading:

---

155 Critics are divided on when the matricide, which must have been an important incident in the *Epigonia* or in the *Alcmaeonis*, took place: I. Krauskopf, *LIMC* 1.1 (1981) 547, thinks it must have been after the return of the Epigoni while Bethe *RE* 1.2 (1894) 1551, 1563, places it before their departure.
156 Toohey 1987: 73–87.

ἀρεταῖ[ς γε μ]ὲν οὐ μινύθει
βροτῶν ἅμα σ[ώμ]ατι φέγγος ἀλλὰ
Μοῦσά νιν τρ[έφει]. (Bacch. 3.90–2)

This is indeed a *topos*. But what it says is that victory requires song to live on. Life is enhanced by victory, but *sub specie aeternitatis* it is no better than death if it is not validated by song. Pindar often says this (e.g., *Pyth.* 3.114–15, *Nem.* 4.1–8). Bacchylides is advertising the power of song to overcome death. Pindar does not do so in this passage. He dwells on the reversals of human fortune but says nothing of death and the poet. The movement is easy from this sober absence of mitigation for the briefness of human felicity to the prayer for a prosperous passage for an unhappy Aegina. Pindar had in lines 67–72 prayed for Apollo's assistance in the presentation of his victory catalogue.[157] Listing previous victories does not normally require assistance of such a powerful divinity, but the case here is unusual and of unwonted difficulty, for the catalogue, tempered with reflections on the mutability of fortune, runs the risk of being overwhelmed by the general pessimism of the context and overall tone. It is a hymn for a victor in a subject city and as such seeks a difficult balance.[158]

5 Unity

Wilamowitz's comment, 'Pindar had too much weighing on his heart to be able to mould the various elements into a whole,'[159] is unfortunate if it implies that we are entitled to look for a whole that could be no more than the expression of a *Grundgedanke*. But there is a danger in treating the poem as simply a collection of passages that may be discussed without relation to the entirety, as many recent treatments have done: the impression gained thereby reinforces Wilamowitz's generally negative assessment of this great poem. If the parts *can* be seen as contributing to an intelligible whole there is much to be gained and the reading is more satisfying. This is not to invoke a false or anachronistic aesthetic.

The Eighth *Pythian* is an epinician ode for a young wrestler from Aegina in 446. The poem is affected by the political situation of that year, and

[157] There is still much debate whether ἑκόντι ... νόῳ (67) is to be taken of Apollo or of the poet: see, most recently, Giannini 1995: 45–53. On the whole I think it likely that ἑκόντι ... νόῳ echoes εὐμενεῖ ... νόῳ of line 18 and so refers to Apollo, but it is not crucial to the argument advanced here to settle the matter, on which there is in any case no consensus.
[158] See Hubbard 1995: 51 n54.
[159] Wilamowitz 1922: 440.

it is the political situation rather than the poet's age that accounts for the subdued tone and dark colours of the canvas. Over a quarter of a century earlier he had composed the First *Pythian* for Hieron of Syracuse and told the myth of the triumph of Apollo and Zeus in heaven and of their representatives on earth, Hieron and Deinomenes, over the foes of Olympus and of Greece respectively. The victory was overt and scored over barbarians. Now Pindar quotes himself[160] and invites comparison with the earlier poem. There is a foe again, symbolized once again by Typhoeus and by Porphyrion, but the lesson to be learned from their discomfiture is given in a timeless, gnomic aorist: βία δὲ καὶ μεγάλαυχον ἔσφαλεν ἐν χρόνῳ (15). Civil concord or Ἡσυχία holds the key to victory and the poet appeals to it. Aristomenes' athletic victory can unite the opposing factions on the island, and an Aegina that is harmonious and without internal dissension will be in a position to make common and successful cause against its enemies. The invocation of Ἡσυχία, which can scuttle ὕβρις (12) and preserve Aegina on a course that is free, shows that the real victory lies in the future, for the Ἡσυχία for which the poet appeals at a time of internal division is a precondition of success against external enemies. The present enemy is not named explicitly, for Aegina is still subject, and among the political parties that need to be reconciled is a pro-Athenian faction. But the aristocrats assembled around the Meidylidae will have had little trouble seeing Athens in the monsters at the beginning of the ode. Pindar reports a personal revelation from the destroyer of Thebes and leaves it open to his audience to imagine that the prophecy was a prediction of the defeat of Athens.

Pindar knows the cost of strife between Greek states. The mood of the poem is without the jubilation of three decades earlier when united Greeks had triumphed over the Carthaginians, Phoenicians, and Persians: the lyre there was a symbol of Hellas itself[161] and would resonate in the σύμφωνος ἡσυχία of a new Dorian foundation (*Pyth.* 1.70). But now Greek will be turned inevitably against Greek and the cost will be great. Pindar's unaccustomed choice of myth for his last Aeginetan poem shows this. It is a tale of internecine war, of destruction of something that he holds dear, and a tale of qualified success because of its cost to the victor. A note of sadness permeates the poem and is evident in the awareness of the loss involved in victory gained. Fate is capricious and often malign, life precarious and for the most part dark. But there is reason for hope. The poem ends with a reminder that the moment of brightness redeems the darkness, and this issues in a prayer for the beloved island, still under the yoke but looking

---

160 Demonstrated in convincing detail by Krischer 1985.
161 Cf. Norwood 1945: 103.

Bacchylides

to a future free of the present travail. The hope is validated by the final litany of Aegina's heroes, the Aeacids; they, like its athletes, including the young man honoured on this occasion, have existed ἀπ' ἀρχᾶς (25–7). They demonstrate the power of inheritance and can be taken as the surest pledge that the future will not be without the glory of the past.

Bacchylides

Bacchylides was born at Iulis on the island of Ceos.[162] He was grandson of an athlete of the same name. His father's name is given as Meidon by the *Suda* and Meidylos by the *Etymologicum Magnum*. We are told that he was the nephew of Simonides and this is generally taken to mean that his mother was sister of Simonides,[163] though it is also possible that his grandmother was twice married, once to Leoprepes, father of Simonides, and once to Bacchylides the athlete, with Leoprepes and Meidon/Meidylos half-brothers.[164] The exact year of his birth cannot be determined with precision. His ἀκμή is placed by Eusebius in the second year of the 78th Olympiad, no doubt because of his most important commission, for the chariot-victory at Olympia of Hieron of Syracuse in 468. The *Chronicon Paschale* place the ἀκμή in 480 but this is certainly erroneous. That he was a contemporary of Pindar is clear from the fact that they wrote for the same patrons. An ancient but unreliable tradition made Bacchylides younger than Pindar.[165] Pindar's birthdate is usually taken to be 518, which will be the approximate date of Bacchylides' birth too.[166] Almost nothing is known of the life of Bacchylides. Plutarch maintains that he was in exile in the Peloponnese. This may be an inference from the fact that Pindar wrote a paean (4, of uncertain date) for the Ceans and this was considered an unlikely commission if Bacchylides had been present on Ceos at the time. Date of death may be 451 since Eusebius mentions him in his entry for that year; and no date after 450s can be assigned to the odes: 6 and 7, for the Olympic victory of Lachon of Ceos, and 1 and 2, for the Isthmian victory of Argeius of Ceos, are from the 450s, most likely from Bacchylides'

---

[162] The standard edition of the poet is Snell and Maehler 1970; all references are to the numbers of this edition: the *epinikia* and dithyrambs are given straight numbers, while fr. is prefixed to the shorter fragments (pp. 82 ff.). Of fundamental importance is Maehler 1982: 1.I. For further bibliography, see Gerber 1990: 67–98.
[163] The testimonia are collected by Snell and Maehler 1970: 130–2.
[164] See Molyneux 1992: 97.
[165] See Maehler 1982: 1.I.1 6–7.
[166] Severyns 1933: 15–30, argues plausibly for 518/517 as birth-date for Bacchylides.

last years.[167] The entry in Eusebius which refers to Bacchylides in 431 is thought to refer to a homonymous pipe-player from Opus.[168]

Poetry

The works of Bacchylides were collected by the Alexandrians, who included him in the canon of nine *lyrikoi*, in nine books: dithyrambs, paeans, hymns, prosodia, partheneia, hyporchemata in honour of the gods, and the epinician odes, encomia, and erotica in honour of men. Only some 100 lines of Bacchylides were known from citation in ancient authors when a papyrus-find in Egypt produced substantial portions of fourteen *epinikia* and six dithyrambs. These fragments were acquired by the British Museum in 1896 and published in an *editio princeps* by Kenyon in the following year.[169] An important edition by Jebb followed shortly thereafter.[170] The discovery allowed an appreciation of Bacchylides' art for the first time since antiquity, but it also caused his reputation to suffer by comparison with the epinician poetry of Pindar, a judgment already voiced by the author of the περὶ ὕψους, 33.5. This judgment has been considerably altered in recent years and Bacchylides is increasingly assessed in his own right, without invidious comparison. Much credit for this is due to the fine commentary of Herwig Maehler.

The papyrus seems to give the full book of epinician odes and the first six poems of the book of dithyrambs, arranged alphabetically. Of the *epinikia*, the earliest appears to be 13. A drinking-song (encomium?) for Alexander, son of Amyntas of Macedon and king 498–54, seems to be from the youth of both poet and addressee and so may be our earliest fragment, dating from before 490. Ode 13 is for the Nemean victory of the young Pytheas of Aegina, for whom Pindar composed *Nem.* 5 in the same year. Pindar's two poems for the brother Phylacides, *Isth.* 5 and 6, contain indications that allow us to date Bacchylides 13 with probability to 485 or 483. The poem, at 230 lines, is the longest we possess, though the first forty lines are badly mutilated. We see that Bacchylides, when writing for Aeginetan victors, drew, as Pindar almost always did in his Aeginetan odes, on myths of the Aeacids.[171] But the poem is also instructive in the comparison it provides

---

167 See Maehler 1982: 1.II.3 125–7.
168 Maehler 1982: 1.I.7 n24.
169 Kenyon 1897.
170 Jebb 1905.
171 Aegina, daughter of the river Asopus, was mother by Zeus of Aeacus, father of Telamon and Peleus. Ajax and Achilles are, accordingly, cousins. This relationship is never brought to the fore in Homer, though it is of paramount importance in the myths told by epinician-poets for Aeginetan athletes.

with Pindar's method of procedure.[172] Pindar in four verses (*Nem.* 5.9–13) gives only a glimpse of the Aeacidae, with a short scene in which Peleus and Telamon and their half-brother Phocus (whom they later slew) stand at an altar, with hands raised to Zeus, praying for the greatness of the island. Bacchylides devotes over sixty lines (100–67) to a description of the central scene of the *Iliad*, the battle at the ships.[173] His elaboration of an individual scene is like what we find in the newly-discovered fragments of Stesichorus. This more discursive style in mythical narration may owe something to Bacchylides' Ionian, rather than Doric, background – Bacchylides came from the world that produced the epic, and Stesichorus probably inherited his Homeric expansiveness from the bardic tradition to which he seems to belong. Bacchylides' style is nonetheless not Homeric but idiosyncratic and very carefully elaborated: he tells the story of Ajax at the ships, presenting the confrontation with Hector and introducing Achilles' name at the outset (101) along with that of Ajax (104) and thus placing the Aeacid cousins together, but then emphasizing the rôle played by Ajax during the absence of Achilles. The scene at the ships is presented in ring-composition (105, 160); at 134 in a flashback we learn of Achilles' withdrawal from action and the quarrel with Agamemnon. The scene given is the turning point of the *Iliad*, and Bacchylides deliberately presents in detail the very incident that will lead to the entry into battle and death of Patroclus with the subsequent return of Achilles to wreak such havoc on the Trojans – the myth ends with the mention of the Trojans turning the waters of Scamander red and thus the valour of both of the Aeacidae can be emphasized again (167). Here as elsewhere Bacchylides is allusive in his art and expects the co-operation of the audience who will know the stories and works of literature on which his narration is based and be able to extrapolate from what he relates. The scene of Ajax at the ships introduces a long simile (124–32) in which the daring of the Trojans while Achilles is out of action is compared to the mood of the sailors who take heart at dawn after a night storm. Again, the simile is wholly individual in that it calls attention to the subjective, to the changing moods of the Trojans; the simile is not an analogue to the action as a Homeric simile would be. The whole central portion of the poem with its myth is preceded and followed, as usual in Bacchylides, by a section praising the city and the victor (67–99 and 182–98). The mutilated first part of the poem (1–58) seems to be a description, perhaps by the nymph Nemea, of Heracles killing the Nemean lion at the site of the games. The two myths, then, enhance the occasion, with the first being a report of a sort

---

172 The comparison is drawn by Jebb 1905: 217.
173 Pindar, by contrast, never in his myths gives a scene we know from our *Iliad*.

of pancration at Nemea that preceded Pytheas' victory in the pancration, reported by Bacchylides, and the second a tribute to the heroism of the Aeacids of Aegina, the boy's island.

Ode 11 also gives us a fine example of the care with which Bacchylidean narrative is composed. The myth (40–112) is placed between an initial and a final praise-section (15–39 and 113–16). It tells of the madness of the daughters of Proetus, their flight from Tiryns (55–7, λιποῦσαι) and their healing by Artemis. The story is told in elaborate ring-composition, the outer ring being the mention of the altar dedicated to Artemis by the maidens (40–2, and 110–12). Within it is the earlier story of the rivalry between Acrisius and Proetus and the flight of the latter from Argos for Tiryns, itself told as a ring (λιπόντες, 60 and 81) and emphasizing the motif, also contained in the outer myth, that an apparently disastrous situation leading to flight may lead to a happy outcome. The story of Proetus continues with the telling of his grief at his daughters' madness and resolve to commit suicide, leading to his healing bath (85–95) which precedes the healing of his daughters. All the narrative is unified by the central rôle of Artemis. She is the patron goddess of Metapontum, the city of the addressee Alexidamus and colony of the cities celebrated in the myth, and she is invoked at the beginning and end of the poem. She is said to have set right the course of the boy's fortunes: earlier he had been cheated of a deserved wrestling-victory at Olympia (24–39) but now his course has been set in a happier direction because of his Pythian victory. The art and limpidity of the myth and the unity of the poem are characteristically Bacchylidean. In a comparable instance in one of Pindar's most brilliant poems, the Seventh *Olympian*, we have a telling of a number of stories associated with Rhodes, the city of the victor, including its colonization, and the same theme of potential disaster averted through divine intervention. But the purport of the myth and its applicability to the victor's case escapes us.[174]

The most famous poems of Bacchylides are those for Hieron of Syracuse: 5 is for the victory of the horse Pherenicus at Olympia in 476, the occasion of Pindar's *Ol.* 1; 4 is for the chariot-victory at Delphi in 470, the occasion of *Pyth.* 1; and 3 is for Hieron's greatest victory, in 468 with the chariot at Olympia, for which there is no song from Pindar. The biographical tradition posits rivalry and hostility between Pindar and Bacchylides at

---

174 The scholiast suggests that the addressee of the poem, Diagoras of Rhodes, had killed a man in the boxing at Olympia. But this is likely no more than a guess, prompted by the lack of obvious relevance of the myths to the occasion.

the court of Syracuse, with Pindar making unflattering allusion to Bacchylides and Simonides in the two jackdaws mentioned at *Ol.* 2.87 and to Bacchylides in the monkey of *Pyth.* 2.72 (the scholiasts on both passages advance this interpretation). The tendency to believe in personal animosity between Pindar and the Cean poets is now not widespread. It must be remembered that there is no evidence for the presence of either poet at Hieron's court that is not based on inference from the poetry, and the proem of Bacchylides 5 *prima facie* seems to indicate in fact that Bacchylides is not present in Syracuse, for he speaks as one who sends his poem across the sea to Syracuse from Ceos (10–12). The dual verb γαρύετον at *Ol.* 2.88 remains perplexing, however, for it is hard to escape the impression that the reference to two jackdaws is a reference to two particular people, whoever they may be.[175] The apparently querulous tone of the ending of the Second *Pythian* is best read within the conventions of praise-poetry and not as biography.[176] But it remains a fact that Bacchylides, not Pindar, was commissioned to write the official ode (3) for Hieron's Olympic victory of 468. In 476 both poets had produced magnificent poems, presumably both on commission; in 470 Pindar composed a splendid offering for official performance in Sicily while the Bacchylidean contribution is the perfunctory 4, a mere 20 lines performed at Delphi immediately after the victory. In 468, for whatever reason, Pindar was not invited to compose a song of celebration.

The ode for the victory of 476 is generally considered Bacchylides' masterpiece. It is constructed, as are the longer poems analyzed above, with a mythical narrative (56–175) placed between initial and final praise of the victor and his city. The dark colours of the canvas are remarkable and seem not to suit the celebration of victory until we remember that Heracles is always appropriate to epinician poetry as the archetypal ἀθλητής.[177] Moreover, the epinician ode, as a hymn εἰς ἀνθρώπους, must have as part of its function a reminder of the limits of mortal felicity since it celebrates men at the moment when the distinction between god and mortal is most susceptible to blurring. Here the long story of Heracles' descent to the underworld to fetch Cerberus and his meeting with Meleager, who recounts the story of the hunt for the Calydonian Boar and of his death because of the anger of his mother Althaea, is introduced precisely as illustration of the adage that 'no mortal is fortunate in

---

175 See Molyneux 1992: 248–51.
176 Most 1985.
177 See n60 above 20 in the section on Simonides.

all things' (54–5).[178] Comparison with the work of Stesichorus and Pindar is illuminating again in this case. Bacchylides' narrative is like that of Stesichorus, with a more discursive style and a fondness for speeches: the encounter between Heracles and Meleager is a set of five alternating speeches, with the third and central one by Meleager the longest, giving the story within a story. It is difficult to escape the suspicion that such poetry was bardic rather than choral, and the suspicion is abetted when we notice that Pindar in his poem for the same victory introduces in self-address (*Ol.* 1.16–18) the very figure of the bard at the feast (like Demodocus in *Od.* 8). Pindar's myth is the tale of Pelops rapt to heaven, while Bacchylides gives us a descent to Hades or *katabasis*, but near the surface of Pindar's tale lurks a tale of descent too, that of Persephone, honoured with her mother in Syracuse.[179] In Bacchylides' myth, probably based on an epic *katabasis* which also left traces in *Aeneid* 6,[180] the story that Heracles hears Meleager tell awakens Heracles' admiration and seals his fate by sending him to the upper world to court Deianeira, with mention of whom (172–5) the myth ends. Here we have another instance of Bacchylidean allusiveness: the hearer must extrapolate from what is recounted to a conclusion outside the poem. Bacchylides evokes the death of Heracles through the indirect agency of a figure in the underworld (cf. Sophocles, *Trach.* 1159–62) and the direct agency of the woman he will marry. One of Bacchylides' dithyrambs (16) tells the story of Deianeira sending the Nessus-shirt to her husband. Through the evocation of the death of Heracles Bacchylides in all likelihood evokes his apotheosis too: Pindar in *Nem.* 1, quite possibly from the same year 476, tells the story of the apotheosis directly, without linking it to the martyrdom and pyre. Characteristically Bacchylidean again is the subjective and pathetic turn to the story: Heracles, on this occasion and for the only time in his life, sheds tears upon hearing the tale told by Meleager (155–7).

In Ode 3, for Hieron's great victory of 468, the structure is what we have come to expect, with a mythical narrative that has a speech at its centre (37–47) placed between two praise-sections. What causes some surprise is to find a figure from recent history placed on a par with figures of myth, for the narrative is of the destruction of Sardis and Croesus' immolation on

---

178 It is remarkable that Pindar's four odes for Hieron (*Ol.* 1 and *Pyth.* 1, 2, 3) all tell stories of the punishment of sinners (Tantalus, Typhoeus, Ixion, and Coronis respectively), while the other ode of Bacchylides for Hieron (3) celebrates the victory, as it were, from a funeral pyre (of Croesus). This may have corresponded to the tastes and predilections of the addressee.
179 See Griffith 1989: 171–3.
180 Lloyd-Jones 1967: 209–29.

the funeral pyre.[181] The relevance of the exemplar in the narrative is not far to seek. Both Croesus and Hieron were rich and powerful despots on the periphery of the Greek world who had ostentatiously honoured Apollo at Delphi. Moreover, it may be that Hieron cultivated the comparison with Croesus: Pindar had in 470 compared the φιλόφρων ἀρετά of Hieron to that of Croesus (*Pyth.* 1.94).[182] Hieron was near the end of his life and ill – the First *Pythian* alludes to his sickness by comparing him to Philoctetes (50 ff.). The translation of Croesus to the land of the Hyperboreans by Apollo at the end of the story suggests the requital of piety and continued life for the great ruler, just as his continued fame is assured by the poetry of Bacchylides (90–3). The reward for virtue is made explicit in Apollo's saving of Croesus from death. Once again the limpidity of Bacchylides' art may profitably be compared to the indirectness of Pindar's. In the Second *Olympian* for Theron of Acragas in 476, Pindar has honoured that ruler's religious beliefs and adumbrated a doctrine of a happy life after death for the righteous. Theron's place is only very indirectly hinted at: the myth ends with a mention of Achilles' translation to the Islands of the Blessed (79–80), and if we keep in mind that Peleus and Cadmus are associated in felicity in line 78 we may expect that a descendant of Cadmus (Theron) will probably have a place beside the descendant of Peleus (Achilles).[183]

Poems 15–20 in the papyrus in the British Museum are called dithyrambs and were presumably so named by the Alexandrians on whose work the manuscript depended. Since they are alphabetical in the order of the initial letter of their titles and these go down only to I (Io and Idas) they must have been part of a larger collection. The problem for modern scholars has been to decide whether these poems are really dithyrambs in the strict sense of poems in honour of Dionysus sung by cyclic choruses or whether they were so classified by the Alexandrians simply because they contained heroic narrative. It seems on balance likely that the Alexandrians had good reason for their classification and that any reluctance on our part to accept these poems as dithyrambs must be based on our very imperfect knowledge of this sort of poetry. We have already seen, in the case of Simonides (above 19), a problem resulting from lack of clear knowledge of the ancient dithyramb. Some of the poems seem too slight to have been performed

---

181 Croesus died in 546 BC.
182 But for Pindar Croesus is a positive example to set beside Phalaris, the tyrant of Acragas at the same period, and so the figures do not quite achieve the stature of mythical paradigms.
183 For the differences between Bacchylides' account and that of Herodotus, and the possible sources of both, see Maehler 1982: 1.II 35–6.

chorally at major festivals, but we can at least see that 16, though only a single triad of 35 lines, was a dithyramb in the strict sense of a poem performed at Delphi in the winter months when Apollo was absent.

The masterpiece of this collection is 17, a long poem for the Ceans to perform at Delos. Since the narrative ends with a ship-board chorus singing a paean to Apollo and since the poem is said to be for performance at Delos, some, including Jebb,[184] have thought it is a paean. But the words 'sang a paean' (128) are not probative since they refer to the activity of the chorus of the narrative. The poem is a superb example of Bacchylidean style, with its central piece a confrontation between Theseus, who is accompanying the youths and maidens to Crete, and Minos, the Cretan king. It contains perhaps the most signal example of all of the subtlety with which Bacchylidean narrative alludes to the outcome without stating it directly. Theseus dives into the sea to retrieve the ring that Minos has tossed into the waves, expecting that the leap will eliminate the defender of the young Athenians. The miraculous return of Theseus corroborates his assertion that he too is god-descended (29–38). Bacchylides, however, ignores the ring and instead ends the scene with the appearance of the young hero embellished by the gifts of the gods (124), bestowed on him by the Nereids in the halls of their father. As in the case of the Heracles-story in 5, the end of the narrative in the poem foretells indirectly the end of the story that the audience can be expected to know: Theseus will be irresistible to Ariadne and this will guarantee the success of the mission to Crete and save the young Athenians.[185]

Dithyramb 18 is vividly dramatic, with an exchange between a chorus-leader and a chorus. There has been much discussion whether this is a survival of the form from which the tragedy allegedly developed (ἀπὸ τῶν ἐξαρχόντων τὸν διθύραμβον, Aristotle, *Poet.* 1449a10) or whether the poem of Bacchylides, doubtless meant for performance at Athens at a period when there were regular tragic competitions, is itself influenced by tragedy.

In addition to the two Theseus-dithyrambs (17 and 18), the most important of the collection, there are in the principal papyrus substantial pieces of narrative that have to do with Antenor (15), Heracles (16), Io (19), and Idas (20). Fragments of other provenance seem to indicate dithyrambs about Cassandra, Meleager (?), Pasiphae (?) Cheiron (?), and Orpheus (?) (23–8).

The language of Bacchylides is the *koine* familiar from the choral poets and Stesichorus, though there is in addition to Homerisms, Aeolisms, and

---

184 Jebb 1905: 223.
185 See Scodel 1984: 137–43.

Doric, a more pronounced Ionic element than in Pindar. This is doubtless to be explained as a local adaptation due to his Cean origin. Bacchylides shows an extraordinary originality in his use of language, with about 230 words that are found only or for the first time in what survives to us of his work. Far from being careless reworkings they are usually significant elements of his word-painting and enhance the often pathetic tone and subjective colour of his narrative.[186] His poetry, especially the epinician odes, is full of *gnomai*, which often serve as bridge between one part of the poem and another.[187] These aphorisms transmit traditional wisdom and, like myth, link the occasion and the excellence of the victors to a wider context. As in Pindar we find strong consciousness of the poet's rôle and of the mutual dependence of poet and patron. This is no doubt closely connected to the circumstances, which we first observe with Simonides, that make the traffic between poet and patron an economy in which praise and immortality are given in exchange for money. Bacchylides' poems are both triadic and strophic, with dactylo-epitritic metre by far the most common, though there is some use of iambic-Aeolic metres. There are few indications that he was popular in classical Athens, but Callimachus knew his work and the papyrus-finds show that he was popular in the Hellenistic and Imperial times. The disappearance of his work led to quite general ignorance of him in the European poetic tradition.

---

186 Segal 1976: 99–130.
187 Cf. lines 3.50–5 (discussed above), which serve to connect the introductory praise-section to the myth.

THE
EDUCATION
OF
ACHILLES

1

READERS of the *Iliad* have ever understood that the well-known story of Thetis' abandonment of Peleus shortly after their wedding is foreign to Homer. Aristarchus thought it a post-Homeric invention of poets,[1] and indeed the version to which he alludes, that Achilles was brought to Cheiron when he was twelve days old, appears very likely to come from a lost poem: the word δωδεκαταῖος which he quotes in his comment is one that would conveniently fill the part of a hexameter line following the bucolic diaeresis.[2] It is frequently and justly observed that in the *Iliad* there are several passages that attest to the presence of Thetis in Peleus' palace while Achilles was growing up. Achilles mentions her boasts which he heard 'in his father's halls' (1.395–6). More important, Thetis herself speaks of having reared her son (18.55–60). She says this in the

---

First published in *QUCC* 45.3 (1993) 7–20.

My thanks are due to Brian Blair, Christopher Brown, Andrew Connolly, Bruno Gentili, Drew Griffith, Bonnie MacLachlan, Nicholas Maes, and Philippa Matheson, all of whom made helpful suggestions.

1 E.g., *Schol.* 16.222b: οὐ δωδεκαταῖον ἀπέλιπε τὸν Ἀχιλλέα γεννήσασα ἡ Θέτις, καθάπερ οἱ νεώτεροι ποιηταί..., and *Schol.* 18.57a: οὐκ ἀπελείφθη τοῦ Πηλέως οἴκου, καθάπερ οἱ νεώτεροι, δωδεκαταῖον καταλιποῦσα τὸν Ἀχιλλέα...; Bernabé (1987: 62) gives these references as *fragmenta dubia* of the *Cypria*.

2 The Hesiodic(?) *Aigimios*, according to the scholiast on Apollonius 4.816, gave the story of Thetis' putting the infant Achilles into a boiling cauldron to learn whether or not he was mortal. Apollonius himself gives in this passage a version remarkably like the story of Demeter's nursing of Demophoon in the *Homeric Hymn*: Thetis puts the infant directly into the fire by night in order to burn away his mortality and make him immortal. In both these versions Thetis fled to her father when she was discovered by Peleus. See M.-W. fr. 300.

very passage on which Aristarchus is commenting when he maintains that the story of her flight is a later invention. We are in addition told that Thetis packed a chest for Achilles to take to Troy (16.570–6).[3]

But the tradition is uniform in telling us that Achilles was at some point under the tutelage of the good centaur Cheiron. This much is certain and is known to the poet of the *Iliad* (11.832, ὃν [sc. Achilles] Χείρων ἐδίδαξε) as well as to the other early poets. The evidence of the visual arts suggests that the vase painters were aware of two traditions.[4] One series of paintings has an infant being handed by Peleus to Cheiron, sometimes to the solemn accompaniment of a procession of Olympian gods, sometimes in the presence of Hermes. The other group shows a young lad being given by either or both of his parents to Cheiron. Thetis is present in the second group. She may be grieving, as on a black figure lekythos in the Museo Nationale in Palermo, or she may be rushing away, as on a late sixth-century cup by Oltos in the Berlin Museum.[5] The important thing is that she is on hand when Achilles, no longer an infant in arms, is consigned to his tutor.

It is the second series that appears to conform to the story as known to the poet of the *Iliad*, for it implies the continuing presence of Thetis in the life of her son. Indeed, the appearance of this motif on Attic vases in the late sixth century may be explained by the popularity of the *Iliad* in Athens, where its recitation became from the time of the Peisistratids part of the Panathenaea.[6] The Oltos cup seems in fact to correspond very nicely to the situation as described in the *Iliad*. Thetis there speaks of her responsibility for Achilles' general welfare (τὸν μὲν ἐγὼ θρέψασα, 18.55) and this is entirely consonant with her having given him into the hands of Cheiron for specific διδασκαλία.[7]

Our *Iliad*, which at one point mentions explicitly Achilles' education by Cheiron, at another gives him a paidagogos in the home of his father (9.485–95, 438–45) in the person of Phoenix, who both dandled him on his knee as an infant and was to instruct him at Peleus' behest (διδασκέμεναι, 442) in the ways of war *after* (!) the departure for Troy. If all this reinforces

---

3 At 11.765–90, however, Thetis is not mentioned in the account of the visit of Nestor and Odysseus to the home of Peleus at the time they were recruiting for the war.
4 Friis Johansen 1939: 181–205, followed by, e.g., Beck 1975: 9–10. Guerrini (1958–9: 43–53) deals exclusively with the later evidence.
5 Description first published by Furtwängler 1885: 2.4220.
6 Friis Johansen 1939. The iconography of the Attic vases is also influenced by Athenian school practice of the time – e.g., Achilles may be carrying an aryballos and javelins: see Beck 1975: 9–10.
7 See Kemp-Lindemann 1975: 14.

the idea that Achilles grew up in a normal home, with parents and paid-agogos in attendance, it somewhat militates against the idea that he was sent away to boarding-school, as the vases suggest. It has recently been argued that Cheiron's part in the education of Achilles is in fact largely post-Homeric invention and that Phoenix's role in Homer is one which is subsequently transferred to Cheiron.[8]

But Cheiron is consistently, and with good reason, portrayed in early Greek poetry as the mentor of young heroes.[9] It is hardly likely that this is an idea that was invented only in the period after the epic and then allowed unaccountably and inorganically to enter our *Iliad*. It must, on the other hand, be remembered that if Phoenix's role in the education of Achilles is memorable in Book Nine of our *Iliad*, it is a role peculiar to that book, very much an *ad hoc* invention in that place and, furthermore, something that other poets or painters were never concerned to exploit. The particulars of Phoenix's account are adduced to suit the occasion of his speech. Within its protreptic frame the Meleager-narrative functions as an αἶνος or story of the κλέα ἀνδρῶν (524), told to one who has himself been singing such things (189) and who might well be expected to listen and understand the relevance of the paradigm. Phoenix makes as strong a case as possible to Achilles in order to persuade him of his claim to be heeded ('I made you what you are today – therefore listen to me,' 485, 496). Details are introduced for an ulterior purpose and are consequently suspect as special pleading, with a somewhat pathetic old Phoenix playing up his own role and importance to Achilles in order to justify and reinforce his plea. Cheiron's part in Achilles' education is mentioned where the detail is quite unforced in its immediate context.[10] Phoenix is, on the other hand, a creation for the purpose of the Embassy to Achilles.[11] It is remarkable that Thetis is nowhere mentioned in Phoenix's account of his flight to Peleus (9.478–95), though she is said to have been with Peleus when Epeigeus came as a suppliant (16.570–6), to be sent subsequently with Achilles to Troy by his parents. Phoenix treated Achilles as a surrogate son from infancy and seems in Book Nine to replace an absent Thetis. This narrative, which is at odds with the other references to Thetis' presence in Peleus' home, fits rather

---

8 March 1987: 23–5.
9 See in particular Brillante 1991: 7–28.
10 Cheiron's instruction is also mentioned in the account of the knowledge possessed by the physician Machaon, who learned his art from his father Asclepius, one of Cheiron's pupils (*Il.* 4.218–19). Both physicians of the Greek army, Podaleirios and Machaon, are sons of Asclepius (2.731–2).
11 The notorious duals of 9.182 ff. show that the Phoenix-episode is imperfectly integrated into our *Iliad*. See Willcock 1978 *ad loc.*; Braswell 1971: 22–3.

the later stories of Thetis' baffled attempts to make Achilles immortal and her disappearance into the sea. Again the Phoenix-episode is seen to sit uncomfortably in the larger context of the poem.

Mention of Cheiron's education of Achilles does not, like mention of Phoenix's, serve the rhetoric of the situation. Moreover, the centaurs are figures of venerable antiquity: they are mentioned at *Iliad* 1.268 as φῆρες ὀρεσκῷοι and at 2.743 as φῆρες λαχνήεντες in a passage where their traditional enmity with the Lapiths is recognized. Nilsson calls attention to the fact that the Aeolic form (φήρ for θήρ) is rare where the Aeolic and Ionic are metrically equivalent[12] – Aeolic, the oldest stratum of the epic,[13] normally survived only where the Ionic could not displace it in the same position in the line. In the first of these two centaur-passages Nestor is referring to the occasion, mentioned again in the second, when the centaurs tried to carry off Hippodameia. The particular incident described is, of course, relevant to the occasion on which Nestor tells it, for Agamemnon like the centaurs is bent on carrying off another man's woman and Nestor is in this case concerned to prevent an outbreak of violence of the sort that occurred when he was a youth and not impartial in a dispute.[14] But the *exemplum* of the centaurs is subtle and has a double reference, for Achilles, if violent, will likewise be behaving in the manner of the reprehensible centaurs, not of his teacher Cheiron, the δικαιότατος Κενταύρων (11.832). Cheiron did not participate in the quarrel between Lapiths and centaurs.

Cheiron, we are told, was also teacher of medicine to Asclepius (4.218–19.[15] But it is not merely as a teacher of medicine that Cheiron figures in the *Iliad*. He is the source of the spear that only Achilles can wield (16.140–4 = 19.388–91). This spear was given by Cheiron to Peleus, clearly on the occasion of his wedding when the gods brought the armour that Patroclus dons and of which he is despoiled by Hector (18.82–5). The passages in Books 16 and 18 together indicate a source, common to the *Iliad* and the *Cypria*, in which the story of the wedding was told.[16] And so Achilles' spear provides a very close link between him and Cheiron.

---

12 Nilsson 1955: 229.
13 The theory of an Aeolic origin for the epic language is not so fashionable now as it once was. But it has been convincingly defended recently by Janko 1982a: 89–92.
14 This was pointed out to me by Nicholas Maes.
15 The celebrated kylix by Sosias from Vulci in Etruria, ca 500 BC, in the Berlin Museum, shows Achilles exercising his medical skill by tending the wounds of Patroclus. See the accompanying illustration (Fig. 1).
16 See fr. 3 of the *Cypria* in Bernabé 1987: 62. Kullmann (1960: 234–6) shows that the *Iliad* and the *Cypria* are in the details of the wedding, as in many others, independent of each other and must thus reproduce older traditions.

Fig. 1 Achilles tending Patroklos' wounds on a hydria from the Leagros group. Berlin F2278.

Cheiron on the vase paintings is regularly carrying a tree, presumably a Pelian ash of the sort that with its branches lopped off could become a spear. The fact that Achilles' spear is the spear given by Cheiron to Peleus calls to our attention the close association of Peleus himself with the centaur who was his neighbour on Mount Pelion and his maternal grandfather – Peleus' mother Endeis was the daughter of Cheiron.[17] Achilles' time spent with Cheiron was thus time spent with his great-grandfather. It

---

17 We are told this by the scholiast on Pindar, *Nem.* 5.7 (12); another tradition (e.g., Apollodorus 3.12.6–7 and Pausanias 2.29.9) makes Endeis the daughter of the brigand Sciron, but this seems to be simply based on a confusion of names, with Sciron for Cheiron. There appears to be some interest on the part of the poets in the women

THE EDUCATION OF ACHILLES 63

is common in Greek society and myth for a boy to be educated outside
the parental home, by the men of his mother's family: Achilles' own
son Neoptolemus grew up on the island of Skyros in the home of his
maternal grandfather (*Iliad* 19.326 ff.) as did Iphidamas (11.221 ff.). And
the young Odysseus is sent to Autolycus, his maternal grandfather who
named him, to be initiated into the hunt *(Odyssey* 19.394, 414, 418 ff.).[18]
Achilles could not easily be sent to Nereus in the sea[19] and so we skip
a generation, with his grandmother's father replacing his mother's fa-
ther. That no one else can wield the spear means that Achilles, when
he re-enters the fray, will be carrying Cheiron's spear, not a substitute,
though he at this point carries substitute divine armour. The poet has
the chance to indulge in a little word-play, with Pelian (the ashen spear),
Peleus, and Pelion brought into close proximity to πῆλαι 'to brandish' —
he seems to be given to word-play in contexts that involve Cheiron.[20]
The poet of the *Cypria*, who knew of Achilles' use of this spear to
wound Telephus, also knew of Achilles' use of the same spear to heal his
victim.[21] The spear that comes from Cheiron both wounds and heals when
wielded by Achilles.

2

There is general agreement on the etymology of Cheiron's name: 'der
Name ist ein Hypokoristikon von χειρίσοφος oder einem andern mit χείρ

---

surrounding Cheiron — his mother (Philyra) and his wife (Chariclo) are named in the
Titanomachy (see Bernabé 1987: 15).
18 See, generally, Bremmer 1983.
19 In Bacchylides 17 Theseus makes a spectacular trip to the marine home of his father
Poseidon. The whole tone of this passage is very foreign to the *Iliad*, which avoids
magic.
20 *Il.* 4.218 seems to contain a rudimentary *schema etymologicum*, with ἤπια alluding to
the name of *Asclepius*. Eustathius 463.33 *(ad Il.* 4.194) derives the name of Asclepius
from ἀσκέω + ἤπια (with an otiose λ). Porphyry *ap. Schol. Od.* 1.68 (on ἀσκελές)
thought that the name Asclepius was a combination of an α-privative with σκέλλεσθαι,
a derivation that seems also to be alluded to at *P.V.* 480–2, where Prometheus puts
himself in the place of the traditional god of healing: ... φαρμάκων χρείᾳ κατεσκέλλοντο
πρίν γ' ἐγώ σφισιν ἔδειξα κράσεις ἠπίων ἀκεσμάτων (I owe this observation to Professor H.
Edinger).
21 See Frazer 1921: 188 n1. The motif of the wound that can be healed only by the spear
that caused it found its way into the grail legend in Wagner's *Parsifal*: see Lloyd-Jones
1982: 131.

zusammengesetzten Wort.'[22] It is clear, I think, that Pindar understands the significance of the name. At *Nem.* 3.53–5 we find:

βαθυμῆτα Χίρων
'Ιασον᾽ ἔνδον τέγει, καὶ ἔπειτ᾽ Ἀσκλαπιόν,
τὸν φαρμάκων δίδαξε μαλακόχειρα νόμον·

This is the clearest instance of a pun.[23] A remarkably similar passage occurs at *Pyth.* 4.270–1:

ἐσσὶ δ᾽ ἰατὴρ ἐπικαιρότατος, Παιάν τέ σοι τιμᾷ φάος.
χρὴ μαλακὰν χέρα προσβάλλοντα τρώμαν ἕλκεος
ἀμφιπολεῖν.

Arcesilaus of Cyrene is here being invited to show, in the application of a healing hand, the διδασκαλία of Cheiron of which Jason, the central figure in the myth of the poem, boasts (102).[24]

And in the Third *Pythian* Asclepius perverts the χειρουργία of his teacher Cheiron by the gold that appears instead of φάρμακα in his hands. Gold appears forthwith in the hands of Zeus as the thunderbolt which strikes the life from Asclepius and the patient he should never have attended (55–8):

ἔτραπεν καὶ κεῖνον ἀγάνορι μισθῷ
χρυσὸς ἐν χερσὶν φανείς
ἄνδρ᾽ ἐκ θανάτου κομίσαι
ἤδη ἁλωκότα· χερσὶ δ᾽ ἄρα Κρονίων
ῥίψαις δι᾽ ἀμφοῖν ἀμπνόαν στέρνων καθέλεν
ὠκέως, αἴθων δὲ κεραυνὸς ἐνέσκιμψεν μόρον.

In the Ninth *Pythian*, Apollo asks Cheiron if he may lay his hand on Cyrene (36):

ὁσία κλυτὰν χέρα οἱ προσενεγκεῖν ...;

---

22 Escher 1899: col. 2302; more recently H. von Kamptz (1982: §72a) looks to a possible Χειρί-μαχος or Εὔ-χειρ.
23 μαλακόχειρα] 'A Pindaric compound, intended to call attention to the meaning of the Centaur's name Cheiron,' Bury 1890 *ad loc.*
24 See Robbins 1975: 205–13 [in this volume 192–201].

The Teubner text of Snell and Maehler follows Fränkel's[25] punctuation of the immediately preceding lines (33–5):

> ποίας δ' ἀποσπασθεῖσα φύτλας
> ὀρέων κευθμῶνας ἔχει σκιοέντων,
> γεύεται δ' ἀλκᾶς ἀπειράντου;

On this reading, the strength of which is its similarity to *Theognidea* 1290 ff., Apollo admires the girl but finds her activity as a huntress unfulfilling for her. He thus asks the centaur if he may assist her to achieve her natural τέλος through union with him.[26] In doing so he defers to the great teacher and asks a question of χειρουργία. The question is erotic, but the placing of a hand on the girl, since it will remedy a deficiency, will be therapeutic, an act of making whole.

The foregoing contexts are medical. But Pindar's Achilles seems to have been instructed in the ways of hunting and war by Cheiron too (*Nem.* 3.43–53, 57–63; my emphasis):

> ξανθὸς δ' Ἀχιλεὺς τὰ μὲν μένων Φιλύρας ἐν δόμοις,
> παῖς ἐὼν ἄθυρε μεγάλα ἔργα· <u>χερσὶ</u> θαμινά
> βραχυσίδαρον ἄκοντα πάλλων ἴσα τ' ἀνέμοις,
> {ἐν} μάχᾳ λεόντεσσιν ἀγροτέροις ἔπρασσεν φόνον,
> κάπρους τ' ἔναιρε· σώματα δὲ παρὰ Κρονίδαν
> Κένταυρον ἀσθμαίνοντα κόμιζεν,
> ἑξέτης τὸ πρῶτον, ὅλον δ' ἔπειτ' ἂν χρόνον·
> τὸν ἐθάμβεον Ἄρτεμίς τε καὶ Ἀθάνα,
> κτείνοντ' ἐλάφους ἄνευ κυνῶν δολίων θ' ἑρκέων·
> ποσσὶ γὰρ κράτεσκε. λεγόμενον δὲ τοῦτο προτέρων
> ἔπος ἔχω·
> . . . .
> Νηρέος θύγατρα, γόνον τέ οἱ φέρτατον
> ἀτίταλλεν <ἐν> ἁρμένοισι πᾶσι θυμὸν αὔξων,
> ὄφρα θαλασσίαις ἀνέμων ῥιπαῖσι πεμφθείς
> ὑπὸ Τροίαν δορίκτυπον ἀλαλὰν Λυκίων τε
>   προσμένοι καὶ Φρυγῶν
> Δαρδάνων τε, καὶ ἐγχεσφόροις ἐπιμείξαις
> Αἰθιόπεσσι <u>χεῖρας</u> ἐν φρασὶ πάξαιθ' ὅπως

---

25 Fränkel 1962: 503 n4.
26 See Woodbury 1982, esp. 251–3.

σφίσι μὴ κοίρανος ὀπίσω
πάλιν οἴκαδ᾽ ἀνεψιὸς ζαμενὴς Ἑλένοιο Μέμνων μόλοι.

While living with Cheiron Achilles is instructed in all things necessary for him to turn his hands to account in the carnage before Troy – and even before departure from Greece he brandishes his missiles to slaughter lions and boars. The underlined words call attention to the teacher's name.

Association with Cheiron is in Pindar essentially what it is in the *Iliad*. It consists in the use of hands to kill and to heal. Pindar also knows of other teaching of Cheiron, but in this case we seem quite certainly to be dealing with something post-Homeric. In the Sixth *Pythian* the young Thrasybulus of Acragas is said to exemplify virtues enjoined by Cheiron on Achilles (21–7). We have to do with moral precepts, with admonitions to honour the gods and to honour parents. The scholiast tells us that these two injunctions formed part of the Χείρωνος ὑποθῆκαι, a collection of didactic aphorisms attributed to Hesiod. This is clearly a secondary development of the tradition of Cheiron as teacher. The primary reputation of the great centaur was, as his name indicates, the work of hands, and he instructed his wards in the ways of hunting and healing. His reputation established, all manner of improving γνῶμαι might be attributed to him, and the result was the ὑποθῆκαι, a collection that was probably in many respects similar to the *Theognidea*, our most famous existing collection of advice for the education of aristocratic youth.[27] Pindar, whose poetry is full of the aphorisms of received wisdom, would doubtless have drawn on this paraenetic tradition as he certainly did on the Homeric epics.[28]

In the Third *Nemean*, extensively quoted above, it is said that in addition to killing lions and boars the young Achilles dragged living animals (σώματα ... ἀσθμαίνοντα 46–7) back to Cheiron's cave. This may very well preserve a detail of a source in the early poets (λεγόμενον ... προτέρων) in which Achilles ate the marrow of living animals in order to gain speed and strength (it appears that in Pindar the young Achilles acquires from his mentor, not from his diet, the training that will give him courage and speed).[29] Such primitive savagery is not far below the surface in the *Iliad* when Achilles tells the dying Hector (22.346) that he

---

27 On the Χείρωνος ὑποθῆκαι and its relation to the Sixth *Pythian*, see Kurke 1990: 85–103.
28 Two recent books investigate in detail Pindar's extensive debt to Homer: Nisetich 1989 and Nagy 1990.
29 See Robertson 1940: 177–80; Huxley 1975: 19. Both think that Pindar is editing an earlier version.

is tempted to cut up and eat his flesh raw.[30] Pindar avoids the sparagmos of living animals as Homer avoids the temptations of cannibalism.[31] We remain aware, though, that the Achilles nurtured by Cheiron is an amalgam of civilization and of savagery, semi-feral like his celebrated centaur-teacher who on some of the vases has animals, killed in the hunt, hanging from the tree he is carrying.[32] It is a puzzling motif in itself, for since horses do not eat flesh the carnivorous aspect of the centaurs must emphasize the beastly, not the human, side of the hybrid.[33] Existing poetry has tamed Cheiron considerably, leaving him as merely provider of and instructor in the weaponry with which men kill animals and each other.

I hope to have established with the foregoing both that the *Iliad* draws on and presupposes sources in which Achilles' connection with Cheiron is of special importance and that the etymology of Cheiron's name is best seen in the use his charges make of their hands.[34]

Hands are omnipresent in the *Iliad*. They are mentioned in connection with eating, praying, supplicating, sacrificing, exchanging pledges, washing, adorning the body, and applying medicines, to name but a few specific activities. They are mentioned in many other contexts too, for the word χείρ in its different cases, singular, dual and plural, fits easily and unobtrusively into the hexameter line. It is most frequently used in battle scenes, where warriors both manipulate their own weapons of destruction and fall at the hands of their foes.

Especially striking is, despite all this, the identification of Achilles with his hands. They dominate the last quarter of the poem where, in conformity with Achilles' own statement at 1.165–6,

> ἀλλὰ τὸ μὲν πλεῖον πολυάϊκος πολέμοιο
> χεῖρες ἐμαὶ διέπουσ'.

---

30 Achilles' most savage act in the poem – it is unparalleled – is the offering of human sacrifice on the pyre of Patroclus at the beginning of Book 23. It has been thought that this whole scene is but a survival of Mycenaean burial customs (cf. Rohde 1925: 12 ff.).
31 See Griffin 1980: 20–1.
32 Cf., e.g., a hydria of the Leagros-group in Berlin, also from the end of the sixth century (= *LIMC* I.2 #22).
33 See Kirk 1970: 161–2. Kirk points out that Pholus, in his encounter with Heracles, eats raw flesh while Heracles eats cooked meat. The man-eating mares of Diomedes provide another strange instance of equine savagery.
34 I think it no accident that on the Achilles-Cheiron vases the boy is often seen extending his hands to the centaur. See, e.g., the cup by Oltos, an illustration of which is included here (Fig. 2), and the hydria mentioned in n32 above.

Fig. 2 Achilles and Cheiron on a cup by the Oltos painter.
Berlin F4220.

When the news of Patroclus' death reaches Achilles the terrified Antilochus must restrain his hands as he lies in the dust, pouring it over his own head with these very hands (18.23, 27, 33). Especially memorable is the scene at 18.317 (the gesture is repeated at 23.18) where Achilles places his hands on the chest of his slain comrade and himself laments as the women wail through the night:

χεῖρας ἐπ᾽ ἀνδροφόνους θέμενος στήθεσσιν ἑταίρου.

This strange gesture is not an embrace but a laying on of hands.[35] Achilles does not cradle the head of the dead man as, e.g., Andromache does to the corpse of Hector at 24.724 and as Thetis does to her son in the

---

35 The laying on of hands is often in itself an act of healing and is associated with Cheiron: see Weinreich 1909: chapter one, 1–62, esp. 11, 16, 34; and, for an early relief showing a doctor healing a patient by the imposition of hands, Chamoux 1953: 363–8, with Plate XXII.3. I do not mean to suggest that Achilles is attempting to bring the dead Patroclus back to life by this gesture (though see 24.756, where Hecuba seems to impute to Achilles a desire to resurrect the dead Patroclus as motivating his maltreatment of

THE EDUCATION OF ACHILLES

pietà that foreshadows his death (18.71). What comes to mind is that the application of these hands could once heal – Cheiron had trained them so to do – but that they are now powerless in the face of the finality of death; the adjective applied to them emphasizes only their connection with death.[36] Their murderous efficacy can still be employed for purposes of revenge, however, and Achilles presently turns to just this. The great spear from Cheiron is wielded (19.386 ff.)[37] for the campaign against Hector, who will be its principal victim. And certainly no one calls attention to Achilles' hands more vividly than does Hector (20.371–2):

> τοῦ δ' ἐγὼ ἀντίος εἶμι, καὶ εἰ πυρὶ χεῖρας ἔοικεν,
> εἰ πυρὶ χεῖρας ἔοικε, μένος δ' αἴθωνι σιδήρῳ.

The epanalepsis is used to great effect.[38]

The climax of the *Iliad* is the arrival of Priam at Achilles' tent where his first act is to approach him and kiss the ἀνδροφόνους hands that have slain so many of the old king's sons (24.478–9, 506).[39] Achilles' hands are ἄαπτοι (20.503); the adjective is used of other hands earlier in the poem, but of no hands other than those of Achilles from the moment of his appearance on the battlefield. And ἀνδρόφονους (479) is nowhere used of hands other

---

Hector's body). The healing taught by Cheiron was not simply the laying on of hands. It was the work of hands or χειρουργία in the fullest sense.

36 Weinreich (1909: 13 with n1) thinks that the gesture of holding hands *over* someone in order to protect them (e.g., *Iliad* 5.432; 9.419) is closely connected to the use of hands in healing.

37 There is no mention of hands in this passage, though there is in others where Achilles is using the spear. Two puns would be too many in a passage that already plays on Peleus/πῆλαι, an invented pun and so more in need of underlining in the text than Cheiron/χειρῶν would be. The mention of hands in Achilles' case is, I think, sufficient to summon up the image of Cheiron: this does not mean that every mention of hands in the poem must work the same way. Similarly, I believe that the use of some form of the noun ἄχος or of the verb ἄχνυμαι may in certain contexts put one in mind of Achilles' name without that name's being directly used (e.g., 1.188: Πηλεΐωνι δ' ἄχος γένετ'; cf. 18.22, 62). But not every use of ἄχος should make us think of Achilles, just as not all hands should make us think of Cheiron. Poetry is not mechanical.

38 It is used on only two other occasions in the poem: 22.127–8 and 23.641–2.

39 Virgil seems to have understood the second of these passages (506) to mean that Priam extended his own hands to Achilles (*Aen.* 1.487). But it is unlikely that the passages refer to different actions.

A magnificent silver cup of the Roman period, found at Hoby in Denmark and now in the Museum in Copenhagen, shows this famous scene from the end of the *Iliad*. The cup is signed in Greek and in Latin by one Cheirisophus (!).

than those of Achilles. It is used only here and in the two passages where Achilles places his hands on the chest of the dead Patroclus.[40]

We know that Achilles' hands, schooled by Cheiron, do both restorative and destructive work. It is common in Greek for a single agent to be possessed of opposing functions: Hesiod's Muses, who know both truths and falsehoods (*Theog.* 25–7), come to mind. And Achilles' own spear is, of course, a signal example. But the best example is Apollo himself, for his province is both pestilence and healing. He sends the plague at the beginning of the *Iliad*. And after its cessation the Achaeans sing the paean in his honour (1.473).[41]

There is this similarity between Achilles and Apollo in the *Iliad*, that both are characterized by their μῆνις (1.1 and 75). They are both connected with healing as well as with death, but this association is at one remove, as it were: Paiëon (5.899 ff.) is the healer among the gods, though Apollo is associated with the paean; and it is Patroclus who exercises the healing arts that originate with Cheiron, though Achilles is the intermediary who learned them from the master (11.831–2).[42] This slight distancing of Apollo and Achilles from the actual practice of healing allows the poem to concentrate, as it must, on the destructive side of both figures. Apollo and Achilles are in addition the only two lyre-players in the *Iliad* (Apollo: 1.603; 24.63; Achilles: 9.186, 194).[43] So similar are they in so many ways that one understands the artistic necessity of having them on different sides in the battle, even though the logic of the war should put Apollo on the

---

40 The genitive singular of the adjective is regular with the name of Hector. There is a complex irony at work here.
41 On the Greek Apollo as combination of a Semitic god of plague and a Cretan god of healing, see Burkert 1977: III 2.5.
42 Podaleirios and Machaon, like Patroclus, have second-hand knowledge (see above n10), but in their case the person with first-hand knowledge (Asclepius) is not present at Troy, indeed is probably not alive.
43 There is a representation of a lyre-player on the shield of Achilles (18.569 and possibly at 604–6, if the latter passage is not an interpolation). But Achilles and Apollo are the only two live phorminx-players in the *Iliad*.

Did Achilles learn his lyre-playing, another use of his hands, from Cheiron? This is a common motif in later art – one thinks in particular of the Pompeian wall-painting that shows Cheiron instructing Achilles in lyre-playing. There is, however, little evidence before Roman times for Cheiron as a lyre-player; see Guerrini 1958–9. Gisler-Huwiler, *LIMC* III.1, p. 238 (s.v. 'Cheiron'), describes an early fifth-century pelike showing a warrior with a shield on which is figured a centaur playing a lyre. It cannot be said with certainty that it is Cheiron who is portrayed. The point is, in any case, not to be pressed.

Greek side.[44] Apollo will in the end kill Achilles (22.359–60). If Apollo is a god of destruction and of healing he is also – and this is the most important facet of his complex personality – epitome of the youthful manhood which he symbolizes and in which he remains the eternal ἀκερσοκόμης (20.39). Achilles is likewise the *kouros* who can never grow old, who will die without dedicating his shorn hair to the river Spercheius in the customary *rite de passage* of youths into manhood (*Il.* 23.144–51).

Apollo and Achilles are so dangerously alike as to be necessary antagonists. This picture, familiar to us from Homer, may be supplemented by the glimpse given in Pindar's poetry of the education of both as pupils in the school of Cheiron. But Apollo, a god, did not need to be instructed by Cheiron. Achilles remains Cheiron's most memorable pupil, as the vase-painters prove to us.

---

44 Apollo has every reason to hate the Trojans for their perfidy, as Poseidon does (*Iliad* 21.441–60). But he nonetheless sides with them. It is often said that Apollo, originating in Lycia, shows continuing evidence of these origins through his Trojan sympathies: the tradition was too strong to be overcome: see Wilamowitz 1931: 1.423 ff; 1932: 2.28 ff. This view has been very influential in this century. It seems to me to have been undercut, however, by Burkert's argument (*loc. cit.* above n41) that the correct derivation of *lykeios* or *lykios* is from wolf, the wolf being a totem for young men who 'run with the pack' until they come of age. The association of Apollo and the wolf is Greek, specifically Dorian. See too Burkert 1975.

ACHILLES TO THETIS: *ILIAD* 1.365–412

For
W.E. McLeod

1

THE LONGEST speech in Book 1 of the *Iliad* is not, somewhat surprisingly, Nestor's attempt to reconcile the quarrelling Achaean leaders but Achilles' plaint and plea to his mother (365–412). G.S. Kirk in his new commentary on the first tetrad of the poem characterizes this speech as 'not very interesting' and, while willing to believe that the lines are the work of the main composer and not a later interpolation by way of résumé, finds that the passage contributes little of value to the *Iliad*, being in large measure a non-dramatic catalogue of events that have been more graphically presented immediately before.[1]

The speech, I believe, repays close attention. Generally, it is a masterstroke to have this concentrated outburst from Achilles before he disappears from the stage of the poem and lapses into the wounded silence that will last until Book 9. And it is psychologically effective to have Achilles reveal the reasons for his sorrow *in extenso* to the mother he loves and trusts – the passage thus establishes the dependence of the hero on the single figure who will be accessible and sympathetic to him throughout the poem.[2]

First published in *EMC/CV* NS 9 (1990) 1–15.

I am especially grateful to Professor W.E. McLeod, Homerist nonpareil, for his advice and encouragement. Professor Martin Cropp and the referees of *EMC/CV* gave much assistance, which I wish to acknowledge. The ideas in this paper originated during the course of a stimulating class in 1987–1988 and it accordingly gives me pleasure to record a debt to my students too.

1 Kirk 1985: 92–3. Lohmann (1970) does not discuss the speech, but there is a sensitive treatment of it from a narratologist's perspective by de Jong (1985).
2 Cf. Edwards 1987: 183. One of the journal's referees points out that, in addition, the speech balances with Achilles' long speech to Thetis in Book 18.

Among the most arresting words in the speech are lines 380–2:

χωόμενος δ' ὁ γέρων πάλιν ᾤχετο· τοῖο δ' Ἀπόλλων
εὐξαμένου ἤκουσεν, ἐπεὶ μάλα οἱ φίλος ἦεν,
ἧκε δ' ἐπ' Ἀργείοισι κακὸν βέλος

These lines are startling, not least because they bring home to us the differences and the similarities between the cases of Achilles and Chryses. Apollo, says Achilles, listened to Chryses because Chryses was dear to him. And so Achilles contrasts himself implicitly with the priest of Apollo. Though Achilles is called 'dear to Zeus' at 1.74,[3] he feels at this moment that he is not valued. Zeus ought to have honoured him (1.353–4) but has not done so. Both Agamemnon and Achilles expect honour from Zeus (cf. 1.175), but Zeus clearly cannot honour both men in the issue that divides them. In Book 9 Achilles will boast that Zeus *has* honoured him (608), and Agamemnon will concede that Zeus loves Achilles and honours him (117–18: love and honour are not, thus, seen as different). In his protestations to his mother he shows that he needs her to re-establish him in Zeus' honour and affection. Zeus will apparently do this because he loves and honours Thetis, hence the mention of Chryses' being dear to Apollo also establishes a paradigm for what Achilles hopes will happen. It prepares for the second part of the speech, in which Achilles moves from recital of past events (365–92) to his request that Thetis go to Olympus on his behalf (393–412). Apollo did what Chryses requested because Chryses reminded him of favours performed in the past (39–41); Achilles provides Thetis with a justification for her right to make a claim. Thetis does not repeat the justification that Achilles provides, though her words at 504, τόδε μοι κρήηνον ἐέλδωρ, are the same as Chryses' words to Apollo at 41.[4] Achilles' mention of Thetis' boast which he heard, presumably as a child (396), provides a moving glimpse of a time when mother and son enjoyed a communion less intermittent than on the plain of Troy (n.b. πολλάκι).[5]

---

3 Achilles is called 'dear to Zeus' five times in the poem (1.74, 16.169, 18.203, 22.216, 24.472), more than anyone else (Hector, 6.318, 8.493, 10.49, 13.674; Odysseus, 10.527, 11.419, 473; Apollo, 1.86; heralds, 8.517; Patroclus, 11.611; Phoenix, 9.168; Phyleus, 2.628).

4 Similar formulas are used elsewhere in the *Iliad* (1.455, 8.242, 16.238). It may be significant that 1.41 and 1.504 are identical – Thetis, after all, will have heard Chryses' prayer to Apollo (Achilles calls attention to her full knowledge of the situation before he begins his recital at 365).

5 The *Iliad* seems to think of Thetis as having performed the normal functions of wife and mother. Thetis speaks (18.55–60) of having reared Achilles, of having sent him

The incident recalled, an attempted palace coup on Olympus when Zeus asserted his authority, remains in our minds, even though Thetis does not mention it again, when another son, Hephaestus, reminds *his* mother of an occasion on which Zeus asserted his authority (586 ff.). At that time Hephaestus was thrown into the Aegean.[6] The contrast between Hera and Thetis, so prominent at the end of the book, is further pointed. Hephaestus intervened unsuccessfully on behalf of his mother; Thetis will intervene successfully for her son. We are not surprised that Zeus likes Thetis better than Hera: we have Hephaestus to tell us that Hera causes trouble for Zeus, Achilles to tell us that Thetis helps Zeus in his hour of need.

The lines quoted above contain the revelation that Apollo sent the plague because he answered Chryses' prayer. It comes as something of a surprise, for we must ask ourselves how Achilles knows this. He did not hear Calchas say it, for Calchas did not mention Chryses' appeal to Apollo. The information is, however, of the first importance as it allows us to see that Achilles is patterning his own behaviour on that of Chryses. Having himself been humiliated by Agamemnon, he will adopt a strategy like that of the priest – he will pray to a divinity to intervene and to cause damage to the Achaean host. For he knows that this works in bringing Agamemnon to make restitution.[7] But he must work through an intermediary since he is himself undervalued and so he enlists his mother, whom he provides with a basis for a claim on Zeus. Achilles, it will be noted, attributes anger to Chryses ($\chi\omega\delta\mu\epsilon\nu\sigma s$, 380). Hitherto we had heard only that the anger was Apollo's (9, 44, 46, 64, 75). This assimilation of Chryses' case to his own is fraught with consequence for Achilles. For the two cases are not, in fact, exactly similar: the absence of anger in Chryses' case made settlement a simple, mechanical matter, while its presence in Achilles' case is what will

---

to war, and of her thwarted hope of receiving him home. We learn of the gifts she gave him upon his departure (16.222–4), though she is elsewhere not mentioned as present at the time of the muster (11.769 ff). For the dramatic time of the poem Thetis' divinity is emphasized as she must be an intermediary between heaven and earth. It is perhaps for this reason that the poet separates her from Peleus and puts her back with her father Nereus in the sea: see March 1987: 23–35.

6 On the occasion referred to by Achilles one hekatoncheir, Briareos, was summoned by Thetis to assist Zeus. He is given another name as well – Aigaion (404) – but the reason for the identification is not explained. There is, however, this possible parallel between the two occasions: in the first case a helpful god was brought to Olympus, probably from the Aegean as his name reminds us, to assist Zeus; on the second occasion referred to, a meddlesome god was cast into the same sea. On Aigaion, see Fowler 1988.

7 See Rabel 1988: 473–81.

make the matter complicated – he will not be able to renounce the anger that has come of his humiliation. There is a fine irony in Achilles' choosing Chryses' solution and assuming identity of motivation in the two cases. But it is a tragic irony, for Achilles' mistaken assumption helps launch him on a course that will prove fatal for Patroclus and thus for himself.

Modern critics have not been unaware of this revelation by Achilles of something that we did not know he knew, i.e., that Chryses had prayed to Apollo.[8] It is the first instance in Homer of what the ancients labelled the σχῆμα κατὰ τὸ σιωπώμενον or pattern in accordance with what is passed over in silence.[9] Awareness of the inconsistencies produced by such a *schema* might trouble an Aristarchus enough to cause him to athetize (e.g., *ad Od.* 17.501: Aristarchus condemned *Il.* 1.366–92 too, but for a different reason – the omniscience of Thetis posited in 365 makes this narrative otiose). Since the phrase σχῆμα κατὰ τὸ σιωπώμενον implies clumsy narrative technique, Bassett prefers the phrase σχῆμα κατὰ τὸ ἤδη εἰρημένον or λύσις ἐκ τοῦ ἀκροατοῦ ('motivation-by-the-audience') – the poet relies on information which he has given the audience and which thereafter characters in the poem are allowed to know.[10]

Satisfactory as this explanation is in some cases, it presents the danger inherent in every coverall explanation: it encourages a tendency to treat as identical situations in which there is at most similarity. In many instances where characters in the poem know something that surprises us, what is known is of small importance for our understanding of the persons involved. This is normally the case when a warrior on the battlefield knows the identity and circumstances of his opponent. But even here all cases are not the same, and it is not intrinsically illogical that warriors who have been enemies for ten years should know each other. The poet emphasizes at times the duration of the war (e.g., Book 2); at times, when it suits

---

8 E.g., Bassett 1938: 132; Bowra 1962: 70.
9 For instances in the *Iliad*, see Erbse 1983: 478–9 (*ad* σιωπᾶν).
10 Bassett 1938: 128–35. Bassett is indebted to Fraccaroli 1903: 397–406. Fraccaroli is led to his conclusion (that the audience, so to speak, communicates things to the actors in the poem) by the *teichoskopia*, for he thinks that the elders on the wall betray knowledge (that they have no way of having) that a duel is to be fought for Helen (3.159–60). I simply do not see that this is the case. A tribute to Helen's beauty is balanced by a wish that she would leave and spare the Trojans the suffering she has brought. The Trojans want the Greeks to go home, but know they will not go without Helen (Book 2 has already shown that the Greeks want to go home). Antenor's speech a few lines later (204–24) surely refers to the occasion when Menelaus and Odysseus came to demand the return of Helen, referred to in the *Cypria* (see below n28).

his purpose to do so, he presents the war as though it were in its initial stages (most of Books 3–7). Priam is thus shown in the *teichoskopia* as, rather illogically, *not* recognizing those with whom he has been at war for a decade! A genuinely surprising case is, certainly, Idomeneus' exultation over the body of the slain Othryoneus (13.361–84), for though Othryoneus is new to the war Idomeneus knows his story. When Diomedes meets Glaucus (5.123), however, he does not know who his opponent is. His ignorance provides the occasion for an important and memorable exchange. Fraccaroli's explanation of this scene is that we know Diomedes well (and thus so does Glaucus), but that we are relatively new to Glaucus (and so Diomedes must ask on our behalf).[11] This seems to me to miss the essential point of the episode. Diomedes has been warned by Apollo at 5.440–2 of the folly of engaging in combat with divinities. His new-found prudence is shown in his inquiry of his new opponent whether he is divine or human, something impossible to tell on the battlefield, where gods assume human guise (and yet, remarkably, Diomedes could see divinities with the naked eye in Book 5!). It is one of the most delicious touches in the poem, and a fine piece of character-drawing.

On occasion the problem sensed by the critics seems non-existent. There are two examples in the *Iliad*, in addition to the instance in Book 1 which is our chief concern here, that are mentioned by Bassett and Bowra.[12] Both are false problems.

1) Patroclus could not have known that Sarpedon was the first to penetrate the Greek wall successfully (16.558). Do we simply say that Patroclus knows because the reader has been told? Patroclus was not with Achilles when the wall was breached but had been sent from Achilles' tent to a point nearer the action where he had seen the attack (15.395). What is most remarkable is that his assumption that Sarpedon was first contradicts the statement of the poet (12.438) that Hector was first (and so the reader has not been told what Patroclus 'knows'). It is an effective piece of rhetoric when Patroclus is exhorting the Greeks to make an all-out effort to capture Sarpedon's body. And it is, I believe, an indication of the ἄτη (16.685) that will carry Patroclus to his own death.[13]

2) At 17.241 Ajax says to Menelaus that he fears lest the body of Patroclus be given to dogs and birds, apparently knowing Hector's intentions as

---

11 Bassett 1938: 398.
12 See above, n8.
13 That Patroclus should understand that Apollo has disarmed him (16.844–50) is hardly surprising: Achilles warned him about Apollo (16.94), and Apollo has already beaten him back three times and addressed him (16.700–9).

expressed by the poet at line 127. This does not seem to me a real problem. Ajax was, after all, facing Hector at the moment Hector was said to have this intention and it is easy to believe that Hector articulated it (Homeric heroes do not fight in silence). Or, alternatively, we may take this as a general and justified fear that Ajax has: the motif of bodies as carrion runs throughout the poem, from its fourth line onwards. Ajax does not in fact attribute the intention to Hector in the passage in question.

Colin Macleod calls attention to the instance we are considering in Book 1 when he is discussing lines 203–5 of Book 24.[14] Hecuba there seems to know Iris' command to Priam, though she has not heard it, for she says that Priam proposes to travel alone (οἷον, 148; οἶος, 203). This seems to me a superb psychological touch. It is natural that a concerned Hecuba make the strongest possible case for the risk that Priam is incurring by going to the Greek camp. Priam has failed to tell Hecuba that he will *not* in fact be entirely alone but has been guaranteed a divine escort and safe passage. His withholding a piece of information somehow augments Hecuba's apprehension and causes her to make what in the circumstances is a natural inference. There is a similar and even more famous instance in Book 9. Achilles' use of the word βασιλεύτερος (9.392) implies knowledge of Agamemnon's use of the same word at 9.160. But Odysseus has not reported this part of Agamemnon's speech. It is, I think, particularly significant that when Odysseus reports Agamemnon's offer he deliberately omits Agamemnon's offensive and inflammatory statement that Achilles should yield to his greater dignity. That Achilles uses the word he has not heard is not to be explained away by the fact that the audience has, after all, heard it but by Achilles' cannily (or perhaps uncannily) accurate assessment of the offer that is being made on the grounds of what he *has* heard and because he knows the ambassador. It is obvious to Achilles that Agamemnon sues for reconciliation without any change of heart. The repetition of a word provides irony for the audience, but we need not attribute Achilles' insight (which is sufficient to explain his sarcasm) to the audience's knowledge.[15] In both the above instances a person who knows

---

14 Macleod 1982: 105.
15 As one of the journal's referees points out, βασιλεύτερος is the sort of thing that Agamemnon would typically say of himself and that Achilles might effectively invoke whether it was used on this occasion or not. Agamemnon has introduced the comparative φέρτερος as early as 1.186 (κάρτερος, 178, is not a comparative) and Achilles regularly admits Agamemnon's superior authority, which clearly rankles (cf. κράτεϊ προβεβήκῃ, 16.54). I do not find the repetition of the verb ἠπεροπεύειν (3.399) at 5.349 very startling. Both Helen and Diomedes revile Aphrodite, and both use the same word. The audience can savour this, but is there any reason to suggest that Diomedes knows

his interlocutor well shows surprising knowledge when that interlocutor has deliberately suppressed something he might have been expected to say. This transparency to the person from whom the information is withheld is a subtle means of characterization.

It is not possible to deal with every instance here.[16] I suggest merely that the principle enunciated by Fraccaroli and Bassett, for all its importance in helping to save the text from simple accusations of illogicality and inconsistency, should not blind us to the advisability of investigating what is particular to individual instances.[17] It does not exhaust the significance of a passage to identify it as an instance of motivation-by-the-audience. If the knowledge displayed by a character in the poem suddenly surprises us, it is just possible that we are meant to be surprised.

Surprised we certainly are when Achilles reveals that he knows that Apollo sent the plague because he answered Chryses' prayer. Rather than argue that in minor matters the poet is not troubled by inconsistencies or invoke the principle of motivation-by-the-audience (the audience after all knows about Chryses' prayer ...),[18] we might ask ourselves how it is possible for Achilles to have known. It is no minor matter, for Achilles has decided to follow the example set by Chryses. The answer, surely, is that it is logical inference on his part. He knows that the offended Chryses is priest of Apollo and might expect that he would appeal to the powerful patron who could take his part. We remember that Achilles claimed to know at the assembly that an angry Apollo had sent the plague (64). This is in itself noteworthy. That the visitation is seen to be caused by a god is not in itself astonishing – anything out of the ordinary is regularly attributed to divine interference – but the categorical certainty that Apollo is the source of the plague comes as something of a surprise. Why should Achilles be certain (unless, indeed, he knows what he later confesses to Thetis that he knows)? It has been pointed out that it is generally the poet who is specific (and he is in this episode), using the divine machinery: his

---

Helen's rebuke? Paris is called ἠπεροπευτά at 3.39 and 13.769. These words simply point to the generally known fact of Paris' elopement with Helen.

16 Bassett (1938: 131) claims to have found over one hundred.
17 This narrative device asks to be studied at length and in detail, for like the formula itself it can provide insight into both consistency and variation in the poet's art. A recurring element is not, for its recurrence, without significance in a given context.
18 Another principle to which appeal might be made is 'The Early Greek Capacity for Viewing Things Separately': see Perry 1937. Again, this is tantamount to arguing that the poet is little concerned with consistency in his narrative or that he does not do things advisedly.

characters ignore it[19] unless, of course, they have good reason to know, as Achilles, for instance, knows of the celebrated case, which he adduces as an *exemplum* to Priam, of the death of the children of Niobe by the arrows of an angry Apollo and Artemis (24.605–6). One might be tempted to argue that Achilles attributes the disease to a god regularly connected with plague. There is, however, no particular indication in the rest of the poem that the Achaeans (or Trojans) think of Apollo as a god of sickness. He is mentioned elsewhere as a god of easy death by gentle arrows (24.759), something quite unlike disease (1.10) resulting, the poet says, from the anger of the hunter-god who strides with clanging arrows over the mountains, menacing as night (1.44–7). The priest at the beginning of the *Oedipus Tyrannus*, speaking for a stricken Thebes, does not assume that the plague comes from Apollo.[20] One might expect Achilles to have some doubt too, unless he has the superior knowledge he later admits to. But if we have any perplexity as to why Achilles should name Apollo as the source of the plague, our perplexity is dispelled when he tells Thetis that Apollo sent the plague because he answered Chryses' prayer. It was, after all, an easy inference. One wonders how many among the rank and file of the Achaean host made the same inference, understanding that Apollo was not aroused to wrath spontaneously by the insult to his priest? The mention of the priest's holy regalia at line 14 calls attention to his standing with the god, whom he asks the Achaeans to honour (21), and we know (22–3) that general opinion was on Chryses' side. Achilles reveals what he has known all along when he has decided to act as Chryses did and enlist a god on his own behalf.[21]

This puts the assembly in a new light. Achilles, says the poet, was impelled by Hera to summon the Achaean leaders because of her concern for the dying (1.54–6). Achilles' expressed concern is somewhat different –

---

19 See, e.g., Dodds 1951: 12. It is not, however, surprising that Patroclus should be specific in attributing his death to Apollo (see above n13).
20 The chorus think that Ares is responsible (190). They may have made this inference for traditional reasons: they know Ares to be βροτολοιγός (*Il.* 5.31), and plague is λοιγός (*Il.* 1.67, 97). Knox (1956: 133–47) thinks that Sophocles, by mentioning Ares, is contriving an allusion to the plague at Athens at the beginning of the Peloponnesian War. But Müller (1984: 31–8) points out a strong objection to this theory: the plague in Sophocles is not an epidemic (as in Thucydides) but a temporary divine punishment (the motif is dropped after the opening of the play). The Sophoclean plague is a purely literary *topos* and the paradigm for it is precisely the plague at the beginning of the *Iliad*.
21 de Jong (1985: 20 n37) says: 'he rightly concluded that Apollo was responsible for the plague (1.64), but as yet did not connect the anger of the god with the events around Chryses.' It is easier to believe that Achilles *did* have a basis for his conclusion and that the basis was his knowledge of the god's connection with Chryses.

he fears that the expedition may fail of its purpose and that the remnants of the army will have to withdraw (59–60). This seems more a preoccupation that opportunities for glory and plunder will be forfeited than a concern for the dying,[22] and it accords well with the presentation of Achilles at the beginning of the poem as a warrior whose paramount interest is his personal honour. In any case, since Achilles knows why the plague has descended it is not really necessary for him to summon Calchas to reveal the truth of the matter. The speculation at line 65 that Apollo has sent the plague because he may be dissatisfied with sacrificial offerings is, in a word, camouflage. It is very likely the case that Achilles knows that Agamemnon will not listen to the truth if it comes from his, Achilles', mouth, and so deems it both prudent and politic to have the real situation revealed by a seer whose integrity and disinterestedness are unimpeachable in the eyes of all. In his passionate outburst in Book 9, Achilles begins by denouncing the man who says one thing and conceals another in his heart (κεύθῃ ἐνὶ φρεσίν, 313). Achilles means the words to refer to himself[23] – it is his intention to speak his mind unreservedly. But as a statement of principle these words must carry a certain piquancy. And Thetis' words to Achilles at 1.363 take on heightened meaning too. She tells him not to conceal anything (μὴ κεῦθε νόῳ). There is no reason for him to do so as he is in the sympathetic presence of one from whom he need have no secrets. In the presence of Agamemnon Achilles fears the effect of a distasteful revelation and seeks to blunt its unpleasant effect, or at least to enhance its authority, by having it made through a voice less likely to be challenged than his own. But his procedure involves an uncharacteristic indirection, and he gains nothing by hiding behind Calchas. Agamemnon's reaction to both Calchas and Achilles is the same (αἰεί τοι τὰ κάκ᾽ ἐστὶ φίλα, 107; αἰεὶ γάρ τοι ἔρις τε φίλη, 177). The two are one in his estimation as the two are one in their knowledge.[24]

---

22 The poet uses the divine machinery while his character acts from personal motives. And so the action is 'overdetermined': see Dodds 1951: 7, 16.
23 The words also apply to Odysseus and to Agamemnon: see the discussion in Whitman 1958: 192–9. Perhaps the best example of Agamemnon's hiding one thing in his heart and speaking another is his suggestion to the army in Book 2 that they flee back to Greece after he has had a dream which he thinks foretokens success: see Owen 1946: 18. Ironically, Achilles is something less than forthright with Odysseus – he says that he will return on the morrow to Phthia (427–30). He later tells the truth to Ajax (650 ff.), that he will return to fight when the battle has reached his ships.
24 The statement that Calchas never speaks anything but bad news is surprising when we remember that at Aulis he predicted the fall of Troy (2.323–9). But Agamemnon, in

2

Achilles' speech to Thetis provides us with another important piece of information. This item will acquire its full importance in the light of subsequent revelations and is thus the opposite of the disclosure regarding Chryses, which sheds a retrospective light. We learn (366–7) that Chryseis was captured on the foray in which Thebe, the city of Eëtion, was taken. This is to prove a telling detail.[25] For the moment we note that Chryseis must have been away from her home (Chryse; 37, 100, 390) when she was taken. This deliberate displacement of the girl from her own city and protection of her father at the time of her capture is curious. As we slowly piece together information in the course of the poem we are able to reconstruct the great *razzia* in which several neighbouring cities were sacked and prisoners taken. These cities were: Hypoplakian Thebe, where Andromache's brothers and father were killed and Andromache's mother captured (6.414 ff.);[26] Lyrnessus, where Briseis was taken (2.690–1) after the killing of her husband and brothers (19.291–4);[27] and Pedasos (20.92), whence Aeneas escaped to Lyrnessus, which was subsequently destroyed

---

the circumstances, shows more forbearance than Sophocles' Oedipus, who when told by a seer that he is responsible for the plague jumps to the conclusion that Creon has base designs and that he has suborned Teiresias to be the mouthpiece for his subversive intentions.

25 For traditional views regarding this detail, see de Jong 1985: 20 n29.

26 Not, as Kirk states (1985: 91), Andromache herself! Andromache came to Ilium before the arrival of the Greeks in the Troad and was never their prisoner. See Sappho 44 (Voigt): the Trojan men and women harness chariots (13–17) to leave the city for the port where they will welcome the bridal couple (6), something that would have been impossible in time of siege unless a truce had been declared (cf. the Trojans pouring out of the city to meet the returning Priam at *Iliad* 24.707). Andromache's marriage to Hector has produced a single child (6.401) and he is an infant in arms. Her marriage seems in this respect to be presented as recent. But the poet does not always ask us to keep in mind that the Greeks have spent ten long years outside the city: the events of Books 3–7 suggests a war that is in its initial stages (cf. above 76 and Griffin 1980: 27–8).

27 Leaf and Bayfield are as confused as Kirk (previous note). In the first volume of their commentary (London 1895) they say, *ad* 9.188, 'Thebe, whence Briseis had come.' Are they thinking of the passage in Book 1, under discussion here, which tells us that Chryseis was taken at Thebe? Anyone who has lectured on Homer will have a certain sympathy for those who confuse the names Briseis and Chryseis. It is also salutary to remember that Chaucer's Cryseyde and Shakespeare's Cressida (= Chryseis) come from Briseida (= Briseis) of Benoit de Sainte-Maure's *Roman de Troie* (Boccaccio provided an intermediate Griseida).

by Achilles (20.193-4 – Aeneas must have escaped a second time).[28] There are no limits, we are continually reminded, to what Agamemnon's army could do in the field when Achilles was fighting alongside the Greeks. The compressing of the several sacked cities into one great foray invites us to compare the fates of the prisoners taken at the same time. Briseis and Chryseis are juxtaposed in Book 1, and doubtless Achilles' knowledge that they were originally taken in the same foray intensifies his sense that his own situation is like that of Chryses. But there is another, more telling, parallel.

When Andromache, telling Hector of his supreme importance to her (6.407 ff.), recounts her family's fate, she speaks of the sack of Thebe. We already know as we listen that Chryseis was taken in this city at this time, for Achilles explained as much to Thetis. Achilles' treatment of the body of Eëtion speaks for his normal chivalry in military action – it is especially moving to learn from the bereaved daughter that Achilles did not strip his victim of his armour and that he gave him the rites of cremation.[29] All this foreshadows by contrast the extraordinary nature of Achilles' treatment of the body of Hector, whom he despoils (22.368) and to whom he denies the privilege he accorded Eëtion. But Achilles' treatment of Eëtion's wife, Andromache's mother, looks back to Agamemnon's treatment of the prisoner he was awarded from the same doomed city.[30]

28 The synopsis of the *Cypria* (see Allen 1912: 105) does not contradict this and seems to imply in addition that Troilus was killed and Lycaon captured on the same foray (distinguished from earlier marauding raids subsequent to an initial Trojan refusal to surrender Helen). It is not clear from Proclus' account that the various cities were sacked and prisoners taken in a single raid, but the events enumerated appear to belong to one episode of the *Cypria*. Leaf (1912: 242-3) thinks that there was originally a distinct poem about this raid and even has a name for it, the 'Poem of the Great Foray.' So too Wade-Gery 1952. The tendency to quarry the *Iliad* for lost pre-Iliadic sources is less fashionable today than it was a generation ago and it seems, certainly, unnecessary in this case: what is consistent within the poem, even if that consistency is perceived only as details accumulate, does not have to point outside the poem.
29 Did Achilles himself commit Eëtion's body to the flames because the sack of the city was so total that there was no one else to perform the obsequies? We know that Lycaon's Pedasos continues to exist after its sack (21.86-7). The action of giving the last rites to one's enemy is, in any case, unusual.
30 Maciej Kowara and Mark Young have pointed out to me that in the division of the spoils of the city captured by Achilles, Agamemnon typically takes the more appealing prize, the young woman, while leaving the older woman to Achilles. At 9.129-30 Agamemnon offers as ransom to Achilles seven women of Lesbos – selected by

For the parallel between the two women is exact and telling. Where Agamemnon refused ransom (ἀπερείσι᾽ ἄποινα 1.13, 372) from Chryses for his daughter, Achilles accepted ransom (ἀπερείσι᾽ ἄποινα 6.247) from Andromache's grandfather for his daughter. This I take to be the point of the otherwise gratuitous detail that she died in her father's halls after being ransomed.[31] If Achilles' consideration for the corpse of the slain Eëtion provides a standard from which he will fall after the death of Patroclus, his treatment of Eëtion's wife is a commentary on Agamemnon's behaviour under similar circumstances – the attempt by a father to ransom his daughter. It is the detail in Achilles' speech to Thetis that allows us to make the comparison.[32]

Agamemnon for himself from an island that Achilles had pillaged! (The juxtaposition of ἔλεν and ἐξελόμην is unwittingly ironic.)

The name of Eëtion keeps coming back in the story of Achilles. Eëtion's Thebe is the source of Achilles' lyre (9.188), his mortal horse (16.153), and his shot-put (23.827). The Eëtion who ransomed Lycaon (21.42–3) is clearly a different man as is shown by the designation Imbrios. The Eëtion whose son Podes is mentioned as a friend of Hector (17.575, 590) must be a third person with this name. Zarker (1978: 148) tries to make Eëtion father of Podes and Eëtion father of Andromache the same person. To get round the problem that Andromache has claimed that Achilles killed *all* her brothers (6.423), Zarker says that Homer is simply narrating the death of this one brother out of sequence (during the fighting over the body of Patroclus). This provides a consistency of nomenclature too dearly bought, for Andromache's words become false in retrospect and their beautiful poignancy is undercut. The alternative to seeing Andromache as exaggerating, if Podes is her brother, is seeing the poet as careless, scarcely a superior solution. We do not need to 'explain the close companionship between Hector and Podes' (Zarker *loc. cit.*) by assuming that they are related by marriage. Podes is simply a ἑταῖρος (577).

31 So, correctly I think, Willcock 1978 *ad* 6.428, πατρός: 'Andromache's mother's father ... ransomed her from the Greek camp; and it was in his house, not in Thebe, that she then died.' It might be possible to take πατρὸς δ᾽ ἐνὶ μεγάροισι as 'my,' not 'her,' father (i.e., Andromache's mother died in Thebe – but see above n29). At 1.396 πατρὸς ἐν μεγάροισιν must mean 'my,' not 'your,' father (see above n5), whereas at 21.475 the phrase means 'your,' not 'my,' father. The phrase need not indicate the father of the speaker in every instance. If πατρός means 'my father' at 6.428, a fine detail in Andromache's narrative is thereby rendered otiose. Andromache's mother was, thus, returned to a city other than the one in which she was taken. In this too she is like Chryseis.

32 I do not think, though some may, that these parallels, which require our remembering something from Book 1 in Book 6, are below the threshold of perceptibility for an audience. We are, e.g., expected to remember 1.26–33 (Agamemnon's anger at a father who has come with ransom) when we witness a similar reaction on the part of Achilles at 24.560. My working assumption is that an oral poet may be as subtle as a literate poet, hence as amenable to close reading and criticism.

Ransom, ἄποινα, in the *Iliad* is of two sorts.[33] It is offered by those who beg for their lives on the field of battle or it is offered off the battlefield by those who beg for something other than their lives. Agamemnon and Achilles are repeatedly contrasted with respect to both varieties of ransom. We see Agamemnon reject the ransom offered by Chryses and learn that Achilles accepted the ransom offered by Andromache's grandfather for his daughter. Achilles at the end of the poem will again accept ἀπερεί-σι᾽ ἄποινα (24.276, 502, 579) from a suppliant father. It is ironic that Agamemnon probably never receives ransom for Chryseis when he is, in the event, obliged to return her. We are nowhere told that he gets the ransom that he was originally offered and there is no reason to believe that he does (Calchas in fact says at 1.99 that Agamemnon will be forced to surrender Chryseis ἀνάποινον). Achilles is similarly obliged by divine intervention (24.133-7) to give Hector back to Priam but he is not, for that, cheated of ransom. When Agamemnon offers ἄποινα to Achilles to return to battle (9.120) it is the single instance in the poem of a Greek's offering ransom – no Greek ever asks a *Trojan* to accept ransom. Agamemnon's offer is rejected by the angry Achilles, but the rejected ransom (19.138) is, of course, later accepted when Achilles has renounced his wrath.

On the battlefield Achilles' regular behaviour is to spare prisoners, for whom he subsequently accepts ransom. He says as much to Lycaon (21.99-102). The taking of prisoners who surrender would appear to be a normal procedure: Thersites claims that he and many another Greek have done it (2.229-31). The speech to Lycaon thus reminds us that the Achilles we see on the battlefield is an abnormal Achilles, one who has departed from his own practice. His initial anger led him to reject the ransom offered by Agamemnon, though he accepted it when that anger was laid aside. When his anger is redirected towards Hector and he returns to battle, he twice refuses supplication and ransom – first for Lycaon and then for Hector himself (22.338-54). Agamemnon twice refuses supplication and ransom on the battlefield too. In this way we see that what is the aberrant behaviour of the temporarily dehumanized Achilles is the regular behaviour of the king.

---

33 ἄποινα is, in effect, simply an intensive form of ποινή, itself a doublet, both etymologically and semantically, of the more common τιμή. The two words appear to be equated at 3.288-90. Both ποινή and τιμή come from IE *q^{u}ei-: see Heubeck 1949. There is a profound and important connection between the two ideas: restitution or indemnity (τιμή) is a form of satisfaction in a carefully calibrated exchange system whose 'satisfactions' include penalties, ransom, and honour.

In Book 6, the hapless Adrestos, when he falls into the hands of Menelaus (37 ff.), begs him to take ransom. Menelaus is disposed to do so but is dissuaded by Agamemnon who, in addition to killing Adrestos (another man's suppliant!), calls down a particularly horrendous curse on pregnant Trojan mothers.[34] The vehemence of this shocks us and is meant to do so. In Book 11 Peisandros and Hippolochos ask Agamemnon to take ransom and he refuses (134). Again, the incident redounds to Agamemnon's discredit, for he invents as an excuse for killing them a fabrication that the poet allows us to see as such: Homer has explained that their father Antimachos took bribes from Paris to side with those in Troy opposed to the return of Helen (11.123 ff.), but Agamemnon magnifies this offence into an attempt on the life of Menelaus. If the two passages refer to the same occasion, as I believe they do, we may notice that Agamemnon's memory of the incident differs crucially from the poet's account and so draw the conclusion that the king has invented a rationalization for killing, a killing described in particularly macabre terms. Achilles and Agamemnon are brought into close juxtaposition in this scene too, for just before his killing of Peisandros and Hippolochos Agamemnon has killed Isos and Antiphos, two sons of Priam for whom Achilles had at some point accepted ransom (101–10): we are told that Agamemnon recognized them from the time they had spent with the Greeks as Achilles' prisoners.[35]

---

34 The slaughter of the unborn is hardly condign punishment for the wrong Menelaus has suffered. On the other hand, Nestor's urging of the Greeks to make the Trojans pay for Helen's sufferings (2.354–6) by having every Greek soldier rape a Trojan woman is, if appalling to us, at least payment in kind and so a form of retributive justice, however exaggerated. Kirk (1985: 153) thinks that Nestor may be urging the Greeks to exact punishment for pains endured by the Greeks 'because of Helen' rather than punishment for Helen's own sufferings: but the genitive is not ambiguous, *pace* (in addition to Kirk) Palmer 1962: 132: a correct understanding of the passage is provided by McLeod 1987: 364. Justice is a matter of reciprocity in the *Iliad* (see previous note) and is so conceived here, whether what the Greeks believe (that Helen was raped) is true or not. The Greeks, as is already evident in Homer, are exacting justice for a figment of their imagination (Helen's own admission is that she went willingly, 3.174). Later authors (Stesichorus, Euripides, Plato) will turn this figment into an actual wraith. On justice as reciprocity see further Gentili 1988: 69.

35 The articulation of a petition to be spared is the essential element in battlefield supplication. Tros' supplication of Achilles (20.463 ff.) remains an intention, mentioned by the poet, but is never uttered. It is thus not parallel to the instances that have been considered above. Gould 1973: 74–103 finds physical contact the primary element in supplication, though he admits, 81, 'figurative supplication,' i.e., supplication through words alone. Tros performs neither act nor speech ($ἥπετο$, 468, is conative).

In Book 10 Dolon asks Diomedes and Odysseus to accept ransom (380). This is an extraordinary situation, not really covered by either of the alternatives I have

3

The foregoing discussion, if somewhat wide-ranging, has had one essential object: to show that Achilles' long speech to Thetis in Book 1, far from being of negligible value in the *Iliad*, provides some intriguing bits of information, apparently casual but of real value for our understanding of Achilles and seeing him in relation to Agamemnon. Most particularly, the revelation that Achilles knows the reason for Apollo's anger colours our understanding of the dramatic presentation of the quarrel, and the information that Chryseis was taken in Eëtion's Thebe will, when added to Andromache's further account of the sack of the city, allow us to make a direct comparison between the behaviour of Agamemnon and that of Achilles in a matter – the ransoming of hostages – in which they are elsewhere compared.[36] This comparison seems carefully designed, for we have to do with two women captives, taken at the same time, whose fathers come to ransom them. The difference in behaviour could scarcely be more pointed. It is a superb touch, hardly surprising in the *poeta sovrano*, to allow us to see, through a few subtle strokes, wherein Agamemnon and Achilles are alike – their hiding of something in their heart – and wherein they differ – their treatment of those who are at their mercy. The dual note is sustained until the end of the poem. Achilles' last speech to Priam contains a deception, albeit a polite and profoundly considerate one, for he tells the king that he must sleep in the courtyard, offering as reason that night visitors may come for strategic discussions.[37] His real reason

---

outlined here. Dolon is asking for his life, but he is on a spying expedition by night, not on the battlefield. Odysseus and Diomedes have no alternative but to kill him. Yet Odysseus allows him to think (383) that he can buy his life back by supplying information. Technically at least, Odysseus does not go back on his word, for he makes no direct promise. But his intent is to deceive. Diomedes, who performs the execution, is not guilty of Odysseus' mental reservation. By the same token, it is not Diomedes who succeeds in eliciting the valuable information. This is subtle and effective characterization.

36 Pedrick (1982: 139) notes that Agamemnon and Achilles are compared with respect to their treatment of suppliants. But comparison points primarily to the similarities between them; what contrast she finds is not between Agamemnon and Achilles but simply between suppliants and the warriors who have them at their mercy.

37 Macleod (1982: 142) translates ἐπικερτομέων (649) as 'teasing, mystifying' and explains, 'it is here used of deception, not mockery.' On this word see now Jones 1989: 247–50. Jones argues that the meaning must always be to 'cut to the quick' and that it is so used here: Achilles' words are wounding to Priam. I cannot believe that Achilles is intentionally wounding, and am not convinced that the word can refer to unintentional wounding (*Od.* 8.153 is offered as an example of unintentional wounding – but since

for the request is, I think, his fear of being together with Priam in the presence of Hector's body, inevitable in the event of a formal farewell but avoidable if the old king is allowed the opportunity to leave under cover of night. The final mention of Agamemnon in the poem (24.687) is put into the mouth of Hermes. We hear, and we hardly know at this point whether to smile or shudder, that Agamemnon, were Priam to fall into his hands, would exact a ransom far in excess of what Achilles accepted for the body of Hector. A few lines earlier (654–5) Achilles has ominously pointed out that there would be trouble with the ransoming of Hector's body if Agamemnon learned of Priam's presence in the Greek camp. Achilles on this occasion means what he says.

---

we have Odysseus' words to Laodamas here, can we know that Odysseus does not think that he is being deliberately provoked?) On κερτομέω in the sense 'delude,' see Dale 1954 *ad* 1125.

ALCMAN'S *PARTHENEION*: LEGEND AND CHORAL CEREMONY

*Und in dem 'Wie,' da
liegt der ganze Unterschied.*
Hofmannsthal

1

The papyrus text of the *Partheneion*, discovered in 1855 and now in the Louvre, consists of 101 lines in three columns. Of these the first 34 lines (column i) are badly mutilated owing to the disappearance of the left-hand side of the column, whereas lines 35–101 (columns ii and iii) can be restored with almost complete confidence. Of a fourth column nothing is legible, though a coronis opposite the fifth line of column iii shows that the poem ended only four lines after our text runs out. The lengths of the existing columns are 34 lines (i), 34 lines (ii), 33 lines (iii). If a full column of 35 lines has been lost before our column i – a pre-eminently reasonable hypothesis – the entire poem will have consisted of 140 lines. Since each strophe consists of fourteen lines, we may thus imagine the whole to have consisted of ten strophes. By a curious coincidence the part of the poem which is almost intact and which deals with the occasion consists of five strophes[1] or seventy lines: it seems to be the case, thus, that the lost or damaged part also consisted of five strophes or seventy lines of choral lyric and dealt with myth: what we can make out, certainly, appears to be exclusively myth and attendant moralizing.

First published in *CQ* 44.1 (1991) 7–16.

1 The strophe, with its metrical pattern abab abab ccddef, may also be construed as our first example of a triad, with strophe, identical antistrophe, and epode. The 14-line pattern is curiously anticipatory of the Petrarchan sonnet if the whole is read as an octave with two identical quatrains containing but two metrical patterns (a and b) followed by a sestet that introduces three new ones (c, d, and e).

If this is the case, the symmetry is remarkable, as is the amount of time spent on the legend.[2] Despite this, studies of the poem have not tried to bring the two halves of the poem together. Indeed, the most penetrating of recent analyses concentrates exclusively on the second part,[3] whereas more comprehensive treatments that have dealt with the myth have not attempted to relate it in any particular way to the rest of the poem.[4] It is perhaps understandable that where so much is lost or damaged and so much obscure there should be reluctance to hazard conjectures about the possible unity of the poem. But though the task must be approached with caution and due awareness of the extreme tentativeness of hypotheses regarding a work that remains both mysterious and mutilated, it is nonetheless a worthwhile undertaking to try to consider the possible interdependence of the two sections of the poem.

The array of conjectures and constructions that purport to explain the five complete stanzas is almost endless.[5] And there is almost no detail of interpretation that commands unequivocal agreement. I shall state here what I believe to be the most likely reading of these stanzas.

Hagesichora and Agido occupy positions of preeminence with regard to a choir, the other members of which are named in lines 70–6. Debate continues on the issue of which of these women (both of whose names are, either accidentally or intentionally, derived from words that mean 'lead') is more important or more beautiful. The preference shown by individual scholars is in every case closely linked to an understanding of the occasion as a whole. But there can be little doubt that both are *fuoriserie*, i.e., stand out from the rank and file of the choir. It is therefore most attractive to take the disputed lines 57–8

---

2 Campbell (1982: 2.195) maintains that 'Alcman spent little time on the legend.' But half of the poem appears to deal with the legend. It might be more correct to say that there is more of the poem devoted to occasion than we find in the epinician odes of Pindar (though perhaps not in his *Partheneia*).

3 Puelma 1977: 1–55, hereafter Puelma. The present article is heavily indebted to Puelma's study.

4 The most exhaustive studies are those of Page 1951a, hereafter Page, and Pavese 1992, hereafter Pavese. The common view is exemplified by D. Clay (1991: 53): 'There seems to be no reflection of the poem's context in the first column of the poem ...'

5 Useful discussions and bibliography will be found in Page, Puelma, Pavese, and in Calame 1983, hereafter Calame; see too Calame 1977b. There is a useful bibliographical article by M. Vetta (1982: 127–36). Volume 1 of Davies *PMGF* also contains much relevant bibliography in the apparatus. And there are valuable observations in Garzya 1954.

ἁ δὲ δευτέρα πεδ' Ἀγιδὼ τὸ ϝεῖδος
ἵππος Ἰβηνῶι Κολαξαῖος δραμήται

as pointing to this fact. The correct construction of these lines is shown by the examples that Puelma adduces from Homer[6] – Ἀγιδὼ must be accusative in a phrase of a type that calls attention not so much to a person's inferiority as to the fact that two people are singled out as being together in a class of their own. The horses run neck and neck, so to speak, something reinforced by the names of the horse-types, names given not because one horse is superior to the other but because both are outstanding.[7] Agido and Hagesichora are apparently singled out as being of virtually equivalent worth.[8] Much is lost by taking the reference to the one who is deemed fit to be mentioned in the same breath as the other as referring to an unnamed member of the choir – the choir in fact busily asserts its inferiority in matters of song and beauty throughout this section of the poem.[9] The horse-simile,[10] moreover, should not be taken to imply that there is an actual contest in running. There is no good reason to believe that there is a footrace – the language of running is the language of contest and emphasizes a point, made metaphorically, that the two leaders, while running neck and neck, outstrip the other maidens. The point of comparison is in fact given and it is beauty, not speed. The future δραμήται, as so often with futures in Pindar, belongs logically to a moment just before the song is sung but is actually a performative utterance.[11] If the two horses are Agido and Hagesichora the horse-references in the poem are confined to these two girls, since the simile at 45–9

6 Puelma 1977: 29–31. See also Campbell 1987: 69–71.
7 ἀμφοτέρω[ν διαπρε]πόντων says the B scholiast, giving Aristarchus as his authority.
8 The inability of commentators to agree, on the basis of the text, which of the two is superior is in the end the most eloquent testimony to this equivalence.
9 Following Puelma we get, 'She (= Hagesichora), second after Agido (accusative) in beauty, will run [alongside her].' Garzya and Calame take Agido as nominative and render, 'She, Agido, second in beauty, will run after (πεδ' in tmesis with δραμήται) her (= Hagesichora).' On both these interpretations the two leaders are placed together and apart from the rank and file of the choir. Most recently, Hansen (1993: 118–19) argues once more that Agido is nominative with πεδ' in tmesis, but emends Ἰβηνῶι to εἰβήνοις, allegedly 'mongrels of dogs and foxes.' The purpose of the comparison is supposed to be suddenly to denigrate Agido, who was earlier praised. This construction of the passage is bizarre, and not tied to any view of the poem as a whole. But it still compares Agido and Hagesichora, the two most important girls, basically to each other.
10 A simile without ὡς.
11 Slater 1969b.

δοκεῖ γὰρ ἤμεν αὐτὰ[12]
ἐκπρεπὴς τὼς ὥπερ αἴ τις
ἐν βότοις στάσειεν ἵππον
παγὸν ἀεθλοφόρον καναχάποδα
τῶν ὑποπετριδίων ὀνείρων·

must again refer either to Agido or to Hagesichora, as must the ensuing ὁ μὲν κέλης Ἐνετικός (49–50). This is a significant point and one to which I shall return.

Just as the language of the race is metaphorical, so too is the language of battle. There is no rival choir, as Page believed: μάχονται (63) is hyperbole, used by the choir to point again to the superiority of the two Peleiades, Agido and Hagesichora, who so surpass the rank and file as to defeat them and make their own unaided attempts to please the Dawn goddess (Ὀρθρίαι 61,[13] Ἀώτι 87, both datives) futile.[14] There is a simile here too – the Peleiades are said to be brilliant as Sirius in the ambrosial night (62–3). The comparison does not suggest a baleful star so much as a brilliant one (see Puelma n66), but combined with the metaphor of battle it suggests invincibility, as when Achilles' spearpoint, at the moment of his final descent on Hector, is compared to a splendid star in the night sky. The choir disparages its own capabilities in this simile just as it did when it placed the stallion among grazing animals.[15] These Spartan maidens exaggerate playfully; to take their words at face value would rob the poem of its quintessential delicacy and lightness of tone.

The scholia to the poem take the Peleiades to be Agido and Hagesichora and there seems something of a consensus now that this is the correct understanding.[16] Whether these Peleiades have the name of the

---

12 So Page in his monograph and Puelma. The word is not accented on the papyrus. Garzya (1954) accents αὗτα. It is wrongly, or, rather, meaninglessly accented as αὖτα by Calame, Davies *PMGF*, and Campbell (1987: 69–71). The error appears to be tralaticious and to originate with Page *PMG*: see Pavese 1992: 58 n52.

13 Ὀρθρίαι as Artemis Ortheia is very difficult – the intrusive ρ and the short ι militate against this identification. But recently Clay (1991) has argued again for the identity of the goddess with Artemis. All of Calame's argument for Helen is circumstantial; there is simply nothing in the poem that suggests her. Other candidates have been proposed: Bruno Gentili thinks that the goddess is Aphrodite (*Addendum* to Clay's article); A.P. Burnett thinks that she is Eileithyia (Burnett 1964: 30–3).

14 The theory of a rival choir has today been all but abandoned: see, e.g., Segal 1983: 262 with n7. Similarly there is little current support for the theory of rival half-choirs, though the idea has recently been defended again by Péron (1987: 35–53).

15 A traditional metaphor for helplessness: cf. Semonides 1.4 West.

16 E.g., Puelma and Calame: so too Segal 1983: 262.

star-cluster,[17] or of Doves, as did, it seems, the priestesses at Dodona, is of less importance here. Both possibilities are puzzling, for both seem slightly inelegant: in the one case a star-cluster is compared to a star while in the other girls whose name is understood to mean 'doves' are compared to stallions.[18]

There seems, in addition, to be considerable agreement now that lines 96–101 of the poem refer to Hagesichora.[19] She it is who sings as sweetly as a swan while the rank and file of the rest can do no better than a screech-owl. Hagesichora comes close to, but does not surpass, the Sirens, for they are after all goddesses (the poem is ever careful to avoid hybris). A problem arises with the number ten in line 99 and the likelihood that the number eleven must, on the basis of the scholia, be inserted into line 98.[20] Puelma and Giangrande[21] quite independently of each other suggested the same solution in the same year. Hagesichora sings *like* ten – the phrase is a topos and alludes, *inter alia*, to Iliad 2.489 ff., where ten tongues represent the imagined acme of human singing skill. Puelma proposes δεκ[ὰς ὡς ἀεί]δει, Giangrande δεκ[ὰς οἷ' ἀεί]δει.[22]

What about the number eleven? If it is restored to the text it is commonly inserted in line 98 in the phrase ἀντ[ὶ ἕνδεκα and the phrase is taken to mean 'instead of eleven.' But, as Puelma points out, the correct translation of ἀντί is in fact 'gegenüber' (1977: 46 n86). Corroboration of his view is, I think, to be found in fr. 41,

ἕρπει γὰρ ἄντα τῷ σιδάρῳ τὸ καλῶς κιθαρίσδην

where the sense of ἄντα is clearly 'gegenüber.' It may well be, in fact, that ἄντα is the word that originally stood in line 98 of the *Partheneion*.[23] If Hagesichora alone sings as a supreme singer over against a choir of eleven, we then have the number of choreuts and it is eleven.

17 Segal 1983: 263–4.
18 Garvie (1965: 185–7), following a suggestion of Bowra's, thinks that Agido and Hagesichora may in fact be πῶλοι or 'foals', a ritual title.
19 Puelma, Calame: see also Vetta 1983: 130–1.
20 Though Davies *PMGF* does not do so.
21 Giangrande 1977: 151–4.
22 Davies *PMGF* prints δεκ[ὰς ἅδ' ἀεί]δει following Page. This will be a self-reference on the part of a choir of ten maidens. But if this is the case φθέγγεται in the following line (there is no change of subject) will also have to refer to the choir of ten and the same girls who were screech-owls in line 87 are now swans!
23 The scholiast's ἀντί is, then, not a lemma but an interpretation in his own prose, in which the word ἄντα does not exist.

I accept Puelma's argument that the stanza from 64 to 77 is devoted entirely to the rank and file of the choir. The rhetorical transition from the previous stanza is then easy and natural. The superiority of the two coursers is first proclaimed and the agonistic metaphor established. It continues in ἀμύναι (65).[24] Eight girls are named directly and their claims to beauty mentioned in a passage that culminates again in a revelation of the superiority of Hagesichora. In addition to Nanno, Areta, Thylacis, Cleesithera, Astaphis, Philylla, Damareta, and Vianthemis there are three unnamed girls, referred to obliquely by elements of their costume – purple robes, an intricate brooch of solid gold, a Lydian mitre. The complete catalogue of the girls' advantages includes the rich adornments of three (those whose chief claim these luxury items are, the girls themselves being, presumably, not physically attractive enough to warrant reference to their beauty) and the sex appeal of eight others.[25] But all of this is as nothing in comparison to the charms of Hagesichora.

The picture that emerges on this reading is, to sum up, the following: a choir of eleven girls that claims to be the cousin of Hagesichora (52) sings in graceful and erotic language of its own desire but fundamental inadequacy satisfactorily to perform a ceremony for the goddess of the Dawn. Set playfully against the eleven is a brace of beauties, virtual twins in excellence, whose pre-eminence, far from redounding to the ultimate discomfiture of those with whom the banter puts them in apparent opposition, will make the ceremony in which all are engaged a success. The two are referred to as horses – but as stallions, not as fillies.

2

The surviving part of the beginning of the poem (i.e., column i) begins with the name of Pollux followed by a catalogue of eleven other names. These

---

24 We find some of the same language in 88–90. The antagonism of the eleven to the two is only playful pretence. In this vein, rivalry is resolved with achievement of the success (or peace) for which the choir strives, and if the choir pleases the goddess it is thanks to the beauty of Hagesichora. ἰάτωρ and πόνων may simply be a continuation of the metaphorical language and point to a resolution that is successful accomplishment of a religious ritual. But this does not exclude its also pointing to a genuine and heartfelt sense that the goddess is beneficent to her devotees. We do not know what services the choir felt she performed for them in their daily lives: the choir is both graceful and grateful.

25 This leaves out Aenesimbrota as a possible member of the choir. But she is clearly not present in any case. I accept West's suggestion (1965: 200), further argued by Puelma, that Aenesimbrota is best explained as a local φαρμακεύτρια to whose talents one might appeal in trying to win a love-object.

eleven names seem to be given in a *praeteritio* which begins in line 2 οὐκ
ἐγὼ]ν Λύκαισον ἐν καμοῦσιν ἀλέγω 'I do not mention Lycaethus among
the dead' and ends in line 12 with παρήσομες 'we omit them' after the
last name.[26] Between the verbs ἀλέγω and παρήσομες there will have been
ten names, as Page carefully and confidently shows (26–30): Enarsphorus
and Thebrus in line 3, one name apiece in lines 4 and 5, Euteiches (from
a quotation) and Areïus in line 6, a seventh name in line 7, Eurytus and
one further name in lines 8 and 9,[27] with a tenth name in line 11.[28] A few
of the names in these lines may be restored with some degree of certainty
because of lists of the Hippocoontidae in Pausanias and Apollodorus, but
accurate prosopography is not crucial here. What is significant is that this
list of eleven, given through disavowal, shows a formal similarity to the
list of the eleven of the choir, for all the entries there are introduced by a
similar repudiation (repeated οὔτε and οὐδέ in lines 64–76). Moreover, the
catalogue of the eleven choir-members ends with the name of the person
who defeats them all, Hagesichora, while the catalogue of the slain warriors
is preceded by the name of him who overcame them, Pollux.[29] And while
the names of the latter list are in the antepenultimate strophe, the names of
the first list occupy a generally symmetrical position if the reconstruction
proposed above is the correct one, for most of the names (eight of the
eleven) will be in the third strophe of the poem.

The eleven slain warriors are generally understood to be sons of the
Spartan Hippocoon. The name of Lycaethus is slightly problematic, for he

26 Calame quite rightly points out (1983: 317) that this is a form of ring composition and
that, with regard to παρήσομες 'cette forme verbale n'est pas forcément accompagnée ...
d'une négation comme l'ont supposé la plupart des interprètes de ce passage.' So too
Pavese.

27 A genitive plural ending in]ν and preceded by a connective in line 8 is one possibility
– this will put the two names in line 9. A connective plus a name ending in]ν in line 8
will put the necessary genitive accompanying ἀγρόταν in line 9.

28 The phrase in line 10 remains puzzling and there is no convincing supplement. But
the line will not have contained a name – the missing cretic at the beginning probably
belongs with]πώρω, which appears to be part of a word in the genitive depending on
κλόνον: see Page *ad loc.*

Pavese (1992: 17–20) seeks to put twelve names where Page says there can be only
ten. He must posit an unwelcome and unparalleled asyndeton in line 9 in order to get
two names in addition to that of Eurytus into lines 8 and 9 (see previous note). And he
must accept πώρω as a self-contained noun in line 10. But, as Page points out, there is
no reason to believe that such a word ever existed. Page's analysis remains, accordingly,
the most convincing.

29 Calame (1983: 317) says that the names which the choir declares its intention of
omitting are those of the heroes τὼς ἀρίστως opposed to the Hippocoontidae (i.e., the
names in the preceding catalogue). I do not understand this.

may be son of one Derites, not of Hippocoon, although Apollodorus lists him as one of the sons of Hippocoon.[30] Our text begins with the name of Pollux. We may believe that his brother Castor was at his side – the twins are ever inseparable – and that the two Tyndaridae were the antagonists who vanquished the eleven Hippocoontidae. Tyndareus was expelled from Sparta by his brother Hippocoon but later regained his throne. There is no source which gives a story that can be equated exactly with the one of which we see the skeleton in the *Partheneion*. Pausanias (3.15.3) and Apollodorus (3.10.5) relate that it was Heracles who killed Hippocoon and his sons and regained the throne for Tyndareus, but they make no mention of any participation of Castor and Pollux in the battle. In addition, Clement of Alexandria (*Protr.* 2.36.2 Stählin) says that Sosibius relates that Heracles was wounded in the hand by the Hippocoontidae; the scholiast on this passage adds that this was mentioned in a poem in the first book of Alcman. While commentators wish to believe that the reference is to our poem, the fact remains that we have in what remains no word about Heracles or his wound and have instead, with the mention of Pollux, reference to a story that does *not* correspond to the battle mentioned by Pausanias and Apollodorus. It is hardly rash to say that the legend recounted in our poem must be a legend having to do with the names that we actually find in our text, broken as it may be. Given the probability that Alcman drew repeatedly on Laconian legend, as Pindar turned with regularity to local Theban stories, he is likely to have turned more than once to stories of the Hippocoontidae.[31] All that we may assert with reasonable confidence is that in our existing long *Partheneion*-fragment we have to do with a quarrel between the two Tyndaridae and their cousins the eleven Hippocoontidae.[32] It was a serious quarrel and it led to the death of the eleven. The parallel

---

30 For the evidence, see Page 1951a: 30–3. The scholia appear to be confused here, with one notice maintaining that the chorus does not include Lycaethus among the Hippocoontidae and another saying that not only Lycaethus but the other sons of Derites are named (does this commentator think that all those mentioned were in fact sons of Derites?). Garzya (1954 *ad loc.*) thinks that the scholiast is simply erroneous in introducing the name of Derites. Either the scholiast or Apollodorus is wrong, certainly, on the basis of what we can make out, and since the scholia are both badly broken and unclear, it is best to follow Apollodorus and believe that we are dealing solely with Hippocoontidae.

31 Or the reference to Heracles, if it was in this poem, may have been a parenthetic reference, of the sort common in Pindar, to an earlier conflict.

32 Hippocoon and Tyndareus were sons of Oebalus and so their own sons are first cousins. Derites is a brother of Oebalus, hence in the (unlikely) case that all the slain are Deritidae we still have to do with consanguinity, though the cousins are no longer first cousins.

with the mock battle between cousins in the rivalry of the ceremonial occasion is striking.

There is only one story known to us that opposes the Tyndaridae to the sons of Hippocoon. The scholiast on Clement tells us further in the passage referred to above that the Hippocoontidae were ἀντιμνηστῆρες, rival suitors, of the Tyndaridae. Though he does not say directly that Alcman told the story (he mentions that Euphorion did),[33] he is providing for us, through this story of rival courtship, not only the hostile link of the sort we need between the actors we know were in our story but also the sort of story for which the gnomic utterance of lines 16 and 17 is appropriate, for it is a caveat against attempting to marry above one's station:

μή τις ἀνθ]ρώπων ἐς ὡρανὸν ποτήσθω
μηδὲ πη]ρήτω γαμῆν τὰν Ἀφροδίταν

This must, then, be the story that was told. Again, it seems to be a local variant of a more familiar legend, for it does not correspond to the version we find in Apollodorus. We learn there (3.11.2) that Castor and Pollux carried off the Leucippides, Phoebe and Hilaeira, from their wedding feast when they were about to be married to the sons of Aphareus, Idas and Lynceus. It was these two who later fought with the twins who had abducted their prospective brides – the reason for the quarrel was the division of the spoils in a cattle-rustling expedition that they had undertaken in common – and this quarrel led to the death of the mortal Castor and of both Idas and Lynceus. The story of the fight over the cattle is the common one: it is mentioned in Proclus' résumé of the *Cypria* and in the myth of the Tenth *Nemean* of Pindar. But the earlier rape of the daughters of Leucippus by the Tyndaridae was a favourite subject in art.[34]

The local (and patriotic) version followed by Alcman would seem to have the following elements, all of them to be found individually elsewhere but in no one place exactly as it was told here: the quarrel was over women rather than over cattle, it led to the death of the rivals, and the sons of Hippocoon, not the sons of Aphareus,[35] were these rival suitors killed for their

---

33 Powell 1925: 35 n29.
34 See Pausanias 1.18.1, 3.17.3, 3.18.11, 4.31.9.
35 It is interesting that the sons of Aphareus, like the sons of Hippocoon, are cousins of the Tyndaridae: Tyndareus is son of Perieres and brother of Aphareus in some versions (Apollodorus 1.9.5), son of Oebalus and brother of Hippocoon in others (Apollodorus 3.10.4).

presumption in competing with the divine twins. It seems to follow that the story can hardly have been one in which the Dioscuri raped the Leucippides, for the moralizing gnomes of the end of the first complete stanza seem to oppose χάρις or grace to ἀλκά or force. The valour referred to is that of the defeated, i.e., the Hippocoontidae, for it is 'without foundation.'[36] The Hippocoontidae, rather, will have been the ones who tried to rape the maidens, who in turn will have been won by the Tyndaridae, presumably by less violent wooing. For grace, not strength, opens the gates of heaven (20–1). Castor and Pollux must here play their familiar role of helpers of the distressed.[37] This role, which includes the rescue of their sister Helen from abductors, was perhaps the motif emphasized by Alcman in the story of wooing. In any case he would seem to have stood the better-known story on its head: the violent were the Hippocoontidae, the gallant, indeed the persuasive, the Tyndaridae.

The reworking is interesting. And a myth of this cast admirably suits the movement of the less lacunose portion of the poem. There too cousins are in competition, in this case playful competition, with a pair of closely matched girls clearly superior to a larger company of eleven. The language purports to be the language of battle, thus echoing the myth, and the triumph is clearly that of grace and beauty, as the moralizing gnomes would have it.

The two girls Agido and Hagesichora, moreover, are repeatedly compared to horses, as we have seen. This is something that further likens them to the Dioscuri, who are preeminently horsemen in myth. It has been suggested that the two chorus-leaders of the *Partheneion* may have been the priestesses of Phoebe and Hilaeira, the Leucippides, and that this would give point to the comparison of these maidens to horses, since the priestesses of the Leucippides at Sparta were in fact called πῶλοι.[38] This is tantamount to maintaining that the divinity of the *Partheneion* is Phoebe and that Phoebe is to be identified with the Dawn. Phoebe is indeed a divinity at Sparta, though there seems to be little hard evidence for equating her with the Dawn. What seems likely to be of importance in the poem is the structural parallel between the two chorus leaders, both horses, and the Dioscuri, who are elsewhere called εὔιπποι or λευκοπῶλοι (Pindar,

---

36 See Campbell's discussion of the passage 1987: 67–9. ἀπ]έδιλος, 'without sandals,' is a curious word and has been much discussed. There seems to be no other possible supplement, however. It is hard to resist a pun here in English translation: 'their valour was bootless.'
37 Burkert 1977 (Eng tr. 1985: 213).
38 Garvie 1965.

Ol. 3.39, *Pyth.* 1.66).[39] The two maidens serve Aotis (the Goddess at the Dawn) or Orthria (the Goddess of the morning twilight) and in so doing are in friendly rivalry with a choir that wishes to serve her too but that finds itself outclassed by the superiority of the pair. The two Dioscuri woo a pair of twins whose names both, certainly, suggest celestial light. And in so doing they vanquish, but lethally, not playfully, the Hippocoontidae. It seems to me quite possible that the myth concentrated in fact on Pollux and Phoebe (for indeed Phoebe became the bride of Pollux), leaving Castor and Hilaeira aside. This would create a neater parallel, with a single divine luminary the object of the strife both in the myth and in the ritual. There is some illogicality to account for in Alcman's myth in any case: eleven are the rivals of two for a prize that cannot have been more than two. That there was such an imbalance suggests that Alcman may in fact have arranged his story to give honour to one bride in particular and that Phoebe was that bride.[40]

If it is not possible to establish with full certainty identification of Phoebe with the Dawn, it is nonetheless tantalizing to remember that the Dioscuri are Greek avatars of an Indo-European pair of divine twins, best known as the Aśvins in Vedic myth (Grk ἵππος = Skrt aśva).[41] These twin horsemen serve and follow the Dawn, or Uṣas (= Grk ἠώς). Indeed they may themselves represent the twilight.[42] This lends some resonance to the idea that both Dioscuri are in the poem essentially at the service of a single goddess, as is often the case,[43] and that Alcman, though presenting them as the rival suitors of the Hippocoontidae for the two Leucippides, may in fact be chiefly interested in Phoebe, the bride of Pollux.

3

Where does this get us?

The poem on this understanding would be a diptych, with its parts having an important thematic connection. The first seventy lines recount a

---

39 That Alcman thought of the name Πωλωδεύκης (the ω is anomalous and peculiar to Laconian) as connected with πῶλος seems to be indicated by fragment 2 (a *schema Alcmanicum*): Κάστωρ τε πώλων ὠκέων δματῆρες ἱππόται σοφοί / καὶ Πωλωδεύκης κυδρός.
40 In Indian mythology both twins woo a single maiden, the Daughter of the Sun: see West 1975: 9 on this *ménage à trois*.
41 See Zeller 1990. The connection between the Dioscuri and the Aśvins is emphasized by Burkert 1977 and by West 1975: 7–9.
42 If one is the Morning Star and the other the Evening Star we have a good explanation of the half-life/half-light in which the Dioscuri are condemned to live in Greek myth.
43 As they frequently are: see Chapouthier 1935.

legend, giving a moral; the second seventy lines, devoted to the ceremony, follow the outlines of the myth closely and put the moral into practice. It is more likely, if this is the case, that the first section of the poem told only one myth and not two. It has been supposed that lines 22 to 35 of the poem recount a story other than that of the Dioscuri and the Hippocoontidae.[44] But there is nothing to recommend this, and the reading I am suggesting goes against it. It looks as though the evil-doers of these lines were more than one, for one seems to have been dispatched with a missile, another with a millstone.[45] But there is reason to believe, as we have seen, that Alcman is introducing features of the story of the battle of the Dioscuri with the Apharetidae into his story of a battle between the Dioscuri and the Hippocoontidae, and we note that Pindar's account of the final battle between the Dioscuri and the Aphraretidae includes, within the space of three lines, mention of both a large stone and a javelin (*Nem.* 10.67–9).[46] In Pindar the stone is in fact the weapon hurled by Lynceus against Pollux.]ώλεσ˙ ἥβα (27) is especially appropriate to suitors cut off in the prime of life. If the myth began with the battle and death, including a list of the victims, to return to this at the end, and if it included in its progress moralizing on the nature of the offence, it would follow a pattern we recognize in Pindar: the first half of another diptych-poem,[47] the Third *Pythian*, contains the story of Coronis, which begins and ends with her death at Apollo's instigation (9–10, 38 ff.) and contains moralizing over the nature of her offence (20–3) – moralizing which, moreover, is directly applicable to the occasion of the poem.[48]

Both sections of the poem set out a battle. The first is in deadly earnest. Two twins are pitted in a fight to the death against eleven rivals. The rivals are doomed, as the gnomes seem to make clear, because they aspire beyond their station and because they use force. The object of all the striving seems to be the divine Phoebe. The second half of the poem – and it appears to be exactly half – shows us a battle in which two 'twins' are pitted against a chorus of eleven. It is not a fight to the death, for the battle is metaphoric, not real. One of the rivals is said to wear down

---

44 See Calame *ad loc.*: suggestions include the Giants, Otus and Ephialtes, Orion, Icarus.
45 A regular weapon in the heroic arsenal: cf. *Iliad* 7.270, 12.161.
46 In addition *Nem.* 10.64–5, μέγα ἔργον ἐμήσαντ˙ ὠκέως / καὶ πάθον δεινόν (of the Aphaterdidae) seems to echo lines 34–5 of the *Partheneion*, ἄλαστα δὲ / ϝέργα πάσον κακὰ μησάμενοι.
47 See my 'The Gifts of the Gods: Pindar's Third *Pythian*' *CQ* 40 (1990) 307–18 [in this volume 175–91].
48 Coronis' story is not unlike that of the Hippocoontidae: in both cases there are rival suitors and punishment.

(τείρει, 76, the last word of the catalogue-strophe) those against whom she and her companion fight (μάχονται, 63, immediately before the catalogue). The language is the language of war (cf. *Iliad* 8.102, τείρουσι μαχηταί), but τείρει also belongs to the language of love: the rivals of the ceremony are in reality united in striving for peace and joy and the contest is one in which the superiority of χάρις is understood. The choir, earnest in its hope to finish the web of its day without tears (38–9), will do just this because it has made its own the lesson it sang in the myth and now greets the goddess of the Dawn with grace, good humour, and love.

If this, or something like this, is at the heart of the exquisite poem, it has not only a profound structural and moral unity but offers us what is perhaps the first instance in Greek literature of something that will become one of that literature's most enduring themes. With their well-known fondness for polarities the Greeks regularly set βία against πειθώ.[49] Alcman in opposing ἀλκά to the Χάριτες gives us the same juxtaposition. His presentation of the contrast is found not only in the gnomic statements within the legend. The poem as a whole is an enactment of the idea that force cedes to grace, for the carnage of the legend gives way in performance to manifestation of the truth that heaven is taken not by storm but by the gentle arts.

---

49 This is the normal disjunction, but it is not exclusive. δόλος may be set against either πειθώ or βία: the *Philoctetes* of Sophocles is a study in the application of these three possibilities.

'EVERY
TIME
I LOOK
AT YOU...':
SAPPHO
THIRTY-ONE

Wer die Schönheit angeschaut mit Augen,
Ist dem Tode schon anheim gegeben.
von Platen

TRANSLATORS and commentators must all[1] face the problem of the τό of line 5. One's understanding of the poem is in large measure dependent on what one makes of this monosyllable. What is its antecedent? The suggestions are several, but they in fact fall into two groups. The antecedent either directly precedes the relative or is to be found somewhere farther back in the first stanza: once an immediately preceding antecedent is rejected, disagreement commences.

The majority, it would appear, take the τό to refer to γελαίσας ἰμέροεν (or ἆδυ φωνείσας ... καί γελαίσας ἰμέροεν). The girl's voice and laughter set Sappho's heart aflutter.[2] There are objections raised against this. It is inelegant, if not illogical, to say, 'I am overwhelmed when I *hear your*

First published *TAPhA* 110 (1980) 255–61. [The epigraph, from August von Platen *Aus Tristan und Isolde* (1825), was added by Emmet Robbins in 2009. Ed.]

1 The following bibliography, though not exhaustive, lists the majority of works mentioned in the course of this article. It is meant to include what has been most influential and what is most recent, if germane. Some further material can be found in Saake's books (1971, 1972), in the edition of Voigt (1971), and in Gerber 1976: 111–13.
  Bagg 1964; Bonelli 1977; Bowra 1961: 185–8; Devereux 1970; Dover 1978: 177–9; Fränkel 1924: 63–127 = 1960: 40–96, 1962: 199–200; Gallavotti 1942, 1966; Gentili 1966; Jachmann 1964; Kirkwood 1974: 120–2; Koniaris 1968; Lefkowitz 1973; Marcovich 1972; McEvilley 1978; Merkelbach 1957; Page 1955: 19–33; Perrotta 1935: 46–9; Privitera 1969; Reinach and Puech 1937; Saake 1971: 17–38, 1972: 53–5; Schadewaldt 1950: 98–112; Setti 1939; Snell 1931 = Snell 1966: 82–97; Treu 1954: 24–5, 177–9; Tsagarakis 1979; Turyn 1929; Wilamowitz 1913: 56–9; Wills 1967. Also influential but not directly relevant to the present discussion is West 1970.
2 The translations of Fränkel (1962: 199) and Reinach and Puech (1937: 194) make it clear that this is how they understand the pronoun. Snell (1931: 78), Kirkwood (1974: 255 n36), Marcovich (1972: 24–5), McEvilley (1978: 10–11), state that it is to be so understood.

voice because when(ever) I *look at you* ...' An item from the first scene is selected (and emphasized with ἦ μάν), then dropped in the phrase that purports to be explanatory.³ A further criticism of this view is that the man exists in the poem solely for the purpose of awakening the girl's laughter – though prominently placed he has minimal importance and disappears immediately.⁴

A second view which has had considerable currency is that the antecedent is the two finite verbs ἰσδάνει καὶ ... ὐπακούει with their expressed subject κῆνος ... ὤνηρ ὄττις. The antecedent, in other words, equals τὸ ἐκεῖνον ἰζάνειν καὶ ὐπακούειν.⁵ This theory forces us to assume that Sappho is expressing her jealousy of the man. The great difficulty with the jealousy theory, and the reason for disliking it as a solution, would seem to be, not that jealousy is unbecoming, but that the following clause, which specifies Sappho's reaction, contains an unequivocal singular pronoun:⁶ 'when(ever) I look at *you* ...' Page (1955: 27) believes that ὠς γὰρ <ἔς> σ' ἴδω means 'when I look at you sitting near him as you are,' but McEvilley (1978: 11) justly observes that this is hardly supported by Sappho's regular practice: what moves Sappho generally is beauty itself, the sight or thought of something she loves rather than its possession by someone else. The same verb ἐπτόαισ' at fr. 22.14 seems to confirm

---

3 Wills 1967: 169. Marcovich attempts to ease the difficulty by saying that the meaning of ὠς γὰρ <ἔς> σ' ἴδω is 'whenever I look you *in the face*' and that the girl's voice and laughter are aspects of the girl's face. The explanation is somewhat circuitous, and the difficulty does not vanish: the laughter is still heard, not seen. And further, as Schadewaldt had observed (1950: 99): 'Das Mädchen wird nicht ins Gesicht gepriesen, auch ihre Stimme wie ihr Lachen erscheinen nur schnell im Vorübergehen.'

4 Wills 1967: 168; McEvilley 1978: 11. This disappearance does not trouble those who believe the poem to be a wedding-song, for in this case the man's presence is quite simply demanded by the occasion, even if the poem scarcely needs him. Most German scholars (e.g., Wilamowitz, Snell, Schadewaldt, Fränkel, Treu, Merkelbach) consider the poem a *Hochzeitslied*. McEvilley's article is essentially an elaboration of the last sentence of the 1966 reprint of Snell's 1931 article: 'Obwohl dem besprochenen Gedicht Sapphos der Makarismos des Hochzeitsliedes zugrunde liegt, möchte ich heute doch nicht mehr annehmen, dass es bei der Hochzeit gesungen sein müsste.'

5 Perrotta 1935: 47, n1; Page 1955: 22.

6 Theander (1934: 83 n2) inclines towards the first solution because 'poetriam animi affectu ... parum honesto liberat.' On the other hand, Perrotta states (1935: 47, n1), 'la gelosia di Saffo è amore.' Bonelli, defending Perrotta's view, simply claims (1977: 493) that the singular pronoun is equivalent to a plural. Italian scholars not infrequently opt for the jealousy theory; e.g., in addition to Ferrari and Barigazzi (see bibl. in Wills 1967: 167), Romagnoli (cited by Perrotta *loc. cit.*), and Gentili (1966: 49, n65), who simply refers to the poem as the 'ode della gelosia.' Bagg (1964: 65) speaks of Sappho's 'savage jealousy' and 'bitterness' without explaining exactly how he construes the text.

this. A further objection, perhaps, is that the phrase ὠς γὰρ <ἔς> σ' ἴδω means 'every time I look at you.' To say, 'your sitting with him stuns me because whenever I see you with him it stuns me,' is a feeble and circular argument.[7]

A number of critics claim that the antecedent is the entire preceding statement, not just the verbs in the subordinate clause. The antecedent is thus construed as τὸ δ' αὐτὸν ἰσόθεον εἶναι φῶτα.[8] Against this third theory the objections made against the second would appear to be valid. For the man's godlike nature is revealed *inasmuch as* he is sitting there with the object of Sappho's preoccupation, and her reaction (ἐπτόαισεν) is still occasioned by his enjoyment of what she lacks, else she would not be affected. And so jealousy is still operative. Moreover, as the most articulate advocate of this theory realizes, the γάρ of line 7 is again illogical: Sappho interjects a statement of her jealousy and explains it by pointing to her regular symptoms when she sees the girl alone. The movement of thought becomes, 'He's godlike, sitting there; *this* affects me, *because* when (ever) I look at *you* I'm reduced.' Since this makes little sense, emendation becomes necessary. Logic is restored by changing μ' ἦ μάν to δή κεν. The sequence is now a sensible, 'Sitting there would have a devastating effect on me, for I'm regularly susceptible.'[9]

But the result of the emendation is to create yet another candidate: the antecedent of the counterfactual verb ἐπτόαισεν is in effect now τὸ ἐμὲ ἰζάνειν καὶ ὑπακούειν. This is exactly what Setti, in his influential article,[10] chose. With the sudden change of subject of the two verbs ἰζάνειν καὶ ὑπακούειν it becomes necessary to create (Wills) or understand (Setti, Welcker) a counterfactual statement.

A view recently put forward is that the τό refers to the entire preceding scene but that the 'woman speaker ... identifies herself with the charming girl sitting close to the godlike man and suffers an emotional breakdown

7 Wills 1967: 170.
8 Gallavotti 1942: 117; Wills 1967: 183; Saake 1971: 26–7.
9 Wills 1967: 183–6. By his emendation he is attempting to create in the Greek the 'würde' of Welcker's 'mir würde es gewiss ... das Herz erschüttern.' Emendation is in any case required, Wills claims, because τό μ' ἦ μάν is impossible Greek: the particles ἦ μάν always introduce the asseverative statement to which they are connected and thus cannot follow τό μοι. Marcovich (1972: 25 n1b) meets this objection, pointing to Alcaeus 344.1, οἶδ' ἦ μάν.
10 His explanation (1939: 214) illustrates his choice: 'Saffo pensa per un momento possibile per sè quello che è reale per l'uomo ... e ne rimane sbigottita e tremante.' Lefkowitz (1973: 120) translates: 'This (i.e., hearing you) terrifies my heart.' The antecedent appears to be taken as the act of hearing, to be τὸ ἐμὲ ὑπακούειν to the exclusion of τὸ ἐμὲ ἰζάνειν. This is the equivalent of taking the antecedent as the girl's voice, and the interpretation probably belongs with those in note 2 above.

... because she does not enjoy what the other does: the company of a man ...[11] This theory, as its author shows, finds indirect support from Greek folksong, but it makes Sappho's choice of words extremely puzzling. There is no real point in mentioning the girl's charms if they have no effect on the singer: the sweet voice and lovely laughter become otiose details. And the girl, not the man, might more reasonably be described as godlike if she enjoys what the singer most ardently longs for. The objection advanced against Page carries force in this case too: the expressed pronoun object is singular.[12]

Each theory presents real difficulties. One critic simply suggests that the attempt to find a clear antecedent is a misguided one: 'l'immagine prevale sulla funzione sintattica' and the ambiguity is intended.[13] One must, it seems, either accept this judgement, or, if convinced that there is a definite antecedent, approach the problem differently.

There has been as much agreement about the γάρ of line 7 as there has been disagreement regarding the τό of line 5. The rival theories all take one thing for granted: that the γάρ introduces an explanation of the immediately preceding clause and nothing else. This is the source of the trouble in every case, the ground on which any objection is based. The word is frequently omitted in translation,[14] or, if it is analyzed, considered directly resumptive of τό ... ἐπτόαισεν.[15] A different approach may solve the difficulty.

Wilamowitz (1913: 57) made the claim that there is a correspondence in the poem between φαίνεταί μοι κῆνος ἴσος θέοισιν ἔμμεν' ὤνηρ and τεθνάκην φαίνομαι. This observation is illustrated by his translation (the same for both appearances of the verb φαίνεσθαι). The point has never been seriously challenged. Many commentators have indicated their

---

11 Tsagarakis 1979: 117.
12 Tsagarakis and Page might better adopt the reading ὡς γὰρ εἰσίδω defended by Beattie (1956: 111), and Bolling (1961: 163). This would at least have the advantage of eliminating the pronoun which specifies the girl as the object of Sappho's attention and would allow us to believe more easily that the presence of the man in the tête-à-tête is what excites Sappho. The unexpressed object of εἰσορᾶν could in this case, as Beattie suggests, be σφώ.
13 Privitera 1969: 54, who gives an idiosyncratic list of five possible antecedents.
14 Wilamowitz 1913: 56; Perrotta 1935: 48; Treu 154: 25; Fränkel 1962: 199; Kirkwood 1974: 121. So too Edmonds 1922b: 187.
15 Snell 1931: 81 n2, who recognizes the problem and translates 'ja auch,' stating that the γάρ is 'explizierend' rather than 'begründend'; Setti 1939: 214 n1; Wills 1967: 168–9; Marcovich 1972: 23 (no. 6); Saake 1971: 28, on the ground that 'Jeder Gedanke unlöslich mit dem voranstehenden verknüpft (ist)' – though two pages earlier he had argued that τό did not go with its immediate antecedent.

agreement,[16] only an occasional voice being raised against it.[17] The publication of the Florentine papyrus, which has restored the adonic of the fourth stanza, has strengthened Wilamowitz' point. For the repetition of the first-person pronoun (μοι ... ἔμ᾽ αὔτ[αι) increases the likelihood that the meaning of φαίνεσθαι is the same in both occurrences. Perhaps the γάρ connects the two principal verbs of the poem, both forms of φαίνεσθαι.

Sappho states that the man who is sitting there and listening to the girl's laughter – laughter which sets her heart aflutter – seems equal to the gods. Why? Because (γάρ) whenever Sappho sees the girl she reacts so strongly that she all but dies. There has been much debate of late whether ἴσος θέοισιν refers to fortitude or beatitude. Critics now regularly feel that it must refer to one to the exclusion of the other.[18] Would Sappho's audience, hearing the words, have restricted their sense? Sappho does not name her emotion[19] – herein lies much of the fascination of the poem – but the symptoms show her distress and vulnerability.[20]

Sappho describes her own reaction in considerable detail. It is easy enough to assume that this reaction is peculiar to her, that it is one which the man does not share. The poem tells us nothing about the man's reaction – we only know that Sappho considers him ἴσος θέοισιν. In all likelihood he is both happy *and* composed.[21] At the end of a crescendo which begins

---

16 E.g., Bowra 1961: 188; Gallavotti 1966: 258; Marcovich 1972: 23 (no. 7a); Kirkwood 1974: 122; Saake 1971: 21; Privitera 1969: 68.
17 Jachmann (1964: 8) finds it artificial, without saying more; Setti (1939: 216 n2) finds the verb φαίνεσθαι so insignificant that a precise verbal echo is impossible. But the echo that Wilamowitz found was not limited to the verb φαίνεσθαι alone – and even Setti admits that 'c'è un'opposizione intima tra la "morte" di Saffo e "l'immortalità" dell'uomo.'
18 E.g., Jachmann 1964: 8, Setti 1939: 211, Page 1955: 21, who maintain that it cannot mean 'strong as the gods' whereas Wills 1967: 181 and Marcovich 1972: 21 say it can mean nothing else. The theory that ἴσος θέοισιν refers to 'Götterkraft' was first put forward by Welcker 1845: 99 n45. It is worth noting that Welcker was not so exclusive as are his *Nachfolger*; he says, 'Der Mann, der dir nahe sitzen ... kann, scheint mir wie ein Gott – nicht bloss glücklich ... sondern auch eine stärkere Natur ...'
19 Her critics do. It has been called jealousy (e.g., Page), love (Marcovich), anxiety (Devereux), terror (Schadewaldt), fear (Turyn), wonder (Saake).
20 A death wish is expressed at a moment of unhappiness in fr. 94.1, the speaker being either Sappho or a departing girl. There seems to be a similar sentiment in fr. 95.11 and perhaps in fr. 23, where μέριμναν (line 8, cf. fr. 1.26) seems to be associated with δροσόεν]τας ὄχθοις (line 11, of Acheron as at fr. 95.12?). Gentili (1966: 57) thinks that we are dealing here with a *topos* of the religious language of Sappho's *thiasos*.
21 So (like Welcker) Schadewaldt: 'Dort jene gelassene Götterkraft, die, ohne Schaden zu nehmen, auch das Glück erträgt – hier jene Ausgesetztheit, für die Nähe der Schönheit lebensgefährlich ist.'

with the individual senses and mounts to encompass the entire body Sappho says that she seems to be on the point of death. Gods enjoy felicity and strength that mortals do not. More especially, they do not die. That is the one certain thing that sets them apart from mortals, the one thing about which there can be no disagreement. At no time is the gulf between gods and men so apparent as at the moment of death: φησὶν ἡ Σαπφὼ ὅτι τὸ ἀποθνῄσκειν κακόν· οἱ θεοὶ γὰρ οὕτω κεκρίκασιν· ἀπέθνησκον γὰρ ἄν· (fr. 201). For Sappho one exposed, as she frequently is, but enjoying the experience – not suffering and expiring – must be more than human. He belongs, for the moment, with the immortals. The reason? Because Sappho, seeing beauty, senses her mortality acutely.[22]

Lines 1–16 of the poem, then, consist of two long sentences, closely connected. The first contains two subordinate clauses, each attached to its immediate antecedent: ὤνηρ, ὄττις and ἰμέροεν, τό. The objections to taking τό with what immediately precedes it, as most commentators and translators would do, vanish when ὡς γάρ <ἔς> σ' ἴδω is relieved of the burden of explaining only the relative clause. The second sentence is periodic too, beginning with ὡς γάρ and ending with φαίνομ' ἔμ' αὔτ[αι. Within it there is an ἀλλά (line 9) joining the negative and positive statements of the same symptom (cf. μή ... δάμνα ... ἀλλά ... ἔλθ', fr. 1.4–6), a list beginning with the first symptom (μέν), seven subsequent δέ-clauses rising to a final verb that echoes the principal verb of the first period. A triumph of careful, balanced, logical construction. γάρ is operative throughout the second period (lines 9–16), finally and fully resolved only in line 16. Similarly, the first and principal statement is held through lines 1–6, to be explained by the following sentence. If it be thought that Sappho, as an archaic poet, is incapable of such calculated effect (two carefully juxtaposed statements), Ibycus should be kept in mind (esp. PMG 266 and 267).[23] Voigt's edition,

---

22 Sappho's words ἴσος θέοισιν thus acquire their full meaning from their context. They are not simply a tag from Homer. In Homer the word ἰσόθεος, like δῖος, θεῖος, ἀντίθεος, ἡμίθεος, is not merely a designation of physical strength. It is a regular attribute of the inhabitants of the Heroic Age. To-day's men have no connection with them, except perhaps for a Xerxes (Aesch. Pers. 79–80) who is χρυσογόνου γενεᾶς ἰσόθεος φώς because he is descended from Perseus and has divine blood in his veins. In a battle epic ἰσόθεος φώς is, of course, naturally used of warriors and thus describes the strong.

23 McEvilley (1971), has shown the extraordinary skill with which Sappho can construct a poem. Fränkel (1924: 70–5) thinks of Sappho's poetry as typical of the archaic 'reihende Stil' in which each element grows from the last and lives in an absolute present which allows no perspective. But this style, in which no overall architectonic controls the relation of the parts to the whole, is no longer practised by Ibycus, whom Fränkel (1962: 325) has to describe as 'nicht mehr archaisch,' the archaic style being, on his definition, incapable of holding things in suspension.

with end of sentence (and end of page!) at ἐπτόαισεν brings out the division in the poem more clearly than does the edition of Lobel-Page (commas before and after τό ... ἐπτόαισεν).[24]

---

[24] Two commentators understand the γάρ of line 7 as argued for here. Koniaris' understanding is marred by his interpretation of the poem, intent as he is on excluding any idea of strength and allowing only bliss to ἴσος θέοισιν. He paraphrases (1968: 185): 'This man appears to me to be in seventh heaven ... since I with one brief look upon you am maddened.' This upsets the balance, destroys the contrast. Dover is also of the opinion (1978: 178 n21) that ' "for whenever ..." explains why "He seems to me ..." ' He interprets the emotions felt by Sappho as the envy and despair felt by a mortal towards a god. But this appears to make the man, not the girl, the source of Sappho's reaction and to be open to at least one objection advanced against the jealousy theory: Sappho responds to beauty itself, as a rule, not to its possession by some other person.

WHO'S DYING IN SAPPHO FR. 94?

τεθνάκην δ' ἀδόλως θέλω·
2 ἄ με ψισδομένα κατελίμπανεν

πόλλα καὶ τόδ' ἔειπέ [μοι·
ὤιμ' ὠς δεῖνα πεπ[όνθ]αμεν,
5 Σάπφ', ἦ μάν σ' ἀέκοισ' ἀπυλιμπάνω.

τὰν δ' ἔγω τάδ' ἀμειβόμαν·
χαίροισ' ἔρχεο κἄμεθεν
8 μέμναισ', οἶσθα γὰρ ὤς <σ>ε πεδήπομεν·

αἰ δὲ μή, ἀλλά σ' ἔγω θέλω
ὄμναισαι [...(.)].[..(.)].εαι
11 ὀσ[- 10 -] καὶ κάλ' ἐπάσχομεν·

πό[λλοις γὰρ στεφάν]οις ἴων
καὶ βρ[όδων...]κίων τ' ὔμοι
14 κα..[- 7 -] πὰρ ἔμοι π<ε>ρεθήκα<ο>

καὶ πό[λλαις ὐπα]θύμιδας
πλέκ[ταις ἀμφ' ἀ]πάλαι δέραι
17 ἀνθέων ἐ[- 6 -]πεποημέναις.

καὶ π.....[   ]. μύρωι
βρενθείωι.[   ]ρυ[..]ν
20 ἐξαλ<ε>ίψαο κα[ὶ [βασ]]ιληίωι

καὶ στρώμν[αν ἐ]πὶ μολθάκαν
ἀπάλαν παρ[   ]ονων
23 ἐξίης πόθο[ν   ]. νίδων

κωὔτε τις [οὔ]τε τι
ἶρον οὐδ' ὐ[   ]
26 ἔπλετ' ὄππ[οθεν ἄμ]μες ἀπέσκομεν,

οὐκ ἄλσος.[   ]. ρος
                 ]ψοφος
29   ]...οιδιαι[1]

First published in *Phoenix* 44.2 (1990) 111–21.

1 The text printed here is that of Voigt 1971. The following works will be referred to by author's name alone: Burnett 1983; McEvilley 1971: 1–11; Page 1955.

THIS LONG FRAGMENT, numbered 94 in our current editions of Sappho, comes from a sheet of parchment, with writing thought to be of the sixth or seventh century AD, published by W. Schubart with the assistance of U. von Wilamowitz-Moellendorff in 1902.[2] The page on which the fragment is written is the left-hand side of a leaf containing two pages. It is likely that this leaf is a *disiectum membrum* of a book, not part of a roll. The right-hand page contains the fragment now numbered 96, and the two poems, 94 and 96, are thought to come from a leaf that was part of a gathering or quire – there is writing on the back of both pages, though this writing is almost illegible and has yielded nothing of consequence. The inner side of the leaf was clearly better protected than the outer, possibly because it remained in contact with other leaves longer whereas the outer side was exposed, the leaf in question having been the outermost leaf of the gathering. The fragment numbered 95 was found sewn to the right-hand side of the leaf, but this seems to have been done after the dismemberment of the book. It is uncertain whether this fragment, which is smaller than either fragment 94 or fragment 96, belongs to one of the inner pages of the gathering or is part of one of the two surviving pages, i.e., the pages of the leaf containing 94 and 96.

The page on which fragment 94 is written is 16 centimetres wide. The text we possess is 12 centimetres high, but the original page is likely to have been double this height. We cannot tell what part of the page we now have, nor could we say, even if we knew with certainty that we had the top of the page, that individual poems began on new pages. This uncertainty has bedevilled interpretation of the poem. Since it is unlikely that we shall ever know beyond doubt how much of the poem is lost, either from the beginning or from the end, criticism must content itself with the remaining portion.

It is the first surviving line – τεθνάκην δ᾽ ἀδόλως θέλω – that has been the subject of repeated discussion in our time. Most critics have been inclined to take it as spoken by Sappho.[3] A number of scholars, however, have

---

2 Schubart 1902: 195 ff.
3 There is a review of the debate in Burnett 292 n38. But Burnett is occasionally misleading in reporting opinions of other scholars on the matter. E.g., in Snell 1976: 8 the words are clearly thought to be spoken by Sappho (though the translator, Zoltan Franyó, puts quotation marks around them and may thus be at odds with the author of the Introduction, presumably Snell). Campbell 1967: 278 mentions both possibilities. In the Loeb edition (Campbell 1982: 1.117) the line is Sappho's, though the possibility that it is the girl's is mentioned in a note. Campbell 1983: 226 unequivocally gives the line to Sappho.

given the line to the departing girl.[4] The first editor, Schubart, originally gave the line to the girl, though he appears to have changed his mind about this when he re-edited the poem in 1907:[5] in 1907 he did not put quotation marks at the end of the first line as he had initially, whereas in both 1902 and 1907 he used quotation marks for the girl's speech in lines 4 and 5. He may have been persuaded by the interpretations of Fraccaroli, Jurenka, and Reinach, whose contributions to the discussion of the poem are listed on page 10 of the 1907 edition and who all thought that Sappho spoke the first line. Or he may have been influenced by Wilamowitz himself, who certainly, though at a later date, gave the line to Sappho.[6]

Recently, Anne Burnett has vigorously argued that the line is to be given to the girl (290–300),[7] and she has found adherents for her position.[8] That this view bids to become fashionable may be suggested by the translation of the fragment (the only piece of Sappho's to be given in full) by Ewen Bowie in the chapter on lyric and elegiac poetry in the new *Oxford History of the Classical World*.[9] Here too the line is given to the departing girl. I still think, however, that the attribution of the line to Sappho is more likely and wish to put that case once again here, in more detail than has hitherto been done.

One thing is certain: there must have been at least one glyconic preceding the line that begins our fragment since that line is the second of a strophe of which the first two lines are regularly glyconic, the third line glyconic with dactylic expansion. The first glyconic must have been spoken by the same person as spoke the second, for the δ' establishes the first

---

ἀδόλως, the single unusual word in the line, does not in itself help in the attribution. It is commonly used in solemn asseveration and to indicate extreme seriousness but it also occurs in erotic and less serious verse: see Page 76–7, and below n30.

4 There are, I realize, assumptions implicit in the use of the word "girl." They are that Sappho is older than the person who is departing and, ultimately, that Sappho was the central figure of a *thiasos* where younger women spent a period of time. These assumptions are not based on the text of fr. 94 itself: a *prima facie* reading of this fragment gives no particular reason to believe that the departing woman is any younger than Sappho. I believe that the assumptions I make are warranted by the remains of Sappho's poetry, though I will not argue for them here, and I consequently use "girl" throughout this article.

5 Schubart 1907: 12.
6 Wilamowitz 1913: 50.
7 Burnett 1979: 16–27.
8 E.g., Fowler 1987: 68; Snyder 1989: 25–6, with n55.
9 Bowie 1986b: 104.

line of what survives as a further statement of the person who spoke the missing line.[10] This flow is broken by the asyndeton of line 2. Asyndeton is regularly used, as Longinus points out (19–21), for emotional effect and in rapid narrative, and so absence of connective in the second line may easily enough be explained as another sign of the turmoil directly expressed in the first line. It is more difficult to account for the asyndeton if we are moving from the girl's despairing cry to Sappho's supposedly cool account of the past,[11] for we would expect a connective with the change of speaker. At line 6 ἄ με becomes τὰν δ' ἔγω: the pronouns of line 2 are juxtaposed once again, this time with the expected connective attending the new speaker. The poised Sappho of the time of parting and consolation, rather, enters the poem here.[12]

If the line is the girl's, we have, on the evidence, a fragment that does not begin in the present but that is simply narrative of a past event. It would be, thus, unlike all the longer surviving fragments of Sappho, none of which (except for fr. 44, the telling of a story from myth) is without some connection to the present of the song. It may be argued that a present for the song was established in missing strophes that preceded the beginning of the poem as we have it, but this is, in the last analysis, not a necessary or helpful hypothesis. We do not need more than a single line to make the poem complete, and the present can be adequately established if Sappho speaks the opening two lines. The departure, in fact, seems to be introduced in what we have and is thus unlikely to have been anticipated, though the

---

10 That Schubart put quotation marks at the end but not at the beginning of line 1 in Schubart 1902 shows that he understood this: the girl will have spoken the missing line of the first strophe.

11 There is a remarkably similar passage at *Od.* 4.663–7:

    Ὦ πόποι, ἦ μέγα ἔργον ὑπερφιάλως ἐτελέσθη
    Τηλεμάχῳ ὁδὸς ἥδε· φάμεν δέ οἱ οὐ τελέεσθαι.
    ἐκ τοσσῶνδ' ἀέκητι νέος πάϊς οἴχεται αὔτως,
    νῆα ἐρυσσάμενος, κρίνας τ' ἀνὰ δῆμον ἀρίστους.
    ἄρξει καὶ προτέρω κακὸν ἔμμεναι·

Antinous expresses strong emotion and then, in a sentence in asyndeton (665), mentions Telemachus' departure.

    Asyndeton is also frequent in explanations (with γάρ suppressed); cf., e.g., Sophocles *OC* 741. This might well be operative here.

12 This presentation of the past lover as not identical with the present singer is what contemporary criticism would term 'focalization': in the long speech we are apparently shown the perceptions of a different Sappho from the one who is now recounting the scene of parting (the 'focalizer' is the narrator here, though of course this need not always be the case): see Rimmon-Kenan 1983: 71 ff.

relation of the past to the present is likely to have played some part in the poem, and will do so if we give the first line to Sappho. Further, a division of the girl's speech into two parts (one of indeterminate length and lost except for a single line) would itself be extraordinary in early poetry, where utterances may be interrupted by the words of an interlocutor but are not normally divided by narrative. It is again easiest to assume that we first hear the girl in the speech that begins with τόδε.

In his fine but unjustly neglected discussion of this fragment, McEvilley showed how carefully and intricately it can be seen to be constructed if we assume an initial line, as did Edmonds, in which Sappho names the girl. Edmonds and Jurenka chose Atthis for the missing glyconic.[13] One hesitates to be so specific, remembering the fate of the once popular Agallis of fr. 31, who departed for all time when the publication of the Florentine papyrus in 1965 gave us the correct reading of line 16 of that poem.[14] But the name of an actual girl would fit with Sappho's practice of naming a beloved of the past (fr. 16, Anactoria; fr. 49, Atthis) but not the immediate beloved (frs. 1, 31). If there is a person named or referred to in the missing line and if it is the first line of the poem, we get the following structure: (a) a line which mentions the singer (presumably Sappho) and the departing girl together; (b) a unit of two lines, doubling the preceding single-line unit, with one line devoted to Sappho's death wish, the other to the girl's weeping departure; (c) a third unit which continues the simple incremental progression – a three-line strophe for the girl, beginning with the introduction of a speech, followed by a parallel strophe for Sappho which carefully echoes it. At this point the deliberate parallel deliberately breaks down, for Sappho takes over the poem.

This is an attractive reconstruction. Even if it is rejected, it should still be borne in mind that the desire for death, or the statement of nearness to death, is elsewhere put into Sappho's own mouth and not into the mouth of others (cf. fr. 31.15–16; fr. 95.10–11). A possible first line, on the analogy of fragment 95, could be something like ζώοισ· οὐδὲν ἔτ· ἄδομαι (providing an appealing contrast, no matter who speaks the second line of the truncated stanza).

The parchment text of the poem offers no punctuation and so provides no help in understanding how the ancients thought the poem was articulated. But the passage from the first to the second stanza is problematic and admits of three readings. It needs to be examined carefully.

---

13 Ἀτθιδ· οὔποτ· ἄρ ὄψομαι, Edmonds 1928: 240; οἴχωκ· Ἀτθις, ἄχος μ· ἔχει, Jurenka 1903: 290.
14 On Agallis see Page 26. Atthis, at least, is attested in the other fragments.

1) If we take the πόλλα of line 3 as dependent on the participle ψισ-δομένα as, say, Bowie does (1986b: 104),[15] we must believe that this is the single instance of enjambment between stanzas in the fragment. If, on the other hand, we take the first stanza as end-stopped we have a second instance of asyndeton following immediately upon the first. Enjambment may be thought to make the opening lines run more easily, for with a pause at the end of line 2 the poem will have six consecutive lines (1–6) that are self-contained (the missing first line of the first strophe was in addition likely a self-contained statement). Some will consider this effect displeasing. The hyperbaton, or postponement and displacement of πόλλα, may, if there is relieving enjambment, be for pathetic effect. But it seems to me simply harsh and more difficult to accept than a second case of asyndeton where there is clearly a first, and a resulting series of halting sentences that give the feelings of two people overcome by powerful emotion. The expected place of πόλλα, if it were to be taken with ψισδομένα, would be before the participle (cf. πόλλα δὲ ζαφοίταισ˙, fr. 96.15). Moreover, if the line is self-contained there will be an exact and careful parallel between με ψισδομένα κατελίμπανεν (2) and σ˙ ἀέκοισ˙ ἀπυλιμπάνω (5). However the case may be, when πόλλα is taken with the participle, the καί of line 3 must join the two verbs κατελίμπανεν and ἔειπε.[16] Burnett (291) simply ignores πόλλα in her translation ('she wept as she went away / murmuring this as well'). She thus uses the καί to introduce a second statement of the girl's, parallel to what she takes as the first. Her translation is in accordance with her understanding of the poem but it does not account for the text, and it gives a wrong idea of the Greek. Bowie's translation, 'so sobbing, many times, she left me,' also gives a skewed impression, for the introduction of 'so' creates a connection

---

15 Page (77) also inclines to this construction of the Greek. Treu 1968: 74, puts a comma after πόλλα, thus emphasizing the enjambment.

16 Note that the καί of κἄμεθεν (7) joins two parallel verb forms (both imperatives) – ἔρχεο and μέμναισ˙ – in the first certain instance of enjambment in the poem. But the enjambment between 7 and 8 is different from the enjambment that would be created by taking πόλλα with ψισδομένα. The earlier instance would be 'unperiodic': the sentence complete at the end of line 2 would be extended by line 3. The latter is 'necessary': line 7 requires the first word of line 8 to complete its meaning (and is within a strophe). See Parry 1971: 251 ff.

Führer (1967: 150–2) maintains that the standard supplement after ἔειπε in this line, i.e., μοι, cannot be correct since, inter alia, it contravenes the rules for enclitic position. But he makes no alternative suggestion, and I cannot think of a reasonable possibility. The supplement need not be monosyllabic – the final ε of ἔειπε is uncertain. ἔειπ˙ ἔμοι is not attractive, there being no reason for an emphatic pronoun, especially after the με of the preceding line (normal enclitic position).

between the weeping girl and the previous line. There is nothing in the Greek that does this.

2) καὶ τόδε may, certainly, mean 'this as well,' with adverbial καί. This is a possibility only if we take the first stanza as end-stopped and construe πόλλα with ἔειπε rather than with ψισδομένα 'she repeatedly said this as well.'[17] But even this reading of the Greek does not oblige us to believe that we are returning, with the words that follow τόδε, to the departing girl's speech rather than hearing it for the first time. A similar passage is to be found in Pindar's Fourth *Pythian*:

> τὸν μὲν οὐ γίνωσκον· ὀπιζομένων δ' ἔμ-
> πας τις εἶπεν καὶ τόδε·
> Οὔ τί που οὗτος Ἀπόλλων   86–7

Here the words εἶπεν καὶ τόδε do not refer to things previously spoken but point to the selection of something (or some things) spoken by a voice that is first heard only after the introductory τόδε (i.e., 'said this among other [unreported] things'). And so even if καὶ τόδ' ἔειπε means 'said this as well,' the first line can belong to Sappho, who reports, after the statement of her reaction to the girl's departure, the fact of that departure, then briefly quotes something selected from the parting speech (τόδε) and follows it with her longer reply (τάδ', 6).

3) The easiest construction of the Greek is, in my estimation, to punctuate at the end of line 2 and not only to take πόλλα with what follows,[18] but to take πόλλα καὶ τόδε together as a unit 'she said much and this (in particular).' The common Homeric phrase πολλὰ καὶ ἐσθλά (e.g., *Od.* 2.312, 4.96, 12.347) is the prototype: there is a slight crescendo, with emphasis on the last word of the three, in Homer on ἐσθλά, in Sappho on the utterance chosen from the many things collected into the single word πόλλα but

---

17 Burnett (1979: 23) translates 'and more than once she said.' This too is an idiosyncratic translation, reversing the πόλλα and the καί. The translation catches the πόλλα, taking it adverbially with ἔειπε, but it also takes the καί as a conjunction. It is not possible to have it both ways at once: if πόλλα is adverbial καί is not copulative but must be adverbial too.

18 There seem to be forms of πολύς at or near the beginning of three other stanzas of the poem: πόλλοις (12), πόλλαις (15), πόλλωι (18, a likely and common supplement). Each of these forms appears to precede the verb with which it goes: περεθήκαο (14), ἔβαλες (17, the usual supplement), ἐξαλείψαο (20). This looks very much like conscious polyptoton and there may be an argument for adding line 3 to the list, i.e., for taking πόλλα with the following verb.

not directly given.[19] καί joins two things and so is copulative as in 1), but this time the two things are neuter accusatives rather than verbs. If this is the correct flow of the passage, then the first surviving line is very unlikely to belong to the girl, for to give it to her would relegate τεθνάκην δ' ἀδόλως θέλω to the position of one of many things lumped together and referred to retrospectively by πόλλα.[20] It is more natural and elegant to take πόλλα as the things passed over in silence before τόδ' announces what the next two lines will report, i.e., what is selected from among many possibilities. No more is needed, for these two lines, 4 and 5, report succinctly the gist of the girl's situation in her own words. She is miserable and she is leaving. I should think that the second asyndeton created by placing punctuation at the end of line 3 might be used much in the manner of the first: both testify, delicately but powerfully,[21] that Sappho's feelings are engaged, and further reveal the consternation that the first line has made explicit.[22] McEvilley's translation of the opening three lines (2) both is fully faithful to the Greek and takes the words in the most direct way:

> Really, I want to die; weeping she left me.
> She said many things, and this: '....

19 Prose amplifies the fundamental idea: cf. γυναῖκας ἄλλας τε πολλὰς καὶ δὴ καὶ τοῦ βασιλέος θυγατέρα, Hdt. 1.1.3 (this example was brought to my attention by Drew Griffith).

20 Franyó (above n3) translates line 3, 'Vieles sagte sie, und auch dies.' I doubt, therefore, that he is really at variance with Snell in their joint edition.
   There remains the remote possibility that there was a long speech by the girl, of which line 1 was the tail end, that Sappho's narrative interrupts it, and that πόλλα refers back to it ('the many things [already reported] plus the following'). But apart from the anomalous practice this would entail (see above 114–15), a πόλλα that refers to a long preceding passage is less likely than a πόλλα that neatly gathers together things left unspecified.

21 In the passage from Od. 4 cited above (n11) there is a second instance of asyndeton (667) following directly upon the first: Antinous' consternation is thus made more vivid.
   The rarity of asyndeton in Sappho itself suggests that it is used in this poem for particular effect (see above 111). Gomme (1957: 260) thinks that the asyndeton of line 2 is an argument for change of speaker there, but he does not elaborate. To me the lack of connective appears to have just the opposite effect, as I have explained.

22 The several short sentences thus coincide with the revelation of Sappho's pain in the present and the girl's in the past. Sappho's valediction, on the other hand, being calmer, is characterized from the outset by longer sentences.

There is no reading, then, of line 3, that favours attribution of the first line to the departing girl. Rather, the structure of what we possess and a close examination of the text make it probable that this line is Sappho's. Our preference in attribution of the first line will be affected, however, by our overall reading of the poet. Burnett's is an upbeat Sappho, cleansed of the *Sehnsucht* and torment that German critics in particular have been wont to ascribe to her. On such a reading we have in this fragment a tranquil and collected, perhaps even a cheerful, Sappho consoling a distraught friend who is departing. The poem is a careful iteration of the activities of the circle the girl is leaving; the pain is entirely the girl's and memory will help her, once she has gone, to overcome her grief. Sappho remains, so far as we can ascertain, unaffected by the departure.

Nonetheless, we have observed that Sappho frequently describes her own pain and her own love, as well as her own desire for, or proximity to, death. In this she is startlingly like the Helen of the *Iliad*, who on all three of her appearances in the poem expresses the wish that she were dead (i.e., had died). On each occasion Helen is looking back. In Book 3 she tells Priam that she wishes she had died before her departure for Troy (173 ff.). In Book 6 she tells the living Hector that she wishes she had died at birth (345 ff.), a sentiment she speaks again to the dead Hector in Book 24 (764). Helen's characteristic utterance is to express sorrow for something that happened aforetime, the *fons et origo* of her present *malorum*.[23] It is tempting to think that Helen is Sappho's model in fragment 94,[24] and tantalizing to try to determine in each case the precise tone of the self-pity.[25]

In the Hymn to Aphrodite (fr. 1), by remembering the past Sappho brings solace to herself and, through memory, checks an initial movement

---

23 Hector, Helen, and Antenor wish that Paris were dead or would die (Hector, 3.40 and 6.281–2; Helen, 3.428; Antenor, 7.390). This is an expression of the general disapproval of Paris within Troy (cf. 3.56–7 and 451–4), not an expression of self–pity. Closer, perhaps, to Helen's own death-wish is Andromache's at 22.481.

Achilles' τεθναίην at 18.98 is complicated. It is partly a response to his mother's prediction of his impending death, but it is also regret for his past action, or inaction (ἐπεὶ οὐκ ἄρ' ἔμελλον ...). Mimnermus' τεθναίην (fr. 1.2, West) refers to the future – the present is not painful.

24 Helen makes everything easy to understand: cf. fr. 16.5 ff.

25 Helen may not be totally self-absorbed and her wish may contain genuine sorrow for the trouble she has caused Trojans and Greeks alike. But she does not say so directly.

There is another significant point of similarity between Sappho and Homer's Helen: both know that they will be remembered (cf. *Iliad* 6.358; Sappho frs. 55, 147).

towards self-pity.[26] In fragment 94 too she is her own physician. She recounts the past at length and remembers its joys in a time of difficulty. The tears and sorrow of the departing girl are, on this understanding, much more than an 'anecdote' (Burnett 293, 295); they are a fiction of the poem designed to elicit Sappho's counterstatement. The counterstatement is a long reverie of self-consolation, for the real grief is her own. Sappho's poem is certainly a love-poem that speaks of mutual joy[27] and mutual pain. But it is in the last analysis a poem about herself.[28]

We need no more than what we can now read to be able to find satisfaction in a superbly crafted poem, all elements of which are to be paralleled in what remains to us of Sappho. There is a present intolerable situation, there is the poet's expressed desire to die (one of many Homeric reminiscences), and there is refuge in memory for the pain of the present. The length of the description of the shared pleasures gains special point if Sappho is really speaking to herself. Schadewaldt wrote memorably of the three time-levels of the poem, the present, the moment of parting in the past, and the more remote past that is summoned up in memory.[29] These

---

26 Fränkel 1969: 201 speaks of 'einen Umschlag von zehrender Qual zu zuversichtlicher Hoffnung.' Fragment 31 also seems to move from agitation to equanimity: ἀλλὰ πὰν τόλματον, ἐπεὶ ... (17).

27 Fr. 96 appears to console Atthis by speaking of mutual joy and mutual sorrow. The sorrow of the departed girl is wishful thinking, for she is across the sea in Lydia and Sappho must imagine her feelings. Distance in 94 is created through time, not space – the girl's sufferings are in the past, not in another land. But in both cases the fiction serves an immediate purpose and that purpose is consolation in present pain.

The 'focalizer' (above n12), when the same person as the narrator, may use the narrator's language. In fr. 94 that language is the language of love, not of detachment, and the first-person plural verbs (8, 11, 26) show the bond that continues to exist. Further, ἐγω θέλω (9) is the language of the present Sappho (cf. θέλω, 1).

28 Rauk, in a fascinating article, argues that Sappho's poem is in fact a lament and as such 'primarily concerned with the speaker's state and emotions, not with those of the companion' (Rauk 1989: 115). Rauk would, thus, also give the opening line to Sappho (107, 111).

The Cologne Epode of Archilochus, with its long central speech replying to a girl, is also primarily a revelation of the speaker himself. It is interesting to note that the reconstruction of this poem proposed by West 1980 is not unlike the interpretation of Sappho fr. 94 argued for here. West recommends joining fragments 196 and 196a and suggests a possible beginning for the poem. The result is a dispirited speaker who in the present recalls an exchange with a girl in the past, the speaker's remembered speech being *prima facie* an attempt to calm the girl but in reality a reflection of his own preoccupation. (Later, West [1989] is not so explicit in connecting the two fragments and does not reproduce the possible beginning for the poem.)

29 Schadewaldt 1950: 113–19.

levels must surely be present on any reading, for even with the opening words in the mouth of the departing girl, we would want missing stanzas to establish the anchor in the present that we find elsewhere in Sappho.

The problem will, no doubt, never be solved to everyone's satisfaction. For our approach to the individual poem depends, inevitably, as I have suggested, on our general reading of the poet.[30] My own inclination is to see her as one who is frequently in love and so frequently in pain, as one who seeks to overcome the tyranny of emotion and of an absolute present by appeal to divinity or appeal to memory (or to both at once). Poem 94 is thus directly comparable to that other ravishing aria, 'Dove sono ...?' Sappho, like Mozart's Countess Almaviva, in her present misery harks back to the 'bei momenti' of shared joy and gathers strength as she does:[31]

> ... se in pianti e in pene
> per me tutto si cangiò,
> la memoria di quel bene
> dal mio sen non trapassò.

[30] On general presuppositions governing interpretation of an individual fragment, cf. above n4. Our interpretation of the word ἀδόλως is coloured by our more general understanding of the poem. If our overall Sappho is the sort of Sappho who can compose poetry to recount an anecdote, the word ἀδόλως may well suggest the 'melodramatic effusiveness' of the girl (Burnett 295); if we think of an earnest and passionate Sappho, the word ἀδόλως gives weight to her utterance.

[31] Fowler (1987: 68) thinks that the poem must have ended with a repeated admonition to remember old friends, and so have formed a ring with line 8. Rauk (1989: 109) also thinks that Sappho's catalogue returned to its beginning and to the 'pose of friend that Sappho assumed there.' He further thinks that such a poem may have been a recognized type (116). I prefer to imagine, however, that the poem returned to the present and in so doing formed a ring with the opening as does fr. 1, the only complete poem we possess: an argument from the poet's observed practice seems to me stronger than an argument from generic composition. But if we are given to speculation about the lost ending of the poem we should perhaps consider the possibility that the poem returned both to the moment of parting and to the present, thus closing two rings – abcba. There are excellent remarks on ring-composition in Kirkwood's chapter on Sappho (1974) – see esp. 116 on the return to the immediate situation.

I am grateful to Christopher Brown, David Campbell, Anne Carson, Drew Griffith, Bonnie MacLachlan, Philippa Wallace Matheson, and the journal's referees, all of whom were perceptive and helpful.

SAPPHO FR. 94: A FURTHER NOTE

In my article 'Who's Dying in Sappho Fr. 94?' in *Phoenix* 44.2 (1990) 111–21 [in this volume 108–18] I outlined three possibilities for construing the crucial passage from the first to the second stanza of what survives of the poem, pointing out that the πόλλα of line 3 is of particular importance for our interpretation. My own preference was, and remains, the third possibility – to punctuate at the end of line 2 and to take πόλλα with what follows, reading πόλλα καὶ τόδε as a unit 'she said much and this (in particular).' But I now realize that the explanatory example that I adduced is unsatisfactory: the Homeric phrase πολλὰ καὶ ἐσθλά is not analogous, for in this phrase the two neuter adjectives are exactly parallel: they refer to the same thing and the word καί could be eliminated without damaging the sense. It would have been more helpful to point to the use of καί explained by Denniston 1959: 291 (6): καί with a sense of climax (= καὶ δή, καὶ δὴ καί; cf. LSJ s.v. A.2).

If this is correct, πόλλα will be a comprehensive reference to what the girl said. The bulk of it is played down by a dismissive πόλλα in order to allow Sappho to concentrate on what follows the τόδε, i.e., on what she will rebut at length. The first surviving line of the poem is not an instance of the πόλλα, alluded to retrospectively – this would, in my opinion, be otiose and inelegant. πόλλα is, rather, a reference to the many things glanced at without elaboration and mentioned collectively inasmuch as the inclusive mention gives point to the one actual quotation singled out and emphasized. Anticipatory examples of the girl's speech would weaken the force both of the succinct πόλλα and of the subsequent quotation.

First published in *Phoenix* 44.4 (1990) 381–2.

I am especially grateful to Robert Fowler for lively debate and criticism. His assistance should not, however, be taken as indication of his agreement with my interpretation.

One further point. If πόλλα is taken in enjambment with ψισδομένα, as perhaps the majority of critics wish, there is simply a reference to much *weeping* along with the utterance. Neither πόλλα nor ψισδομένα (Hsch. ψιζομένη· κλαίουσα) is a reference to articulate sound, much less a reference to earlier speech, and the normal Greek distinction between intelligible utterance and wailing would be observed in this case too: cf., e.g., the Homeric ὣς ἔφατο κλαίουσ᾽ (*Il.* 24.746).

SAPPHO, APHRODITE, AND THE MUSES[1]

φησὶν ἡ Σαπφὼ ὅτι ἀποθνήσκειν κακόν· οἱ θεοὶ γὰρ οὕτω κεκρίκασιν. ἀπέθνησκον γὰρ ἄν.

Sappho says that death is an evil: the gods have so decided, otherwise they would die.[2]

The sub-title of the present volume is 'Women in Ancient Greek Cult.' It would thus be only natural to find this final chapter a discussion of the cult of Aphrodite as we see it portrayed in the poetry of Sappho. But cult cannot be taken for granted; indeed just to posit cult-association in connection with Sappho's poetry is to draw the scorn of much contemporary criticism, which feels that the poetry loses its marvellous erotic intensity to the degree that it is read as the expression of religious feeling and communal worship.

And so an old question must be opened afresh here, despite the fact that it has given rise to one of the most envenomed and inconclusive debates of the twentieth century in the field of early Greek poetry. The problem is, fundamentally, that there is no external evidence and little helpful context to assist in interpreting the fragments of Sappho. Everything we say is ultimately a deduction from the poetry itself. It has come down to us in such tattered and sorry pieces that it demands hypotheses that will help us see a coherent pattern. Moreover, just to talk about this poetry is to have to face a sexual issue that is heavily charged in any age, and one's interpretation will thus inevitably betray, and betray quite strongly, certain aspects of the *Zeitgeist* of the period in which one is speaking or writing.

First published in *Ancient World* 26.2 (1995) 225–39, a volume containing the proceedings of a conference entitled 'Women in Ancient Greek Cult.'

1 I am grateful to Brian Blair, Christopher Brown, and M. Owen Lee for their helpful comments.
2 Arist. *Rhet.* 1398b (fr. 201). All references to Sappho are to the edition of Voigt 1971, which follows the numbering established by Lobel-Page. The edition of Campbell 1982 (Loeb) contains, for the most part, the same numeration and a reliable translation of all the fragments and testimonia.

For most of the Victorians homosexuality was the 'love that dare not speak its name'; it could be ignored or even banished from the fragments.³ The Victorian era was, incidentally, the very period in which the few actual quotations that had come down through ancient authors and that had up to that time constituted the pathetically small 'text' of Sappho began to be supplemented by considerable papyrus discoveries. In our age, an age of Women's Studies and Gay Pride, when homosexuality is no stigma and eagerness to discuss erotic questions openly is a badge of liberation and sophistication, Sappho's poetry is read with the same conviction that it contains just what we are intent on finding, though what we now expect to find is likely to be the very opposite of what our grandparents found. Like Narcissus, we see ourselves in the pool.

The point of departure for twentieth-century discussions of Sappho is, as for so many other problems in Greek literature and poetry, Wilamowitz. Exactly 100 years ago, in 1895, the French poet Pierre Louÿs published a collection of poems entitled *Les chansons de Bilitis traduites du grec pour la première fois*. These purported to be part of a collection of poems found the previous year in the grave of one Bilitis. Half Semite (as the name shows), half Greek, she had spent time with Sappho on Lesbos and had been Sappho's rival in a passionate affair with the Mnasidika whose name was already known from the fragments. She retired to be a hierodule of Astarte and a poet at Amathus on Cyprus. There she died, leaving her literary legacy to await the sort of discovery that was becoming familiar to Europeans in the nineteenth century.⁴ This whole fiction was supported by an elaborate pseudo-scholarly apparatus and sustained by an archaizing patina on what was explicitly homoerotic poetry. The book aroused much interest, for Pierre Louÿs was a literary figure of some importance (one need mention only Debussy's exquisite settings of some of the poems two years later in 1897).⁵ The French reading public, at least, with sensibilities educated by Gautier and Baudelaire, was comparatively tolerant of lesbianism. But this work differed from any of its predecessors in purporting to depict the historical Sappho. This it was that prompted Wilamowitz's outraged review of the collection of poems in 1896 in *Göttingische gelehrte Anzeigen* – one remembers his successful assault, 25 years earlier, on Nietzsche's *Birth of Tragedy*, when his massive armament of *Wissenschaft* trained on a work

---

3 See Dover 1988.
4 See Turner 1968: Chapter 1. The actual discovery of papyri of Sappho began two years after Wilamowitz's review.
5 See DeJean 1989, esp. 276–80.

lacking in philological rigour left him in full possession of the scholarly field. Wilamowitz continued to think about Sappho and returned, on the eve of the First World War, in *Sappho und Simonides* (Berlin 1913), to the matters he had discussed in 1896. In this book he sets out in detail the theory he had only adumbrated 17 years earlier – that Sappho was mistress of a girls' school and president of what he labelled a *thiasos* (the word is Wilamowitz's and is not found in the fragments). This was a religious group which devoted itself to the cult of Aphrodite. The poetry is the natural expression of the intense but innocent feelings of a teacher for students to whom she is attached and this love is made legitimate and innocent by the common but chaste service of a goddess. Sublimation of the sexual drive certainly appears to play an important part. There is throughout a fascinating, and, I might add, quintessentially German-Romantic, emphasis on unsatisfied longing, 'unbefriedigtes Sehnen' (40). One of the most personal, moving, and truly memorable passages in the book is Wilamowitz's account of the later fictions of Sappho's unhappy love for the handsome boatman Phaon and her consequent love-death: he explains the story as the fabrication of someone closely attuned to the inner motions of Sappho's soul as expressed in her poetry and able to capture this understanding in a story of unfulfilled passion and suicide.

It is this document that has set the terms for nearly all later discussion. It focuses quite explicitly on the issue of cult. Most subsequent German scholarship has followed Wilamowitz down to the details. Such distinguished scholars as Snell, Fränkel, and Merkelbach accept the *thiasos*-theory in its smallest particulars: the most notorious instance is well known – all these critics have maintained that fragment 31, φαίνεται μοι κῆνος ἴσος θέοισιν 'He seems to me equal to the gods,' is an epithalamium or marriage-song, not a love-poem.[6] Ranged with these Teutonic heavyweights is Anne Pippin Burnett. Burnett, while not going so far as the above-mentioned Germans, accepts the *thiasos* so fully that she even entitles one of her chapters 'Circle' (= German 'Kreis,' the usual translation of *thiasos*).[7] She reads, for instance, poem 94, the long address to a departing girl with its catalogue of shared pleasures, as a virtual statement of the curriculum of the *thiasos* that Sappho headed.

But most British and American criticism has been hostile to Wilamowitz and has delighted in fastening on the most extreme passages in the book to discredit the whole. A generation ago Denys Page mounted a celebrated

6 See Robbins 1980: 255–61 [in this volume 101–7].
7 Burnett 1983. Cf. the title of Merkelbach's famous essay (1957), 'Sappho und ihr Kreis.'

attack in his book *Sappho and Alcaeus*.[8] A recent American book,[9] to give but one further – and typical – example, states, 'A[n] ... effort to imbue Sappho with Victorian respectability centred on the equally insupportable fancy of the great classical scholar Wilamowitz that she was the official religious leader of a cult of female worshippers devoted to Aphrodite .... The tenacity of the idea is astounding; even in the new (1970) edition of the *Oxford Classical Dictionary*, Sappho is described as "the centre of some kind of θίασος [religious guild] which honoured Aphrodite and the Muses and had young girls for its members." *There is simply no evidence for this notion in either the fragments themselves or in the ancient biographical material*' (italics mine).

It is easy to make fun of Wilamowitz as protector of Sappho's chastity: Aphrodite is not a goddess of chastity. It is equally easy, and follows all too easily after the first step is taken, to reject what is compelling in his arguments. I find it ironic and inconsistent that the critic who calls Wilamowitz's cult-theory an 'insupportable fancy' says five pages after what I have just quoted, of the famous fragment on the sherd now numbered 2 in our collections, that 'we can safely assume that the description [of the grove] reflects some sort of experience involving a communal rite in honour of the goddess.'[10] She adds the necessary if slightly contradictory disclaimer that we need not believe in anything official, of course. But rites or cults are not casual happenings; the people who perform them are bound by a sense of shared purpose and do not form haphazard agglomerations. Virtually every critic, even those professedly hostile to the cult-theory, sees incontrovertible evidence of cult of some sort in this fragment. I shall return to examine this crucial poem. It was discovered on a sherd only in 1937 and so Wilamowitz could not have known it except for what is the final stanza on the sherd, a stanza quoted in antiquity by Athenaeus. Interestingly, Wilamowitz did not use this stanza as evidence for cult, as critics since him have done. As will be seen below, I think Wilamowitz's intuition very close to the truth about the poem.[11]

Let us avoid the word *thiasos*, since it is not found in Sappho's poetry. Sappho speaks of her ἔταιραι or 'companions' (160, τάδε νῦν ἐταίριας ταὶς

---

8 Page 1955. See especially 110–12 and 143–6. What is most extraordinary is that this attack comes from a critic who approvingly quotes the perfumed prose of John Addington Symonds, the verbal equivalent of the paintings of Alma-Tadema, as an 'insightful' description of Sappho's world!
9 Snyder 1989: 12.
10 Snyder 1989: 17.
11 Wilamowitz 1913: 43 n1.

ἔμαις τέρπνα κάλως ἀείσω 'I shall now sing these songs beautifully to delight my companions'). An Attic red-figure hydria[12] of the last quarter of the fifth-century shows this ἑταιρεία: Sappho is in the company of three other women, one of whom is extending a lyre to her as she sits in a chair reading a scroll of poetry, the first word of which seems to be θεοί 'gods.'[13] The women are apparently of an age with Sappho, though people discussing the vase are wont to call them her 'pupils.'[14] Evidence of this sort suggests an association of women interested in poetry and music, but it probably says more about fifth-century Athens than about seventh-century Lesbos: there are other similar vases where the women are not named.[15] But Sappho *does* refer to παῖδες 'young people' and παρθένοι 'maidens,' in particular those whom she prepared to sing epithalamia for the marriages of their peers (e.g., 30, 49). Himerius calls the epithalamia Ἀφροδίτης ὄργια 'rites of Aphrodite' (194), but this seems a figurative use of the word, for weddings were never considered rituals that formed part of a cult of the goddess. And a lament for Adonis, which must have belonged to a women's festival of a sort familiar to us from other sources, is addressed to 'maidens' (κόραι [140a]). The mediaeval encyclopedia known as the *Suda* specifically distinguishes between Sappho's ἑταῖραι or friends (test. 253) and her μαθήτριαι or pupils, whom it lists as coming from Miletus, Colophon, and Salamis. A papyrus published in 1974[16] and so not included in Voigt's edition is a commentary on Sappho that gives an extraordinary boost to the school-theory: it says that 'Sappho lived in peace and quiet teaching the noblest girls not only from local families but also from families in Ionia, and was so esteemed that Callias of Mytilene ...' (there is a break at this point). The papyrus' association of Sappho's school with the name of a local historian, known from Strabo to have written a work about Sappho and Alcaeus (test. 41 Campbell), is important. It is impossible to believe that Callias' opinions are not based on good knowledge of the poetry and of local tradition regarding Sappho. And it is gratuitous to insist that he is simply engaged in apologetics, in whitewashing someone from his home town – a Wilamowitz before Wilamowitz. The name of Callias is followed on the papyrus by a lacuna and then

12 Athens 1260; Beazley 1963: 1060 §145.
13 For an attempt to reconstitute the writing on the scroll as a poem, see Edmonds 1922a: 1–14.
14 Beck 1975: 57–8 §366; H.R. Immerwahr 1964: 26.
15 E.g., the slightly earlier Athenian vase shown in Berard et al. 1989: 90, fig. 124: here we see a scene of poetry, singing, and music in the home of a well-to-do Athenian woman.
16 Gronewald 1974 = fragment 214B in Campbell 1982 (Loeb).

by the name of Aphrodite; the papyrus column breaks off, as almost all papyrus fragments seem to do, at the critical point. Clearly there was something further about the school or about the poetry, perhaps about both.

A school is not a cult. But neither is a school a casual organization for the satisfaction of sexual urges; it suggests some structure and a programme. It is interesting, then, that there *does* appear to be evidence for a cult of Hera on the island of Lesbos and for the formal participation of Sappho and her coterie in it. The scholiast on *Iliad* 9.129, the passage in which Agamemnon is offering seven women of Lesbos, famous for their beauty, to Achilles, says that there were regular beauty contests on Lesbos at a shrine of Hera. And Alcaeus in his exile (129) mentions a shrine of Zeus, Aeolian Hera, 'glorious goddess, mother of all,' and of Dionysus which seems to be the very shrine referred to in another of his exile poems (130b). There he talks of a shrine of the gods

> where Lesbian women with trailing robes go to and fro
> being judged for their beauty and around rings the
> wonderful sound of the annual cry of women.

An anonymous epigram in Book 9 of the Palatine Anthology guarantees Sappho's participation in these ceremonies:

> Come to the shining precinct of gleaming-eyed Hera,
> women of Lesbos, whirling your delicate footsteps
> and set up there the beautiful dance to the goddess;
> and Sappho will lead you, her golden lyre in hand.   (9.189)[17]

There is a papyrus fragment (17), moreover, that seems to be a hymn invoking Hera (what we call a 'cletic' hymn). It may be personal and not a ceremonial prayer, but it talks of arrival, perhaps at a shrine.[18]

The activities of the school seem to have included instruction on deportment and dressing: Sappho often mentions clothes and garlands (22, 29, 39, 57, 92, 98, 101) and the way they are worn, and we remember both Aphrodite's own toilette in the *Cypria* (fr. 4) and the toilette of Hera (who has enlisted Aphrodite's assistance) for her seduction of Zeus in *Iliad*

---

17 Page (1981: 338) thinks that the epigram is 'manifestly Alexandrian in style and spirit, and may be as early as some of Meleager's authors.'
18 If Martin West's supplement (adopted by Campbell) ἶρ˙ is correct in v. 20. The word π]αρθ[εν occurs a few lines earlier.

14.[19] Both goddesses were concerned with these matters, clearly. But the evidence, such as it is, connects the cultivation of beauty more with Hera than with Aphrodite. The Graces, so regularly Aphrodite's companions elsewhere in matters that regard beauty (cf. the *Cypria*-passage above), in Sappho's poetry, interestingly enough, are regularly associated with the Muses, not with Aphrodite (44A[b], 103, 128, 208).

There is enough in the fragments to suggest that young women who spent time with Sappho left, after their time with her, to become brides. But we have no way of knowing whether the public occasions on which the poetry commemorating such departures was sung were meetings of other students or of a group of like-minded women in Mytilene who listened to Sappho and perhaps themselves sang. (I take for granted that the 'publication' of the poetry was, in the first instance at least, performance before a group of some sort.) Of the long fragments found in modern times on parchment and papyrus, 16 recalls the departed Anactoria who is mentioned in the *Suda* as a pupil, 94 marks the departure of someone unnamed who has clearly spent time with Sappho and other women, while fragment 96 dwells on the love-longing of a woman now in Lydia who thinks back with tenderness to the Atthis she has left behind and whom Sappho consoles with her poem. Are these women students who left to be married? This seems far more plausible than to imagine them the wives of businessmen or diplomats who found themselves temporarily on Lesbos and who later went home or to other postings. Sappho's poetry is full of departures; some of the departures are depicted with acrimony rather than with sadness, for they seem to be defections of girls to rival groups very like her own: the names of Gorgo and Andromeda appear to be the names of competitors (cf. 130, 155). Such rivalries and censure seem only too Greek. But from the poems that offer consolation, either through memory or through metaphor, there breathes a spirit that is unique in early Greek poetry: these women cared for each other tenderly and there is nostalgia and sympathetic imagination in Sappho's account of them.

It is hard not to place all this under the aegis of Aphrodite, who is a ubiquitous presence in the poetry, and there is no reason not to think that Aphrodite had a place of special honour in the life of the group as well as in Sappho's own life. The word 'official' becomes in fact meaningless. The school will hardly have had certification, course-credits, and graduation ceremonies, like modern high schools or universities. School is, or should be, preparation for life. I confess, though, that I often wonder if the sort

---

19 The archetype for all these scenes of a goddess adorning herself is Astarte or the Sumerian Inanna: see West 1978 *ad* vv. 73–5.

of life lived by the young people under Sappho's tutelage was in fact a preparation for the lives they must often have led after they left her and found themselves married to men who were fundamentally misogynist and may have been brutal to boot. Many will have looked back to their time on Lesbos as the only time of real happiness in their lives. Any group, in order to be a community and not just an aggregate, must have shared ideals, ideals that transcend the individuals that constitute the group. Such ideals for the early Greeks were almost certainly not exclusively secular; our best parallel for the activities of Sappho's school is the life of the groups of girls portrayed in the fragmentary maiden-songs or *partheneia* of Alcman. These come from Sparta of the same period. Here cult, love, clothes, song, and perhaps even contests, come together in one exquisite amalgam. It would be perverse not to associate all these same things with Aphrodite in Sappho's world.

But even when all this is said, there remains the central fact: that Aphrodite dominates Sappho's *personal* life. Whatever importance the divinity may have had for the group, the intense, loving, and intimate communion between a devotee and a divinity in Sappho's poetry is something I find here and here alone in early or classical Greek poetry. There are brief flashes of it elsewhere (e.g., the relation of Hippolytus and Artemis at the beginning of Euripides' *Hippolytus* – though Hippolytus' devotion strikes the audience as not only singular but unbalanced).[20] On the whole, though, I find nothing directly comparable. My students, whose ideas of religious experience are generally unsympathetic to ritual and whose notions of religion, if they have any at all, are created within a Judeo-Christian tradition where there is personal encounter between god and the individual, tend to find Greek religion lacking in just those things that seem to them to constitute real religion. This may be an unfair judgement, for doubtless there was at the popular level much fervour and love governing the relations between individuals and the gods they trusted and served. But the traditional religion as it appears in the literary documents is a social phenomenon, something which concerns the state. Priests are magistrates, prayers official, temples dedicated to civic gods, sacrifices punctiliously and mechanically performed, prescribed festivals routinely celebrated. The usual word in classical Greek for 'believe' ($νομίζω$) is derived from the word for 'law' or 'custom' ($νόμος$): belief or worship is little more than civic custom. Sappho stands out in a world where we see works, not faith: in her we get, as we do not elsewhere, some sense of the attitude in which the various $δρώμενα$ were performed. Elsewhere when religion is personal

---

20 For a sympathetic assessment see Festugière 1960: Chapter 1.

it is normally 'quid pro quo,' with sacrifices performed to win favour and reciprocity.[21] Whatever artifice and self-consciousness there may be in Sappho's utterance – and there is some in all good verse – the poetry burns with the sense of a woman who lives easily and confidently with her divinity at all times. She talks to her goddess by day (1, 60, 86: cf. 33 αἴθ᾽ ἔγω, χροσοστέφαν᾽ Ἀφρόδιτα τόνδε τὸν πάλον λαχοίην 'Golden-crowned Aphrodite, if only I could obtain this lot') and by night (134 ζά <τ᾽> ἐλεξάμαν ὄναρ, Κυπρογένηα 'I spoke with you in a dream, Cyprogeneia'). She spoke to her in the past and speaks to her in the present (esp. fr. 1). And Aphrodite offers hope for the future too. For me the most significant word in the Hymn to Aphrodite is the twice-repeated ἀθάνατος (lines 1, 14): – it is an adjective normally used only of Zeus or collectively of the immortals as a group, ἀθάνατοι, but not of individual Olympians apart from Zeus.[22] But here the poet who, we shall see, is ever concerned with her own immortality, recognizes what she seeks for herself in the face of the goddess. Elsewhere Aphrodite's face is characterized by its beauty and by its smile (cf. *Hom. Hymn* 10.2 ff.), not by its immortality. The poem gives Sappho confidence in the immediate future. In it there is perhaps an arcane and more distant promise too, delicate and beautiful as Beatrice's to Virgil when she descends from her heaven to *his* hell (Dante, *Inferno* 2.74).[23]

It is, I admit, bold to read in the Hymn to Aphrodite a covert intimation of immortality. But this much we can say with certainty about the poem, in any case: its central section, with the recollection or *hypomnesis*, both reveals Sappho's easy familiarity with her goddess and establishes a perspective which makes the present bearable and comprehensible as part of a just and coherent universe. Pain is overcome and a pattern discerned. Art here involves recollection, but the occasion of recollection is immediate pain.[24] Everywhere in the longer fragments I find a device that allows the poet to establish a perspective on the present and that gives it its richer meaning. The Hymn to Aphrodite uses the past epiphany to reestablish equilibrium in the here-and-now. Fragment 16 uses myth, and the example of Helen, to lend credibility to the statement that love

21 See, e.g., Blundell 1989: 46–7.
22 Wilamowitz 1913: 44.
23 See Torraca 1926 *ad loc.*: Beatrice seems to hint at Virgil's eventual release from Hell.
24 Marcel Proust's aesthetic in his great set of novels, *A la recherche du temps perdu*, seems to me identical: involuntary memory is triggered by immediate sensory experience; reflection gives meaning and invites the reconstitution of experience in art. The title of the second novel, *A l'ombre des jeunes filles en fleurs*, might serve as a designation for Sappho's entire oeuvre.

is all-important. Of the several competing interpretations of this poem,[25] I continue to find most compelling the idea that Helen's departure and forgetting of Menelaus 'best of husbands,' Helen's dereliction of family, is an example that cuts two ways. Her surrender to Aphrodite is a tribute to that goddess, but we are also left contemplating this 'most beautiful of women' from the point of view of the abandoned family and so can move easily to remembering the absent Anactoria and her supreme value: οὐ παρεοίσας 'absent,' is in emphatic position as the adonic of its strophe and comes with the first mention of Anactoria. A note of wistfulness enters this happy song – *surgit amari aliquid* in the famous Lucretian phrase (4.1133–4) – for it is, in the final analysis, a poem about separation. Fragments 94 and 96 do not function very differently. In 94 pain is eased through memory, and memory is in effect an epiphany of the goddess, for the joyful activities of lovers are recalled. I believe that Sappho is consoling *herself* primarily, not the girl whose departure is reported.[26] And I think too that in fragment 96 Sappho's own longing for the departed girl is palpable in her consolation of Atthis, whom she is *prima facie* addressing.[27] The hushed moonlit landscape at the heart of the poem establishes the perspective that offsets the pain of separation. Sappho, we know, coined the word 'bitter-sweet,' and the word is applicable to all the longer fragments. Let me offer yet another instance, no less real if less immediately apparent.

Fragment 44 consists of thirty-five lines so apparently joyous that critics continue to wish to take them as an epithalamium.[28] They depict the Trojans pouring from their city jubilantly to greet prince Hector as he arrives bringing his lovely bride Andromache. Fine and good. But there is a spectre – 'something of bitterness' – at the feast. For we know that Troy is a doomed city and cannot read without remembering the very end of the *Iliad*, where the whole population of Troy pours through these same gates within which they have been pent up for ten years, streaming across what has been, since the moment evoked by Sappho, a blood-soaked battlefield. Troy now raises the threnody as Hector's body is brought back to the city from the Achaean camp, Andromache cradles Hector's head in her arms and begins the lament. The poignancy of Sappho's picture is wonderfully subtle. And wrenching, despite the apparent joy of the scene. For it cannot but be read with the more famous picture from the end of the *Iliad* in

---

25 See Most 1981: 11–17.
26 Robbins 1990: 111–21 [in this volume 108–18].
27 Macleod 1974: 217–20.
28 Fränkel 1962: 196. So too, most recently, Contiades-Tsitsoni 1990: 102 ff.

mind. The pain of Hector's last return to Troy (does any one of us ever stop feeling it?) is for a moment banished by a memory of an earlier, joyous return. That joy is in this case too the province of Aphrodite, for the poet is Sappho.[29]

This reading of Sappho emphasizes the shadow, I admit, and goes against most current understanding. But I confess to finding much contemporary reading of Sappho suspect, for I sense in it a political agenda. This runs as follows: those who find sorrow in Sappho are thought to be passing implicit judgment on her and her unnatural or doomed love;[30] but since homosexuality is perfectly normal and good we have to see proof of this in Sappho's happiness (the very word 'gay' as synonym for 'homosexual' itself shows the determination to escape the stigma). We discredit the value judgment by denying its basis. My reading, however, simply sees poetry of passion as poetry of suffering. It has virtually all the love-poetry of the western tradition to support it. I see no need either to deny the homosexuality, with Wilamowitz, or to ignore Sappho's own pain, with, say, Burnett (n7 above) or Winkler (n45 below). My own favourite summary of Sappho is from one of the few poets worthy of mention in the same breath – Rainer Maria Rilke.

In a famous phrase Alcaeus is said to have addressed Sappho:

ἰόπλοκ᾽ ἄγνα μελλιχόμειδε Σάπφοι

violet-tressed, holy, sweetly-smiling Sappho.[31]

Or at least 'violet-tressed' is how all commentators insist on translating ἰόπλοκ᾽ – the word, which does not occur elsewhere, is said to be the equivalent of ἰοπλόκαμος, which does. But Rilke, in a letter to his wife,[32] seems to be thinking of Sappho's own usages, δολόπλοκος 'weaver of wiles' (1), μυθόπλοκος, 'weaver of tales' (188), when he translates 'Weberin von Dunkel,' 'weaver of darkness.' That is both good philology and intuitive understanding.

29 The loss of the context of the passage might be as important as our knowledge of the sequel in myth in establishing the poignancy of the scene.
30 Devereux 1970 is the *reductio ad absurdum*; but for the attitude see also McEvilley 1978.
31 Voigt eliminates Sappho's name from this fragment; Lobel-Page retain it (Alcaeus 384).
32 Rilke 1930: no. 149, July 25, 1907: '... Und nun einiges als Erklärung für Dich: Alkaios war ein Dichter, der auf einer antiken Vase, die Leier in Händen, vor der Sappho steht, das Haupt gesenkt, and man weiß, daß er zu ihr gesagt hat: "Weberin von Dunkel, Sappho, Reine mit dem Lächeln der Honigsüße, Worte drängen zu meinen Lippen, aber eine Schäm hält mich zurück."'

Sappho's mechanism is, as I see it, a fairly constant one. Pain (Wilamowitz's 'unbefriedigtes Sehnen') is stilled and given meaning by memory, by epiphany, or by both (i.e., the memory may involve epiphany as in 1, may be memory that is communal as in the myth of 16, or the epiphany may be veiled as in 94 and 96). But everywhere the tyranny of the more immediate is allowed to open onto a larger world, a world in which the goddess rules and to which she gives meaning. Fragment 31 reverses the mechanism, for the paroxysm at the heart of the poem (an epiphany of eros if ever there was one!) is made bearable in the lost ending of which the first words are ἀλλὰ πὰν τόλματον 'but anything can be endured.' Only the deepest thinkers among the early poets can see the larger whole: Homer's Achilles learns, and is able to tell Priam, that compassion is superior to mere endurance, Archilochus knows that a rhythm (ῥυσμός) governs the affairs of men, and Pindar can see that a life dominated by darkness (πόνος) is redeemed by intermittent flashes of light (αἴγλα). Sappho's consolation and joy are unique in being part of her intense attachment to her goddess.

Aphrodite in the first fragment, the famous 'Hymn to Aphrodite,' is the source of the hurt and of the healing consolation. Generally in Sappho I think it is the beneficent side of the goddess that dominates and corrects the pain, while Aphrodite's son Eros is sensed as more oppressive (ἀλγεσίδωρον, 'paingiver' 172, λυσιμέλης δόνει, γλυκύπικρον ἀμάχανον 130 [in which the pain seems to predominate over the pleasure]):

Ἔρος δ' ἐτίναξέ μοι
φρένας ὡς ἄνεμος κὰτ ὄρος δρύσιν ἐμπέτων

Love shook my heart like a wind falling on oaks on a mountain.   (47)

Among the other early poets only Alcman appears to make the same distinction between a wanton or destructive Eros and Aphrodite:

Ἀφροδίτα μὲν οὐκ ἔστι, μάργος δ' Ἔρως οἷα <παῖς> παίσδει,
ἄκρ' ἐπ' ἄνθη καβαίνων, ἃ μή μοι θίγῃς, τῶ κυπαιρίσκω.   (58 PMG)[33]

It is not Aphrodite, but wild Eros plays like a boy, coming down over the galingale flowers: do not touch them!

---

[33] On a possible connection between Sappho 130 and Alcman 58, see MacLachlan 1989: 95–9. Easterling 1974: 37–41 discusses the fragment from Alcman.

It is possible that these words are a woman's utterance too, since they may come from the voice of maidens singing a partheneion. They at least appear to suggest that the goddess is not violent like the god. Ibycus (286 *PMG*) certainly makes Aphrodite herself source of the same fierce winds that Sappho attributes to Eros. For Sappho Eros is Aphrodite's son (198).[34] In Hesiod he was an independent cosmic principle, antecedent in birth, like Aphrodite, to the other divinities of Olympus. No genealogy is given for him, though he keeps company with Aphrodite (*Theogony* 201). Sappho seems to emphasize the subordination of Eros to her personal goddess by making him Aphrodite's son – this filiation may be her own idea.[35] And when she calls Eros Aphrodite's θεράπων or attendant she puts him on a par with herself (159). Eros is never other than violent in early Greek poetry – Anacreon documents this with special force: the young boy is a blacksmith who hammers hearts on his anvil, a gambler whose dice are madness and battle (376, 398, 413 *PMG*). But Aphrodite, who is primarily the goddess of the joyfulness of love, is more comprehensive than her son. Eros can never console as can a mother. It is Sappho who understands this best.

A goddess to whom Sappho has an intense personal relationship, then, and one who has the power to control pain and transmute it into joy. This brings us to fragment 2. It is by far the oldest written testimony we have to Sappho's poetry, the calligraphy being of the second or third centuries BC,[36] (all the parchment and papyri are of the Roman period).

> Hither to me from Crete ...
> holy shrine where is a lovely grove
> of apple trees and altars smoking
> with incense.
>
> There cool water murmurs through
> apple-branches; the whole place
> is dusky with roses and from the rustling leaves
> enchantment takes hold.
>
> There a meadow where horses graze
> burgeons with spring flowers, and breezes
> breathe sweetly ...

---

34 She seems, if Pausanias is correct, to have tried other genealogies (198).
35 She made Peitho, 'Persuasion,' Aphrodite's daughter (201); this looks like her own invention too.
36 Norsa 1937: 8–15, second century; Page 1955: 35, third century.

> There take garlands, O Cyprian,
> and in golden cups nectar
> that belongs to celebration –
> pour it out gently.

Again we sense the intimacy and the confidence that the goddess will respond to a summons. It is remarkable – and I have already called attention to this above – that even the critics most hostile to Wilamowitz's general interpretation, which centres on cult-association honouring Aphrodite, are willing to find evidence of a rite here. Francis Cairns thinks that the poem may have been chorally performed![37] The garden is taken as a real garden; the θάλιαι, which regularly receive the adjective 'our' in translations, are a communal celebration (Martin West breezily speaks of a 'picnic,'[38] admittedly not a rite of much solemnity). But critics are also obliged to point out that it is a rite in an uncanny garden, in a season that is no specific season.[39] Even West must admit of the *locus amoenus* where the picnic is being held that 'we scarcely believe in such perfection in this world.'[40] Wilamowitz, as I said earlier, knew of this poem only the lines in which Aphrodite is asked to pour wine which she brings in golden cups (not, as most translations would have it, to pour wine into golden cups):[41] golden Aphrodite, who lives in a golden house (fr. 1.8) might well herself have golden cups for this ritual, but would Sappho's companions, on the other hand, take golden cups on a picnic? – if the cups belong to Sappho's companions, one has to assume transubstantiation, with the picnic cups *becoming* gold. Wilamowitz thought that the banquet was taking place in heaven.[42] This is just about right, I believe – I am reminded of Heracles in heaven participating in the θάλιαι of the immortals (*Od*. 11.603). In any case, there is no mortal but Sappho mentioned in the poem, her presence indicated by the single letter μ᾿ (= μοι) in line 1.[43] David Campbell complains that the phrase 'nectar mingled with our festivities' 'lacks Sappho's customary

---

37 Cairns 1972: 192.
38 West 1970: 317.
39 Burnett 1983: 263.
40 West 1970: 317. There are elements here that recall an actual τέμενος or sacred precinct, of course. See Barrett 1964 *ad* vv. 73–6 and the meadow from which Hippolytus picks his garland for Artemis.
41 Fragment 96.27–8 makes it clear that Aphrodite pours from golden cups (her own).
42 Wilamowitz 1913: 43 n1.
43 ὔμμε was read in the first line by Norsa in the original publication 1937: 13, but this has not found followers. She thought the poem was addressed to Cretans and that it was written during a period of exile which Sappho spent on Crete.

clarity.'[44] It does so only if we insist on introducing the adjective 'our.' Nectar belongs to the goddess and to heavenly banquets (it is united to or mixed with, i.e., is inextricably part of, them), nectar belongs in golden cups, and nectar from these cups, when shared with mortals, makes them immortal (cf. Pindar, *Ol.* 1.62–4). It is a private world. I do not mean by this the private world of women that Winkler posits when he sees 'double consciousness' in Sappho's poetry, where the garden provides an elaborate code for lesbian sexual pleasure, allowing language superficially innocent enough to get past the male censors: 'the accumulation of topographic and sensuous detail leads us to think of the interconnection of all the parts of the body in a long and diffuse act of love' (with reference to this poem).[45] I am in agreement with Winkler that the garden is not to be taken literally. Where I disagree is that I do not see Sappho's Aphrodite as merely a goddess of sexual encounter; she has a wider function in the life of the group and she commands a personal devotion that is not limited to acts of love-making, though it may certainly include them. The garden here is an imaginative garden. But it is the imaginative garden where a devotee and her divinity meet: that is why it is no earthly garden at all, as West understands.

The poem on the sherd is, in my opinion, incomplete (see Endnote). Its author was not a school boy taking dictation but a person of accomplished calligraphy who transcribed on a sherd part of a favourite poem. We have in the excerpt a scene invoking the goddess (who was undoubtedly named earlier) to a garden where she will commune intimately with Sappho. And the nectar is here as important as the immortal face in fragment 1, the Hymn to Aphrodite. There is only one other detailed garden scene in Sappho, and that is the simile that extends over three stanzas of fragment 96: here the moon pours its light over the gardens and the sea. These two passages are directly comparable. The garden of fragment 96 is unquestionably an imaginary garden, and it has always seemed to me an epiphany of the goddess at the heart of the poem, not a tasteless and uncontrolled digression in a love poem, as Page would have it.[46] We need not be as frightened as we once were to attribute to Sappho imagination rather than mere ability to report on the world around her. Most people today would, for instance, accept that 'He seems to me the equal of the gods' is an imagined, not a real scene.[47] And, as we have noticed, Sappho is good at bridging distances by imagining those she loves. The epiphany

---

44 Campbell 1967 *ad loc.*
45 Winkler 1990: 186.
46 Page 1955: 94–6.
47 Latacz 1985: 67–94.

in fragment 2 is, in a word, as real – or as imaginary – as Aphrodite's long, slow descent from heaven in her chariot across three strophes of fragment 1.[48]

The best analogues I am able to find for such poetry are in fact in great mystical poets, who use garden imagery to speak of their communion with the god they meet and are joined to. The thirteenth-century Sufi mystic Jelaluddin Rumi writes:

> Come to the orchard in Spring.
> There is light and wine,
> and sweethearts in the pomegranate flowers.
> ...
> Poles apart, I'm the color of dying, you're the color of
> being born. Unless we breathe in each other,
> there can be no garden.[49]

This strikes me as extraordinarily Sapphic – the fruit trees, wine, the nearness to death, and the communication of life in the garden. But even more arresting to my mind is the garden of St John of the Cross's poem on the Dark Night of the Soul:

> Within my flowering breast
> Which only for himself entire I save
> He sank into his rest
> And all my gifts I gave
> Lulled by the airs with which the cedars wave.
> ...
> Lost to myself I stayed
> My face upon my lover having laid
> From all endeavour ceasing
> And all my cares releasing
> Threw them amongst the lilies there to fade.[50]

---

48 C.G. Brown points out to me that the passage of Himerius (194) which gives particulars of the Ἀφροδίτης ὄργια is in all likelihood an imaginative description rather than a description of real 'rites.' The details of the wedding ceremonies are not a narration of acts that Sappho performed; Himerius is, rather, drawing on Sappho's poetic description of marriage – the introduction of Aphrodite on her chariot, for instance, is as it is in fr. 1, and the rest of Himerius' description is similarly based on verse, not on practice.
49 Tr. Moyne and Barks 1984: Quatrains 914, 921.
50 Tr. Campbell 1960: 27. Bowra 1936: 195 compares Sappho to St Teresa of Avila.

At the very least these poems show, like Sappho's, the mingling of erotic and garden language in a religious poem.

St John's poem is, I remind you, the Dark Night of the Soul; the poem in its entirety makes this apparent. I have already said that I find a sense of longing or pain in all the more substantial fragments of Sappho that we possess, with the divinity, i.e., love, also able to function as consolatory. I am thus inclined to think that something of the sort may have been operative here too: the bittersweetness everywhere evident in the other long fragments would have characterized the whole, even though what remains to us is only the sweetness. I point to the fact that if we had on a sherd only the garden scene of fragment 96 we would never guess that its context is someone who is eating out her heart (or whose heart is heavy).[51] I should like to point out too that we have an allusion to a garden in fragment 95, that the garden in this case is the banks of Acheron with their dewy lotus and that the description seems to come from a trance or dream which is combined with a death-wish. But I have another, and I believe more compelling, reason for thinking that the context of the sherd poem might be self-consolation.

There is only one piece of poetry from Greek antiquity that seems to me to show the incontrovertible influence of this poem of Sappho's. It comes from nearly a thousand years later and is by one of the great doctors of the Eastern Church in the 4th century AD, St Gregory of Nazianzus.[52]

Gregory describes how in a moment of despondency, eating out his heart (θυμὸν ἔδων), he sat alone (οἶος ἀπ' ἄλλων) in a grove and meditated. Many of the details of his poetic garden, though similar to details in Sappho's description, could be paralleled from other pictures. But there is one phrase in particular that seems to me to guarantee that his model is Sappho:

αὖραι ἐψιθύριζον ...
καλὸν ἀπ' ἀκρεμόνων κῶμα χαριζόμεναι,
καὶ μάλα περ θυμῷ κεκαφηότι. (5–7)[53]

51 On the two different understandings of βόρηται see Page 1955: 92.
52 The verbal echoes were first noticed by Q. Cataudella 1940: 199–201.
53 Text in PG 37: 755–6. (There is a direct quotation from Archilochus [19 IEG] in the poem on page 683 of the same volume.)
    Gregory had an actual garden with shady groves on his estate at Nazianzus, where he retired in AD 384: his religious poetry belongs to this period. But biography does not eliminate the existence of literary models – any poetic garden will be described to some degree in terms of the author's experience of actual gardens (see above n40).

> The breezes whispered ...
> lavishing enchantment (κῶμα) from the tips of the boughs
> on my soul though it was sorely afflicted.

Κῶμα is an unusual word and has given rise to much discussion.[54] These breezes that waft enchantment and that come from the treetops are certainly patterned on the κῶμα that in Sappho comes down from the rustling leaves of the orchard: the exact verb in line 8 of Sappho is very uncertain,[55] but Gregory's poem makes it quite certain that the verb, a compound with κατά, must govern αἰθυσσομένων δὲ φύλλων, which is thus not a genitive absolute, as many have thought. And Gregory's understanding provides, *inter alia*, an appropriate meaning for κῶμα, making the elaborate explanations of so many critics unnecessary. Burnett, for example, makes of κῶμα the torpor of *après sexe* ('the trance of desire allayed').[56] This seems to me to leave a very fundamental problem – if the assembled girls are sated and sluggish at this point in the poem, the epiphany has already occurred and the sacramental wine has been prematurely spilled before the last stanza, which is clearly the communion banquet. (I do not believe for a moment, moreover, that Sappho, of all poets, would have been coy enough to suggest that sexual satisfaction comes from the treetops.)[57] It is further remarkable that Gregory mentions Crete in his line 49; Crete is for him, like another place which he does not name but where cold and snow are not known, a never-never land. The unexpected occurrence of this place-name (the single geographical reference in his poem) again suggests Sappho, where Crete is the place whence Aphrodite is summoned (this has

---

54 Cf. Wiesmann 1972: 1–11.
55 καταγρει [καταίρει ed] 'takes hold of,' best corresponds to the traces on the sherd. Most editors have resisted it because there is no expressed object, though Turyn 1942: 308–18 approved of it (the alternatives are intransitive and cause no problem). I am inclined to think, on the basis of Gregory's poem, that the object is Sappho; Gregory supplies an *indirect* object pronoun here.
56 Burnett 1983: 273. What she envisages is something like the lethargy of Mars lying in the lap of Venus at the opening of Lucretius; what I have in mind is more like the magic of the lyre that holds Ares in a κῶμα at the beginning of Pindar's First *Pythian*. Wiesmann 1972 translates 'Benommensein,' which seems to me to give just the right sense.
57 St John's poem gives, in the phrase 'Suspended every sense with its caresses' (*todos mis sentidos suspendía* – in the stanza omitted between the two given above), and in the phrase quoted above, 'Lulled by the air with which the cedars wave' (*Y el ventalle de cedros aire daba*), a sense very close to the sense Weismann 1972 thinks correct for κῶμα; here too the enchantment seems to waft down from the branches.

often been found an embarrassment and some, like West, wish to emend it away).⁵⁸ Sappho's poem, it seems, contains a contrast between a distant home of the goddess and a present garden of encounter. Gregory's poem presents a contrast between a distant land of peace and calm and a grove where, troubled, he sits and summons his divinity: the Holy Trinity is in fact invoked in the words "Ἰλαθί μοι, βασίλεια κεδνή,' 'Be propitious to me, gracious queen' (line 119). This poet prays that his μέριμνα may cease (vv. 125–6) – 'Sois sage, ô ma Douleur, et tiens toi plus tranquille.'⁵⁹ Gregory's *Recueillement* succeeds in stilling his *douleur*. Somewhat cheered, he leaves the grove. But the effect of his poem is bittersweet.

Strange tribute from one who is reported to have ordered Sappho's works burned wherever he found them in his diocese. It suggests, at the very least, that he was deeply involved with Sappho's poetry, which he, as one of the best educated men of his century, will certainly have known well: Gregory is extraordinarily adept at following the school models that he studied with the pagan sophist Himerius, an enthusiastic admirer and frequent paraphraser of Sappho's poetry. And it makes it even more plausible that one of his own poems is a reworking of one of hers. If the movement of Sappho's whole poem is mirrored in Gregory's, we may well have a further instance of the goddess providing, in intimate encounter, release from an oppressive and absolute present. What I most wish to emphasize, in any case, is that the religion of Aphrodite is not only personal, but that it foretokens, in its ability to instil peace or bliss, a world beyond death and pain. The goddess of the immortal smile pours nectar. I see a connection between this and the abiding sense that Sappho shows in her poetry that she will be immortal, for Aphrodite is the substance of that deathless poetry. In her belief that poetry confers immortality Sappho is a good Greek.

Sappho identifies with Helen of the *Iliad*, the Helen who is given to expressing a death-wish and at the same time knows that future generations will speak of her.⁶⁰ Time and again Sappho talks of her immortality. In fragment 55 she pities or castigates someone who, not a poet, will be unremembered and unattended in death:

58 West 1970: 316, following Schubart 1938: 299 and 303, prefers ῥήτας 'appointed.' Among those who accept Crete there is a division between Crete as the place from which the goddess comes (so the majority) and Crete as a place to which she has been known to come in the past (reading αἰ Κρήτεσσι following Lanata 1960 – so Kirkwood 1974: 114 and, apparently, Burnett, judging from her translation if not from her text).
59 Baudelaire, *Recueillement*, in *Les Fleurs du Mal*.
60 See Robbins 1990 [in this volume 108–18].

Sapphic Fragment

'Thou shalt be – Nothing.' Omar Khayyám
'Tombless, with no remembrance.' W. Shakespeare

> Dead shalt thou lie; and nought
> Be told of thee or thought,
> For thou hast plucked not of the Muses' tree.
> And even in Hades' halls
> Amidst thy fellow thralls,
> No friendly shade thy shade shall company.
>
> (tr. Thomas Hardy)

Fragment 147 is the haunting 'Someone, I say, will remember us in the future.' In the very lacunose fragment 58 Sappho appears to turn the myth of Tithonus' abduction by the Dawn to her own purpose by insisting that though her body ages and decays her voice will continue strong and unravaged by time: she exploits the traditional story, which made of the immortality a *curse* inasmuch as it was unaccompanied by the countervailing gift of youth.[61] And Aelius Aristides (193) says, 'I think you must have heard Sappho too boasting to some of those women reputed to be fortunate and saying that the Muses had made her truly blessed and enviable, and that she would not be forgotten even when she was dead.' Again we remember immortal Aphrodite and her nectar. Really, then, Sappho's ultimate consolation is her knowledge that despite pain, and even with its relief or redress (I think of Aphrodite's ability to punish Sappho's brother Charaxus and Doricha, the Egyptian prostitute who ensorcelled him [5, 151]),[62] the Muses with their attendant Graces offer the only assurances that truly matter. There is a short fragment that brings together perfectly everything I wish to say. It is number 150:

> οὐ γὰρ θέμις ἐν μοισοπόλων οἰκίᾳ
> θρῆνον ἔμμεν· οὔ κ' ἄμμι τάδε πρέποι.

It is not right that there should be lamentation in the house of those who serve the Muses. That would not be fitting for us.

We see determination to triumph over sadness. We see a community of people with a shared purpose (I take the plural to mean what it appears to

---

61 *Hom. Hymn* 5.218 mentions Tithonus' φωνὴ ... ἄσπετος.
62 On redress and justice see Giacomelli 1980: 135–42.

mean).[63] The service is to the Muses. The second part of μοισοπόλων, 'servants of the Muses' (again the compound appears to be Sappho's coinage), is from the verb πέλω/πέλομαι, (from Indo-European *q^{u}élo and thus the exact twin of *colo*,[64] the Latin verb that gives us *cultus* and 'cult'). This is the significant cult for Sappho. The divinities of whom she is the mediator are the Muses, for she is first and foremost a poet.

The Muses remain, so far as I am able to judge, the most distinctive Greek contribution to the world pantheon. Sappho served them well. And in the end the Muses took her unto themselves. Let us give the last word to Plato, as we gave the first to Aristotle:

ἐννέα τὰς Μούσας φασίν τινες· ὡς ὀλιγώρως·
ἠνίδε καὶ Σαπφὼ Λεσβόθεν ἡ δεκάτη.   (*Anth. Pal.* 9.506)[65]

Some say there are nine Muses: how careless! Look – Sappho of Lesbos is the tenth![66]

Endnote: The Sherd and its Contents

Norsa makes, in her original 1937 edition, the following puzzling statement regarding the sherd: 'Quando fu scritto era a *quattro* lati ineguali, si staccò poi l'angolo in alto a destra, e pure il margine destro dovè subire ancora un piccolo consumo per attrito, dato che spesso mancano o sono, soltanto in parte conservate le lettere finali di alcuni righi' (italics mine).[67]

She must be saying that the right-hand side of the original ostrakon was one of four sides of a trapezoid and that this long side, which extended

---

63 Maximus of Tyre, the source of the quotation, says that Sappho addresses these words to her daughter. But his words are suspect, since he is intent on adducing a parallel for another situation within a family (Socrates' death and Xanthippe). But even if he is right, ἄμμι may include people other than Kleis, Sappho's daughter.
64 'deckt sich formal genau:' Frisk 1970 *s.v.*
65 The ascription to Plato is traditional and not beyond doubt.
66 A recent article, Parker 1993, makes a number of points very similar to those presented here (see § XIII, p. 346): Sappho is primarily a poet and her poetry should not be read differently from other poetry; and her group is better called a *hetairia* than a *thiasos*, though cult and ritual may well have played a part in the activities of the group. We differ in that I am not prepared to dismiss the ancient testimonia as valueless and in that I do not feel that Sappho's 'school' is a mere fabrication of ancients and Victorians who impose male-hierarchical obsessions with control and power on women's groups (322), as though associations where the younger learn from the older were *per se* male ideas. Where there is love, there are inevitably hierarchies – both Sappho and Anacreon remind us forcefully that the beloved has power and control over the lover.
67 Norsa 1937: 9.

upwards in an unbroken line, was broken off after the ostrakon was inscribed, creating our fifth side. But if a piece was broken off from such a long right-hand side, a large triangle would be missing (it clearly is not missing, for a triangle of the sort would have taken away much more of the inscription than we have actually lost – and we can get *four* sides only by imagining the missing piece to be this sizeable triangle which if present would continue the line of the edge that now angles sharply to the left just above ψύχρο[in the sixth line of the inscription). All five lines above the line ending with ψὐχρο[are lacking letters, as many as five in the most extreme cases (lines 1 and 2 if the very first line is numbered 1a); none of the subsequent lines is deficient. The sherd, then, must originally have had the five-sided form it now has – the small piece broken off, thus eliminating two letters and a space from 1a, several letters from lines 1 and 2, and two from 3 and 4, may originally have appeared as a *sixth* side in fact.

Though the poem is not complete, the first line on the sherd (usually 1a) does not belong to the poem – apart from being incapable of satisfactory supplement to make of it the end of a preceding Sapphic stanza,[68] it contains the word κατιου[σα, not Aeolic, where we would expect κατιοι[σα. It is common to criticize this scribe for inaccuracies of transcription, but it may be said in that scribe's defence that he, or perhaps it was she, in two other places in the poem gets the similar dialect forms right: πνέοισιν, line 11 (= Attic πνέουσιν) and ἔλοισα, line 13 (= Attic ἐλοῦσα). The unimpeachably standard Greek of the first words on the sherd seem thus to be a title, or a *résumé* of something preceding.[69] It is to be noted that κατιου[σα is missing two letters. If the detached piece eliminated nothing from 1a other than the ending of κατιου[σα, there would originally have been some space left on the sherd – the line must have stopped well short of the very right-hand edge. This might be, perhaps, an added argument that the line did not belong to a preceding strophe, for the transcription on the sherd is run-on; the scribe does not elsewhere begin a new line for a new strophe as he does in line 1 (though admittedly the other strophes do not end quite so near the right-hand edge).

---

68 καράνοιθεν is both feeble and is otherwise unattested; ὠράνοθεν will not fit metrically, though οὐράνοθεν would be fine in prose.

69 Siegmann 1941: 418 suggested that the entire ostrakon was written as a 'Gedächtnishilfe,' with the first stanza in a non-poetic and abbreviated form since that stanza was better known to the scribe than was the rest of the poem. This strains credulity, but the understanding that the words preceding the first full stanza are Attic prose and somehow connected with the rest of the poem, whether as *aide-mémoire* or as title, seems to me basically correct.

It is easy to dispose of the idea that the words τούτοισι τοῖς ἑταίροις ἐμοῖς γε καὶ σοῖς 'for my companions and yours,' which follow the quotation in Athenaeus, conceal a stanza in the original that refers to Sappho's companions.[70] The line is not Aeolic (Sappho's dialect), it is not verse, and five words are in the masculine, i.e., in the wrong gender. The last letter of τούτοισι is the single thing that might suggest a lyric original, but it can also be shown that Athenaeus is wont to continue his verse quotations with prose influenced by the language of the preceding quotation.[71] Schubart thought that the added words in Athenaeus were a *résumé* of a following strophe;[72] in this he is like Siegmann, who sees line 1a as a *précis* of what precedes the first full stanza on the ostrakon.

The belief that the poem ends where the inscription on the sherd ends depends on one of a number of arguments.

1) The poem ends here because this is the last of a series of sherds on which it was inscribed and line 1a is part of the continuing inscription. But we have seen that 1a is unlikely to be part of the poem, and there is no good reason to believe that a series of sherds was used for a single poem (or for an anthology).

2) Sappho's poems in Book One contained five stanzas each (Siegmann); if we can make of 1a the vestiges of a first stanza, we get five. But apart from the improbability that 1a is not the vestige of a single earlier stanza, we cannot maintain that we should be looking for a poem complete in five stanzas. We know that Book One of Sappho, to which this poem belonged, contained 1320 lines (i.e., 330 stanzas)[73] but we do not know how many poems it contained, therefore cannot speak confidently of 'average' length. The single complete poem we possess, fr. 1, contains seven strophes.

The poem seems complete. But it is normal to introduce the name of a divinity before the last stanza of a cletic hymn. Even if this is not a formal hymn but a song that imitates a hymn, the formal invocation is appropriate; fr. 1 makes this very clear. There remains the problem of the

---

70 If this prose concealed an original verse line, the translation 'our' with θαλίαισι would of course be impossible.
71 See McEvilley 1972: 326. But the added letter, which seems to suggest that the word is poetic, is not found in all the manuscripts in any case and it could be the error of a scribe whose eye was caught by the previous θαλίαισι. It is surprising that this dative is not consistent with those that follow, which lack the -ι. It is also grounds for suspicion that the phrase is so similar to the phrase Athenaeus quotes earlier (160, τάδε νῦν ἑταίραις ταὶς ἔμαις τέρπνα κάλως ἀείσω 'I shall now sing these songs beautifully to delight my companions': see above 124).
72 See above n58.
73 P. Oxy. 1231, fr. 56 *subscriptio* (= fr. 30).

first line on the sherd for those who think the poem complete in four stanzas: the first line is then best explained as part of another poem in another dialect, from an anthology on sherds – or perhaps as the title of the whole, not of an excerpt.

[In 2004 M. Gronewald and R. Daniel brought to the attention of the classics community the text of a papyrus located in the University of Cologne that had been recovered from Egyptian mummy cartonnage (*ZPE* 147, 1–8; *ZPE* 149, 1–4). The papyrus contained fragments of three poems of Sappho, the earliest recorded texts known to date (3rd century BC). The second poem, in which Sappho addresses younger girls, contains her reflections on the loss of vitality that comes with age. This important text corroborates Emmet Robbins's contention 1) that Sappho was a leader of a group of women and 2) that the poet's consciousness of the bittersweet nature of life was central to her work. Ed.]

HERACLES, THE HYPERBOREANS, AND THE HIND: PINDAR, OL. 3

1 The Structure of the Narrative

THE Third *Olympian* tells of the olive-tree, source of the victor's crown, which Heracles brought from the land of the Hyperboreans to Zeus' precinct at Pisa. This myth includes the further information that Heracles visited the Hyperboreans when he went to fetch the hind, customarily called 'Cerynean' or 'Cerynitian' because of accounts in Callimachus and Apollodorus.[1] There is no unanimity on the question whether Pindar is telling of one or two trips on the part of Heracles. Most editors of Pindar since Boeckh assume that Heracles' trip to fetch the hind preceded that on which he brought the olive to Olympia.[2] But

First published *Phoenix* 36.4 (1982) 295–305.

1 Pindar's is the first literary version of this myth. Euripides, *Her. Fur.* 375 ff., places the labour at Oenoe (in the Argolid). Callimachus, *Hymn* 3.109, places the hind in Achaea (Cerynia). There has been much debate as to which is the earlier tradition: see Gruppe 1918: 1039–1040. The version given by Apollodorus (2.5.3) is confusing: the hind is Cerynitian but is at home at Oenoe. Pschmadt 1911: 26–7, advances the hypothesis that the hind is in origin an import from the Semitic East and that its horns represent the moon, with the Greek name concealing the Hebrew *qeren* (both 'horn' and 'ray of light'): lack of understanding of the non-Greek name led Callimachus to associate the hind with Cerynia. For a not dissimilar line of approach, see Friedländer (1907: 126 n2), who, following Curtius, thinks that the association with Cerynia was made because of the similarity of the name to the Greek word κέρας. Pschmadt eliminates the confusion in Apollodorus' account by claiming that κερυνῖτιν (MSS κερυνήτην or κερνῆτιν) is an inherited non-Greek appellation and not a geographical reference. In any case, there is no justification for speaking of the 'Cerynean' hind in the Pindaric account.
2 Boeckh 1821: 139; Dissen 1830: 47; Mezger 1880: 174; Fraccaroli 1894: 214; Gildersleeve 1885: 156; Jurenka 1894: 22; Sandys 1919: 35; Farnell 1930–2: 1.20; Kakridis 1930: 475

many others hold, implicitly or explicitly, that Heracles brought the hind back to Eurystheus and the olive-tree back to the racetrack at Olympia on the same trip.³ Illig is alone among the latter group in providing the grounds for his belief. Pindar, thinks Illig, returns with θάμβαινε (32) to the moment previously mentioned with αἴτει (17): the two verbs refer to one occasion, with αἴτει reporting the event ('der äussere Vorgang') and θάμβαινε giving its psychological motivation ('der innere Vorgang'). The wonder of the hero leads directly to his request.⁴ Following this line of argumentation one might, I suppose, further argue that the references to θυμός (25) and ἀνάγκα (28) provide an example of the familiar phenomenon of 'overdetermination': the same action is product of both an inner impulse and an external force.⁵

Illig's argument is attractive, but a heavy price must be paid for the advantage gained. Pindar stands convicted of a certain sloppiness for having fused two stories, that of the olive-tree and that of the hind, somewhat imperfectly. Tell-tale details have been left lying about carelessly, for we are told that Heracles proceeded from Arcadia, in bondage to Eurystheus, when he went for the hind (27), whereas we know that he came from Olympia for the olive (23–5).⁶ And, presumably, we must not analyze other elements in the narrative too closely. By line 26 we have learned that Heracles, having set up altars and founded the games at Olympia, wished to protect the precinct from the glare of the sun.⁷ It was on this occasion (τότ', 25) that he set out to the land of the Hyperboreans to acquire the tree. He must, thus, have known of the existence of the trees

---

n50; Puech 1931: 50; Fernandez-Galiano 1956: 165; van Groningen 1960: 352; Méautis 1962: 65; Hamilton 1974: 61; Nisetich 1980: 92; Jaufmann 1977–8: 35 n14; Lehnus 1981: 66 (with reservations).

3 Before Boeckh: Heyne 1798: 12. After Boeckh: Mommsen 1852: 14; van der Kolf 1923: 39; Wilamowitz 1922: 238; Illig 1932: 58 n2, 66 n2; Fehr 1936: 37–9; Guthrie 1950: 76; Segal 1964: 235; Devereux 1966: 295; Duchemin 1970: 81; Arrighetti 1981: 89.

4 Illig 1932: 66 n2.

5 Cf. Dodds 1951: 16

6 In the sequence given by Apollodorus (2.7.2), the killing of Augeas, necessary preliminary to the establishment of the games, is subsequent to the completion of the twelve labours. We cannot assume, however, as does Mezger 1880, that Pindar knew the events of Heracles' career in the order to which we have become accustomed. Heyne (above n3, *ad* 29 ff.) realizes that if there is a single trip it presupposes a sequence unlike the familiar one: 'post ludos aetos ad Cervam aeripedem capiendam profectus est: qui fuit proximus ab Augea labor secundum nostrum; diversa narrant alii.'

7 And of the full moon, according to the scholiast on 19–20 (Drachmann *Scholia* 1.115).

and this is most easily accounted for if we assume that he had been among the Hyperboreans on a previous occasion.

Kakridis has called attention to a difficulty in the two-trip hypothesis (above n2). We are forced to assume that δέξατ᾽ (27) functions as a pluperfect and mentally to supply a ποτέ, the usual sign in Pindar that an aorist introduces an anterior stage of the narrative. But the problem is more apparent than real. The pluperfect, never common in Greek, is all but non-existent in Pindar,[8] who is generally content to use the simple aorist of past action and to supply other temporal indicators to locate events in a narrative in relation to each other. In this case ἐλθόντ᾽ Ἀρκαδίας ἀπὸ δειρᾶν ... εὖτέ νιν (27–8) is an elaborate specifying phrase that clearly shows this to be not the occasion of the founding of the games but an earlier trip.

The ancients knew a division of the exploits of Heracles into ἆθλοι, performed at the behest of Eurystheus, and πράξεις undertaken voluntarily.[9] This division corresponds nicely to a distinction between the ἀνάγκα of the quest for the hind and the θυμός-prompted voyage for the tree. And these two trips provide a parallel with the normal Pindaric progression of the victor from πόνος (analogous to ἀνάγκα) to the victory in which he can indulge his θυμός (cf., e.g., Nem. 7.74, εἰ πόνος ἦν, τὸ τερπνὸν πλέον πεδέρχεται). On another level the two trips correspond to the poet's own progression from ἀνάγκα to θυμός in the course of his song. The first thirteen lines of the poem are a prayer for grace amidst the sense of compulsion (χρέος, 7) generated by the crowns that demand praise of the victor.[10] Grace and joy are present subsequently in the return of Heracles (ἵλαος, 34) and in the feast which the poet's own θυμός (38) now prompts him to celebrate.

In Pindar's narrative, then, ἤδη γάρ (19) introduces the occasion on which Heracles decided to obtain the olive-tree for Olympia. This ἤδη γάρ is picked up by δὴ τότ᾽ (25), a reference to the same occasion and a marker that, conjoined with ἤδη γάρ, binds 19–26 into a unit. What is subsequent in the narrative is anterior in time, i.e., is an earlier visit of which the narration ends at σταθείς (32). ἵμερος (33) harks back to θυμός (25): what intervenes is a digression that introduces (a) the earlier visit in pursuit

---

8 κέκρυπτο, Ol. 6.54, is, I think, the only instance.
9 The division between voluntary and involuntary is given by Pausanias (3.17.3) as part of a description of the Temple of Athena Chalcioecus (ca 500 BC). Robert (1921: 429) thinks the distinction goes back to Pherecydes.
10 On this motif, see Schadewaldt 1966: 20 [278] n1. Arrighetti (1981: 90–1) calls attention to the parallel between the poet and Heracles, both of whom act to enhance the Olympic victory.

of the hind, and (b) Taygete's dedication of the animal on a still earlier occasion. But lines 32–4 have bothered commentators. Hamilton (above n2) finds that τόθι (32) with its reference to χθόνα (31) and the first trip is confounded by τῶν (33), which appears to continue the reference to the sighting of the trees on the trip for the hind, but is found, as the sentence unfolds, to refer to a second trip, since the racecourse did not exist on the earlier visit. Lehnus (above n2) finds that τῶν, if taken to refer to the second trip, introduces 'un violento calo cronologico.' I detect neither confusion nor violence. The article in Pindar is regularly a hinge. Most frequently it opens a door onto the past (e.g., τάν, 13), but the door can also swing forward and propel the story ahead. In this passage τάν (31) moves the narrative from the point most remote in time (Taygete's dedication) to Heracles' first visit to the Hyperboreans while τῶν (33) advances it a step further to the time of the second trip. And the two references to desire (ἵμερος and θυμός) secure the backward reference of 33 to 25 before mention of the racetrack corroborates it.

The sentence δὴ τότ᾽ ἐς γαῖαν πορεύεν θυμὸς ὥρμα / Ἰστρίαν νιν (25–6) has a pivotal position in the narrative. ἵμερος (33) refers back to it, closing a ring. But this sentence itself closes a ring which began at 14, for Ἰστρίαν νιν clearly picks up Ἴστρου ἀπὸ ... παγᾶν (14). The extended backward movement of the myth is temporarily broken by a return to the point of departure. This is something not without parallel in Pindar.

H.J. Rose observed that in the Seventh *Olympian*, 'the myth of Helios' acquisition of Rhodes and of the birth of Athena are thrust into ... Apollo's advice to Tlepolemus,' i.e., that lines 34–76 are a sort of digression in the structure of the poem.[11] We have something remarkably similar in the Third *Olympian*, with a digression that also includes two distinct steps backwards. In the Seventh *Olympian* the digression which begins at ἔνθα (34) comes after the story of Tlepolemus, itself contained within the verbal frame Ἀσίας ... νᾶσον πέλας / ἐμβόλῳ ... Ἀργείᾳ σὺν αἰχμᾷ (18–19, mention of Argos and periphrastic description of Rhodes) and Λερναίας ἀπ᾽ ἀκτᾶς ... ἐς ἀμφιθάλασσον νομόν (33, oracular description of Argos and Rhodes). In the Third *Olympian* (26), the story of the olive-tree is interrupted by a digression, introduced by ἔνθα which likewise includes two earlier events – Heracles' first visit to the Hyperboreans and, still more remote in time, Taygete's dedication of the animal to Orthosia. In both poems the receding perspective, slightly foreshortened by a verbal

11 Rose 1931: 159. Rose actually claims that the digression is lines 32–77, but this is surely just a slip – it begins at 34. ἔνθα is not part of the oracle: see Verdenius 1972: 16 (108).

echo, moves insistently back to an ἀρχή. In the Seventh *Olympian* the poet dwells expansively on the earliest episode in the triptych (the marriage of Rhodes and the Sun) whereas in the Third he gives the ἀρχή (Taygete's dedication) only briefly. But the poems are alike in their sustained backward motion followed by an abrupt return to the present. There are other poems (e.g., *Pyth.* 4) where the poet cuts short a long narrative to return to the addressee, other poems (e.g., *Pyth.* 3) where extended movement backwards is followed by a corresponding forward progression and the closing of many rings. *Olympians* 3 and 7 are unique in having a dominant central section, essentially tripartite, which moves slowly backward and then leaps forward.[12] In no other poem is the backward movement so pronounced. And in both poems the most distant point in the past is connected in a particular way with the opening of the poem. The wedding of Rhodes and the Sun in the Seventh *Olympian* recalls the wedding-scene of the proem. Taygete's appearance in the Third *Olympian* is hard to explain until we remember that she is genealogically linked to the Tyndarids and Helen, with whom the poem opens.[13]

2 The Stories

There are three myths: (a) Heracles' acquisition of the trees, (b) Heracles' labour, (c) Taygete's votive-offering.

(a) We have no other account of Heracles' winning of the olive for Olympia and so no way of knowing with certainty whether this story was current in Pindar's time or was an invention of the poet's, as some

---

12 In Bacchylides 11 there is regressive movement through three episodes (foundation of the sanctuary, madness of the maidens, departure of Proetus from Argos for Tiryns), but the return ἀπ' ἀρχᾶς (65) is effected in a leisurely fashion.

13 See M.-W. frs 169, 175 (with apparatus), 199.8. Apollodorus (1.7.3 and 1.9.5) accepts a different tradition, making Tyndareus a descendant of Aeolus. There is a good deal of confusion regarding Tyndareus' ancestry (see Frazer 1921: 174 *ad* 3.10.4). The connection between Taygete and the Tyndaridae is the earliest version we know and it appears to receive special attention in the Catalogue.

The Tyndaridae restore Helen to Sparta after her abduction to Athens by Theseus: this rescue is, in fact, the only incident in Helen's biography in which she is associated with her brothers. The scholiast (Drachmann *Scholia* 1.120–1) says that Taygete dedicated a hind with gilded antlers to Artemis for her help after escaping abduction by Zeus. There *is* a remarkable similarity between these stories of unsuccessful abduction: on the 'schéma mythique caractéristique des mythes ... du viol' see Calame 1977a: 281–5.

ὀρθώσαις of the opening (3) seems to find an echo in Ὀρθωσίας (30) but I am unable to see any connection other than verbal.

have thought (e.g., Wilamowitz, above n3). I suspect that the story is not original with Pindar.

Cazzaniga claims that Heracles, the olive, the hind, and the games are on the early staters of Caulonia (550–480 BC).[14] These show on the obverse a naked archaic male figure, right arm raised and holding a branch, left arm extended and bearing a small figure running, in the right field an antlered deer. These are the emblems of *O1*. 3 and, says Cazzaniga, demonstrate that the mythical material was not new with Pindar. It is noteworthy too that Herodotus (4.34.2) mentions that an olive-tree was seen to grow over the tombs of the 'Hyperborean' maidens in the shrine of Artemis on Delos. This may have been connected with the notion that the tree was Hyperborean in origin and the gift of this northern people. Had Pindar wanted to produce an original aetiology that brought from the land of the Hyperboreans a tree whose foliage was used to crown victors in the Greek contests he could have claimed that the Delphic laurel was identical with that worn by Apollo's devotees (*Pyth.* 10.40). He does not,[15] nicely as it might have served his purpose in a poem where he is concerned, as Köhnken has demonstrated, to show the continuity, not the discrepancy, between the victor and the Hyperboreans.[16] It looks as though Pindar exploited the connection between the olive and the Hyperboreans in the Third *Olympian* because it was already to hand.

Heimsoeth was, I believe, the first to suggest that in telling the story of Heracles' winning of the olive for Olympia we have the poet's correction of an old tradition in which the hero behaved badly towards this pious folk, wresting their precious tree from them against their will.[17] The phrases πείσαις λόγῳ (16) and πιστὰ φρονέων (17) gain point if this insistence rebuts an incorrect version. πειθοῖ καὶ οὐ βίᾳ is the comment of the scholiast (Drachmann *Scholia* 1.113), who is aware of the special emphasis the poet places on the peaceful acquisition of the tree. The problem of presenting the savage Heracles of tradition is frequent enough in Pindar, who has to come

14 Cazzaniga 1968: 371–8. For an alternative see Kraay 1976: 168–9, 174.
15 The laurel brought from Tempe to Delphi in the festival called the Septerion (var. Stepterion), put Plutarch (*De mus.* 1136B) and Aelian (*Var. Hist.* 3.1) in mind of the Hyperboreans, but they do not claim it came thence. The earliest temple at Delphi, built of laurel from Tempe, was transported to the Hyperboreans (see Pindar *Pae.* 8.63 with Snell's supplements). For other examples of trees in sacred precincts propagated from trees elsewhere see Williams 1978: 16.
16 Köhnken 1971: 154–87.
17 Heimsoeth 1847: 6. His view is shared by, *inter al.*, Jurenka (above n2); Dornseiff 1921: 126; Bowra 1964: 302; Huxley 1975: 16.

to terms with Heracles' murder of his children (*Isth.* 3/4.79–82), Heracles' fight with Poseidon, Hades, and Apollo (*Ol.* 9.28–39), and Heracles' brutal attacks on Diomedes and Geryon (fr. 169 Snell-Maehler).[18]

(b) In the case of the earlier trip for the hind to the land of the Hyperboreans we have a similar problem. The pursuit of the hind is a regular labour, but did Pindar transfer this from the Peloponnese to the North? A black-figured amphora in Boulogne shows, apparently, Heracles departing from the Garden of the Hesperides, represented by a fruit-bearing tree beside which stand two maidens and under which stands a deer.[19] It is not an exact parallel for the version in the poem: the genitals show that the animal is male,[20] and Hesperides are not Hyperboreans.[21] But the amphora may reveal the existence of a tradition in which Heracles went for the animal to a paradise at the ends of the earth and in this story too there may be little Pindaric invention.

For this second myth, there are vase-paintings which make it clear that Heracles fought with a divinity for possession of the hind. Devereux has collected some of the evidence and proposes that, since the story of Heracles' violence was well known, the poet introduced this story with a

---

18 See Dornseiff 1933: 72; Huxley 1975: 17–18.
19 Reproduced as 'Herakles und die kerynitische Hindin' in Meuli 1960 Chapter 4 and 1975 Tafel 38 facing page 810.
20 The animal of Heracles' labour is sometimes female, sometimes male. Brommer (1972: 24) thinks that the artists of three famous series of metopes in the fifth century, on the Athenian Treasury at Delphi, on the Temple of Zeus at Olympia, and on the Theseum at Athens, are portraying a stag. Cf. the relief in archaizing style from the late first century BC (Meuli 1975 Tafel 37 facing page 799), no doubt modelled on the fifth-century Greek examples: in this instance, where the relief has not been damaged, the animal is undoubtedly male. Pindar stresses the sex of the animal in his version: the relative pronoun ἄν would be sufficient to indicate the gender of ἔλαφον (29), but Pindar adds the adjective θήλειαν, showing that he is aware it is an extraordinary creature. The scholiast's comment here (Drachmann *Scholia* 1.120), that poets commonly give horns to the female, seems inadequate. Some see in the horned hind a significant link with the north, reindeer being the only well-known species of *Cervidae* in which the female has antlers: see Burkert 1979: 94, who gives Meuli as his source. Ridgeway suggested in 1894: 14–15 that the animal was a reindeer, but his suggestion is, curiously, ignored by both Meuli and Burkert. Taygete appears to have dedicated the hind in Arcadia, her birth-place (Apollodorus 3.10.1), whence Heracles' pursuit began; but the hind seems to be of northern origin and to be returning, in its flight to the Hyperboreans, whence it came.
21 Though Apollodorus (2.5.11) says that these apples were among the Hyperboreans. Brommer (1942: 107) thinks that the painter of this vase was mistakenly conflating motifs that belong to different stories. Schefold (1978: 101–2) accepts a northern origin for the hind but believes that this vase shows Cerynean nymphs, not Hesperides.

deliberately ambiguous δέξατ' (27).²² But δέκομαι. the regular word for 'welcome' in Pindar (cf. πανδόκῳ, 17) is hardly ambiguous. There are versions on the vases that show Artemis acquiescing, possibly even assisting, in the performance of this labour.²³ Pindar, in this passage, is surely presenting another case in which Heracles is understood to be behaving πειθοῖ καὶ οὐ βίᾳ. The δέξατ' is not conscious ambiguity but deliberate presentation of the true version and δέκομαι should be allowed its normal Pindaric force. It is hard to imagine what possible reason Pindar might have had for conscious ambiguity in this passage in any case. There would be little point in his simply serving notice that he is aware of conflicting traditions. It would be more likely and more in keeping with his regular practice of interpreting myth by giving correct versions that he is here presenting an unequivocal account creditable to both divinity and hero.

(c) The third and earliest myth is presented succinctly and, for us at least, somewhat mysteriously. Taygete dedicated the hind to Orthosia. We cannot know whether the scholiast's Ovidian tale of the nymph's pursuit by an amorous Zeus, her metamorphosis by Artemis into a hind to escape him, and her grateful dedication of an animal with gilded horns was a folktale known to Pindar.²⁴ If it was, then we see once again a version which is silent about the discreditable elements in other contemporary versions.

The scholiasts and most modern commentators are correct, I think, in taking the Orthosia to whom the hind is given to be Artemis.²⁵ Identification of Orthia (= Orthosia) and Artemis seems to have begun at Sparta as early as the sixth century,²⁶ and the names Orthosia and Artemis are certainly coupled in Herodotus (4.87.2). It is most economical to believe that the goddess who gives Heracles the hind in the land of the Hyperboreans is the goddess to whom the animal was originally dedicated and who thus has the right to bestow her sacred animal as a gift.

---

22 Devereux 1966: 294–5. He claims that the verb may mean 'to receive as an enemy' but adduces no instance in Pindar. He argues (293) that line 28 presents an alibi which would be unnecessary unless the preceding δέξατ' suggested hostility and thus created the need to present the extenuating circumstance: Heracles pleads compulsion and therefore personal innocence for his violent act. But line 28, the εὖτε-clause, is, as we have seen, the temporal specification that identifies, in the absence of a ποτέ, the separate trip for the hind.
23 E.g., the black-figured amphora (Cat. No. B 231) in the British Museum.
24 The rape of Taygete was represented on the Amyclaean throne (Paus. 3.18.10).
25 Calame (1977a: 284) and Lehnus (1981: 61) think they are distinct divinities.
26 See Wace 1929: 282 ff.

Artemis is regularly a goddess to whom blood-sacrifice is made:[27] Artemis Orthia especially so, for Artemis Orthia is linked to the northern or Taurian Artemis to whom human sacrifice was offered (Her. 4.103.1). The Spartan shrine of Artemis Orthia, where boys were ritually scourged, had the best claim to possess the image of Artemis brought from the Taurians by Orestes (Paus. 3.16.7).[28] Since Artemis accepted a hind in place of Iphigeneia (Eur. I.A. 1587), whom she translated to the Taurians, it is tempting to see in the hind of the Hyperborean Artemis along the Danube in Pindar an animal substitute for human sacrifice. Mommsen suggested, in fact, that in this passage in the Third *Olympian* we have just such a substitute.[29] Perhaps, but any hint of human sacrifice is deeply submerged in Pindar's account. Pindar's point appears to be that there is no sacrifice at all. The gilded horns would normally foretoken the animal's death – gilding was traditionally put on the horns of sacrificial animals (cf. Pindar fr. 329 Snell-Maehler).[30] Significantly, the hind is not sacrificed but is available to Heracles when he arrives on the scene at a later date. There may be, in this, some accommodation to Acragantine sensibility and practice. There is evidence at Acragas for worship that carefully avoided blood-sacrifice, and Pindar may be respecting in the Third *Olympian*, as he certainly is in the Second, Theron's religious beliefs.[31]

---

27 See Burkert 1977: 237: 'In der Tat ist und bleibt Artemis eine Herrin der Opfer, gerade der grausamen, blutigen Opfer.'

28 See Farnell 1896: 453 n2. Other places also claimed to have this cult-statue: see Graf 1979: 33–40. At Tyndaris in Sicily ritual abuse replaced human sacrifice, but at Halai in Attica blood was still drawn.

   Northern Apollo has similar associations with human sacrifice. The scholiast on *Ol*. 10.19 (Drachmann *Scholia* 1.316) says that Cycnus built a temple for Apollo at Pagasae out of human skulls. On Cycnus as priest of Hyperborean Apollo see Farnell 1907: 272–3. See too Krappe 1942: 353–70 on the connection between swans and Hyperborean Apollo.

29 Mommsen (above n3); so too Gildersleeve 1885: 160. Henrichs (1981: 203–7) warns against seeing in stories of animal substitution proof of increased moral sensitivity. After all, Iphigeneia, who is spared through the substitution of an animal, becomes the slaughterer of human victims among the Taurians.

30 Cf. Onians 1954: 106, 236.

31 See Demand 1975: 352–3. The hind dedicated with an inscription to a goddess (ἄν ... Ταϋγέτα ... ἔγραψεν, 29–30) is a γραπτὸν ζῷον (for γραπτός = 'with an inscription' see, e.g., Achaeus *TrGF* 20 F 19.3). Empedocles says that γραπτὰ ζῷα were offered to divinity in the Golden Age when there was as yet no blood-sacrifice (Diels-Kranz 31 B 128). The but half-civilized Thessalians will have noted, on the other hand (*Pyth*. 10.33), that the Hyperboreans sacrificed hecatombs.

3 Acragas and Rhodes

The Third and Seventh *Olympians* share a structure and a mood. In both there is a prolonged regressive movement and three myths; in both there is a remarkable emphasis on the goodwill governing the relation between gods and men.[32] We are reminded that there is a close connection between the cities of the victors, Theron and Diagoras.

Gela, the parent-city of Acragas, was a Rhodian foundation (Her. 7.153; Thuc. 6.4.3). Memorable lines in the Second *Olympian* (8–12) speak of the arrival in the Promised Land in the West of the Emmenidae, the clan to which Theron of Acragas and his brother Xenocrates belonged:

> καμόντες οἳ πολλὰ θυμῷ
> ἱερὸν ἔσχον οἴκημα ποταμοῦ, Σικελίας τ' ἔσαν
> ὀφθαλμός, αἰὼν δ' ἔφεπε μόρσιμος,
>   πλοῦτόν τε καὶ χάριν ἄγων
> γνησίαις ἐπ' ἀρεταῖς.

Theron, we know from the Second *Olympian*, traced his line back to Thersander, son of the Polyneices who fell with the Seven against Thebes and bulwark of the expedition of the Epigoni, the Argives who later sacked the Thebes their fathers had failed to take. This Thersander, son of an Argive princess (daughter of Adrastus) and married to an Argive (daughter of Amphiaraus), died in the first Trojan expedition, according to Proclus' *résumé* of the *Cypria* (Allen 5.104). His Argive descendants, the Adrastidae (*Ol.* 2.45), established themselves in Rhodes, much in the manner of Tlepolemus, who also sailed from the Argolid (*Ol.* 7.18–19, 33). Didymus, in fact, calls attention to Theron's Argive patrimony (Drachmann *Scholia* 1.107): he claims that the Theoxeny, which the scholiasts take as the occasion of the Third *Olympian*,[33] was an inheritance from Argos. The migrations of the Emmenidae brought them from Thebes and Argos to Rhodes and thence to Gela and Acragas.

Pindar is our best source for the early history of the Emmenid house. He must have got his information directly from Theron[34] and so will already have been contemplating Rhodian history in 476 BC, twelve years before

---

32 On the mood of *Olympian* 3 see esp. Segal 1964: 228–52. The four poems for Hieron of Syracuse are, by contrast, remarkably sombre.

33 Correctly, I believe; I hope to return to this question elsewhere. [See 'The Divine Twins in Early Greek Poetry' 238–53 of this volume.]

34 van Compernolle 1959: 380.

the Seventh *Olympian*. Lines 8–12 of the Second *Olympian* are echoed in fr. 119 (Snell-Maehler), part of an encomium for Theron and generally ascribed, like *Olympians* 2 and 3, to 476:

> ἂν δὲ 'Ρόδον κατῴκισθεν ...,
> ἔνθεν δ' ἀφορμαθέντες, ὑψηλὰν πόλιν ἀμφινέμονται,
> πλεῖστα μὲν δῶρ' ἀθανάτοις ἀνέχοντες,
> ἕσπετο δ' αἰενάου πλούτου νέφος.

It is fascinating to see in the attendant 'cloud of wealth' (ἕσπετο ... πλούτου νέφος) not only an echo of the contemporary αἰὼν δ' ἔφεπε ... πλοῦτον ἄγων but an anticipation of the clouds of the Seventh *Olympian*, so crucial to the story of the Heliadae in that poem. The Emmenidae, like the Heliadae, lived under a cloud – perhaps one which had followed them from Rhodes.[35] Rhodian history was known and appreciated at Acragas and Pindar could hear it there.[36]

Pindar's choice of Heracles as the principal subject of the mythical portion of the Third *Olympian* does not, as is sometimes suggested (e.g., Duchemin [above, note 3]), show his indifference to local tradition and choice of material of indiscriminate applicability. He was clearly well informed about the history of Theron's house and his city. And part of the spiritual legacy of the Acragantines included the poetry of Pisander of Rhodes, probably the first to organize the canonical cycle of the ἆθλοι of Heracles.[37] The earliest of the great succession of temples that have made the remains of Acragas among the most splendid of antiquity was a Temple of Heracles (ca 520).[38] The Acragantines had, in fact, an unusually strong claim on Heracles: as self-conscious Dorians[39] they could style themselves Heraclids (descendants of Hyllus) in the traditional manner. And there

---

35 Cf. Young (1968: 89 n1). The Acragantine cult of bloodless sacrifice seems to have come from Rhodes; cf. *Ol*. 7.47.
36 The famous decadrachms minted at Acragas 412–10 BC appear to contain a reference to Rhodian history. The traditional Sicilian motif of *quadriga* with Nike-figure has been adapted to show a young male god (no Nike) driving a chariot across the vault of heaven (the ground-line has been suppressed and the chariot-wheels put on a slant). The coin may well show Helios driving through the sky: see Seltman 1948: 1–10, Kraay 1976: 226.
37 Huxley 1969: 101 ff. Friedländer (1907: 45–59) even claims that it was Rhodian epic and the importance it gave to Heracles that were responsible for bringing a non-Boeotian hero to Thebes.
38 See Waters 1974: 10.
39 Diodorus (11.48.8 and 49.3–4) says that in 476 Theron quelled a revolt by the citizens of Himera and repopulated the city with Dorians.

were doubtless among them descendants of another son of Heracles – the Tlepolemus who, the Seventh *Olympian* tells us, was the *oikistes* of Rhodes.

The Acragantines, and in particular their ruling princes, were proud of their Rhodian heritage and kept it alive. They brought their traditions to the attention of Pindar when he was at the Sicilian courts in 476. When Pindar was composing for Theron in the *annus mirabilis* of *Olympians* 1–3 he was already meditating on matters to which he would return twelve years later at the other end of the Greek world.[40]

---

40 I am grateful to Professor L.E. Woodbury and Mr C.G. Brown for much illuminating discussion. This paper also profited from the helpful comments of Professors D.E. Gerber, W.J. Slater, and of a *Phoenix* referee.

INTIMATIONS OF IMMORTALITY: PINDAR, OL. 3.34–5

In several of Pindar's epicinian odes, the victory seems to be celebrated as part of a wider festival. In the Eleventh *Pythian* we find in the proem a convocation of local Theban divinities at a shrine for a regular ceremony to which a victory-celebration for Thrasydaeus has been added.[1] The Ninth *Olympian* was sung at Opus at a festival of Ajax, whose altar the victor crowned.[2] The Fourteenth *Olympian* seems to be a processional-hymn to a temple of the Graces in Orchomenus.[3] And commentators have not infrequently supposed that the Fifth *Pythian* forms part of a festival of the Carneian Apollo at Cyrene, mentioned in lines 79–81.[4]

The Third *Olympian* has traditionally been thought to belong to a theoxeny of the Dioscuri at Acragas. The scholiast believed this to be the case and, indeed, his opinion is enshrined on our manuscripts, where we find εἰς θεοξένια in the title of the poem. Certainly *Olympians* 2 and 3, for Theron of Acragas, honour the same victory. The longer of the poems, the Second *Olympian*, gives the impression of being the more private of the two, while the shorter, the Third *Olympian*, seems to be the more public. These two poems are, in this, much like *Pythians* 4 and 5, also composed to honour a single chariot-victory. Here too the longer poem addresses more personal issues while the shorter belongs to a great civic occasion.

First published in D.E. Gerber (ed.), *Greek Poetry and Philosophy: Studies in Honour of L.E. Woodbury* (Chico CA 1984) 219–25.

1 See Burton 1962: 61.
2 Gildersleeve 1885: 201, 210–11.
3 Wilamowitz 1922: 150–1.
4 Burton 1962: 135.

The opinion that the Third *Olympian* is for performance at a theoxeny was challenged by Hermann Fränkel in 1961.[5] He had, in fact, been anticipated in this view a century and a half earlier by Heyne, who likewise took the inscription of the title to be an unwarranted inference from internal evidence.[6] Heyne's suggestion remained ignored by the nineteenth-century commentators, but Fränkel's has met with a measure of acceptance: the current editors of the Teubner text, for instance, now bracket the inscription εἰς θεοξένια in the title of the poem.

Fränkel claimed that the Dioscuri are honoured in the first line of the Third *Olympian* only as patrons of athletic contests, not because the occasion is a festival in their honour. There is a very real difficulty with this explanation. It is, quite simply, the presence of Helen, with her brothers. Helen has no part to play in athletic contests, but she is regularly associated with Castor and Pollux at theoxenies, as the close of Euripides' *Helen* makes clear:

> ὅταν δὲ κάμψῃς καὶ τελευτήσῃς βίον
> θεὸς κεκλήσῃ καὶ Διοσκόρων μέτα
> σπονδῶν μεθέξεις ξένιά τ' ἀνθρώπων πάρα
> ἕξεις μεθ' ἡμῶν. (1666–9)[7]

The scholiast's opinion may be a deduction from the text, as Fränkel thought, but it is the most reasonable one. That theoxenies for the Tyndarids were regular events at Acragas appears to be implied in lines 39–40. Aristarchus and Didymus maintained that the Dioscuri were held in special honour in the city (Drachmann *Scholia* 1.105–6). We have no incontrovertible evidence for this, but again it is a reasonable assumption on the basis of the poem. The popular 'Temple of Dioscuri' to be seen in Agrigento today has no connection with the twins: this name is modern, just as the remains themselves are a 'delightful piece of 19th century landscape gardening.'[8] But the best-observed temple in Agrigento, the so-called 'Temple of Concord' from the fifth century, may originally have been a temple of the Dioscuri.[9] In the Middle Ages it was a church of Saints Peter and Paul, who are frequently portrayed in art as the Dioscuri.[10] Continuity of

---

5 Fränkel 1961: 394–5.
6 Heyne 1807: 36–7.
7 See the edition of Kannicht 1969: 2.432–3 for discussion with references literary and artistic, and Calame 1977a: 1.347 n341.
8 Guido 1967: 127.
9 See Gruben 1976: 304. For a different identification see Alzinger 1974: 295–9.
10 Lowrie 1947: 148.

cult is a well-known phenomenon throughout the Mediterranean, and it is intrinsically likely that the twin pillars of the Christian Church should have taken as their temple a site sacred to the Dioscuri.

The Third *Olympian* was in all probability performed at a public festival of a sort that was frequent at Acragas.[11] Most commentators before Fränkel assumed that in the ἐς ταύταν ἑορτάν of line 34 there is a reference to the occasion of performance.[12] Fränkel, disbelieving in the theoxeny, claimed that this phrase refers to the Olympic festival, and in this belief he has found followers.[13] In favour of Fränkel's interpretation it should be pointed out that Pindar commonly uses ἑορτά to refer to festivals at which athletic contests are held: of nine instances of the word, seven have an association with games (*Ol.* 5.5, *Ol.* 6.69, *Ol.* 10.58, *Pyth.* 8.66, *Nem.* 9.11, *Nem.* 11.27, fr. 193) while one refers to a religious festival unconnected with games (*Ol.* 6.95) and one case, the one under discussion here, is disputed. It should also be observed, however, that in the majority of cases where ἑορτά refers to a festival which includes contests, Pindar distinguishes between the ἄεθλοι or ἀγῶνες and the ἑορτά of which the contests form a part.[14] The religious sense of ἑορτά remains paramount.

It is neat and tempting, given this distinction, to assume that ἑορτάν (34) refers to the Olympic festival in its religious aspect and that ἀγῶνα (36) refers to the athletic competition. So considered, lines 34–8 (καί νυν ... διφρηλασίας) would continue the mention of Olympia, to which we have returned from the Hyperboreans of the myth with δρόμου / ἵππων

---

11 Nilsson (1906: 419) warns against thinking that a cult of the Dioscuri was ever more than a house-cult. He thinks that the Third *Olympian* was meant for private performance. Nilsson is much influenced in this by his general view of the Dioscuri (see Nilsson 1967: 1.409 and 1949: 34–5) as Minoan-Mycenaean tutelary household *daimones*. Burkert (1977: 324–5), on the other hand, stresses their Indo-European origins and their similarity to the Aśvins of the Vedic myth. His arguments are extremely compelling. The Aśvins are the twin horsemen like the Dioscuri (cf. *Pyth.* 1.66), performing many similar functions (see Oldenburg 1923: 213–14). They are, in particular, associated with celestial bodies, especially the sun. E. Bethe, *RE* 5.1 (1903) 1090–1, sees the solar connection of Castor and Pollux in *Nem.* 10.49, where the Dioscuri, because of their connection with Παμφάης (a name for Helios), continue to visit his descendants. Interesting too the association of the Dioscuri with the daughters of Leucippus, Φοίβη and Ἰλάειρα (for ἰλάειρα as an epithet of the moon cf. Empedocles, Diels-Kranz B 40.

On theoxenia as public feasts, see Gill 1974: 122–3.
12 E.g., Gildersleeve 1885: 160; Wilamowitz 1922: 237; Farnell 1930–2: 2.29.
13 E.g., Jaufmann 1977–8: 39; Lehnus 1981: 67; Köhnken 1983b: 59, n44.
14 E.g., *Ol.* 5.5–6, ἑορταῖς θεῶν μεγίσταις / ... ἀέθλων τε ... ἀμίλλαις; *Ol.* 6.69, ἑορτάν τε ... πλειστόμβροτον τέθμον τε ... ἀέθλων; *Ol.* 10.57–8, πενταετηρίδ᾽ ... ἑορτὰν σὺν Ὀλυμπιάδι; *Nem.* 9.11–12, νέαισί θ᾽ ἑεορταῖς / ἰσχύος τ᾽ ἀνδρῶν ἀμίλλαις.

φυτεῦσαι (33–4), and would recapitulate, by mention of the ἑορτά and the ἀγών, the regular distinction between festival and games already suggested by μεγάλων ἀέθλων ... κρίσιν καὶ πενταετηρίδ᾽ (21). Nonetheless it is more likely that those critics are right who take ταύταν ἑορτάν to refer to the theoxeny. Given the religious sense of the word in Pindar, and given the likelihood, established on the basis of the opening line of the poem, that the occasion is a theoxeny, it is most natural to assume that 'this religious celebration' (ταύταν ἑορτάν) means the one which the audience hearing the Third *Olympian* was attending as it listened. Fränkel gives *Nem.* 5.37 as a parallel instance of an Olympian visiting the site of the games.[15] But the parallel is not compelling, for in this passage the crucial demonstrative pronoun is lacking. Bundy has called attention to the common Pindaric practice of referring to the scene of celebration by means of the demonstrative pronoun.[16] Further, καί νυν is regularly used by Pindar to refer to the actual time and place of the singing of the ode (cf. *Ol.* 7.13, *Ol.* 10.78, *Pyth.* 11.7).[17] If the reference were to Olympia and not to Acragas, καί νυν would refer to a generalized present (now as opposed to the time of the foundation of the games), whereas if the ἑορτά is the festival being celebrated in the song, καί νυν means, more naturally, 'now, on this occasion of festivity.' And if we set any store by Mezger's theory of the importance of recurrent words in Pindar,[18] we may in addition find some significance in νίσεται of the line in question. In line 10 songs come (νίσονται) to honour the victor, who has just been named. Heracles and the Dioscuri come to honour the victor too. This advent-motif, coming immediately before and after the myth, frames it exactly as the κλέος-motif frames the myth of Pelops in the First *Olympian* (23, 93).

Wilamowitz remarked that Pindar's claim that Heracles entrusted the administration of the games at Olympia to the Dioscuri (36) is a genial invention of the poet's.[19] A plausible reason for Pindar's making this connection might be his desire, given the importance of the twins at Emmenid Acragas (1, 40), to provide an additional reason for their presence at the

---

15 Fränkel 1961: 396.
16 Bundy 1962a: 23 n53. The pronoun most frequently used is ὅδε. For οὗτος = ὅδε, see Slater 1969a: 401–2. That the scene of celebration is not Olympia is clear from line 9: τᾶς ἄπο shows that the performance is *'procul ab Olympia'* (Boeckh 1821: 135).
17 Cf. also *Pyth.* 4.42. καὶ νῦν is a common formula in cletic hymns: cf. Sappho 1.25, Soph. *OT* 167. Theocritus 15.143–4 is remarkably similar: Adonis comes ἴλαος ... καὶ νῦν to a great public festival (with *trapezômata*) celebrated by a monarch.
18 Mezger 1880: 36–41. Young (1970: 27) considers the theory 'the greatest single aid for an understanding of a Pindaric ode.'
19 Wilamowitz 1922: 238.

victory celebration: they are welcome participants in the city's rejoicing because (γάρ, 36) they have an official connection with the games where the victory was won. This connection is given as closer and more specific than their general patronage at all athletic events.

But Castor and Pollux are present in the poem not simply because they attended the celebration, as Aristarchus seemed to think. This is poetry, not the Court Circular, and Pindar is a poet, not merely a reporter. Details are neither irrelevant nor extrinsic to his artistic purpose. What, then, is the particular reference of the Dioscuri to Theron?

There seems, from what we learn in Pindar, our only source, to have been a remarkable harmony between the tyrant of Acragas and his brother Xenocrates, who were, so far as we know, both alive and present at the performance of *Olympians* 2 and 3. In 490 Pindar, writing of Thrasybulus, son of Xenocrates, finds the boy outstanding by both his father's and his uncle's standard (*Pyth.* 6.45–6). In the Second *Olympian*, though Theron is ostensibly honoured, we learn that κοιναὶ Χάριτες have brought victory ὁμόκλαρον ἐς ἀδελφεόν (49–50). This may suggest that Theron's brother was equally successful, or it may mean that the victory at the Isthmus, of uncertain date,[20] was considered a victory of both brothers together.[21] The latter is rendered the more plausible by the curious statement in the Second *Isthmian* (28–9) that Theron and Xenocrates had shared the honours at Olympia, presumably in 476, as we know of no other Olympic victory of the Emmenids. In the Second *Isthmian* (35–40) Pindar appears to allude to the name of Xenocrates, who surpassed all others in hospitality (ξενία and κρατέω in the sense of ὑπερέχω 'to surpass' or 'be superior'). Pindar here mentions the ξενίαν ... τράπεζαν at Acragas (40), as he does at *Ol.* 3.40. These are the only occasions on which Pindar joins ξένιος and τράπεζα, and the juxtaposition is surely not fortuitous.[22] Coming as it does directly after a reference to Theron and the Emmenids, the phrase may well contain an allusion to Xenocrates in the Third *Olympian* too: ξενίας ... τραπέζαις refers, in effect, to surpassing hospitality. This close association of the

---

20 The victory celebrated in the Second *Isthmian* is in all probability the victory at the Isthmus mentioned in the Second *Olympian* (50). The victory at Olympia mentioned in the Second *Isthmian* (23–9) is the victory of 476. The Second *Isthmian* is generally regarded as the later of the two poems, written some years after the victory it celebrates and after the death of Xenocrates.

21 van Compernolle (1959: 355) speaks of the 'victoire isthmique remportée au quadrige par Xenocratès et son frère Théron.'

22 The ξενίαν τράπεζαν of Acragas has an interesting counterpart in the φίλαν ... τράπεζαν of Syracuse (*Ol.* 1.16–17). Here too the adjective is significant, anticipating φίλαν (38), φίλια (75), φίλαν (85).

brothers is certainly noteworthy: Pindar elsewhere uses ὁμόκλαρος only of the twins Apollo and Artemis (*Nem.* 9.5), and the word is sufficiently like the phrase πότμον ἀμπιπλάντες ὁμοῖον (*Nem.* 10.57, of Castor and Pollux) to merit comment. We know nothing about the respective ages of Theron and Xenocrates. There is no reason to believe that they were twins except in what matters most for the poet, their success in the games and the immortality it conferred. But the Dioscuri are ideal emblems for these scions of the Emmenid house.[23]

The point gains some support if we consider neighbouring Syracuse. Hieron and his brother Polyzelus were, at the time of Pindar's presence in Sicily, not on the best of terms. In the year of the *Olympians* 1, 2, and 3, a war between Hieron and Theron had just been averted, a war springing from a family feud between Hieron and Polyzelus, who had taken refuge in Acragas. Direct mention of Polyzelus would have been indiscreet in Syracuse, even though Polyzelus was a Pythian victor.[24] Pindar refers to Hieron's brothers only through allusion in the First *Pythian* (48, 79) to the great military victory over the Carthaginians, when the late Gelon, founder of the dynasty at Syracuse, had led the Greek troops at Himera.[25] The reticence with regard to Hieron's living brother Polyzelus is in marked contrast to the insistence on the closeness of Theron and Xenocrates.

But there is another, more important, point. The heavenly twins come to the theoxeny in the company of that Heracles who, the myth of the poem tells us, twice visited the land of the Hyperboreans.[26] This people lives beyond the boundaries of the known world, on the shores of the encircling ocean. Their land, like that of the Ethiopians, the Garden of the Hesperides, the Isles of the Blessed, is a place unaffected by the vicissitudes of the sun, whose weary struggle with darkness characterizes the world under the vault of heaven.[27] The normal rule of suffering and age does not hold

---

23 Professor T. Martone has called my attention to an interesting parallel. In the Ducal Palace at Urbino there is a painting of Duke Federico da Montefeltro and his brother Oddantonio by Justus van Ghent, the iconography of which depends on a visual allusion to the Dioscuri. Federico and Oddantonio were, like Theron and Xenocrates, not twins after the flesh.
24 See Wade-Gery and Bowra 1928: 161–4.
25 εὑρίσκοντο (48) and παίδεσσιν ... Δεινομένεος (79) are most easily understood as referring to Hieron, the ruling tyrant, and Gelon, tyrant in 480.
26 See Robbins 1982: 295–9 [in this volume 145–56].
27 Vermeule 1979: 134. A convenient map of the northern part of this world may be found at the back of Bolton 1962: Pindar is likely to have envisaged the northland much in the manner of this map, which gives a largely traditional picture. Cf. the description in Sophocles fr. 956 Radt (870 Nauck[2]):

ὑπέρ τε πόντον πάντ' ἐπ' ἔσχατα χθονὸς

among the Hyperboreans (*Pyth.* 10.41–4; Sim. 570 *PMG*).[28] Bacchylides' Croesus was saved from death and translated to the Hyperboreans for his piety (3.58–61). Ordinary mortals could no more reach this land than they could scale heaven (*Pyth.* 10.27–30), but Perseus and Heracles were no ordinary mortals. Perseus made a single visit with Athena's guidance (*Pyth.* 10.45); Heracles made two.[29] Perseus is a type of the victor in his

---

νυκτός τε πηγὰς οὐρανοῦ τ' ἀναπτυχάς,
Φοίβου τε παλαιὸν κῆπον

This passage gives an orderly description of the outward journey: 1) the sea to the ends of the earth; 2) the place where night originates and ascends the firmament; 3) the land beyond, which is that of the Hyperboreans. In the traditional picture Rhipaean Caucasus and the Cave of the North Wind were at the end of the earth – the word Rhipaean may well come from ῥιπαί, the blasts of the North Wind. It is not clear whether Pindar places the source of the Danube near the Hyperboreans (*Ol.* 3.14) because he thinks of it as rising in the Rhipaean Caucasus as does the Don (see Bolton's map and Wilamowitz 1922: 238, n2, who points out that Pindar must have thought of the Danube as running north-south, not east-west, into the Black Sea), or because he knows that the great rivers are the children of Oceanus (Hes. *Theog.* 338 ff.) and finds it fitting that their springs should be located beside it. Stesichorus in the *Geryoneis* (7 *SLG*) puts the springs of the Tartessus near the Ocean Stream and the Island of the Hesperides. Apollonius makes the Danube a branch of the Ocean rising in the Rhipaean Caucasus at the back of the North Wind (4.282–7): see the edition of Livrea 1973: 96–7.

28 Köhnken (1971: 163–8) argues that Pindar is presenting, in the Hyperboreans of the Tenth *Pythian*, a picture of people who are immortal. This, he claims, is the meaning of the phrase φυγόντες / ὑπέρδικον Νέμεσιν (43–4). For a different interpretation, see Slater 1983: 130.

29 There is some difference of opinion with regard to the timing of Perseus' visit to the Gorgons, mentioned in *Pyth.* 10.46. Köhnken (1971: 177) places it before the visit to the Hyperboreans. This has the merit of providing a link between the two events mentioned by Pindar: Perseus is given a Hyperborean holiday as reward for his heroic deed. Burton (1962: 9) also puts the slaying of the Gorgon before the visit to the Hyperboreans, though he finds it an irrelevant detail, of no consequence to the main myth (cf. Wilamowitz 1922: 469–70). Slater (1979: 64, n5) thinks that the decapitation of Medusa is subsequent to the visit to the Hyperboreans. His reasons are formal: the myth in the Tenth *Pythian* is of a common Pindaric type, which he labels 'complex lyric,' in which the 'end of the myth is posterior to its beginning.'

Whichever came first, the killing of Medusa or the visit to the Hyperboreans, it is probable that the two episodes took place on the same trip and the the Gorgons and the Hyperboreans are neighbours (cf. Illig 1932: 92). See Bolton 1962: 181, and, for other possible instances of Pindar's knowledge of the *Arimaspea* of Aristeas, also 1962: 50, 71 ff., 127.

The myths of the Tenth *Pythian* and the Third *Olympian* function in similar fashion. In the Tenth *Pythian* Perseus returns from his visit to the north bringing back death (θάνατον φέρων are the final words of the myth). We are reminded that life and death characterize our world while those beyond its bourne are exempt from these vicissitudes. Heracles' planting of the olive-tree at Olympia, through loyalty

brief exaltation. Heracles is a type of the victor too. He could apparently visit the Hyperboreans at will – this is what the second trip implies – and he found in the land of the Hyperboreans a foretaste of the permanent beatitude of Olympus, where he later came (*Ol.* 3.36). On his second visit Heracles brought the olive-tree back to Olympia. Since Theron wears the crown of an Olympic victor, his garland is, thus, an import from this happy land[30] and a clear sign that he is, though otherwise unable to travel past the pillars of Heracles to the lands of the Ocean Stream (*Ol.* 3.44), touched by their light and so elevated to the company of the Blessed.

The scholar we are honouring has, in an important article, elucidated the great eschatology of the Second *Olympian* and shown the importance of the equinox for understanding that poem.[31] Now, the Dioscuri are the mythical emblems of the perfect, equinoctial balance of day and night which is mentioned in the Second *Olympian* (61–2), for they inhabit an eternity in which light and dark are present in precisely equal amounts (cf. *Nem.* 10.55–6 and 87–8, *Pyth.* 11.63–4). When they grace Theron's board they come from this eternity along with Heracles who, in turn, visits from an Olympus of unalloyed brightness.[32] It is an especially happy inspiration on Pindar's part: the pre-eminent patrons of athletes (Heracles and the Dioscuri) are also the pre-eminent mediators between mortality and immortality.[33]

---

    to Zeus (*Ol.* 3.17), may be meant to symbolize the rule of this world, kingdom of Zeus (*Ol.* 2.58), in which light and dark, good and evil, are inextricably mixed (*Ol.* 2.32–4). Heracles, in providing shade at Olympia to contrast with the previous relentless brightness there, is creating what is characteristic of the climate in which mortals live: uninterrupted sunshine is unnatural and unbearable under the vault of heaven (cf. Köhnken 1983b: 57 who emphasizes the bringing of shade to Olympia).

    The scholiast on Theoc. 2.121 (Wendel 1967: 290) says that Heracles garlanded himself in the Underworld with the white poplar which was growing on the banks of the Acheron (the source of the story may be Eratosthenes' work on the chronology of Olympic victors). This tree grew in the precinct at Olympia. Pausanias (5.14.2) has Heracles bring it there from the Acheron in Thesprotia. The white poplar or abele (*bicolor ... populus*, Virgil *Aen.* 8.276) symbolizes, with the silver underside and green upper side of its leaf, light and darkness (see Gransden 1976: 119, for a discussion of the symbolism). The importation of the poplar to Olympia, like that of the olive, establishes there a symbol of the light and dark which characterize our condition.

30 Schwenn (1940: 254) imagines the olive wreath, Theron's crown, displayed on an altar for all to see during the performance of the Third *Olympian*: Theron's link with the land of the Hyperboreans is visible, tangible.
31 Woodbury 1966.
32 For epiphanies of Heracles, see Nilsson 1906: 446.
33 Cf. Burkert 1977: 327. The immortality of the Dioscuri is imperfect, that of Heracles perfect: cf Proclus' statement in his summary of the *Cypria* (Allen 5.103): καὶ Ζεὺς

And they body forth concretely the ideas of equinox and eternal light honoured at Acragas and explained in the eschatology of the Second *Olympian*.

The Second and Third *Olympians* celebrate, on two occasions, the same victory. In the Second, Pindar sets out a doctrine not to be found elsewhere in the Odes. We find a description of the hereafter as it will be experienced by the just, of whom Theron is one (*Ol*. 2.6). This is doctrine that was in all probability current in Sicily, especially at the court of the Emmenids, for it is conspicuously unlike the theology in the other epinicians. We hear of a place where light and dark alternate in equal proportions and also of the island to which the justified make their final escape from the cycle of reincarnation. As might be expected, this island is remarkably like the land of the Hyperboreans: the flora is golden, the winds are gentle, and the inhabitants weave wreaths for their hair (*Ol*. 2.74, *Pyth*. 10.40). All this in a land which mortals do not normally reach, though Theron might well believe, hearing the Second *Olympian*, that it was the road he would travel after death. It was arcane doctrine, to be heard by initiates, unquestionably strange for normal adherents of the religion of the Olympian gods (85–6). The Third *Olympian*, on the other hand, keeps well within the bounds of normal Pindaric theology.

And yet the doctrine of the Third *Olympian* is remarkably similar to that of the second.[34] In the Third, at the theoxeny, representatives of eternal equinox and of eternal light are with Theron, the first in the person of the Dioscuri, the second in the person of the Olympian Heracles and in the Hyperborean olive. Theron is told that he has reached the summit of human expectation, and we twice hear of crowns (6–7 and 13–14): they are nothing less than the motor of the song and the subject of its myth. The olive-crown that Theron has won assimilates him, still in this world, to whose who dwell in the Isles of the Blessed and to the Hyperboreans, similarly crowned. Theron has no further distance to travel. His ἐσχατία (43) is, in the words of modern theologians, a 'realized eschatology':[35] that same kingdom which the Second *Olympian* placed in the next world is, in

---

αὐτοῖς ἐτερήμερον νέμει τὴν ἀθανασίαν. The land of the equinox is likewise an imperfect foretaste of full beatitude.

34 Menander Rhetor 415.15–30 links the figures we find in the eschatology of the Second *Olympian* (Rhadamanthys, Achilles) with those we find in the Third (Helen, the Dioscuri, Heracles) as appropriate to a speech of consolation: they all suggest a blessed destiny. (I owe this reference to Mr C.G. Brown.)

35 Cf. Dodd 1961: chapter 2 esp. 41 ff.

the Third, a matter of actual experience. Theron's ultimate destiny may lie beyond history, but the pattern of the metaphysical is given in a historical event, in a visitation of the Dioscuri and of Heracles, in the celebration at Acragas of a chariot-victory at Olympia in 476.[36]

---

36 If the Third *Olympian* hints at a gaining of immortality, it is not surprising that Pindar should take the trouble to emphasize the antlers and sex of the hind (29). Horns are life-power and life-potency (cf. Onians 1954: 106); given the unquestionable supremacy of the female in the cycles of life it is symbolically most appropriate for the hind to have antlers, even if it is zoologically incorrect. It is well worth considering in this respect the recently discovered funerary chests from Armenoi Rethymni and Episkopi in Crete (see Tzedakis 1971: 216–22, and Vermeule 1979: 66–7 for pictures). On these we see horned animals being hunted. On some of the Armenoi coffins the horned animals, including the females with their young, are unquestionably deer. So common is the deer-motif, in fact, that the artist is called the τεχνίτης τῶν ἐλάφων. On the larnax from Episkopi the animals being attacked have horns while the animal conveying the dead to the beyond has lost its horns, which, curiously, seem to reappear as the boat on which the dead travel. The animal appears to have communicated life in the next world through the gift of its horns. The crescent form that is here a boat is the regular way of portraying a single horn, either cervine or bovine. It occurs as a repeated motif along with an animal frieze on one of the Armenoi coffins, where it also appears as the horns of an animal with its head lowered before an altar of the Double Axe. On these chests there appears to be an association between hunting horned animals and life beyond the grave, with the horns or antlers supplying the link between the two motifs.

Many of Heracles' labours, in particular his going to the Underworld to fetch Cerberus, are doublets of his final apotheosis. In the Κατάβασις Ἡρακλέους or Κέρβερος Pindar apparently mentioned Heracles' acquisition of Amaltheia's Horn (fr. 249a/70b Snell-Maehler). Perhaps this tale reinforced the main theme of the Harrowing of Hell.

THE BROKEN WALL, THE BURNING ROOF AND TOWER: PINDAR, OL. 8.31–46

*Leonard Woodbury
in memoriam*

IN THE Eighth *Olympian*, for Alcimedon of Aegina, Pindar recounts a story (31–46) that, according to a notice in the scholia, is not found in earlier Greek literature.[1] Aeacus was summoned from Aegina to Troy by Apollo and Poseidon to help in the construction of the city's fortifications. Smoke, says the poet, would one day rise from the very battlements Aeacus built. The wall newly complete, a portent appeared: three snakes tried to scale the ramparts but two fell to earth while one succeeded in entering the city. Apollo immediately interpreted this sign: Troy would be taken 'owing to the work of Aeacus' hand' and would, moreover, be taken 'by the first and the fourth generations.'

If there is literary invention here,[2] it would seem that Pindar has drawn inspirations from three passages of our *Iliad*: 1) 7.452–3, Apollo and Poseidon toiled to build a wall for Laomedon; 2) 6.433–4, there was one spot in the wall of Troy that was especially vulnerable; 3) 2.308–29, the seer Calchas declares an omen involving a snake to signify the eventual destruction of Ilium.

The general import of the passage is clear enough – descendants of Aeacus play a prominent part in the Trojan war and in the capture of the city. But the details of the portent and of the prophecy have caused much perplexity, for they cannot easily be made to correspond to the history they prefigure. It is the numbers in Pindar's account that are the chief source of confusion.

First published in *CQ* 36 (1986) 317–21.

1 Drachmann *Scholia* 1 *ad* 41a.
2 Some commentators are unwilling to believe that Pindar's story is in any way original, despite the scholiast's claim: cf. Dissen 1830: 100; Wilamowitz 1922: 405; Farnell 1930–2: 1.45.

On the model of the omen interpreted by Calchas (where a snake eating nine birds represents a lapse of nine years before the sack of the city) the three snakes in the Pindaric story might reasonably be expected to represent the lapse of three generations before Aeacus' great-grandson Neoptolemus played his conspicuous part in the final agony of Troy.[3] But this interpretation of the portent forces us to explain away the fact that Troy was also destroyed by Aeacus' son, Telamon, as Pindar repeatedly insists in his Aeginetan odes (*Nem.* 3.37, 4.25; *Isth.* 6.26–31):[4] if the snakes are taken to represent generations, one of the unsuccessful snakes in fact represents a successful conqueror. This is a disturbing inconcinnity.

A second expedient, adopted by many modern commentators, is to take the two unsuccessful snakes as representative of Achilles and Ajax, Aeacids who died before the final capture of Troy, and to take the third as Neoptolemus.[5] The numbers no longer refer to generations; rather they count the unsuccessful and the successful Aeacids. But there are still problems. The successful Telamon is left aside; more important, the successful Teucer (Telamon's son, *Nem.* 4.46) is also ignored, though he was with Neoptolemus in the Trojan horse.[6] Gildersleeve, though he accepts the interpretation, wrily notes that ἀτυζόμενοι (of the two dying snakes, 39) 'hardly seems applicable to the representatives of Achilles and Aias.'[7] This reading of the passage about the three snakes derives its authority from the scholia, where it is mentioned three times.[8]

A more satisfactory solution is to take the number three as pointing to the number of collaborators in the building of the wall. The chthonic snakes are opponents of the Olympian order, whose construction they

---

3 So, e.g., Beattie 1955: 1–3.
4 Euripides in the *Andromache* (796 ff.) says that Peleus was with Telamon and Heracles during the first sack of Troy, but Pindar nowhere mentions Peleus in this connection.
5 E.g., in addition to Farnell 1930–2: 1.45, Gildersleeve 1885: 196; Boeckh 1821: 182; Fennell 1879: 70. Hill (1963: 3) refers to this as 'the traditional view.'
6 It is almost universally assumed by modern commentators that Pindar is including in the prophecy Epeius, artificer of the Trojan horse (the lineage would be Aeacus–Phocus–Panopeus–Epeius). This is not impossible: Asius, the 7th- or 6th-century author of genealogies and epic poetry, apparently made Epeius a descendant of Aeacus (cf. Pausanias 2.29.4). But it involves identifying Aeginetan Phocus, son of Aeacus (this Phocus died prematurely on Aegina, *Nem.* 5.12), with a different Phocus (see *RE* 20.497–8) who along with Panopeus is an eponym in Phocis. I am not convinced that Pindar made this identification. Intent as he is on illustrating the number and glory of the descendants of Aeacus, he never mentions Epeius.
7 See Gildersleeve 1885: 196.
8 See Drachmann *Scholia* 1 *ad* 51 (with apparatus), 52a, 53e.

cannot overset. The participle ἀτυζόμενοι (39) becomes appropriate, for it explains the impotent rage of the two creatures confronted with the work of the gods: in the First *Pythian* this same verb (13) expresses the frustration of the enemies of Zeus and introduces a description of the serpent Typhoeus and his unavailing rebellion against divine dispensation. The wall is impregnable where gods laboured; where a mortal laboured Troy will be taken. This reading frees us from having to try to reconcile the numbers of the portent with the numbers of Apollo's prophecy. What it leaves unexplained is Apollo's precise knowledge of the time when Troy will fall. But I think there is another way of understanding why the poet has Apollo append to his prophecy information not gleaned from the omen, and I shall suggest it below. The interpretation of the portent outlined here is to be found in the scholia too.[9] Among modern Pindarists only two explicitly associate the three snakes with the three workers on the wall.[10] It is not, I think, a serious objection that the numbers in the omen no longer correspond to the lapse of time before the taking of Troy as do the numbers in the omen interpreted by Calchas in the *Iliad* – Pindar is not bound by all the details of the Homeric passage.

The god, speaking to Aeacus, tells him that Troy will fall by reason of his work (42). Aeacus' responsibility is incontestable. But Apollo goes on to add that Aeacus' descendants will be involved too (οὐκ ἄτερ παίδων σέθεν, 45, in emphatic position at the beginning of the triad), and this comes as a surprise. Apollo further specifies the generation that will collaborate with Aeacus in the destruction of Troy. In computing time and indicating the joint responsibility Apollo includes Aeacus as part of his own family. By a method of reckoning that must seem somewhat strange to us, Aeacus is the first generation of his own descendants. There are, however, excellent analogies in Pindar. In the Fourth *Pythian*, a poem that is concerned more than any other in the corpus with reckoning generations,

---

9 *Ad* 49b, 53b.
10 Dissen 1830: 100; Fernández-Galiano 1956: 242. Lehnus (1981: 139) claims that this is the commonly accepted interpretation, but he does not refer to specific commentators. It appears to be problematic for him because he senses a necessity of reconciling the one and two of the snake-prodigy with the one and four of lines 45–6. He entertains the possibility that the two falling snakes symbolize the two times that the wall would fall (in the first generation after Aeacus and in a later generation). But what are we then to make of the successful snake? That it represents the *building* of the wall? This seems quite strained, and the correspondences would be inexact, for if the wall falls twice, it is also built twice (by Aeacus and the gods, and after the first sack by Heracles and Telamon).

Medea (likewise prophesying) includes the Argonauts as the first part of their own descendants (47–8),[11] Jason refers to himself and Pelias as the third generation sprung from their grandparents (143–4), and the poet addresses Arcesilaus of Cyrene, seventh (for us) in line from the Battus who founded the city, as eighth of the first king's descendants (65). The portent that Apollo interprets points to a single sack of Troy; his interpretation also refers to a single conquest.[12] The taking of the city will be a work of συνεργία as was the building of its wall. When Neoptolemus breaches the wall of Troy, Aeacus will be collaborating through his handiwork.[13]

It is not necessary, then, to emend τετράτοις in line 46 to τερτάτοις. τερτάτοις, first proposed in 1860,[14] has been accepted by, inter alios, the current Teubner editors, presumably because they think that the prophecy refers to two sacks of the city (by Telamon and by Neoptolemus). But since the portent contains no reference to Telamon, the prophecy should not be understood as including him either. There are other difficulties as well –

11 Medea refers to the 'blood' or offspring of the fourth generation. This is the fifth generation by her reckoning though it would be the fourth by our (exclusive) reckoning, since she is in fact referring to great-great-grandsons of Argonauts (the generation of the returning Heraclids; cf. Herod. 6.52).
12 Beattie (above, n3) understands that Aeacus and Neoptolemus are referred to, but his interpretation is very difficult to accept: he emends ἄρξεται to ἀέξεται which is supposed to have double meaning and to refer to 'building' by Aeacus and 'sacrifice' by Neoptolemus. His case is further weakened by his wishing to introduce Telamon and Peleus into the portent. Hill (above, n5) likewise correctly understands the reference to Aeacus and Neoptolemus, but his statement is marred by his acceptance of the numbers of the omen as referring to Aeacids between Aeacus and Neoptolemus (i.e., Achilles and Ajax). I cannot make sense of Bowra's claim (1964: 299) that Troy 'will be captured *first* by Aeacus, and *later* by his descendants' (italics mine).
13 Though we might expect ἅμα (45) to be a preposition, parallel to the ἄτερ that precedes it, it is, I believe, more likely adverbial, the datives being datives of agent (cf. 30). ἅμα when accompanied by καί is not normally a preposition: cf., e.g., Isth. 2.11, κτεάνων θ' ἅμα λειφθείς καὶ φίλων; Od. 3.111, ἅμα κρατερὸς καὶ ἀμύμων. The words imply close conjunction, often with a sense of simultaneity. This is what we want here, for Aeacus' contribution to the fall of Troy will be manifest at the time of Neoptolemus' victory.

If πρώτοις and τετράτοις are datives of agent, the case for a strong passive verb is made more likely. ῥάξεται was suggested independently by Gildersleeve (loc. cit., above, n5) and Wilamowitz (1922: 404 n3) and has been defended by von der Mühll (1964: 51–3). This seems preferable to the weak ἄρξεται of the codices, for which no convincing translation has been offered (Aeacus and Neoptolemus can scarcely be said to have 'ruled' in Troy). It is, moreover, a satisfactory synonym for ἁλίσκεται (42), to which it is parallel in this passage.
14 Ahrens 1860: 52.

τέρτατος is an unattested form,[15] and the exclusive reckoning that does not include Aeacus in his own family is anomalous too.

There is another remarkable instance of συνεργία in the myth of the poem. Apollo is depicted not as an omniscient god but anthropomorphically as a seer. It is not uncommon to find mantic Apollo as Διὸς προφήτης (Aesch. *Eum.* 18–19), mouthpiece of his father (cf. *Hymn. Hom. Ap.* 132, *Herm.* 471–2). But it is unusual to see him functioning as a human seer who must interpret signs. In this he is like the μάντιες ἄνδρες of the beginning of the poem (2) who seek to understand the will of Zeus and to predict the future through divination by means of the altar flames at Olympia. Zeus is the source of the greatness of the Aeacids as of the addressee's family (15–16, 83–4), and generally of the truth that his seers declare (3). But here Apollo's prediction shows some independence, for as a mantis interpreting a sign he goes beyond what may legitimately be extracted from the portent by his prediction of the exact timing of the fall of Troy. There is nothing in the omen, on the reading suggested here, that indicates *when* the wall will be breached – this information is, as a recent commentator has put it, a 'precisazione autonoma.'[16] If the prophecy is a work of concerted effort, with Zeus providing the φάσμα (43) and Apollo interpreting it, there is a virtuoso cadenza in the concerto.

Apollo is variously presented in Pindar's odes, always in a manner that is harmonious with the poem as a whole. In the First *Pythian*, a poem celebrating the close bond between father and son in the earthly dynasty of the Deinomenids, Apollo and Zeus provide a divine paradigm of this union. In the Third *Pythian*, a meditation on human destiny and on the possibility of mortal knowledge (possible because Apollo, the god of truth, guides human fortunes), special care is taken to emphasize the god's independence and omniscience: the raven that in the Hesiodic account[17] told of Coronis' infidelity is eliminated, presumably as unnecessary to a god whose grasp of truth is immediate and total. Apollo in the Ninth *Pythian* is portrayed as a well-bred youth on the eve of marriage; he is like the other suitors of the poem, including the addressee Telesikrates, who has wooed and won victory. The brief glimpse of Apollo in the Eighth *Olympian* is a glimpse of a humanized Apollo whose performance is in part dependent on co-operation, in part an individual achievement.

15 τέρτατος would be an Aeolic form of τρίτατος. But Pindar's regular word for 'third' is in any case τρίτος.
16 Lehnus (above, n10) *loc. cit.*
17 M.-W. fr. 60.

He is in this not unlike the ultimate conqueror of Troy, Neoptolemus, whose feat is his own, though possible only because of the assistance of Aeacus.

To recognize this motif of co-operation or assistance is to grasp an important key for understanding the poem. Aeacus is, of course, important as progenitor of the race that made Aegina so dear to Pindar's heart. But this is a general consideration, relevant to virtually any one of the Aeginetan odes, where stories of the Aeacids may be told to remind the audience of the past glories of the island race whose scions in the poet's time are winning victories in the Panhellenic games. The general appropriateness of the brilliant exploits of the Aeacidae in Aeginetan odes does not explain why Pindar tells any individual story as he does.[18] But if we note the repeated insistence in the myth on the theme of collaboration, we may also note the surprising prominence accorded in the poem to the victor's trainer. Though Pindar elsewhere (*Nemeans* 4–6) mentions trainers, he nowhere else devotes so much of a poem to direct eulogy of a trainer (including a catalogue of that trainer's victories). So important is Melesias, in fact, that a scholiast could consider him a co-dedicatee of the ode.[19] Melesias has experience and foreknowledge (59–60) and so is an important contributor to the ἔργα (63) that are at the heart of the poem (cf. 19, 32, 42, 85). The γέρας of Alcimedon (11) is the γέρας of Melesias as well (65). Pindar elsewhere shows that he is interested in the διδασκαλία of youth. His regular position, as is widely recognized, is that mere learning or training can accomplish nothing if native ability be not present. In the Third *Nemean* we hear that

ὃς δὲ διδάκτ᾽ ἔχει, ψεφεννὸς ἀνήρ
ἄλλοτ᾽ ἄλλα πνέων οὔ ποτ᾽ ἀτρεκεῖ
κατέβα ποδί, μυριᾶν δ᾽ ἀρετᾶν ἀτελεῖ νόῳ γεύεται (41–2)

But this very poem, which appears to denigrate διδακτά, contains a myth given over to the διδασκαλία of Cheiron's pupils Jason, Asclepius, and Achilles. Under the tutelage of the centaur Asclepius learned the φαρμάκων ... μαλακόχειρα νόμον (55). And the training of Achilles was undertaken that he might make proper use of his hands in the slaughter before Troy

---

18 'Il est clair que ce mythe n'a aucun rapport avec Alcimédon personellement,' says Puech (1930: 104).
19 Drachmann *Scholia* 1.236.

(62; cf. 44). διδασκαλία is, we see, a matter of χειρουργία,[20] and so it is not surprising to find that Melesias himself is described by Pindar as χειρῶν ... ἀνίοχον (Nem. 6.66), 'guiding to a proper use of hands',[21] while the triumph of Alcimedon is a χειρῶν ἄωτον (Ol. 8.75), 'the flower of his hands.'

Aeacus' place in the poem is especially interesting. His own χειρουργία ensures (42) the triumph of his race, and so he may be seen as assisting in the fall of the city he helped build. Mortal weakness (to which the snake-portent calls attention) establishes the vulnerability of Troy, but this weakness is hardly reprehensible since the fall of Troy is fated (33–6) and, moreover, the weakness is the direct cause of the success of one of Aeacus' descendants. Aeacus assists Neoptolemus to victory; he is also the collaborator of Apollo and Poseidon in much the same way. For Apollo and Poseidon built the walls of Troy as an *athlos* (cf. *Il.* 7.453, ἀθλήσαντε), in thrall to King Laomedon, and the garland of battlements is the crown of their labour. Homer refers to the towers of Troy as its κρήδεμνα or veil *(Il.* 16.100); Pindar has made the towers (38) a στέφανος or crown (32). The image is perhaps not original – the scholiast on this passage quotes Anacreon *(PMG* 391) as speaking of a στέφανος πόλεως.[22] But it is most effectively employed here, for the coronation of Troy, result of the labour of building, is like the στεφανοφορία of the athlete and his rejoicing *komos* (10). Aeacus is the συνεργός of Apollo and Poseidon in the placing of the crown as he is later the συνεργός of Neoptolemus in its destruction. And as burning entrails are the source of the prophecies mentioned at the beginning of the poem, burning battlements (36) are the substance of Apollo's vision in the myth.

The poem, if read as I suggest, is not a curious amalgam of badly co-ordinated elements, but an exquisite tribute to a boy-victor and to the τέκτων of his success. The myth is limpid and appropriate, and there is in it something of great importance to the poet. The execution of noble deeds requires the contribution of God and of inborn nature: Pindar regularly stresses the decisive role of θεός and φυά. He stresses too the exertion (πόνος) and the expense (δαπάνα) necessary for the achievement of

---

20 So too Jason's education: see Robbins 1975: 205–13 [in this volume 192–201]. Asclepius perverts his teaching χρυσὸς ἐν χερσὶν φανείς, *Pyth.* 3.55); Zeus takes the matter in hand with the thunderbolt (χερσὶ δι' ἀμφοῖν, *Pyth.* 3.57).
21 See Farnell 1930–2: 2.287–8.
22 Sophocles twice uses the image of the garland of towers that crowns a city, at *Ant.* 122 and at *O.C.* 14–15 (reading στέφουσι with Wakefield and Dawe).

greatness. But Pindar also honours – and this may too easily be overlooked – the part played by a mentor or trainer in the παιδεία of the young – of gods, heroes, and mortals alike. The Eighth *Olympian* is a joint tribute to Alcimedon and Melesias. The myth of the poem, in keeping with this, is a tale of co-operation.[23]

---

23 In the poem we learn that the Blepsiads (Alcimedon's family) are descended from Zeus (16). There is thus some analogy with the Zeus-descended Aeacids: both families are guided and protected by Zeus. We do not know whether Alcimedon's family was descended from Zeus through Aeacus or traced its line back to Zeus independently of Aeacus. It is interesting, however, to note that Melesias is an Aeacid. Pausanias (2.29.4) tells us that the family of Cimon and Miltiades was descended from Aeacus, Telamon, and Ajax. Wade-Gery (1958: 246) has traced the descent of Melesias from Cimon. I do not wish to press this point, but I think it a sobering counter-consideration to the common belief that Melesias, as an Athenian, was *persona non grata* in 460 in Aegina. I find no foundation in the poem for this view; it is certainly not supported by line 55, which is perfectly intelligible as normal Pindaric preoccupation with φθόνος in a passage of eulogy.

THE GIFTS OF THE GODS: PINDAR'S THIRD *PYTHIAN*

1

HIERON of Syracuse was the most powerful Greek of his day. He was also, and the two facts are not unrelated, the most frequent of Pindar's patrons. A singular feature of the four poems for this Sicilian prince is their obsession with sin and punishment: Tantalus in the First *Olympian*, Typhoeus, Ixion, and Coronis in the first three *Pythians* – all offend divinity and suffer terribly. But even in this company, where glory comes trailing clouds of pain, the Third *Pythian* stands out. The other three odes are manifestly epinician and celebrate success, both athletic and military. The Second *Pythian*, for instance, is a sombre canvas, and a motif of ingratitude dominates the myth. Yet it rings at the outset with praise of Syracuse and of Hieron's victory. The Third *Pythian*, by comparison, is not obviously a victory ode.

For victory, in the Third *Pythian*, seems remote and is mentioned only in passing. This, ironically, has been one of the principal reasons for the ode's popularity. It can be appreciated even by those who feel distaste for the conventions of epinician poetry, so little does it say about victory.[1] Wilamowitz thought the poem a poetic epistle to an ailing tyrant, not worrying whether such a genre was credible for late Archaic Greece.[2] Recent criticism, on the other hand, has found in the poem conventions that link it to others that are indubitably epinician, and has consequently

---

First published in *CQ* 40.2 (1990) 307–18.

1 See Young 1968: 27–68.
2 Wilamowitz 1900: 48 and 1922: 280. I can find no reference to the Third *Pythian* as a letter before Wilamowitz in 1900, but he mentions the idea so casually that it scarcely seems an innovation.

been more inclined to view the Third *Pythian* as a normal epinician ode.[3]

It is my belief that the older, more naive, reading must be the correct one. The poem is consolatory, not celebratory, and no attempt to isolate features of style common to many Pindaric poems will turn it into a convincing victory ode.[4] A victory is mentioned only once, in a contrary-to-fact condition at line 73, and the mention includes the information that the victory alluded to was ποτέ 'once upon a time.' I shall return to this later. For the moment it is important to review indications that help to determine the date of the poem.

Pherenikos, the renowned stallion named in line 74, won for Hieron at Olympia in 476. This, the most illustrious of his victories, is the occasion of both the First *Olympian* and Bacchylides 5. Bacchylides mentions (5.41) that Pherenikos had before this date won at Delphi. He seems to be referring to a single victory. The First *Olympian*, on the other hand, says nothing about previous contests. The scholiast to the Third *Pythian* maintains that Hieron won twice at Delphi with the single horse, in 482 and in 478.[5] He does not name Pherenikos as the victorious courser, but since he appears to be extracting his information from the poem he may have misread what is a poetic plural (στεφάνοις) in line 73 and have concluded that Pherenikos won on two occasions.[6] The evidence for two victories at Delphi is, therefore, not strong, though the fact that victories in 482 and 478 are also mentioned by the scholiast to the First *Pythian* may carry some weight (if the basis of this scholium is not the same misreading of the Third *Pythian*'s plural).[7] It seems certain, then, that Hieron won at Delphi with Pherenikos in 478. He may have won there in 482 as well, but there is no compelling reason to believe that he did, and it is certainly unlikely that Pherenikos was victorious in 482. In 482 Hieron's brother Gelon was king of Syracuse and Hieron was in all probability ruling in Gela where the dynasty originated. Gelon died in 478 and was succeeded in Syracuse by Hieron, who then reigned for eleven years and eight months (Diod. 11.38.7). If Hieron came to the throne before the Pythian festival was held, his victory in 478 will have been a victory as king of Syracuse. He is called king in line 70, though this means, of course, only that the Third *Pythian* was composed subsequent to his accession.

3 Young 1983: 31–42; Slater 1988: 51–61.
4 So too Lefkowitz 1976: 142–57.
5 Drachmann *Scholia* 2.62 *ad* Inscr. a.
6 For the poetic plural of στέφανος cf. *Ol.* 6.26, *Pyth.* 2.6, *Isth.* 3.11.
7 Drachmann *Scholia* 2.5.

The ποτέ of line 74 certainly seems to indicate a date later than 478 for the poem, with a passing reference to the victory of that year. Farnell wanted the date of composition to be earlier than 476 since there is no mention of the victory at Olympia in 476.[8] But this is not at all convincing, for none of the odes of Pindar for Hieron contains a reference to a venue other than that of the specific occasion, much less a catalogue of earlier victories. Farnell was untroubled by the ποτέ but he will likely have thought of it as harking back to both the recent 478 and the more distant 482, accepting what on the whole we have seen to be improbable – that Pherenikos won both times. Young thinks, however, that the ode is the victory poem of 478 and that the ποτέ does not refer to the past but is to be understood from the point of view of generations to come who will read, or hear, the ποτέ as referring to days of yore. What we have here is the language of inscriptions.[9]

But can this feature of dedicatory inscriptions simply be understood as operative in Pindaric poetry? Inscriptions are directed to posterity in general, whereas occasional verse has a specific addressee and its primary audience is immediate. The end of our poem looks to the future when it refers to the immortality that poetry conveys, but it does so *para prosdokian*, as a surprise after the burden of the preceding strophes which emphasize the impossibility of immortality (explicitly at lines 61–2, among the most famous in Pindar). The force of the end of the poem depends on the force of the doctrine that this ending corrects: the πρόσω suddenly possible for Hieron at line 111 contradicts the πόρσω that characterized the company of fools at line 22 (the echo is sealed by the repetition of ἐλπίς, 23 and 111). Important too is the Homeric precedent for ποτέ in an 'inscriptional' context:

> καί ποτέ τις εἴπησι καὶ ὀψιγόνων ἀνθρώπων
> νηΐ πολυκληΐδι πλέων ἐπὶ οἴνοπα πόντον.
> 'ἀνδρὸς μὲν τόδε σῆμα πάλαι κατατεθνηῶτος,
> ὅν ποτ' ἀριστεύοντα κατέκτανε φαίδιμος Ἕκτωρ.'
> ὥς ποτέ τις ἐρέει. τὸ δ' ἐμὸν κλέος οὔ ποτ' ὀλεῖται.   *Il.* 7.87–91

Hector imagines someone yet unborn gazing upon the barrow of Ajax. The framing future ποτέs (87 and 91) establish the time of the backward look to that day, given with the ποτέ of 89, when Hector slew Ajax.

---

8 Farnell 1930–2: 2.135. Young (1983: 42 n33) is also inclined to see the silence as significant.
9 Young 1983: 31–42.

This is what we would expect in poetry and what is missing in the Third *Pythian*. Without some assistance we can hardly be expected to recognize the retrospective ποτέ as spoken in time to come, the time of 'coloro / che questo tempo chiameranno antico' (Dante, *Par.* 17.119–20). There is nothing to suggest that the words Hector attributes to the future speaker are to be read on an inscription – since they are spoken by someone sailing on the Dardanelles, reading must in fact be precluded.[10]

There are other considerations that make 478 unlikely. Hieron is called Αἰτναῖος (69) and this is most easily understood as an allusion to his re-foundation of Catania as Aetna in 476 (Diodorus 11.49.1). That the tyrant of Syracuse was intensely proud of his new city is clear from Pindar: in 470, when he won with the chariot at Delphi, Hieron had himself proclaimed Αἰτναῖος (*Pyth.* 1.30–3). We cannot argue with certainty from appellations of this sort,[11] but there is a *prima facie* case for accepting Diodorus' date for the foundation of the city and for taking the use of the adjective as pointing to a subsequent year. Another consideration, not conclusive in itself but suggesting a time of composition in the latter part of the decade, is Hieron's illness, the central fact of the Third *Pythian*. While not impossible that Hieron was ill in 478 when he ascended the throne, it is significant that the only other reference to Hieron's illness is in the First *Pythian* of 470, the latest securely datable of Pindar's poems for this Syracusan patron. In a remarkable passage

---

[10] Young (1983: 38 n24) refers to this passage from Homer but thinks that it means that Homer was aware of inscriptional practice. This begs very large questions – the date and literacy of Homer. It is much more likely that the writers of epitaphs in the sixth and fifth centuries were familiar with hexameter poetry and with passages such as this one. The ποτέ of inscriptions may be considered a legacy of epic poetry in another way as well. Those who are thought to have died 'in the olden days' are thereby assimilated to the Heroic Age. Their natural company is the great of the past, not the lesser men of the present (this understanding gives the ποτέ of an inscription erected after a battle immediate relevance – it does not have to wait for future generations before it acquires meaning).

Hector typically thinks of what people will say 'at some point in the future': cf. also *Il.* 6.459, 479; 22.106. His mother speaks this way too at Eur. *Troades* 1188–91. Lefkowitz is surely right, *pace* Young 1983: 38 n24, to see the ποτέ of 1188 as relevant to the ποτέ of 1190 – when Hecuba imagines Astyanax's future we remember Hector's doing the same at *Il.* 6.479. Euripides will have known epitaphs and their language (and we are clearly in the world of writing in these lines), but in the context the passage functions like the passage from Homer quoted above: poetry makes explicit the future point for the backward glance.

[11] Young (1983: 35 n18) makes light of them. He must do so, as they are inconvenient for his theory.

Hieron is compared to Philoctetes, who took the field despite his infirmity (50–5). We must not fail to notice that there is a strong contrast here between the mention of the battle of Himera in 480, when Hieron waged war in the company of his brothers and of Theron of Acragas against the Carthaginians (47–9), and a time (νῦν γε μάν, 50) closer to the date of the victory that this poem celebrates. It is at the later time that Hieron is like Philoctetes. The most attractive hypothesis is that the reference to an ailing conqueror is a reference to Hieron's decisive intervention in the affairs of Acragas in 472,[12] when, shortly after the death of Theron, Theron's son Thrasydaeus led the Acragantines in a war against Hieron. The war led to the expulsion of Thrasydaeus and a restoration of democratic government in Acragas. Whether this explanation is correct or not, Hieron's illness is, on the evidence of the First *Pythian*, not long before 470.

All in all, then, the circumstantial evidence points to a date fairly late in the decade. If the poem is subsequent to the First *Olympian*, it is silent about Pherenikos' victory at Olympia in 476, but this silence is not especially surprising, given that the First *Olympian* is silent, as Bacchylides is not, with regard to an earlier Pythian success. The First *Pythian* similarly mentions no previous agonistic triumph (it mentions only previous military triumphs). Three of the poems for Hieron mention only one victory, the occasion of the poem in each case. The Third *Pythian* likewise mentions only one, I think, and it seems to be treated as a relatively remote victory.[13]

The ποτέ of line 74 looks back a few years to a victory of 478. We are in a poem that advocates the acceptance of distances, both spatial and temporal, and decries the folly of trying to bridge them (distance is also absence: cf. ἀποιχόμενον, 3).[14] Acceptance of distance is, in fact, a moral obligation, and failure to accept it the root of Coronis' sin ἤρατο τῶν ἀπεόντων, 20). And so the gap in time between the victory of Pherenikos and the time of the song is indicated by the word that introduces the story of Asclepius

---

12 Vallet 1985: 311.
13 Another reason that has been advanced for a date of 474 for the Third *Pythian* is its resemblance to the Ninth *Pythian*, a poem that can be securely dated to that year. Both odes (they are the only two in the corpus to do so) take stories from the *Ehoiai* of Hesiod dealing with the loves of Apollo. On the similarities between the two poems see Bernardini 1983: 62–7, and Köhnken 1985: 77. Köhnken, however, without discussion simply dates the Third *Pythian* to 476, the year of the First *Olympian*,
14 Young (1968) has an excellent discussion of these themes in his literary essay on the poem.

(5), on whose death and consequent unavailability the poet dwells.[15] If we take Pindar's words at their face value, he is saying that he can bring neither a healer nor a κῶμος. Lines 72–6 are perhaps the most problematic of the poem. The counterfactual condition has been taken in a variety of ways.

1) The first person is the first person of the chorus.[16] This interpretation relies on the assumption that the first-person utterance in the poems of Pindar is the voice of the chorus as well as that of the poet. The contrary-to-fact condition cannot, in this case, be genuinely contrary to fact, for it would be patently absurd for a chorus to be chanting in effect, 'I'm not really here!' And so the counterfactual condition that begins at line 72 must apply not to the arrival-motif but only to that of health. Most current opinion is, however, against taking every first-person utterance in Pindar as including the chorus.[17]

2) The first person is the poet, but his arrival is not denied.[18] Indeed, it is wrong to try to elicit biographical information from traditional motifs, and the arrival-motif is traditional. The counterfactual condition is there to create a mood but is not to be taken literally. Part of the unreal condition must still be taken as literally true, though, for it remains a fact that the poet is unable to provide a healer. Against this, and similarly against 1), it is important to point out that even if we interpret this second unreal condition as saying 'I haven't come *bringing health*' (rather than simply 'I haven't come'), the earlier of the two contrary-to-fact conditions (63–9)

---

15 I do not claim that the ποτέ is significant enough for there to be an echo of line 5 in line 74. ποτέ is a word Pindar regularly uses in introducing mythical narrative. But it appears here in the very phrase that associates Cheiron with Asclepius. When they are next brought together (63 ff.) Pindar has himself understood the undesirability of desire for the absent.

16 E.g., Slater 1988: 59.

17 Burton (1962: 146) observed that the first-person singular pronoun in the epinician odes of Pindar never excluded the poet. About the same time Lefkowitz (1963) investigated the matter in detail and concluded that the first person could refer only to the poet and that there was no choral 'I' at all in the epinicia. She returned to this question in 1985: 47–9, and in an article (1988): her conclusion here is that not only does the first person not include the chorus but that the odes were for the most part not performed chorally. Two further articles that appeared at almost the same time as Lefkowitz's and that share her conclusion – that there is little reason to believe in choral performance of the epinician odes – are Heath 1988 and Davies 1988. Most recently, Carey 1989 and Burnett 1989 have defended the traditional belief that the poems were sung chorally. But even if this is the case, the first person is not necessarily the voice of the group. Carey (1989: 561 n41), for instance, believes that lines 63–79 of the Third *Pythian* refer to the poet himself and not to the chorus.

18 E.g., Young 1968: 45–6.

ends with a bald and unqualified apodosis – Pindar says that because he cannot provide an Asclepius or an Apollo for Hieron he has not come. And so on this interpretation too the passage as a whole must be taken to mean the opposite of what it appears to say.[19]

3) Pindar has remained at Thebes and cannot send a healer (this is consonant with a literal understanding of the first of the two counterfactual conditions). But he nonetheless announces or celebrates a victory.[20]

The above interpretations all assume that the poem is in the last analysis epinician since it mentions a victory. But the victory mentioned is distant, past, as we have seen, and a κῶμος no more possible than health, to which the κῶμος is parallel.[21] It is well to remember that the basic meaning of κῶμος is revelry, something totally foreign to the spirit of this song. The poet has not come – and since he has not come he cannot be bringing (ἄγων) anything. The poet, who is not present, states that he has in this case neither health nor a κῶμος to bring. It is further specified that the κῶμος he might have brought would have been for an old victory. This puts it in a class with other things the poet has abjured – an old triumph joins the dead Cheiron, the dead Asclepius, and a trip to a far-away land. Pindar turns his back on all of these even when they are, like the provision of a healer, distinct desiderata. There is, of course, a difference in scale of distance. Cheiron is dead (ἀποιχόμενον) and his recall impossible. Health is not impossible in the same way, but it is not πὰρ ποδός despite the vivid description of the positive potential of medicine in the strophe devoted to the cures dispensed by Asclepius (47–53). The victory mentioned is simply ἀπεόν: hence its celebration is, like Coronis' desire, inappropriate in the circumstances. The only reference to it is in the section of the poem that emphasizes concentrating on the immediate. It is not mentioned as a source of Hieron's εὐδαιμονία (84–5) but only in the company of what is distant or denied.

---

19 Of both the foregoing interpretations it is tempting to say with Gow (1965: 130, re the Seventh *Idyll*): 'A theory based upon the assumption that he means the reverse of what he says starts at some initial disadvantage.'
20 E.g., Herington 1985: 190–1.
21 At *Ol.* 4.9–10 κῶμος appears to mean 'celebratory song' and to refer to the poem that is being sung since, unlike festal dance-κῶμοι, this one is a χρονιώτατον φάος. Gerber (1987: 16) thinks that κῶμος at *Pyth.* 3.73 is similar and means simply 'song.' But *Ol.* 4 is quite clearly a short processional (whether at Olympia or Camarina is disputed). The κῶμος, if it is a song, is also a procession, perhaps a dance: it is mentioned with the deictic pronoun (and with the reception- and arrival-motifs discussed by Heath 1988: 185–90). It is a κῶμος very like that of *Ol.* 14, another short processional ode which refers to τόνδε κῶμον (16).

This reading is, I think, the only one that will adequately fit the tone of the poem. It is, moreover, a poem that can be considered epinician only if we take the single reference to victory as unaffected by the unreal condition in which it is embedded. A former victory (presumably only one) is mentioned because it contributes to an important theme of the poem.[22] And the Delphic victory of 478 is mentioned rather than the Olympic victory of 476 because it is more remote. But there is, perhaps, another reason that this victory at Delphi is mentioned.

If the poem is from 474, it is from a year in which Hieron did not win. Did he compete? There may be here a discreet allusion to Hieron's unsuccessful participation in the games of that year.[23] If he competed with Pherenikos and lost, the mention of that horse's name makes good sense. Hieron won prizes in the equestrian contests of mainland Greece at two-year intervals from 478, the year of his accession in Syracuse, until his death, with the exception of 474: 478 at Delphi, 476 at Olympia, 472 at Olympia,[24] 470 at Delphi, 468 at Olympia. The regularity of the pattern seems to demand an entry for Delphi in 474. Pherenikos' career, on this reconstruction, would include two victories (478 and 476) and a loss (474).[25] Beneath the mention of a former victory may lie the reality of a present disappointment tactfully passed over in silence: ... τὸ

---

22 *Ol.* 10, *Nem.* 3, *Nem.* 9, and *Isth.* 2 are poems which seem to celebrate a victory at a subsequent date. If it is felt that *Pyth.* 3 is simply another such instance, the question of the dating will be immaterial – it will be a commemorative poem at a date after the victory, but exactly when it was composed will be unimportant. My argument is, basically, that the rhetorical stance of *Pyth.* 3 is internally consistent and that its mood is unique. Special explanation is, consequently, necessary.

23 See Wilamowitz 1922: 282–3. So too Most 1985: 67 with n42.

24 Pausanias (8.42.9) gives a dedicatory epigram from Olympia that accompanied a monument erected by Hieron's son, Deinomenes. This epigram records Hieron's two Olympic victories with the single horse and one with the chariot. The victor-list from Oxyrhynchus (*P. Oxy.* II 222 Col. I 19) gives the dates 476 and 472 for the κέλης-victories. This corroborates a scholium on the First *Olympian* (Drachmann *Scholia* 1.15–16), where the chariot victory of 468 is also mentioned (this chariot victory was the occasion of Bacchylides 3).

25 If there was a victory at Delphi in 482 the pattern is not so neat. But, as I have argued, the case for victories in both 482 and 478 is not strong, and 478 seems certain. 482 is in any case not during Hieron's reign in Syracuse.

On the length of the career of a racehorse in antiquity (and in modern times), see Maehler 1982: 79 n6. If we accept that Pherenikos was not Hieron's horse at Delphi in 482 and that he was in 474, we have certain victories in 478 and 476, when he was at his peak, and no victory in his final competition. There is no reason for thinking that the victory of 472 was a victory of Pherenikos.

σιγᾶν πολλάκις ἐστὶ σοφώτατον ἀνθρώπῳ νοῆσαι (Nem. 5.18). This is a poem of consolation in illness – the illness is clear from the text. It may also be a poem of consolation in defeat, the defeat implicit in the fact that the only victory mentioned as a possible source of celebration is old. The last epode of the poem expresses hope for the future. Perhaps, like the final epode of the First *Olympian*, its hope is for future victory and for the poet's association with Hieron in the celebration of that victory. If this is so, it is easy to believe that the poem was sung at Hieron's court, by proxy or indeed by a chorus, much as a normal epinician poem might have been sung, and easy to account for the mood. My own hunch, for what it's worth, is that Hieron, who had won with Pherenikos at Olympia in 476, retained Pindar for 474. Great patrons may well have approached poets in advance of the games, and it is not difficult to imagine that a man who named his horse Pherenikos would have planned a victory celebration beforehand. Pindar had, it is generally agreed, been in Sicily in 476 and knew Hieron personally. In the event Pindar produced a song and mentioned an earlier victory at Delphi.[26] It was not a κῶμος for a recent victory. There was no recent victory to celebrate.[27]

2

Formally the Third *Pythian* falls into two sections. The first part begins with an unattainable wish and ends with the two counterfactual conditions we have noted. Linguistically the εἰ-clause of line 2 is echoed by the εἰ-clauses of lines 63 and 73, and the εὔξασθαι of 2 by the ἐπεύξασθαι of 77. This section contains the meditation on the impossible and the distant. Line 80 forms at once the climax of the first part and the beginning of

---

26 I prefer this explanation to the idea that the poem is an unsolicited offering.
27 If the first person of the poem is the voice of the poet and not that of a chorus and if the poet has not come to Syracuse, παρ' ἐμὸν πρόθυρον would appear to refer to Thebes. But the primary implication of the phrase is that the poet is making a public prayer: cf. the prayer of the Locrian maiden πρὸ δόμων at *Pyth*. 2.18 and the presence of the Cyrenean kings πρὸ δωμάτων during the festal procession at *Pyth*. 5.96. Pindar has already drawn attention to the public nature of his prayer in line 2 with the word κοινόν (proleptic, 'so daß es alle hören können'; cf. Schroeder 1922: 27).

Victory and peril belong to the world of men, ignominy and ease to the world of women: a defeated athlete returns home to his mother, *Pyth*. 8.85. The prayer to the mother goddess is, thus, especially appropriate if there has been an actual defeat. Cf. Robbins 1987: 25–33, esp. 32 [in this volume 229–37, esp. 236–7].

the second.[28] Hieron is now directly addressed for the first time and an alternative is set out in a new εἰ-clause. The second part, like the first, contains a double myth, for the first tells the cautionary tales of Coronis and Asclepius while the second tells the consolatory stories of Cadmus and Peleus. This second part also issues, at the conclusion of the myth, in two εἰ-clauses (103 and 110), slightly closer together than those of the first part, just as the second section is shorter than the first.[29] Line 80 is, thus, the hinge on which the poem turns. It introduces a quotation which Hieron is said to be able to understand aright: ἓν παρ' ἐσλὸν πήματα σύνδυο δαίονται βροτοῖς / ἀθάνατοι (81–2).[30] The line is a paraphrase of Achilles' famous words to Priam about the urns on the doorstep of Zeus:

δοιοὶ γάρ τε πίθοι κατακείαται ἐν Διὸς οὔδει
δώρων οἷα δίδωσι κακῶν, ἕτερος δὲ ἐάων·   Il. 24.527–8

Even the immediate application helps to secure the reference to Homer, for Pindar in admonishing Hieron, like Achilles in his pity for Priam, applies the general truth to two old men made sorrowful through their children. Peleus is common to both paradigms.

But Pindar appears to make something specific that is left unclear in Homer. The majority of commentators, beginning with the Pindaric scholiast,[31] say that Pindar has misunderstood the Homeric passage, which should be taken to mean that there are two, not three, urns from which allotments come (Plato took the passage to mean that there were only two and at *Rep.* 379D he gives a version that changes line 528 to κηρῶν ἔμπλειοι, ὁ μὲν ἐσθλῶν, αὐτὰρ ὁ δειλῶν).[32] Pindar apparently understands

---

28 Pelliccia 1987, in a subtle and sensitive analysis of the rhetorical articulation of the first part of the poem, has shown that the ἀλλ' of line 77 is not the alternative to the preceding impossible conditions but that this function is fulfilled by the new condition of line 80.

29 The importance of conditional statements in the Third *Pythian* is noted by Greengard 1980: 107 n66.

30 The practice of quoting a poetic text and then commenting upon it first becomes common in Greek poetry about this time: see West 1974: 180.

31 Drachmann *Scholia* 2.82. Cf. Macleod 1982: 133. Among editors of the *Iliad*, Monro, Leaf, Ameis-Hentze, and Willcock, e.g., maintain that the proper understanding of the passage is that there are but two urns.

32 Cannatà Fera (1986: 85–9) maintains that controversy over the correct understanding of the lines from Homer already existed in Pindar's time.

Plutarch is fond of the passage and quotes or alludes to it five times in the *Moralia*. Only once (105c) does he give the version we find in our texts of Homer. He quotes Plato's text at 24A–B and at 600D provides a commentary obviously based on Plato's

that there are three urns, two of bad things and one of good, when he makes explicit a 2:1 ratio. Why? Such a formulation is not necessary if all Pindar wants to suggest is the preponderance of evil in the world[33] – this much was never in question. It is a reasonable answer that the particular form of the quotation (not a misreading, as so often charged, but one of two possibilities implicit in the original) is important for the poem.

Each of the mythical sections might be expected to illustrate the adage. Gildersleeve, somewhat whimsically, was tempted to apply the numbers to the children of Cadmus and Peleus but found he could do so only loosely. He points out that in the case of Cadmus there is 'one joy to three sorrows' and that in the case of Thetis the death is of an only son 'and so more than a double sorrow.'[34] If we press these numbers we have, of course, 3:1 and 1:1. And the story of Cadmus' daughters is puzzling, for it is not an ideal example of a good set alongside evils. The mention of Thyone (= Semele) seems to offer something positive, a momentary respite from the woe that Agave, Autonoe, and Ino caused old Cadmus through their madness and murder of Pentheus. This is, after all, another marriage of a mortal with divinity and since the divinity is Zeus there is recall of the Διὸς χάριν of 95. Mention of Semele is, however, an odd interruption in a narrative that moves from joy to ensuing sorrow – the death of Achilles follows forthwith, and Cadmus and Peleus have been adduced because they are strictly parallel in the unhappy fates of their children (τὸν μὲν ... θύγατρες, 97; τοῦ δὲ παῖς, 100) as they were parallel in their fortunate marriages, each having taken a goddess as a bride. The unexpected reprieve, if reprieve it is, proves ambiguous on closer inspection.[35] The story of Semele is a third instance of the union of divinity with a mortal, but in this case the sexes are reversed and it is the bride who is mortal. We are, thus, more likely to be put in mind of Coronis' liaison with Apollo than of the marriages of Cadmus and Peleus. Pindar's audience was, moreover, unfamiliar with the story, known to us from Callimachus (*Hymn* 5.107–18) and from Ovid (*Metam.* 3.138 ff.), of Actaeon's death for disturbing Artemis at her bath.

---

version. It is unclear which version he has in mind at 369c and 473B, but quite clear that here too he thinks that there are but two jars in all.

33 As Friis Johansen and Whittle (1980 *ad* 1070) believe. One of the scholia to *Ol.* 1.60, μετὰ τριῶν τέταρτον πόνον (Drachmann *Scholia* 1.40–1), tries, not very convincingly, to bring the expression into line with the passage in *Pyth.* 3. For a discussion of this phrase, 'the most controversial in *O.* 1', see Gerber 1982: 99–103.

34 Gildersleeve 1890: 269.

35 Though the ἀτάρ is adversative it is not strongly so: for a similarly weak contrast between ἀτάρ and μέν cf. *Pyth.* 4.168–9. The δέ of line 100 also provides continuity rather than contrast.

Actaeon was, for them, punished on Zeus' orders for wooing Semele (see, e.g., Stesichorus 236 *PMG*), and they may have recognized Semele's death as punishment for the sin for which Coronis died, i.e., seduction by a mortal when she was carrying the seed of a god.[36] The λέχος of Semele (99) recalls the λέκτροισιν of Coronis (26). In this way a link is provided with the earlier myths of the poem. And the name of Semele inevitably conjures up in imagination one thing more than any other – *her* death by fire and the saving of a child from *her* womb. Fire is prominent in the account of the deaths of both Coronis and Asclepius (36, 40, 58), as it is in the death of Achilles (102).[37] Semele is, like Achilles, whose example follows, an instance of a child's being a source of both joy and sorrow.

The numbers of the children may support a fundamental idea of the preponderance of pain (cf. the use of numbers to reinforce a basic idea at *Ol.* 1.79, *Nem.* 7.48, 104). But the exact pattern 2:1 is discernible more generally in the shape of each of the mythical sections of the poem. Cadmus and Peleus move from indeterminate sorrows (ἐκ προτέρων καμάτων, 96) to joy (the joy is marital) and then to sorrow again. The triple rhythm is emphatic: κάματος (πῆμα), χάρις, πῆμα again. And there is a similar rhythm in the first section, where we find the death of Coronis, elaborately told at the outset (accounts of her death begin and end her story), the brilliant medical career of Asclepius, and finally his death by the blazing thunderbolt. The moment of cheer between the framing fires that consume Coronis and Asclepius is a detailed account of Asclepius' cures extending through the entire third strophe (47–53). The aretalogy (Asclepius' successes are listed in this poem, not Hieron's!) is, then, the ἐσλόν between πήματα. This list

---

36 See Janko 1984: 299–307.
37 Achilles was, like Asclepius, taught by Cheiron (cf. *Nem.* 3.43–55). Both mythical sections of the poem thus end with the fiery death of a ward of Cheiron, and both deaths are followed by a gnomic reflection about what mortals must (χρή: 59, 103) expect from the gods.

There are two actual pyres in the poem, that of Coronis and that of Achilles. Coronis is killed τόξοισιν ὑπ' Ἀρτέμιδος (10), Achilles τόξοις (101) of an unnamed assassin. The parallelism is surely deliberate, and another connection is thus established between the two mythical sections of the poem. Pindar suppresses direct mention of the agent of Achilles' death. That agent was Apollo, who also had Coronis slain. Apollo is mentioned neither as the source of the arrows that killed Achilles nor as having sung at the wedding of Peleus and Thetis (cf. *Nem.* 5.22–5 and *Il.* 24.63), perhaps because the one would suggest the other and Pindar's presentation of the wedding as a moment of unalloyed felicity between ills would thereby be damaged: the wedding redounds to the discredit of Apollo in Homer (*Il.* 24.63) and in Aeschylus (cf. *TrGF* 2.350, where Apollo speaks dishonestly). On the wedding of Peleus and Thetis in Pindar and earlier, see March 1987: 3–26, esp. 20–3.

of cures includes mention of Asclepius' power to restore from wasting fire, and it ends with the words ἔστασεν ὀρθούς (53). We remember these words at the moment of joy between sorrows in the second myth (ἔστασαν ὀρθὰν καρδίαν, 96).

Are we also entitled to seek further relevance in Hieron's own situation? The nineteenth century, with its penchant for biographical criticism, felt most emphatically that we were. Dissen, quoting Tafel, says, 'carmen ... plane ineptum esset, nisi re vera Hiero tum duo mala uno cum bono habuisset.'[38] The list of *duo mala* found by the commentators makes fascinating reading.[39] Boeckh, for instance, discusses the matter at some length and decides that one of the most striking things about the Third *Pythian* is the emphasis on the death of children in the myths. And so the poem must be a sort of *Kindertotenlied*, with a biographical referent in the death of some otherwise unknown child of Hieron's.[40] I am inclined to think that we *are* invited to find in Hieron's own fortunes the *duo mala* that are the artistic and emotional centre of the poem in Pindar's reformulation of Homer. Hieron's invitation to right understanding frames the second part of the poem in two εἰ-clauses (80, 103). ὀρθάν (80) is characteristic of his understanding as it is characteristic of the moment of brightness in both illustrative myths.

It should be clear, I hope, where this is leading. σύνδυο πήματα picks up διδύμας χάριτας (72). Both phrases are striking: twin joys, a brace of woes. But the twin joys are known by their absence, I have argued, and are thus πήματα. To Theron of Acragas Pindar had pointed out that ἐσλῶν ... ὑπὸ χαρμάτων πῆμα θνάσκει (*Ol.* 2.20).[41] This is an ode where much the same myths are arranged in rather more characteristic Pindaric fashion to show the dominant light – the stories of Ino and Semele end with apotheosis, the story of Achilles with his translation to paradise. In the Third *Pythian* we are left wondering what the ἐσλόν is beside which the πήματα of sickness and absence of victory, possibly actual defeat, are set. The phrasing of the

---

38 Dissen 1830: 211.
39 For a selection, see Mezger 1880: 65–6.
40 Boeckh 1821: 255: 'De ipsa filii vel filiae morte ne dubites.' The second *malum* for Boeckh is, of course, Hieron's illness.

Boeckh's interpretation at least has the merit of trying to bring the myths of the two sections of the poem together. For a recent discussion of the problem of the unity of the two sections of the poem, which remains broken-backed in most interpretations, and for a proposed solution, see Buongiovanni 1985: 327–36, esp. 331 ff.

41 Mullen (1982: 100–9) has studied the interaction of χάρις and πῆμα in the odes. His statistics show (not altogether surprisingly) that *Pyth.* 3 is exceptional in its emphasis on πῆμα.

famous maxim emphasizes that there must be ἓν ἐσλόν for it is given the emphatic position.

In Achilles' description of the gifts of Zeus, the verb is δίδωσι. Pindar uses δαίονται. The choice of verb is once again deliberate and significant, for it emphasizes one of the principal themes of a poem which gives a clear and consistent picture of man's fate. μοῖρα (84), αἶσα (60), and πότμος (86) are all roughly equivalent terms for expressing what the gods award. And since the gods are repeatedly δαίμονες (34, 59, 109), there is probably an etymology suggested by δαίονται.[42] The gods grant good and bad fortune alike – Coronis' misfortune came from a δαίμων (34), hence her story is not simply a lesson about the mistake of longing for the distant but an example of the gods' direction of human affairs. δαίσαντο (93), which further underscores the theme of divine participation in the lives of mortals, fits into the pattern. Immediately after the passage that tells of the gifts of the gods Hieron is told to contemplate his share of εὐδαιμονία (84) rather than his sorrows. His εὐδαιμονία is, generally, his high station. But this is, I think, made more precise.

It is the δαίμων that makes a man μέγας (86, 107).[43] By paying attention to its dispensation we find our ἔμπρακτον ... μαχανάν (62, 109). Hieron's god-given πλοῦτος (110) can give his εὐδαιμονία permanent form despite the winds of change (104–6), for it enables him to engage a poet.

And so the real answer is given, with customary Pindaric delicacy, in the surprise ending: the ἓν ἐσλόν is the poem itself. The final εἰ-clause repeats the idea of divine dispensation from the conditional sentence of line 80 and advances a hope for future κλέος for the addressee. Since this κλέος is, primarily, what Hieron wins in the great games (cf. Ol. 1.23),

---

42 A correct etymology, as it happens: see Frisk 1973: 341. But for purposes of the poem it is the word-play that is important. The correctness of the etymology is not.

If we are tempted to look for a *Grundgedanke* in the poem, the quotation from Homer, with its strategic position in the structure and its resonance in the language and the myths of the poem as well as in the personal situation of the addressee, would be an excellent candidate. Young, though he is critical of the theory of *Grundgedanken*, finds the Third *Pythian* more amenable to this theory than the other odes of Pindar. But the *Grundgedanke* that has traditionally been found in this poem is something rather different, i.e., γνῶθι σεαυτόν (see Young 1968: 65). The fundamental idea of both good and bad fortune's being of divine origin suits the myths of both parts of the poem, however, whereas the idea of self-knowledge or self-restraint is less applicable to the stories of Cadmus and Peleus than to the stories of Coronis and Asclepius (for a discussion of the inadequacy of most analyses of the poem to account for the myths of the second section, see Buongiovanni 1985). There is a more sympathetic treatment of the idea of *Grundgedanken* now by Heath (1986).

43 Lines 103–4 say much the same thing: prosperity comes πρὸς μακάρων.

there may be here a covert prayer for future victory. More certainly, the theme of singing, so delicately woven into the poem (cf. 17, 64, 90), reappears at the end to remind the king that poetry *does* allow the distant (πρόσω, 111) which up to this point it appeared folly to seek. Hieron's εὐδαιμονία comes into final focus. It is a supreme paradox, we learn at the close, that immortality, which is the future and the distant, is given in the present in the form of the poem: it is ἐοικότα and πὰρ ποδός (59–60) after all. Alongside it there may be the two sorrows that dishearten the ailing Hieron, and Pindar cannot remedy these directly. And so he has not come to Syracuse. Nonetheless Pindar has, for Hieron, changed his absence to delight.[44]

Appendix: Hieron and Polyzelus

The dynasty founded by Gelon in Syracuse lasted not quite twenty years, from 485 to 466 (Diod. 11.38 and 68.5–7). Gelon left three brothers at his death – Hieron, Polyzelus, and Thrasybulus. Hieron and Thrasybulus both ruled Syracuse, Hieron from 478–67, Thrasybulus from 467 until his expulsion a year later. Polyzelus, of whose enmity with Hieron we learn from both Diodorus (11.48.3–5) and the Pindaric scholiast,[45] never ruled at Syracuse. The inscription that was found in 1896 with the charioteer of Delphi names, in the mutilated second of its two lines, Polyzelus as the dedicator. A different version of the first line is still legible *in rasura* beneath the emended line which has been inscribed over it. In the original Polyzelus was called Γέλας ... ἀνάσσων; in the second version all reference to his kingship has been suppressed.

---

44 '... en délice il change son absence ...' The phrase is from Paul Valéry's *Le Cimetière marin*, a poem that takes its epigraph from *Pythian* 3. Another fine poem that shows the direct influence of the Third *Pythian* is Hölderlin's hymn, *Der Rhein*: see the study by Seifert (1982–3).

45 Drachmann *Scholia* 1.68 *ad Ol.* 2.29c. Diodorus and the scholiast agree on the essential point, that Hieron wished to get rid of Polyzelus by sending him to fight in a mainland war, but disagree on other points (e.g., whether Polyzelus actually went).

Polyzelus and Gelon are never mentioned in Pindar's poetry – the situation at Syracuse was strikingly different from that at Acragas, where Theron and Xenocrates were on the best of terms and both patrons of Pindar. At *Pyth.* 1.48 the plural εὑρίσκοντο is surprising immediately after the singular παρέμειν· (referring to Hieron). No subject is expressed, but the reference is to the leaders at the battle of Himera where it is likely that both Polyzelus and Hieron were with Gelon. Line 79 is likewise vague, with the plural able to accommodate a Polyzelus and a Hieron who are not mentioned by name.

It may be inferred that Polyzelus came to rule in the ancestral Gela after Hieron succeeded Gelon in Syracuse. Polyzelus presumably predeceased Hieron. We do not know how or when he died. He disappears from the literary sources after the incident mentioned above: when Hieron tried to get rid of Polyzelus, he took refuge with Theron of Acragas, at once his father-in-law and son-in-law. This episode nearly led to the outbreak of war between the two royal houses but the strife was apparently composed peacefully and led to Polyzelus' establishment in Gela.

474 was, in all likelihood, the year in which Polyzelus won the victory for which he dedicated the charioteer at Delphi. This is the date proposed by Chamoux[46] and it appears to be generally accepted.[47] The year cannot have been 482, certainly, for in that year Hieron, not Polyzelus, was lord of Gela. 478 is not so good a candidate as 474 since, as we have seen, it is the year of Hieron's accession in Syracuse, and Polyzelus may not have been securely established in the Geloan viceroyalty immediately upon Gelon's death and in time for the Pythian festival of that year. As guardian of Gelon's son and commander of the Syracusan army he may well have had designs on Gelon's Syracusan throne but found himself forced by events to take Gela as a consolation prize (that it was a second-best that he only grudgingly accepted is suggested by the stories of his falling-out with Hieron and his appeal for help to Theron). In 470 Hieron was the quadriga-victor. This victory is recorded in the First *Pythian*.

Two supreme masterpieces – the Third *Pythian* and the Charioteer of Delphi – may well date, then, from the same year. It adds a certain piquancy to our contemplation of either or both if we consider the possibility that one issues from defeat, the other from victory in the equestrian games at Delphi in 474 and that the works commemorate two hostile brothers. Wilamowitz aptly remarked that the chariot victory of Theron of Acragas in 476, being a more splendid victory than Hieron's with Pherenikos in the same year, was something that Hieron cannot have contemplated without envy.[48] His envy must have been even greater in 474 when, no victor himself, he contemplated the victory of his hated brother. It is sometimes believed that it was Hieron who, since he survived Polyzelus, was responsible for the re-writing of the inscription in such a way as to exclude reference to

46 F. Chamoux 1955: 26–31.
47 See, e.g., Woodford 1986: 86; Mattusch 1988: 127 ff.
48 Wilamowitz 1922: 237.

any kingship of Polyzelus.[49] He could not, of course, eliminate the reference to the victory which the charioteer proclaims.

The praise-poet regularly sees it as his duty to counter the φθόνος that attends the victor. Pindar's sense that Hieron was the victim of envy that worked from within as well as from without may have contributed to the general darkness of the poems in his honour.

[49] E.g., Mattusch 1988: 127 ff. n48. Jeffery (1961: 266) thinks that the change was made by the Geloans about fifteen years after the date of the original inscription.

I am grateful to an anonymous referee for valuable criticisms and suggestions. My thanks are also due to Professors C.I.R. Rubincam and M. B. Wallace and to Mr Robert Nickel for much helpful discussion.

JASON AND CHEIRON: THE MYTH OF PINDAR'S FOURTH *PYTHIAN*

Nothing from the extant remains of Greek lyric is more impressive than Pindar's Fourth *Pythian* Ode. It is the longest complete poem remaining from the period between the epic and Attic tragedy. Even in the Pindaric corpus it stands unique in its length and unsurpassed in its brilliance. Thirteen full triads make it well over twice as long as its closest rivals, which have only five. Of these thirteen triads eight are devoted to the story of Jason and the Argonautic expedition. This, the first surviving version of the myth in European literature, is told with an amplitude of detail astonishing for Pindar. Moreover, the notorious difficulties of the Pindaric style – allusiveness, extreme compression, subtlety of transition – are, if not totally absent, less sensed than elsewhere, and the intrinsic interest of the story, ever one of the most popular of the Greek myths, combines with the vividness of the individual scenes to produce an effect especially splendid. Pindar has given us other poems equally dazzling within a smaller compass, perhaps, but no other where the impression left by the central myth is so memorable.

And yet, despite the relative absence of obscurities in a poem of such proportions, real problems have arisen when critics have attempted to relate the myth of the poem to the occasion of its composition and performance. If we are not to agree with the scholiast that the work simply suffers from a lengthy digression which occupies the bulk of the poem,[1] or to abandon with Wilamowitz the attempt to seek any unity in the work,[2] we must try

---

First published in *Phoenix* 29.3 (1975) 205–13.

1 Drachmann *Scholia* 2.92.
2 Wilamowitz (1922: 384) speaks of 'die lange Erzählung der Argofahrt, in jeder Hinsicht ein Hors d'oeuvre, von der sich Pindar doch nur wieder gewaltsam zu Kyrene zurückfindet, 261.' See also his further comments 392.

to understand the function of the myth in its context. About the addressee of the ode and the reason for its composition we know a fair amount, most of it ascertainable from the words of the poet himself. A brief rehearsal of the known facts will be helpful here.

Pythians 4 and 5 were both written to commemorate the victory of King Arkesilas of Cyrene in the chariot race at Delphi in 462 BC. The Fifth *Pythian* is, correctly speaking, the actual victory ode for the king. The Fourth, a much longer poem, says almost nothing about the victory. The victory is, in fact, only the ostensible reason for the ode – the real reason, which emerges in the last two triads, being to advance a plea on behalf of a banished subject whose name, Damophilos, is told to us by the poet in line 281.[3] Damophilos, it is clear from the poem, had spent part of his exile in Thebes, where he had known Pindar (299) and had enlisted the poet's support in his attempt to secure his recall to North Africa. It is unclear whether the ode was commissioned officially by a member of the royal house, in which case Pindar will have taken advantage of the opportunity to introduce something which his patron is unlikely to have requested,[4] or whether it was a peace offering on a magnificent scale from the refugee who had himself asked for the poem and paid the poet.[5]

It is precisely this plea for the recall of a political exile with which the poem ends that makes the choice of myth somewhat surprising. King Arkesilas claimed descent from one of the Argonauts, Euphemus: hence the tale of the quest for the Golden Fleece is legitimately part of the history of the royal house of Cyrene.[6] Euphemos, of no particular importance in other accounts of the voyage of the Argo, is especially prominent in the

---

[3] The common belief (see, e.g., Boeckh 1821: 264–05; Wilamowitz 1922: 376) that Damophilos was a kinsman of the king rests entirely on a notice in the scholia (Drachmann *Scholia* 2.103): ἦν δὲ αὐτῷ καὶ πρὸς γένους. It may be nothing more than an inference based on the fact that the poet emphasizes the relationship between Jason and Pelias, the two chief figures in the central portion of the myth (e.g., lines 142–5). But the notice is unclear, for αὐτῷ can and has been taken to mean that Damophilos was related to Pindar (see Wilamowitz 1922: 376, esp. n2). The exact nature of the rebellion in which Damophilos was involved is unclear too. Some, seeing significance in the name of the exile, have assumed that it was a democratic rebellion (e.g., Wade-Gery and Bowra 1928: 102); others (Gildersleeve 1885: 278) have believed that it was an aristocratic uprising. The latter view has found recent support from Chamoux 1953: 195–8.

[4] Chamoux 1953: 178–9.

[5] Gildersleeve (1885: 278), who also thinks (280) that an ode of such length must have cost a fancy price.

[6] Boeckh (1821: 281) argued that Damophilos was descended from Jason, thereby seeking to establish an even stronger link between the myth and the occasion of the poem.

Pindaric version. It is he who, on the return of the Argonauts with Medea from Colchis, receives from a mysterious stranger in North Africa a clod of earth, which betokens a return by his descendants to that continent. Much of the first three triads of the poem is an explanation, cast in the form of a prophecy by Medea to the crew of the Argo, of just how the pledge will be redeemed in the colonization of Cyrene by Battos of Thera seventeen generations later (10). And eighth in line from Battos is the ruling monarch whom Pindar addresses.

The theme of return (νόστος) is certainly emphasized throughout the poem. We hear of the return of the Argonauts to their fatherland (32), of the desire of the soul of Phrixos to be escorted back to the country whence he departed on the miraculous Golden Ram, much against his will (159–62), of the desire of Jason to be reinstated on the throne of his ancestral kingdom which he too had been forced to leave (109–16). Even the colonization of Cyrene is seen as a return to a Promised Land,[7] perfectly appropriate in a poem which ends with an appeal for the recall of an exile to his native land. But herein lies the difficulty. For the mythical paradigm which Pindar proposes to his audience appears to be that of a chivalrous young hero deprived of his rights by a tyrannical king. A prima facie identification of King Arkesilas with King Pelias and of Damophilos with Jason seems almost inevitable. It also seems intolerable, of course, for Arkesilas is hardly likely to have been delighted with a pointed suggestion that in banishing a countryman he has behaved as did Pelias in dispatching the gallant Jason on a mission meant to ensure that the king need never again be troubled by the meddlesome upstart.[8]

Commentators have not ignored this problem. Indeed, much of the modern criticism of the poem has been concerned with attempting to show that the import of the myth is not offensive to the addressee. In Jason we have the most detailed portrait in all of Pindar. Is he a type of the exiled Damophilos longing to be restored to his patrimony, as a naive reading might imply, or can we see in him an idealized version of the king? Those who have been inclined to see Damophilos in Jason have been at pains to point out the harsh lesson that Arkesilas might learn from Pindar's presentation. Boeckh, for instance, while insisting that no invidious comparison of Damophilos and Arkesilas was intended by the

---

7 The νόστος theme is noted by Burton (1962: 168, 173) and by Ruck and Matheson (1968: 19).
8 Gildersleeve, in a slightly different context (the interpretation of the parable of Oedipus at lines 263–70), notes that the equation of Arkesilas and Pelias, Damophilos and Jason is 'monstrous' (1885: 302).

myth, still thought that Pindar was showing the king an example of a tyrant come to a bad end at the hands of one deprived of his rights and sent away, and was warning the king against duplicating the fate of Pelias.[9] Those, and in recent years they have been the majority, who have looked to find the possible links between Jason and Arkesilas have emphasized the character of the Pindaric hero rather than the personal opposition between the two chief figures in the myth: Jason is courteous and conciliatory and bases his claim to the throne on divine right (105–8), as do the Battiads of Cyrene (51, 63, 260).[10]

It is not surprising that commentators should have sought to explain the similarities between the mythical *exempla* of Jason and Pelias and the principals in the quarrel in Cyrene. For there is an obvious parallel of situation between the two pairs. In addition there is the necessity of accounting for Pindar's way of telling the story of the voyage of the Argo. Pindar in the Fourth *Pythian* comes closer, it is true, than does any other Greek poet in any surviving work to answering Quintilian's famous description (10.1.62) of Stesichorus as *clarissimos canentem duces et epici carminis onera lyra sustinentem*, but despite the epic theme and unusual length of this choral ode the treatment of the myth is totally lyric and characteristically Pindaric, with the story told in a succession of *tableaux vivants* rather than by discursive, ongoing narrative. And at the very heart of the poem we find Jason facing Pelias. Far from avoiding any confrontation between the two, Pindar elevates their encounter to a position of pre-eminence in his long poem. It is the main canvas in an exhibition of pictures paraded before our eyes and the one which King

---

9 Boeckh 1821: 264–5, 281. So too Mezger 1880: 219: 'wie nahe lag die Gefahr, dass der verbitterte Verbannte einem künftigen Aufstand in Kyrene seine mächtige Unterstützung lieh, wenn er plötzlich wie Jason zurückkehrte.'

10 The views of the nineteenth-century critics are conveniently summarized in Mezger 1880: 204–5. Of more recent critics, Wilamowitz (1922: 384–5) sees no special connection between the myth and the plea for Damophilos' recall. Norwood (1945) is equally silent on the matter; so too are Farnell (1930–2), Méautis (1962), Bowra (1964). Lattimore (1948: 19–25) sees the dominant motif as one of the folly of delay and, with this, the necessity of decisive action at the opportune moment: the restoration of Jason's patrimony, like that of Damophilos, has been too long put off (22–3). But Lattimore warns against the identification of Jason with Damophilos that this might seem to imply. By offering Jason as a model of gentlemanly behaviour for the king Pindar more than redresses the balance (23–4). So too Burton 1962: 168, who in addition feels it necessary to warn against the temptation to read the myth as a parable. Despite Burton's warning, and with obvious awareness of the inherent difficulty, Sandgren (1972: 12–22) pleads, albeit briefly, for the Jason = Damophilos, Pelias = Arkesilas theory as 'noch einiger Gedanken wert' (18).

Arkesilas, like ourselves, will probably have found most impressive.[11] The two figures, Jason and Pelias, are held up for the king to view and he is left to reflect on them. If analogies could be sought between the antagonists of the legendary past and those of the contemporary dispute in Cyrene, the two portraits could equally well be viewed *per se*, without necessary external reference. Or, at least, the only reference might be left for the king to create by voluntary association, through similarity of behaviour, with one or other of the two actors in the central *tableau*. This too would be in the best Pindaric manner. At the very end of the First *Pythian*, addressed like the Fourth to a reigning monarch on the fringes of the Hellenic world, Pindar had offered the examples of Croesus and Phalaris to Hiero for his consideration. There we have only brief sketches, not the full portraits of the Fourth *Pythian*. But their import, and Pindar's preference, are clear enough. Croesus is remembered with affection while posterity accords only its hatred to Phalaris. Hiero may be remembered either way and is fully free to choose which reputation he will enjoy. Not dissimilarly, Arkesilas has two models set before him.

It is likely that Arkesilas will have found the picture of Jason more attractive than that of Pelias.[12] Is there any indication that Pindar is asking the king to take Jason to heart in a special way, or does he simply leave him to contemplate the alternatives without deliberately nudging him in one direction? In the First *Pythian* the poet's priorities would be evident even without direct recommendation of one choice over the other. The pictures speak for themselves.

So they do in the Fourth *Pythian*, to a great extent, but there is something very particular that Pindar and Jason have to say to Arkesilas that commentators have generally not noticed. That this is something dear to both Pindar and Jason there can be little doubt, for they both tell us as much.

---

11 Duchemin (1967: 98) compares the ode to a Doric pediment with the statues of Pelias and Jason centrally placed. Chamoux (1953: 190) divides the myth into four sections, the first of which, the visit to Pelias (lines 71–168), is, he remarks, as long as the other three together.

12 The first words of Pelias (97–100) are generally taken as disrespectful if not positively insulting and have, more than anything else in the poem, cast Pelias in an unfavourable light. But there is room for doubt whether they should be so taken: see Shorey 1930: 280–1, Burton 1962: 155. If Shorey is correct and Pelias' words are not uncomplimentary, the comparison between Pelias and Jason is not so invidious as that between Croesus and Phalaris in the First *Pythian*.

Jason begins and ends his first speech with mention of the centaur Cheiron. His very first concern is to state that he is proud bearer of Cheiron's teaching; his last words introduce Cheiron again, this time not as the one who gave him his education but as the figure who was responsible for his very name (102, 119):

Φαμὶ διδασκαλίαν Χίρωνος οἴσειν.
φὴρ δέ με θεῖος Ἰάσονα κικλήσκων προσαύδα.

The exact nature of the teaching of Cheiron has been variously interpreted. The scholiast understood it to be ἡ ἀλήθεια;[13] Gildersleeve took it to be 'reverence for Zeus, and reverence for one's parents,' using Pyth. 6.23–7 to shed light on this passage.[14] No doubt Cheiron, as the great preceptor of young heroes, did include truth and reverence for gods and parents in the curriculum of his academy. To these might be added good manners in dealing with the fair sex, for Jason goes on to say in his speech that he has never behaved churlishly or spoken in a manner offensive to the mother, the wife, or the daughters of Cheiron.

But Pindar informs us in two other poems about Cheiron's teaching, and it seems clear that one aspect of it was of outstanding significance to him. In the sublime Third *Pythian*, intended to console the ailing Hiero of Syracuse, Pindar mentions the education of Asclepius at the hands of the old centaur. Apollo snatched his son from the womb of Coronis on her funeral pyre and committed him to Cheiron's care (45–6):

καὶ ῥά νιν Μάγνητι φέρων πόρε Κενταύρῳ διδάξαι
πολυπήμονας ἀνθρώποισιν ἰᾶσθαι νόσους

It is precisely this act of healing that Pindar himself would like to be able to perform for Hiero with the gift of the poem which he is offering him. In the Third *Nemean* we are told (43 ff.) of the education of Achilles, another of Cheiron's distinguished pupils. Pindar says, in a particularly revealing passage (53–5):

---

13 Drachmann *Scholia* 2.123.
14 Gildersleeve 1885: 291. As Gildersleeve remarks (318) the passage in the Sixth *Pythian* in all likelihood alludes to the Ὑποθῆκαι Χείρωνος or *Precepts of Cheiron*, a series of didactic aphorisms attributed to Hesiod. Almost nothing of this work has come down to us: Merkelbach and West (1967) give only one direct quotation as certainly from this work (fr. 283), lines preserved by the scholiast on the Sixth *Pythian*. On the Ὑποθῆκαι Χείρωνος see Jaeger 1945: 25, 194.

βαθυμῆτα Χίρων τράφε λιθίνῳ
Ἰάσον᾿ ἔνδον τέγει, καὶ ἔπειτεν Ἀσκλαπιόν,
τὸν φαρμάκων δίδαξε μαλακόχειρα νόμον.

Once again he mentions healing as the teaching of the master. And he reminds us that Jason was educated by the same tutor as was the god of healing. The tradition that Cheiron taught healing to his pupils is well established: in the *Iliad* we are told that Achilles learned about ἤπια φάρμακα from Cheiron (11.832),[15] as did Asclepius (4.218–19). Healing, then, appears to have been a regular part of Cheiron's teaching.

It has often been remarked that Jason's very name calls attention to this aspect of Cheiron's instruction.[16] That the name Jason meant 'The Healer' for Pindar seems quite likely from the consideration that Pindar's Cheiron not only taught the art of healing but also chose the name to be worn by the bearer of his teaching.[17]

Names were fraught with meaning for Pindar. In the Fourth *Pythian* Medea alludes to her skill and her name (μήδεσιν ... ἁμοῖς, 27) just as does Jason.[18] The name of Cheiron appears to have been a *nom parlant* for the

---

15 Cf. too the red-figured kylix by Sosias, ca 500 BC, in the Staatliche Museen, Berlin, with Achilles tending the wound of Patroclus: Grant and Hazel 1973: 317.

16 E.g., Kirk 1970: 159; Brelich 1958: 117, 197, who argues that the cult of Jason is in origin one of healing, hence the name of the hero. So too Jessen 1916: 759: 'Der Name (von ἰᾶσθαι) kennzeichnet I. als alten Heilgott ..., wie man schon im Altertum erzählte, Chiron habe I. die Heilkunst gelehrt und ihm den Namen I. = ἰατρός gegeben (Pind. Pyth. IV 119 nebst Schol. 211; Schol. Apoll. Rhod. I 554).' Pinsent (1969: 79) calls attention to the famous kylix by Douris in the Museo Gregoriano Etrusco in the Vatican: 'if Jason was swallowed and regorged by the snake it suggests that his quest was, as befits a man whose name is "Healer," for immortality, and that he ... died and was rejuvenated. Vases ... often depict earlier versions of a myth than are preserved in the literary tradition.'

17 Corroboration is offered by the scholiast (Drachmann *Scholia* 2.127): παρὸ ἰατρὸς ἦν, τὸν ἐκτραφέντα ὑπ᾿ αὐτοῦ φερωνύμως Ἰάσονα ἐκάλεσε παρὰ τὴν ἴασιν. Nowhere in Pindar is it suggested that Cheiron chose the names of his other wards. It is all the more likely, then, that the name deliberately assigned has special meaning. Apollodorus (3.13.7) claims that the centaur gave Achilles his name of 'Not Lips' (from α-privative and χείλη 'lips') because the child fed on the entrails of wild animals, and had never put his lips to the breast. This grotesque explanation appears to be original with Apollodorus.

18 Other obvious examples of punning are ζαθέων ἱερῶν ἐπώνυμε πάτερ of fr. 105 Snell[3] and the name Iamos of *Ol.* 6 (from ἰός, 47, and ἴον, 55). For other interesting possibilities see Norwood 1945: 125 (on Ἰσμήνιον) and 131 (on Θήρων). Lloyd-Jones (1973: 129, esp. n117) discusses the tremendous significance Pindar attributes to names, while Sandgren (1972: 14–15) points out that Jason, in his first speech to Pelias, carefully avoids announcing his name until the very end, thereby giving a 'fast

poet too: it is hard to escape seeing an allusion to Cheiron's name in the μαλακόχειρα of Nem. 3.55.[19] That Cheiron's name actually does come from the word χείρ is generally accepted.[20] Pindar's etymology is thus perfectly correct. It would matter little if it were not, though, for what is important is only what he appears to have seen in a name, not the philological accuracy of the derivation.

Cheiron, He of the Skillful Hands, is the teacher of Jason, The Healer. A pupil of Cheiron's will be adept in the work of hands and it is very likely that his skill will be therapeutic.[21] And so there is a wonderful resonance to the words of the poet when he addresses Arkesilas directly (270–1):

ἐσσὶ δ' ἰατὴρ ἐπικαιρότατος, Παιάν τέ σοι τιμᾷ φάος
χρὴ μαλακὰν χέρα προσβάλλοντα τρώμαν ἕλκεος ἀμφιπολεῖν

Ἰατήρ recalls Ἰάσων and μαλακὰν χέρα, like μαλακόχειρα of Nem. 3.55, the διδασκλία, indeed the very name, of Cheiron.[22] The laying-on of hands is apposite to Arkesilas not so much because 'his kingdom of Libya is the

---

mystische Bedeutung' to his revelation. Sandgren does not suggest what that meaning might be.

19 Cf. Bury 1890: 56.

20 E.g., Robert (RE 3:2302), Frisk 1970: 1083. Among modern editors Snell-Maehler and Bowra print Χίρων, Turyn Χείρων in the text of Pindar. Both appear to be attested forms even before Pindar's time: see Kretschmer 1919: 58–62, West 1966: 431.

21 Robert (RE 3.2302) calls Cheiron 'der Gott der schmerzmildernden, kunstgewandten Hand.' The work of hands that Cheiron taught could be the alleviation of pain, but it could also be the skills of hunting or spearmanship in the case of an Achilles, as the passage from Nem. 3 proves. It is interesting to observe that in the Ninth Pythian Apollo asks Cheiron if he may lay his hand upon Cyrene (36): ὁσία κλυτὰν χέρα οἱ προσενεγκεῖν. Apollo is, throughout this passage, another young pupil of Cheiron's, as Woodbury (1972: 561–73) has pointed out. Is this further proof of the fact? For a pupil of the centaur will best show his education by the use he makes of his hands. H. Fränkel (1962: 503 n4) has suggested that the word ἀπείραντος which Apollo uses of the ἀλκά of the maid Cyrene at line 35 of this passage means 'unerfüllbar': the virginal Cyrene, like Atalanta in a strikingly similar passage in Theognis (1287–1294), has hitherto shunned marriage, the natural τέλος of women. She is thus 'unfulfilled,' as we would put it, and the god is proposing to remedy the girl's deficiency by translating her to North Africa where she will bear him a child. On this interpretation the context of Apollo's questions at Pyth. 9.35–7 would be medical, for the laying-on of hands would heal or make whole. But even if Fränkel's interpretation of ἀπείραντος is not accepted, we still see Apollo making an inquiry of the master with regard to a matter of χειρουργία.

22 Of commentators only Fraccaroli (1894: 410) is aware of the significance of Jason's name for this passage. He does not, however, make anything of the probable allusion to Cheiron.

mythological child of that Epaphos who was born of Io by the touch of Zeus,'[23] but because Arkesilas can show himself to be in fact what Jason is in name – a healer – and can reveal, through the use of his hands, the teaching of Cheiron. The wound on which he is asked to place his hand is a wound in the body politic.[24] He can make that body sound again by recalling and being reconciled to Damophilos, himself suffering from the terrible disease (οὐλομέναν νοῦσον, 293) of exile as a result of his quarrel with the king.

Cyrene was famous in antiquity for its physicians. It is noteworthy that Apollo is called Παιάν, or Healer, in the Fourth *Pythian* (270) and that its companion piece, the Fifth, mentions the healing power of Apollo of Cyrene (63–4). Herodotus says (3.131) that the physicians of Cyrene were the most renowned in the Greek world after those of Croton,[25] and a fine bas-relief, dated by Chamoux to the second quarter of the fifth century, thus exactly contemporary with the Fourth *Pythian*, shows a doctor healing a patient by the imposition of hands on the patient's shoulder.[26] The mysterious plant silphium which made the fame of Cyrene in antiquity from the very foundation of the city and which even appeared on its coins was noted in particular for its medicinal properties.[27] There is a special appropriateness to the introduction of the healers Jason and Cheiron into the myth of the Fourth *Pythian*, for the art of healing appears to have been held in high honour in the kingdom of Arkesilas. In the Seventh *Olympian* Pindar had let the images of growth and flowering control much of the myth and his choice of language, for these images had special meaning on the Island of Rhodes where the Ode was to be performed.[28] Perhaps it was his knowledge

---

23 Ruck and Matheson 1968: 25. Medea mentions Epaphos at line 14, it is true, but it is Aeschylus (*PV* 848–52), not Pindar, who suggests an etymology for the name. In the Ninth *Pythian*, where the motif of touch is often repeated (11, 120, in addition to 36), no mention is made of Epaphos.

24 The word ἕλκος was first used in a metaphorical sense by Archilochus, fr. 13.8 West: see Gerber 1970: 18. Archilochus also uses the word ἰᾶσθαι with reference to what we would consider a non-physical wound, fr. 11 West.

25 Some editors consider this passage an interpolation, either a later addition by Herodotus himself or the work of a scholiast. See How and Wells 1.297. The lines are in all the manuscripts.

26 Chamoux (1953: 363–8 and Pl. XXII.3) has a thorough discussion and photograph of the work.

27 Chamoux 1953: 246–63.

28 On Rhodes as a rose plant see Norwood 1945: 138–45; Duchemin 1955: 240–1; Lawall 1961: 33–47; Young 1968: 69 ff., esp. 76; Verdenius 1972: 117, 119. All critics accept some connection between growth and flowering and the island of Rhodes in *Ol.* 7, though some see it as much more pervasive than others.

of the importance attached to healing in Cyrene that led him to tell the story of the quest for the Golden Fleece in the manner he did.[29]

We shall never know what was Arkesilas' reaction to Pindar's tale and ensuing plea. But whether he found it agreeable or distasteful, the Fourth *Pythian* must have given him much to think about. And if he listened attentively he will have understood just how much Pindar was offering him. After all, to Hiero of Syracuse the poet had been able to offer immortality but no cure for his immediate affliction. Cheiron was dead, Asclepius was dead, and all hope of a healer was vain. King Arkesilas of Cyrene enjoys the same immortality as Hiero of Syracuse. And thanks to Pindar he could also derive the comfort of knowing that the power of healing, transmitted from the old centaur to his pupils, was alive and present in his own hands.

---

[29] It is noteworthy in this respect that Medea is referred to as φαρμακώσαισ', 221, and παμφαρμάκου, 233, and that the Argonauts seek a φάρμακον ... ἀρετᾶs, 187.

CYRENE AND CHEIRON: THE MYTH OF PINDAR'S NINTH *PYTHIAN*

CYRENE and its victors called forth Pindar's finest efforts. *Pythians* 4, 5, and 9 are the longest complete poems in the Pindaric corpus, if we judge length by the number of lines in our modern editions. But they are not merely of exceptional length. They are of particular beauty too, and critics have been unanimous in their praise of the Cyrenean odes, far fewer in number than the Sicilian or Aeginetan poems but equally impressive as a group. Of the three poems two (*Pythians* 4 and 5) were composed for King Arkesilas, victor in the chariot race in 462 BC. The third was written twelve years earlier for Telesikrates, victor in the hoplite race. In all three there breathes a special grace, appropriate to the 'land of fair women' (*Pyth.* 9.77), 'Aphrodite's sweet garden' (*Pyth.* 5.24).[1] The Cyrenean odes are all in major keys, just as the Syracusan are predominantly in the minor mode with their darkling myths of suffering and punishment (Tantalus in *Ol.* 1, Typhoeus in *Pyth.* 1, Ixion in *Pyth.* 2, Coronis in *Pyth.* 3).

The Ninth *Pythian* is resonant with happy harmonies. In a major key, it might aptly be described as a sonata with extended coda: Exposition, Development, Recapitulation[2] in lines 1–78, with the last fifty lines introducing

First published *Phoenix* 32.2 (1978) 91–104.

1 Women figure largely in all three Cyrenean poems: see Norwood's remarks, 1945: 41. All references to Pindar are to the edition of A. Turyn (Cracow 1948).
2 To press the musical analogy further, lines 1–13 form the Exposition with its two 'subjects': first subject Telesikrates; second subject Cyrene, whose story is given economically in its main outline. Lines 14a–72 are the Development, the second subject elaborated and expanded. The Recapitulation of first and second subjects comes in lines 73–8: the son of Karneiades (first subject) is mentioned, followed by Cyrene (second subject), and with this the ode seems to come to a natural end. If the musical analogy seems forced, it might be pointed out that sonata form is really only a

new myths but familiar themes. The first three triads seem to form a complete poem. What follows is not so formal in its construction but is clearly related, through its imagery of vegetation and its motif of marriage, to what precedes. In the Fourth *Pythian* too the first three triads appear to constitute a well-rounded whole, a perfectly complete epinician in themselves. But there, because of the extreme length of the ode, the musical analogy is surely overture and following *melodramma*, not sonata with pendant coda.

Of particular interest is the 'Development' section of the Ninth *Pythian*. For here we see Pindar at work transforming a story from the Hesiodic *Eoiae* or *Catalogue of Women*. Only two lines of the *Eoia* of Cyrene are preserved for us by the scholiast, hence we are unable to say with any certainty just what changes Pindar made in adapting his source. The most memorable parts of Pindar's lyric treatment – the scene of Cyrene wrestling with the lion on Mount Pelion and the conversation between the god Apollo and the centaur Cheiron – may or may not have been in the original. We have no way of knowing. One commentator, for instance, feels that the lovely scene of Cyrene's bare-handed combat with the beast cannot have formed part of the *Eoia* where it would have been 'redundant and purposeless.'[3] It is thus Pindaric invention. Another influential commentator feels that Apollo's encounter with Cheiron is, in Pindar, 'unnecessary'[4] and so must simply have been transposed wholesale from the Hesiodic catalogue. Critics have been troubled by the question of the central myth's relation to its source. More recently than the two Germans cited above, R.W.B. Burton has stated that two passages in Pindar's version of the story of Cyrene – her lineage and the cult-titles of her son Aristaeus – 'give the impression of undigested epic material.'[5] The question is in all cases the same: What is intrinsic to Pindar's version and what is the source material that has been, perhaps pointlessly, incorporated?[6]

---

highly-wrought example of what is generally recognized as 'ring-composition' in archaic, especially Pindaric, poetry. Themes sounded at the outset are developed and then repeated for the listeners. Pindar, like Mozart, was meant to be heard, not read, and so it is not surprising that similar forms of composition should be natural to both.

3 Drexler 1931: 464.
4 Studniczka 1890: 41, followed by Malten 1911: 9.
5 Burton 1962: 38.
6 Even if there is some feeling in certain critics that Pindar has not completely assimilated his source, there is nonetheless no lack of admiration for the poem as a whole: see Burton 1962: 32, 59.

Since Pindar's relation to his lost source-material must remain a matter of conjecture for the most part, it may be more profitable to consider the story of Cyrene *per se*, as we find it in the Ninth *Pythian* and without reference to a work we no longer possess. External reference may help us, but only reference to other poems of Pindar.[7] Where we have Pindar's actual words, either in the Ninth *Pythian* or elsewhere, we may draw conclusions more satisfactorily than when we reconstruct lost sources.

The Development section of the Cyrenean Sonata gives us the centaur Cheiron. Whether or not he was in the Hesiodic version he is certainly accorded extraordinary prominence in Pindar's poem. Thirty-seven lines (30–66) are devoted to him. He is summoned from his Thessalian mountain cave by the young god who marvels at Cyrene's strength and courage. He sanctions the union which Apollo so ardently desires, compliments him for his deference to age despite his omniscience, predicts the outcome of the union – the birth of Aristaeus in Libya – and concludes with a prophecy of the child's nurture and an enumeration of the names by which he will be known.

Cheiron was obviously a figure of extreme importance to Pindar. Understandably, for there is scarcely a more interesting figure in all of Greek myth.

---

7 Young (1964) has criticized Hermann Fränkel for seeking the 'unity' of Pindar in the whole corpus and not in individual poems (64–7). Young would treat each poem as a self-contained unity, not as a facet of a larger whole in which we can see the consistency of the poet's preoccupations and the continual recurrence of a few basic themes (Fränkel's position). It is valuable to be reminded that each poem is a unit and that some internal consistency must be sought in individual Pindaric odes. But it is perhaps to be influenced excessively by the 'new criticism' or by F.R. Leavis to take poems as discrete units with no external reference, even to other works of the same poet. Modern poets too (W.B. Yeats and Wallace Stevens are outstanding examples) resist this sort of treatment. Pindar's style is extraordinarily allusive: he expects an enormous amount from his audience, but he supplies supplementary glimpses throughout his work of the way in which he is working in any particular ode. And so it seems legitimate to accept additional evidence from other poems that help to shed light on a particular passage in a particular poem. Lloyd-Jones (1971: 124) reminds us of something we all too often forget, that Greek myth was a 'vast, intricate and loosely coherent web' with all its parts interconnected. One part suggests another, and sometimes, especially in Pindar, we have the poet's own words in poems other than the one we are considering to help us understand a myth. The same is true of the parts of a Pindaric ode that are not myth, and Fränkel is surely right to consider the whole Pindaric corpus as a 'vast, intricate and loosely coherent web,' with certain themes more obvious in the ensemble than in the parts. On this point see also the valuable remarks of Slater 1977: 194.

Healer, prophet, teacher, he is in many respects a type of the poet himself, as the Third *Pythian* makes clear. As well as being preceptor of young heroes – Pindar mentions Jason in the Fourth *Pythian*, Achilles and Asclepius in the Third *Nemean* – Cheiron appears to be a model son, husband, and father, if we can believe Jason when he tells us the high standard of decorum and decency that obtained in the cave where the centaur lived with Philyra his mother, Chariclo his wife, and his unnamed daughters (*Pyth.* 4.103–5). This unfailingly gentle and courteous relationship with women is most remarkable.[8] Also remarkable is his regular appellation in Pindar's poetry by his matronymic, Philyridas. Elsewhere in Greek myth only Apollo is regularly designated by a matronymic, and this is so unusual that the name Letoides has been used to argue the non-Hellenic origin of the god.[9]

Given his association with young heroes, it is not surprising to find him close at hand when the maiden Cyrene is displaying her heroic prowess. Apollo has apparently stumbled on the scene of her exploit (κίχε, 27) but Cheiron lives nearby. And Cheiron, in fact, teaches exactly the skills in which Cyrene excels. She is a huntress (*Pyth.* 9.20–1). Cheiron teaches hunting: *Nem.* 3.41–7 describe the childhood of Achilles in the cave of Cheiron and the boy's precociousness in spearmanship and the chase. Cyrene is a wrestler with lions. This too is something in which, we learn from Pindar, Cheiron could give advice: it was the counsel of Cheiron that enabled Peleus to overcome the lion into which Thetis changed herself to avoid his embraces (*Nem.* 4.60–5).

Other considerations suggest a natural connection with, or interest in, Cyrene on the part of Cheiron. As son of Philyra he is grandson of Ocean.[10] Pindar explains in some detail – this is part of the 'undigested epic material' – that Cyrene's father Hypseus was a grandson of Ocean (*Pyth.* 9.14b). Here we can profitably compare Pindar's account with the *Eoia* on which the scholiast says he drew, for the two surviving lines are helpful:

ἢ οἵη Φθίῃ Χαρίτων ἄπο κάλλος ἔχουσα
Πηνειοῦ παρ' ὕδωρ καλὴ ναίεσκε Κυρήνη.

---

8 For a discussion of the relations between men and women in Greek myth, see Slater 1968. Gildersleeve (1885: 341) speaks of the 'refined environment' of Cheiron.

9 Guthrie 1950: 83–4. Hermes is referred to as Μαίης υἱός, but he has no matronymic appellation corresponding to Letoides.

10 See Wendel 1958: 47–8 (scholion on A.R. 1.554). The scholiast's source is a lost *Titanomachia*. Pindar does not say that Philyra was an Oceanid, but he does not give any alternative parentage for her. Nor does anyone else. It is probably safe to assume, then, that Philyra was generally recognized to be a daughter of Ocean.

The *Catalogue* tells us merely that Cyrene dwelt alongside the Peneius river. Pindar tells us that Peneius was her grandfather and that Oceanus was her great-grandfather.[11] Pindar makes a genealogical relationship of what is only a geographical one in the epic material. And Cyrene thus becomes a relative of Cheiron.

Further, Cyrene's father Hypseus is, we are told (*Pyth.* 9.14a), king of the Lapiths. The Lapiths were famous in story and in art as the enemies of the centaurs, those wild and licentious centaurs descended from Ixion (*Pyth.* 2.40–7) and sharply distinguished from Cheiron. The west pediment of the temple of Zeus at Olympia, contemporary with the Ninth *Pythian* and in all likelihood known to Pindar, shows the great battle of the Lapiths against the barbarous intruders at the wedding of Peirithous, like Hypseus a Lapith king, and Hippodameia.[12] The scholiast on *Nem.* 4.60, quoting Hesiod,[13] explains that the centaurs were suborned by Acastus to kill Peleus, and Pindar himself says that Cheiron saved Peleus from the trap laid for him.[14] It is not hard to imagine that Pindar, by taking the trouble to inform us that Cyrene's father was king of the traditional enemies of the centaurs, suggests a certain affinity with Cheiron, himself at odds with his more ferocious brethren: Cheiron and Hypseus are allies by virtue of the well-known principle that one's enemy's enemy is one's friend. The Lapiths themselves are described in the Ninth *Pythian* as Λαπιθᾶν ὑπερόπλων (14a). It is difficult to say whether the adjective

---

11 The Hesiodic lines do not preclude the possibility that Cyrene was granddaughter of Peneius, but this seems unlikely. The scholiast on Apollonius 2.498–527a (Wendel 1958: 168) says:

τινὲς δέ φασι τὴν Κυρήνην Πηνειοῦ
θυγατέρα γενέσθαι, κακῶς· ἔνεμεν γὰρ παρ' αὐτῷ
θρέμματα, οὐκέτι δὲ καὶ θυγάτηρ αὐτοῦ ἦν.

This appears to be a criticism of someone who, knowing the Hesiodic lines and reading more into them than was there, made Cyrene the daughter of Peneius. Since the scholiast merely repeats what the two lines of the *Eoia* state and does not go on to provide a genealogical relationship, he seems to imply that no descent from Peneius is specified in the source. It is interesting to note that Apollonius himself reverts to the simple geographical relationship we find in the *Eoia*: Cyrene lives ἕλος πάρα Πηνειοῖο (2.500).

12 On the date, see Ashmole and Yalouris 1967: 7. At *Il.* 1.263–8 Peirithous and Caineus are said to have fought with φηρσὶν ὀρεσκῴοισι; at *Il.* 2.743 the enemies of Peirithous are called φῆρας ... λαχνήεντας. Peirithous is the father of Polypoetes, one of two Lapiths mentioned at *Il.* 12.128–30.

13 Drachmann *Scholia* 3: 80–1; M.-W. fr. 209.

14 Escher (1899: 2306) finds this the determining incident in Cheiron's biography: it was his rescue of Peleus that set him apart from the other centaurs.

simply suggests their recurrent troubles with their traditional enemies, the centaurs, or is used *malo sensu* to point to a certain savagery in their demeanour.[15] Either would be instructive. If the first meaning is intended, their quarrels with their troublesome neighbours are no doubt underlined; if the second meaning is the stronger, something is revealed about Cyrene's background.

The relationship between Cheiron and Cyrene may be schematized as follows:

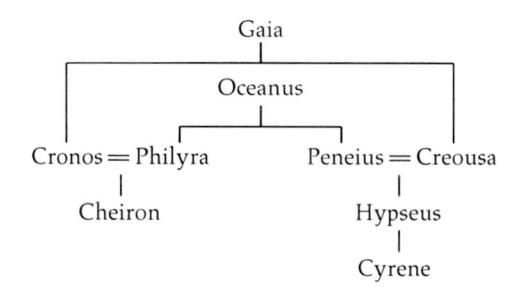

```
                         Gaia
                          |
                       Oceanus
          _____|_____
         |                                 |
  Cronos = Philyra                Peneius = Creousa
         |                                 |
      Cheiron                          Hypseus
                                           |
                                        Cyrene
```

Hypseus and Cheiron are both grandchildren of Ocean on one side, grandchildren of Gaia by their other parent.

None of this is absolutely conclusive, but it does at least help us understand why Pindar provides the genealogical information he does and points to a curious but real connection between Cheiron and Cyrene in Pindar's imagination. Most important of all, perhaps, is the bond created between the two by Pindar's use of the word ἀγρότερος. Norwood glosses the word with his customary sensitivity: 'it regularly means "connected with the open country" (ἀγρός), often with a secondary notion of "hunting" (ἄγρα).'[16] At *Pyth.* 9.6a Cyrene is called παρθένον ἀγροτέραν. The word is also used at *Pyth.* 3.4b of Cheiron himself: he is φῆρ᾽ ἀγρότερον. There are only two further instances of the word in Pindar, once in a Cheironic context: Achilles, Cheiron's ward, fights with λεόντεσσιν ἀγροτέροις at *Nem.* 3.44. The fourth and last instance of its use, at *Ol.* 2.60, remains an extremely vexed problem.[17]

---

15 Rumpel 1883: 460 takes the word in a good sense; Slater 1969a: 521 translates 'insolent.'
16 Norwood 1945: 130. Page (1955: 263–4) calls attention to the rarity of the word as a literary epithet.
17 Attempts to explain the word in *Ol.* 2 (e.g., von der Mühll 1954: 55–6; Erbse 1960: 27–31) remain unconvincing. One is tempted to accept Norwood's suggestion of a pun

Cheiron lives in the country, isolated and away from the society of even his fellow-centaurs. He is the supreme exemplar of civilized arts but he is also a beast of the wild wood to whom the adjective ἀγρότερος may be applied. Geoffrey Kirk has a fascinating discussion of the place of the centaurs in Greek myth. He contrasts the licentious tribe at enmity with the sociable Lapiths and the δικαιότατος (Il. 11.832) Cheiron in an attempt to find the Lévi-Straussian dichotomy between nature and culture, so basic to mythic thinking in all times and all places according to modern structuralists.[18] The mythopoeic imagination sends up binary or antithetical symbols and these, when decoded, reveal fundamental polarities and suggest a mediation.

This is wonderfully suggestive, but just slightly out of focus if applied to Pindar. Cheiron and the other centaurs are polar opposites when viewed in relation to each other and Cheiron is therefore a symbol of justice and society. But when seen in relation to man, Cheiron, as Pindar sees him, is the bridge between the opposites. He is not one of the antithetical poles but a mediator between them. He may be civilized *'par excellence'* (Kirk's phrase) by comparison with other centaurs, but he remains wild (ἀγρότερος)[19] by comparison with man in society. Another set of polarities emerges in Lévi-Strauss's investigation of the Pueblo Indians.[20] Here hunting appears to be a mean between warfare and agriculture, relying with the former on weaponry in order to kill and being with the latter a way of amassing food.[21] In the light of these polarities, or something quite like them, Cheiron can be seen to mediate as well. He teaches the use of weapons – weapons that may be used for martial or for peaceful purposes, in warfare as well as in hunting. The great ashen spear that Cheiron gave to Peleus (Il. 16.143–4) was destined specifically φόνον ἔμμεναι ἡρώεσσιν.

---

on Theron's name or to emend with Wilamowitz, for whom the word ἀγρωτέραν was 'nonsense, arrant nonsense' (1922: 246 n3).

18 Kirk 1970: Chapter 4, esp. 152 ff.
19 Kirk 1970: 159. ζαμενής, used of Cheiron at *Pyth.* 9.39, is intriguing in its ambiguity. It may mean 'inspired,' as it seems to mean when used of the prophetic Medea at *Pyth.* 4.10, but it may also suggest 'wild': the word appears to be used of the savage tyrant Diomedes at fr. 169.35 (Snell-Maehler).
20 Lévi-Strauss 1963: 222.
21 Burkert (1972) in sections 1 and 2 of Chap. 1 has interesting comments on the ambivalent position of weapons in the evolution of the species. Great problems ensue upon man's first learning to use weapons: 'intraspecific' aggression (aggression directed towards other men) must now be channelled outward against animals and the hunt must take precedence over internecine use of the newly acquired weapons.

Achilles learned spearmanship from Cheiron and turned his teaching to spectacular account in the carnage before Troy (Pindar even says at *Nem.* 3.56 ff. that this was the *purpose* of his education). And Apollodorus mentions (3.13.6) that Cheiron fed Achilles on the innards of wild beasts. This may well derive from an epic source that is also reflected in Pindar, whose child Achilles drags σώματα ... ἀσθμαίνοντα back to Cheiron's cave. Why animals not yet dead unless the child was to feed on their living flesh?[22] Cheiron, though perhaps a hunter, is neither warrior nor conspicuous carnivore himself. In fact he appears to have been a gardener. Herbs found on Pelion near his cave were named after him: presumably they were important in the potions and poultices he taught Asclepius to use (*Pyth.* 3.52–3). Cyrene, a huntress who has special affinities with Cheiron, uses her skills to protect her father's kine (*Pyth.* 9.23–4). In a word, Pindar's Cheiron seems to look both ways, whichever set of polarities we use.

This throws considerable light on the juxtaposition of Cheiron and Cyrene. The *enfant sauvage* shuns the company of her fellows and domestic pursuits (*Pyth.* 9.18–19) to hunt ἀγρίους θῆρας. Cheiron, of course, understands this side of her well. He understands too that she is not yet fully civilized[23] and predicts her future in North Africa. Married, she will be fruitful, will know the rule of law in a country where she will, if she chooses, continue her hunting activities among a herding people (cf. Νομάδων δι' ὅμιλον, 127–8, of the Cyreneans):

ἵνα οἱ χθονὸς αἶσαν
αὐτίκα συντελέθειν ἔννομον δωρήσεται
οὔτε παγκάρπων φυτῶν νήποινον οὔτ' ἀγνῶτα θηρῶν   (58b–60).[24]

---

22 See Robertson 1940: 177–80. The centaur Pholus eats raw flesh (Apollodorus 2.5.4); perhaps Cheiron does too, though we nowhere hear that he does.

23 It is interesting to note that Ἄγριος is the name of one of the centaurs at Apollodorus 2.5.4. Is it too fanciful to imagine that Cyrene, defending the interests of her Lapith father, fought off the predatory centaurs and so showed herself as ally of the Cheiron who was himself at odds with them? Fränkel (1962: 503 n4) points out the similarity between Pindar's Cyrene and Theognis' Atalanta (1288–1291), suggesting that both are taken from an identical archetype in Hesiod. Atalanta shot and killed centaurs who tried to rape her (Apollodorus 3.9.2.).

24 Drexler (1931: 455–64) thinks that the story of Cyrene's fight with the lion is native to North Africa. Callimachus certainly thought so (*Hymn* 2.91–3). If so, it is a local Cyrenean legend that will in all likelihood have been transmitted to Pindar by Telesikrates when he presented his dossier to the poet he commissioned. Or Pindar may have visited Cyrene and heard the story there. Chamoux (1953: 169–73) argues that

Again Cheiron mediates. He knows both sides, nature and culture, solitude and civilization, foraging for food and the tendance of crops. He is expert in νόμος as well as being ἀγρότερος. At *Nem.* 3.53 he teaches τὸν φαρμάκων ... νόμον. And his short sermon to Apollo in the Ninth *Pythian* is, in fact, a lecture on νόμος, on the traditional method of procedure for men and gods. Cyrene must move from the darkness into the light, from the shady glens of Pelion (35) to the golden halls of Libya (58, 71), from maidenhood to motherhood, from the lone struggle on the mountain (μούναν παλαίοισαν, 28) to life in community, which she has hitherto shunned.[25]

If Pindar has taken special care to show a certain sympathy between Cheiron and Cyrene, he has also underlined the master-pupil relationship between Cheiron and Apollo in this ode. The matter has been convincingly discussed elsewhere.[26] What is particularly enchanting in the passage at 26 ff. is the tone of intimacy and affection that characterizes the exchange

---

Pindar had not yet visited Cyrene when he wrote the Ninth *Pythian*. He also excludes the possibility that Pindar could have seen a limestone sculpture of Cyrene wrestling with a lion on the Cyrenean treasury at Olympia. This work of art is generally accepted as one Pindar must have known: see, e.g., Burton 1962: 43. Chamoux argues (379–85) that this famous relief never existed: it was created by Studniczka (1890) and is the result of an overheated imagination arbitrarily misinterpreting hopelessly inadequate evidence.

25 As a lone huntress who avoids society and marriage and who usurps an essentially masculine role, Cyrene is quite clearly immature: cf. the interesting article by Vidal-Naquet (1968: 49–64). According to Vidal-Naquet the ephebe must pass from his youthful condition in which his exemplars are the heroes, models of individual prowess, to membership in the hoplite phalanx where personal glory is subordinate to action in concert. The heroes of old remain the pattern for Pindaric athletes, of course, but one must remember the degree to which for Pindar prowess revealed in athletic victory is something performed for the common good (τό γ᾽ἐν ξυνῷ πεπονᾱμένον, *Pyth.* 9.96). We see, in the Ninth *Pythian*, Cyrene's 'rites de passage.' Perhaps Telesikrates is at a similar time in his life. It is admittedly dangerous to extrapolate from Pindar's poetry to a supposed biography of the addressee of the poem (see below n38), but it is worth remarking that Telesikrates bears a certain resemblance to the boy Hippokles of *Pyth.* 10 (see *Pyth.* 10.59 with Gildersleeve's remarks, 1885: 355): i.e., Telesikrates is in all likelihood young. He is nonetheless a *hoplitodromos*, fully adult by Vidal-Naquet's criteria. D. Carne-Ross (1975: 180–1) aptly remarks that Apollo's wonder at the wrestling skill of the young Cyrene and his desire to marry her are echoed by the wonder of the women who watch Telesikrates at the games (100–4) and desire him as son or husband. Perhaps this parallel suggests that Cyrene and Telesikrates are of an age.

26 Woodbury 1972. The discussion by Stéfos (1975a: 48–58) throws no light on the subject; nor does his article (1975b).

between the god and the centaur and the courtesy with which Apollo, temporarily waiving his own omniscience, seeks advice from the great teacher. It is of small importance, ultimately, to be able to ascertain whether or not Cheiron was in the Hesiodic original. We see with ample clarity why he is in Pindar's poem. He possesses a pre-eminence and dignity before which even Apollo bows. He stands, in a way, in the same relation to both the youth and the maid to whose union he good-naturedly gives his approval, for he understands the young Olympian as he knows the huntress in the glades of Pelion. It is especially interesting to note the way in which Cheiron pays tribute to Apollo's knowledge. Totally in terms of nature: Apollo, says Cheiron, knows the number of leaves that the earth puts forth in spring, the number of sands that in the seas and in the rivers are driven before the waves and the gusts of the winds (47-50). Beautifully apposite to the young divinity who stands in the wilds before the cave of the ἀγρότερος! In the land of Libya another aspect of Apollo's personality will come to the fore. The centaur predicts the civilizing of Cyrene. That will take place in North Africa. Similarly, in Libya Apollo's knowledge will show another side, a side more closely linked with civilization. There is perhaps only one other passage in Pindar in which tribute to Apollo is so magnificently paid as in the passage in the Ninth *Pythian* in which Cheiron speaks. In the Fifth *Pythian* Apollo is the patron of the North African city. In this case the terms are especially appropriate to civilization:

> ὃ καὶ βαρειᾶν νόσων
> ἀκέσματ' ἄνδρεσσι καὶ γυναιξὶ νέμει,
> πόρεν τε κίθαριν, δίδωσί τε Μοῖσαν οἷς ἂν ἐθέλῃ
> ἀπόλεμον ἀγαγών
> ἐς πραπίδας εὐνομίαν
> μυχόν τ' ἀμφέπει
> μαντεῖον   (63-9a)[27]

This is the Apollo of culture, as the Apollo of Pelion was the Apollo of nature. Pindar, then, in the Ninth *Pythian* looks at both the young lovers in the same light. It is the twilight of the Thessalian morning. And Cheiron sees them in this light too, Cheiron who understands all things that the future holds for bride and groom. Children, νόμος, medicine,

---

[27] Healing is the teaching of Cheiron: see *Phoenix* 29 (1975) 205-13 [in this volume 192-201]. In this too, then, Apollo shows the teaching of the master.

prophecy: all are part of Cheiron's province. For the young couple they are still in the realm of potentiality, to be translated into the brightness of day with *their* translation to Libya. Apollo on Pelion is a *Naturmensch*, ready to learn from Cheiron; in Cyrene he will be hymned as god of culture and civilization, bringer of εὐνομία. Cyrene on Pelion is seen as a huntress. But even there she brings εἰρήνη to her father's cattle through her hunting. The pastoral and agricultural side of her, incipient in Thessaly, will be fully revealed in North Africa where she will be πολυμήλου καὶ πολυκαρποτάτας ... δέσποιναν χθονός (6b-7) and where her son Aristaeus will be a protector of flocks, ἄγχιστον ὀπάονα μήλων (66b), in a land of herdsmen. It is not so much a question of something being added as of something embryonic or not fully developed being brought to realization. The imagery of dark and light in the poem reinforces this.

Cheiron's prophecy to Apollo ends with a prediction of the birth of Aristaeus. Here, as in the case of the relationship of Cyrene to Peneius, it does appear possible to say something definite about the relationship of Pindar to his source. Pindar's Cheiron says that the child will be brought to the Horae and to Gaia for nurture (62), that he will be called Zeus and Apollo, Agreus and Nomios (66–7). The names probably come from Hesiod, for Servius (on Virgil G. 1.14) says: *Aristaeum invocat, id est Apollinis et Cyrenes filium, quem Hesiodus dicit Apollinem pastoralem.*[28] *Pastoralem* is in all likelihood a translation of Νόμιον. Apollonius (2.507) calls Aristaeus Ἀγρέα καὶ Νόμιον too and it is likely that he is following Hesiod rather than Pindar here.[29] In Apollonius' account Aristaeus is brought back to Thessaly and nurtured in the cave of Cheiron. This incident may have been in the Hesiodic source. Certainly Apollonius did not find it in Pindar, who leaves the child in North Africa, the place of his birth, and makes the only connection of Aristaeus with Cheiron the prophecy put into the centaur's mouth.

Lines 61–7 then, which at first appearance may seem an unassimilated chunk of source material, make excellent sense in terms of the movement of the poem. Aristaeus will bear his father's name, Apollo. Zeus' name is given to him too, and though this seems startling it at least calls to mind the place of his birth, the Διὸς ἔξοχον ... κᾶπον (55). Ἀγρέα καὶ Νόμιον are perfect, for he is the child of the huntress (the word recalls ἀγροτέραν

---

28 M.-W. fr. 216. Fr. 217, a recently discovered papyrus, may be the actual passage to which Servius is referring.

29 See above n11 for a clear instance of Apollonius' dependence on the Hesiodic source.

and ἀγρίους) in her new home, the land of Nomads and of νόμος (59).[30] The wild and the civilized meet in the child just as they do in Cheiron. No one, not even Apollo as he is presented in the Ninth *Pythian*, is so able as Cheiron to speak of the boy's birth. For he, like Cheiron, will be something of a mediator.[31] This is suggested by his names, his background, the place of his birth.

It is also suggested by the names of his nurses. Pindar leaves Aristaeus in Libya in the charge of the Horae and of Gaia. Gaia is the great-grandmother of Cyrene and was especially prominent in the genealogical material at the beginning of the ode.[32] We are reminded of his mother's Thessalian descent, of her 'natural' side. The Hours, Δίκη, Εἰρήνη, and Εὐνομία[33] are especially suitable to civilization. Εὐνομία in particular is associated with Apollo in his role as patron of Cyrene and giver of culture (*Pyth.* 5.67). Again we discern how the details of a myth in Pindar may reinforce a

---

30 Νόμος in Pindar is the traditional belief or ordinance that binds members of a community: see Ostwald 1965: 127 ff. F. Heinimann (1945) discusses the occurrences of the word in Pindar and draws the same conclusion. Νόμος is 'die traditionell gefestigte und geltende Ordnung' (71), always with overtones of community: 'νόμος ist ... das bei einer Gruppe von Lebewesen "Geltende"' (65). Cultural relativism could undermine the belief that there was any νόμος that applied to all men, but even when the absolute validity of νόμος was challenged it retained a kernel of its initial meaning: it continued to apply to a group. The word νόμιος 'pastoralis,' comes from νομός, which in turn comes from the same root *nem-* that produces νόμος. The problem of the semantic relationship between the two words νόμος and νομός is notoriously difficult and no conclusive explanation has been advanced (see Heinimann 1945: 59–61; Laroche 1949). But perhaps the idea of community, especially of civilization, informs both. The 'Neolithic Revolution' was the result of the herding and domestication of horned beasts and, with this, the cultivation of fodder. This produced the first sizable fixed communities. Palaeolithic man had been a hunter and consequently his social life was limited: 'it was only through the control of breeding of animals and plants that early man was able to ensure himself a reliable and readily expandable source of food and thereby establish a secure basis for cultural advance' (Clark 1962: 76–7). In other words, νομοί make cities possible and cities (civilization) are particularly prone to develop νόμοι. Cf. Lloyd-Jones 1972: 56: 'as the polis developed, law and law-abidingness acquired a special sanctity.' In the Nomads we see a very special phenomenon, pasturing people without fixed homes: animal husbandry has not led to agriculture. There were Nomads in Cyrene and presumably the patronage of Cyrene's son extended to them. But at the same time it is emphasized that Cyrene's African settlement will be a city (*Pyth.* 9.71). Pindar, ever an advocate of civic virtue and life in community, makes no exception in the case of Cyrene.
31 This structuralist view of Aristaeus Agreus and Nomios as a mediator between extremes is put forward by Detienne 1971: 18–19. Detienne sees Aristaeus as the mean between Orion (excessively savage) and Orpheus (unnaturally gentle).
32 Γαίας θυγάτηρ stands at the beginning of the epode of the first triad.
33 Cf. Hesiod, *Theogony* 902. Pindar mentions them too at *Ol.* 13.6–7.

central theme. Cheiron is mediator between nature and culture. He gives his blessing to Apollo and Cyrene, both of whom will, in North Africa, show new, civilized facets of their personalities. The fruit of their union will be both Ἀγρεύς and Νόμιος and nurtured by a plurality of goddesses that represent nature and culture just as Cheiron himself does. If Cheiron is forgoing his right to educate the child he is at least promising nurses who are fully adequate to their task.

The contrast between nature and culture which the structuralists find so helpful in analyzing myth is not something of which the Greeks were themselves unaware. The distinction between *nomos* and *physis*, so discussed by the sophists, is a very similar formulation of polarities. The sophistic debate is not one in which Pindar participated,[35] but the contrast between law or custom and nature, which in the late fifth century developed into a radical conceptual antithesis, is adumbrated in Pindar's Cheiron, a mythical figure in whom both terms of the antithesis are contained. The greatest attraction of the structuralist school is that it asks us to take myth seriously and to see it as a vehicle through which important and complicated issues are expressed. Myths are not simple entertainment nor the bumbling and inarticulate formulations of people who have yet to grow up and discover philosophy. Pindar's myths are not just purple patches that adorn his odes nor the product of a childish mind.[36] Pindar is a serious thinker whose thought is presented through poetry and myth. The figure of Cheiron seems to have haunted his imagination. With good reason, for Cheiron embodies something central to the thought of all men, if Lévi-Strauss is correct.[37]

34 See Kirk 1970: 152.
35 Ostwald 1965; Lloyd-Jones 1972.
36 Norwood's phrase (1945: 184) is memorable: 'after his death it was no longer possible to think like a child and sing like an archangel.'
37 Kirk's intriguing discussion of the centaurs (above, n18) has a sequel in an equally fascinating discussion of Heracles as an embodiment of the nature-culture dichotomy in 1974: 170 ff. Heracles is a figure in whom contradictions meet. He is a paradigm of raw brutality and a supreme culture hero. Pindar's fascination with Heracles is as great as his attraction to Cheiron: κωφὸς ἀνήρ τις, ὃς Ἡρακλεῖ στόμα μὴ περιβάλλει he exclaims at *Pyth.* 9.90. These words are surely spoken by the poet, not, *pace* E.L. Bundy (1962a: 18, esp. n43), by the victor. Bundy's analysis of the conventional elements in this catalogue is for the most part convincing, but his claim that 82 ff. is the second entry in the catalogue, a victory in the Iolaia at Thebes, and that 90–2b represent the third item, a victory in the Herakleia, is puzzling, there being only one known set of games at Thebes in honour of the two heroes: see the scholiast on *Ol.* 7, Drachmann *Scholia* 1.232; Farnell 1915: 194; Péron 1970: 58–78. Just as Cheiron, prophet and healer, is a type of the poet, so is the suffering Heracles a type of the ἀθλητής. He is also a fellow-Theban, and Pindar's preoccupation would be fully justified on these grounds

In the coda of the Ninth *Pythian* we are told of an ancestor of Telesikrates, one Alexidamos. He won a race, as did Telesikrates, and his prize was a bride.[38] Within the story of Alexidamos is told the story of the forty-eight daughters of Danaus who were, like Alexidamos' bride, won by their second husbands in a footrace. Is there a connection between this myth and that of Apollo and Cyrene?

R.P. Winnington-Ingram thinks there is. He suggests that the moral of Pindar's poem is that 'the sexual relations of men and women should not

---

alone. But perhaps Heracles fascinates Pindar because he, like Cheiron, is a mediator between nature and culture. Pindar knows Heracles' violence and is troubled by it (fr. 169 Snell-Maehler). But he also thinks of him as a great benefactor of humanity: see the prophecy of Teiresias at *Nem.* 1.60 ff. Heracles is a famous lion-wrestler: the first of his labours is the strangling of the Nemean lion. And perhaps his most important single exploit on behalf of mankind is his killing, in a wrestling-match, of Antaeus (*Isth.* 3/4.70–3). This took place in Libya, Cyrene's home. Pindar may allude to this in the Ninth *Pythian*: if line 110 is punctuated, with Turyn, Ἴρασα πρὸς πόλιν Ἀνταίου, the reference is to the famous giant, not to a later namesake (cf. Gildersleeve 1885: 347). This punctuation is attractive because 1) Ἀνταίου now precisely defines the expression πρὸς πόλιν, which by itself adds nothing to Ἴρασα, 2) Telesikrates is no longer the descendant of a monster, as he would be if Ἀνταίου modified κούραν (110b), 3) it eliminates the chronological difficulty that so embarrassed the scholiast that he was forced to posit a second Antaeus, totally unknown elsewhere: see Chamoux 1953: 284–5. Antaeus' name means 'adversary,' pure and simple (cf. ἀντάεις at line 96 of *Pyth.* 9, unique occurrence of the word in Pindar). The ἁλίοιο γέροντος of line 97 is Nereus, and this may hint at another wrestling-match. According to the scholiast on Apollonius (above, n10) 315 (on 4.1396) Heracles' match with Nereus, who like the Thetis of the Fourth *Nemean* assumed a variety of forms to escape his antagonist, immediately preceded that with Antaeus. The same story is told by Apollodorus, 2.5.11. These possible allusions to Heracles the wrestler may be calculated echoes of Cyrene's wrestling. And it is remarkable to find Cheiron and Heracles both so important in the Ninth *Pythian*. Nowhere else does Pindar bring them together.

38 The theme of winning a bride is central to the poem. Apollo wins a bride. Alexidamos wins a bride. Forty-eight suitors in Argos win brides. Commentators have thought that this insistence on the theme of marriage says something about the victor's private life (see Gildersleeve 1885: 337–8 for a critique of this view). But Telesikrates' bride is victory, which he brings back to Libya just as Apollo brought his bride back to North Africa: ἀγαγόντ', 78, seems to suggest this (cf. ἀπάγεσθαι, 123). For the active used rather than the more usual middle cf. Aeschylus *PV* 500. Just as Libya will welcome Apollo and Cyrene (δέξεται ... πρόφρων, 58–8b) so will Cyrene welcome Telesikrates and his bride (εὔφρων δέξεται, 76). The δέξεται of line 76 does not prove that the ode was performed at Thebes: see Gildersleeve 1885: 335, Bundy 1962a: 21–2, esp. n48. The future tenses with present meaning given by Bundy are all, with the exception of the δέξεται of the present passage, in the first person. ἀντιάξει of *Ol.* 10.88 should be added to his list to strengthen the case for the use of a person other than the first in futures of this sort: see Schroeder 1922: 80. See also Slater 1969b: 86–94, esp. 88.

be based upon force, upon *bia*'[39] and thinks that this is just the lesson of the Danaid trilogy of Aeschylus too.[40] The trouble with this interpretation is that it assumes that Apollo is asking Cheiron's permission to go out and rape Cyrene and that he is dissuaded by the centaur from so doing. But there is no discussion in the poem of rape or force as the basis of sexual relations.[41] Similarity between the myth of Cyrene and that of the Danaids there undoubtedly is, however. In both cases, girls who have elected virginity (and the use of weapons)[42] come to accept marriage. Rather than a single and simple-minded moral, 'wooing is better than rape,' we have two subtle myths that complement each other; girls who use murderous swords – there is something harsh and forbidding about them – become brides. The motifs heard in the coda are familiar, as they should be. But the composer knows variant harmonies and it is these we hear at the close.

---

39 Winnington-Ingram 1969: 13. This is oddly re-evocative of L. Dissen's interpretation of the poem (1830: 302), though Winnington-Ingram's moral is general whereas Dissen's is levelled at the victor. Dissen found a 'summa sententia' or 'Grundgedanke' in each ode. His attempt to extract morals from the myths has been harshly dealt with: Young (1964: 7 ff.) considers it the most perniciously misleading theory in the history of modern Pindaric criticism; Norwood (1945: 76) is simply scornful.
40 Winnington-Ingram 1969: 10. Mette (1963: 52–3) thinks that the Aeschylean trilogy may have ended with the marriage of the daughters of Danaus as in the Ninth *Pythian*: fr. 125 (Mette) would be a bridal song for the occasion. Garvie (1969: Chapter 5) finds that the material at our disposal allows no probable conjectures.
41 See Woodbury 1972; Gildersleeve 1885: 337.
42 The Danaids murdered their first husbands with swords, all except Hypermnestra who, μονόψαφον ἐν κολεῷ κατασχοῖσα ξίφος (*Nem.* 10.6), spared Lynceus, and Amymone, whom Pindar appears to exclude also. The very mention of the Danaids would inevitably bring to mind their use of their swords on their first wedding night. Cyrene's sword flashes in the darkness too (21–6), like the swords of the Danaids. Death by the sword is a motif that is heard at 83–4a: Iolaus kills Eurystheus. His use of the sword, like Cyrene's, is to rid the world of a beast. Stroke of sword may do good or ill: cf. Fränkel's comments (1962: 565) on *Ol.* 7 – the stroke of Neoptolemus brings death, that of Hephaestus life.

PINDAR'S ORESTEIA AND THE TRAGEDIANS

'No other poem of Pindar's has baffled the interpreter so much as this,' says Farnell of the Eleventh *Pythian*.[1] The problems are legion, as are the interpretations. What is the date of the poem? What is its relation to Aeschylus' *Oresteia*? The principal difficulty perhaps (certainly the one that first strikes even the most casual of modern readers) is the apparent inappropriateness of the myth. What place has this tale of murder and counter-murder in a poem of praise for a victor at Delphi? Not a few commentators, beginning with the scholiast,[2] have found some consolation for their bafflement in the fact that Pindar accuses himself of irrelevance as soon as he has told his story, and they are content with the poet's own admission of incompetence (38–40):

> Truly, friends, I have been whirled along
>   ever since
>   the road divided –
>   all was well till then;
>   or was it a sudden gust
>   blew me off course
> like a boat at sea?[3]

First published in Martin Cropp, Elaine Fantham, S.E. Scully (eds), *Greek Tragedy and Its Legacy: Essays Presented to D.J. Conacher* (Calgary: University of Calgary Press, 1986) 1–12.

1 Farnell 1930–2: 2.225.
2 Drachmann *Scholia* 2: 259, followed by Farnell 1930–2: 2.228, for example.
3 Translations are from Nisetich 1980.

In 1968 David Young announced his solution to the problem posed by the myth.[4] It is, he claims, an extended negative example.[5] The poet recounts the horrors of the House of Atreus in order to give point to his utterance in lines 52–3:

> having searched
> into the city's ways, and having learned
> that moderation blooms
> with a longer happiness,
> I have no fondness for the tyrant's lot.

Moderation is, Young claims, 'the life traditional to Thrasydaios' family.'[6] On this reading everything falls neatly into place.

The difficulty with this interpretation is the import assigned to the myth. Pindar does, certainly, use negative examples: the Second *Pythian* provides the best-known instance. But in this dark canvas we are left in absolutely no doubt as to the meaning of the myth: Ixion is a notorious sinner, his sin ignorance of *charis*, and the example instructive for poet, patron, and audience. There is no comparable stigma attached to Agamemnon and Orestes in the tradition.[7]

The importance of Orestes as good son *par excellence* is fixed in pre-tragic art and literature.[8] The tone is set by the *Odyssey*, where

---

4 Young 1968: 1–26.
5 The idea that the myth is a negative example was earlier put forward by Dissen 1830: 348. It seems to have been novel in 1830 and found little acceptance until Young reintroduced it in 1968. Since then the view has been widely accepted: e.g., Nisetich 1980: 48; Newman 1979, who says (55) that 'the deadly narrative of murder and lust is *contrasted* with the shining victory of Thrasydaeus' (Newman's italics). See also n34 below.

It was Dissen who introduced into Pindaric criticism in 1830 the idea that the essence of a Pindaric poem can be given in a single brief formulation (*Grundgedanke, summa sententia*). Young (1964: 3) criticizes this theory as 'the most infamous idea in the history of modern criticism.' But Young's own reading of the Eleventh *Pythian* is itself ultimately a *Grundgedanke* ('tyranny is a bad thing') and here too he is close to Dissen.
6 Young 1968: 21. In 1964: 9, Young rejects Boeckh's interest in the lives of Pindar's patrons and his belief that the poems say something about those lives as only slightly less misleading than Dissen's approach. Yet his own interpretation is, we see, supposed to have biographical relevance.
7 In the case of Odysseus Pindar takes an unfavourable view of the hero, one that is at variance with the Homeric picture: see *Nem.* 7.21–4. But in this Pindar is not unique. Odysseus is much less favourably regarded from the fifth century onwards than he was in epic: see Stanford 1974: 139 ff.
8 On Orestes see Davies 1960: 214–60; Vermeule 1966: 1–22; Schefold 1966: 14, 47–8, 94–5; Schefold 1978: 260–2. I have not been able to see A.J.N.W. Prag, *The Oresteia:*

Orestes is held up as a model for Telemachus by Nestor (*Od.* 3.193–200) and by Zeus himself (*Od.* 1.35–41). This Orestes is a matricide (*Od.* 3.310; cf. Hesiod fr. 23a. 30M.-W.).[9] There is no indication before the tragedy that his murder of Clytemnestra is reprehensible or morally ambiguous. As early as the *Nostoi* (Allen 1912: 109), where Orestes comes with Pylades from Delphi, the act of revenge has Apollo's sanction. Aeschylus makes Apollo's justice, like all the other partial forms of justice in his *Oresteia*, questionable and imperfect, but this questioning of Olympian standards is not an intrinsic part of the story. Orestes rids the world of an evil, traditionally, and is in this not very different from Perseus, who killed the Medusa. It might in fact be argued that Orestes is superior to Perseus, for Perseus killed a perfectly innocent creature who was minding her own business and whose death-dealing career was *initiated* by his act.[10] Clytemnestra's was *terminated* by Orestes. J.D. Denniston, in his introduction to the *Electra* of Euripides, says of Clytemnestra:

> The Greeks of the fifth century ... thought of women not so much in the light of a gentle, weak creature, needing protection, as of something passionate and crafty which in the absence of restraint might prove infinitely dangerous.[11]

More recently, this attitude has been further elucidated and shown to be by no means new in the fifth century.[12]

Pindar's version is entirely consistent with this earlier understanding. In lines 22–5 he puzzles over two versions of the legend. One is the version we know from the *Odyssey*: Clytemnestra took a lover in her husband's absence and abetted or performed the murder on his return. The other version, which we find in the *Cypria* (Allen 1912: 104) and in the Hesiodic

---

Iconographic and Narrative Tradition (Warminister 1985). The sudden appearance of Orestes, frequently in the company of Pylades or Talthybius, on early red-figure vases around 500 BC (see Vermeule 1966: 14) coincides with the prominence of tyrannicides in the Attic scholia. This is probably not fortuitous: Orestes and Pylades suggest Harmodius and Aristogiton.

9 Denniston 1939: ix repeats the suggestion first made by Robert (1881: 163) that Clytemnestra's funeral in the *Odyssey* follows her suicide. This idea has been generally discredited: see Lesky 1967: 5–21. Orestes' matricide is visible on, *inter alia*, a bronze relief from Olympia (about 570) published by Daux 1960: pl. 18.2, and on a late 6th-century metope (see Schefold 1978: 261).
10 See Vermeule 1979: 139.
11 Denniston 1939: xviii–xix.
12 Carson 1981: esp. chap.3 .

fragments (fr. 23a.17 M.-W.) tells of the slaughter of a daughter. Neither of these sources, nor Pindar in recounting this tradition, makes Agamemnon the actual murderer of his own daughter: in the tradition Calchas is the butcher, and Pindar's version is perfectly consonant with this.[13] It was for Aeschylus, it seems. to make Agamemnon the killer of his own child, no doubt to increase the culpability of the king.[14]

Pindar's procedure in lines 22–5 has been seen as mirroring the influence of Aeschylus' *Oresteia*. Farnell again:

> It has not been sufficiently observed that in telling this story Pindar departs from his usual straightforward style of epic-lyric narrative ... There is no parallel elsewhere in his works to this method of handling an epic tale ... In fact, lines 22–30 can be best explained if we assume that Pindar wrote them under the strong impression made on him by the *Agamemnon* of Aeschylus, where the Iphigeneia sacrifice is a prominent motive and is made the ground for this casuistic problem: whether it accounted for and extenuated the guilt of Klutaimestra?[15]

But Pindar's procedure here is not so unparalleled as Farnell claims.[16] We frequently find Pindar casting about, looking for a true *logos* among dis-

---

13 Séchan 1926: 86–101, claims that in the *Cypria* Agamemnon sacrificed his own child. This is almost certainly wrong: see Henrichs 1981: 213, who points out that the officiant is traditionally a seer (Calchas). The words of Proclus in his account of the *Cypria* (Allen 1912: 104) do not point to the agency of Agamemnon. Janko 1982b: 25–9 tentatively reconstructs the relevant passage of the *Cypria*: Agamemnon is sitting to one side at the sacrifice. See also Vermeule and Chapman 1971: 285–93: this vase very likely shows the sacrifice of Iphigeneia. The authors think (293) that Agamemnon may have been present with a sacrificial knife but there is no visible evidence for this and it goes against what we glean from the literary accounts. The Hesiodic Ἰφιμέδην μὲν σφάξαν εὐκνήμιδες Ἀχαιοί (fr. 23a.17) is echoed by Pindar's Ἰφιγένει᾽ ... σφαχθεῖσα (23). See also Dyer 1967: 175–6.
14 Henrichs 1981: 198 believes that the tragic version of Iphigeneia's sacrifice is new in the early fifth century, with Pindar and Aeschylus. But Solmsen (1981: 353–8) convincingly argues that the Hesiodic lines describing the rescue by Artemis are not part of the original narrative and that the tragic version is at least as old as Hesiod. This reinforces the view presented here that Pindar is recording traditions inherited from earlier poetry.
15 Farnell 1930–2: 2.223–4.
16 Though modern commentators, like Farnell, commonly speak of this passage in *Pyth.* 11 as showing an otherwise unparalleled Pindaric interest in motivation, Pavese (1975: 248) more correctly observes that the disjunctive question πότερον ... ἢ is 'per introdurre varie versioni ... della leggenda.'

crepant versions. In *Ol.* 1 he combines true and false stories of Pelops' disappearance in a way that still leaves commentators in disagreement as to what he really believes the true story to be.[17] This is common enough on his part.[18] For Pindar myth is history and there must be a true account of the events of the past. The problem of knowing what is true is intensified by the fact that conflicting accounts are transmitted orally; a true *logos* exists among competing *logoi*. Whereas the tragic poet is presenting a *mythos* that need not have a literal validity outside the drama, Pindar is responsible for giving an accurate account of the events of the past. The tragic poet is free to analyze a complex character like Clytemnestra and probe the reasons for her action, just as he will investigate the moral ambiguities in the actions of Agamemnon and Orestes. Pindar, in seeking historical fact, frequently allows us to watch him sifting the evidence until he finds the true account among variant versions.

In this case Pindar's choice seems to be quite clear: the version we know from Homer is correct. In 25–7 the poet dilates on the evils of adultery, an ἔχθιστον ἀμπλάκιον. Clytemnestra is indeed 'passionate and crafty'! And the adulteress suffers with her paramour in Orestes' act of revenge. By killing the lovers Orestes presumably silences the *kakologia* that adultery has awakened (28). It is probably not too fanciful to see a parallel between the Orestes of the myth and the victor Thrasydaeus: if revenge silences *kakologia*, victory in its turn calls forth praise to counter the *phthonos* that inevitably attends the great (29, 54).

Orestes is, as Wilamowitz understood, an agent of Delphic justice in this poem, which extols Πυθῶνα ... ὀρθοδίκαν.[19] The νηλὴς γυνά (22) is presented in the blackest terms. She is worse than the Clytemnestra of Homer and Aeschylus, for she would have murdered her own son had he not been saved through the good offices of his nurse. And so Clytemnestra's death is deserved. The mythical narrative is, in fact, nicely framed by φονευομένου (17) and πέφνεν ... φοναῖς (37). It provides an excellent

17 See, e.g., Köhnken 1983a: 66–76.
18 On 'the device of mentioning and then abandoning what has just been said' (without explicit disavowal), see Gerber 1982: 69–70. It may be that Pindar rejects the tradition according to which a child was sacrificed, considering it at variance with the true (Homeric) story. In *Ol.* 1 Pindar rejects the traditional story according to which Tantalus killed his child Pelops. He may also, in *Ol.* 1, even reject the common story that Pelops had an ivory shoulder, though he does not *explicitly* repudiate this (cf. Gerber 1982: 56).
19 Wilamowitz 1922: 261. Burton (1962: 63) disagrees; but see Egan 1983: 194.

example of δράσαντι παθεῖν: Clytemnestra is killed for the husband she killed, by the son she would have killed. It is worth mentioning that the Orestes of the Eleventh *Pythian* is more than slightly reminiscent of the Jason of the Fourth. This Pindaric hero was similarly threatened with death as a child and deprived of his patrimony, was smuggled away and reared in exile to return as a young adult to reclaim his patrimony and bring about the death of a usurper.

Condemnation of Clytemnestra there certainly is in the poem. But even those who show a willingness to exempt Orestes from censure extend condemnation to Agamemnon. The basis for this is ὄλεσσε κόραν (33). Translators into English regularly make Agamemnon responsible for the death of Cassandra at this point.[20] But ὄλεσσε here is simply 'lost,' a common enough meaning.[21] Pindar begins his narration by recounting Clytemnestra's heinous deeds (including the murder of Cassandra, 19–20). He reverts to the death of the Trojan maiden in 33 when he is telling us once again that the heroic son of Atreus was laid low. The brief and brilliant account of the destruction of Troy at the end of the myth is what some Pindaric critics call 'terminal exploits'[22] (cf. Pelops in *Ol.* 1, Achilles in *Ol.* 2, Bellerophon in *Ol.* 13, Perseus in *Pyth.* 10), and they increase Agamemnon's stature. But the sacker of Troy lost his life and his prize on his return home.

Both Agamemnon and Orestes are in Pindar what they were in Homer. We have a heroic father, with a son who is a 'chip off the old block' (Orestes' 'terminal exploits' follow those of Agamemnon). This offers the key to the poem under discussion. Pindaric insistence on φυά and τὸ συγγενές is well known (e.g., *Pyth.* 8.44, *Pyth.* 10.12). And if we look at the Eleventh *Pythian* we note that the youthful Thrasydaeus has bestowed a crown on the paternal hearth (14) and that his father was a victor before him (41–5). Interpretation of 41–5 is difficult, but the simplest and the most satisfactory understanding is given by assuming that Pythonicus is the name of the father of Thrasydaeus, not a Pindaric allusion to a Pythian victory won by that father (who if he is not Pythonicus is not named in the poem). 'Pythionikos' and not 'Pythonikos' is, in any case, Pindar's regular form for the adjective (*Pyth.* 6.5, *Pyth.* 8.5, cf. *Pyth.*

---

20 Sandys (1919: 301) 'caused the destruction'; Bowra (1969: 220) 'brought death on'; Lattimore (1947: 91) 'brought to her death.' These are representative. Slater (1979: 66) uses 'kills(!)'.
21 E.g. *Od.* 9.566; Anacreon *PMG* 419; Eur. *Andr.* 1236.
22 See Slater 1983: 129.

9.1). A problematic notice in the scholia to the Eleventh *Pythian* gives two dates for the victories of Thrasydaeus, 474 and 454 (sixteen years before Aeschylus' *Oresteia* or two years after Aeschylus' death).[23] Bowra argued that the references are to victories by father and son, both named Thrasydaeus, and that this poem is to honour the son in 454.[24] But according to the most common Greek practice a boy would be named after his grandfather, not after his father.[25] We get excellent sense if we assume that the addressee's grandfather (Thrasydaeus?) was a victor at Delphi and that he named his son Pythonicus in honour of his victory. This Pythonicus, father of the addressee, is himself a victor (perhaps at Olympia, 47); he is unusually closely associated with his son in victory (καταβάντες ἤλεγξαν, 49).[26] This son was victorious in 474. Three victorious generations explain τρίτον ... στέφανον, 14. And the myth, with its mention of Atreus-Agamemnon-Orestes, provides a parallel instance of φυά over three generations. Our Thrasydaeus, victorious in 474, may well have won another victory twenty years later.[27] If any poem was composed for the occasion it has not survived.[28]

23 Drachmann *Scholia* 2: 254.
24 Bowra 1964: 402–5 (Appendix 1).
25 See Dover 1968 on Aristophanes' *Clouds* lines 46, 65.
26 Pindar elsewhere uses a plural verb to mark a close association between two victorious members of the family e.g., *Isthm.* 2.29 (of Theron and Xenocrates).
27 Alternatively, the Thrasydaeus victorious in 454 may have been an entirely different person. There is, admittedly, some difficulty believing that someone who as a boy won a victory in the *stadion* in 474 could have won another victory in a short-distance event twenty years later (when he was over thirty). V.J. Matthews calls to my attention, however, that our standards for 100–400 metre events are largely determined by American college athletes who retire after graduation since there are few short-distance events subsequently open to them (a situation very different with long-distance events). An aristocratic Greek athlete would have no economic difficulty in continuing to compete as long as he retained his interest and his ability. Even in modern times there are examples of sprinters competing effectively into their thirties (e.g., M. Larrabee, 400 m [*diaulos*] winner in the 1964 Olympics). On Greek victors in running events who competed successfully over fifteen years, see Gow 1965 on Theocritus 2.115.
28 Egan 1983: 194, while finding Orestes a positive example, is inclined to view *Pyth.* 11 as critical of Agamemnon. He adduces *Ol.* 1 as also having a myth that censures a father (Tantalus) while praising a son (Pelops). But that negative example is of a famous sinner, like Ixion in *Pyth* 2. In *Ol* 1, where the addressee is an adult and his father is not mentioned, there is no possible parallel between the father/son of the myth and the addressee's family. Pindar would be lacking his accustomed tact if in praising Thrasydaeus by adducing Orestes he were to censure Orestes' father in the presence of Thrasydaeus'. *Pyth.* 6, on the other hand, gives a good analogy with *Pyth.*

If we admit the bond between fathers and sons to be important in the Eleventh *Pythian*, there is a further advantage to be gained. The word *xenos*, used twice (16, 34), is applied once to Pylades and once to his father Strophius. This too reinforces the thrust of the poem: like father like son.[29]

The myth is, then, not 'irrelevant.' And the poet's self-accusation is not without parallel. The primary function of epinician poetry is praise, and Pindar elsewhere as well calls himself abruptly back from mythical narrative to more direct praise by the suggestion that the myth has been a digression. *Pyth.* 10 provides an exact analogy, with a similar nautical metaphor:

> Stay the oars now!
> Heave the anchor overboard
> before we splinter
> on the bristling reef. (51–2)

But what of 52–3 and the mention of tyranny? Wilamowitz, accepting the early date, saw in these lines Pindar's repudiation of charges levelled at him personally upon his return from the courts of the Sicilian tyrants where he had been in 476/5, the previous year (the year of *Olympians* 1–3).[30] This is improbable, as Young realized. But Young's own solution,

---

11; here the myth of Nestor and Antilochus provides a parallel for Xenocrates and his son Thrasybulus.

29 Slater (1979: 65–8) finds in *xenos* a key to the significance of the myth. Orestes was a *xenos* at Delphi and, the audience will have known, Thrasydaeus was too, for the Delphians honoured their victors as *xenoi* with a banquet in the Prytaneum. This is an arresting idea, but it yields a very tenuous connection (and one outside the poem at that) between the myth and the victor. It is difficult to acquiesce in Slater's belief that the entire myth is about *xenia*. Slater states for instance (67 n11) that Pindar takes it for granted that Cassandra was cheated of her rightful *xenia* by her murder (but does an enslaved captive have a right to *xenia*?). In the interpretations of Young and Slater Orestes is introduced by what Méautis (1962: 264) calls a 'subterfuge géographique': Delphi, place of victory, is made a spring-board for a myth connected to the victor solely by a point of geography. If this is so it is easy to understand why the scholiast speaks of a digression.

Slater 1983: 129 also says of *Pyth.* 11, 'The final exploits of Orestes are the murder of his mother and her lover. One hopes that the boy-victor did not feel himself to be addressed directly.' This embarrassment is sensed only if we consider myths to have paraenetic function ('go thou and do likewise!'). But if the function is paradigmatic the problem disappears: Orestes is an example, typically Pindaric, of progress through *ponos* to triumph over adversity. Myths, like parables and metaphors, must not be nailed to a Procrustean bed of one-to-one correspondences.

30 Wilamowitz 1922: 263.

which makes the poem self-contained and requires the condemnation of tyranny to be an explicit statement of the meaning of the myth, is no more satisfactory. The strong dislike of Young and the other critics for references in Pindar to contemporary politics[31] is intensified, in Young's case, by hostility to Boeckh's doctrine of historical allegory of something in the victor's own life.[32] Historical allegory was alive in a curious incarnation at the very time Young was writing: Bowra, who supported the later date, saw in Clytemnestra the Athens of 454, soon to be humbled by the defeat at Coronea (447).[33] The tide of hostility to historical allusion in Pindar has ebbed somewhat in the last few years. Gentili refers the lines in question here to the political situation in Thebes in 474.[34] Thucydides provides the clue: at 3.62.3 the Thebans describe their internal politics at the time of Plataea:

> The affairs of our city were at that time in the hands of a small group of powerful men – the form of government most opposed to law and moderation, and closest to a tyranny (ἐγγυτάτω δὲ τυράννου).

An external reference to contemporary Theban politics seems the best explanation. It is not, however, original with Gentili but was the explanation of most critics until Wilamowitz propounded the less attractive idea that the lines are a palinode on the part of a poet who had recently flirted with the great tyrannies of the west.

The Eleventh *Pythian* is not a self-referential poem. The opening lines make clear beyond doubt that the occasion of performance is a local festival in Thebes about which we know nothing. There may be other Pindaric poems in which the victory is celebrated as part of a wider festival.[35] But none of these other cases is absolutely certain, whereas we are here

---

31 See Bundy 1962b: 35.
32 See above, n6.
33 Bowra 1964: 154–6, 405.
34 Gentili 1970: 153–4. Gentili, though he reads Pindar's personal reflection on contemporary politics into the criticism of tyranny, seems to take the whole house of Atreus as a bad example ('la tirannide, impersonata dalla figura di Atreo'). So too Newman (1979) who takes the myth as a negative *exemplum* but finds in the political vocabulary of the poem possible allusion to the situation mentioned by Thucydides: see also Newman 1982: 193. Pindar elsewhere (*Isthm.* 4.35–6, 8.11–12) alludes in passing to the unfortunate consequences for Thebes of its 'official' pro-Persian policy. The allusions are necessarily brief, for families of Pindar's patrons may well have been among the medizing faction: see Podlecki 1984: 218.
35 E.g. *Ol.* 3, for a theoxeny of the Dioscuri at Acragas, and *Pyth.* 5, part of a festival of the Carneian Apollo at Cyrene.

obliged to believe in such an occasion: καί νυν (7) shows that we have a convocation of local divinities at a local shrine for a regular event to which a victory-celebration has been added. External reference is built into the poem. The opening lines allude to the festival, lines 52–3 to the recent political climate. Pindar, like Thucydides' Thebans, repudiates tyranny; the *mesa* he desires is presumably government by the *sophoi*, a group between tyrants and the *labros stratos*. He made this tripartite division for Hieron (*Pyth*. 2.87–8). Whether this middle way was 'the life traditional to Thrasydaios' family' we cannot know. But it is the poet's preference, and his is the voice of the community gathered to give praise.

The earlier of the two dates suggested by the scholiast is, then, the more likely. Thrasydaeus was in all probability a boy in 474. And there is no compelling reason to believe that Pindar was influenced by Aeschylus. It is, in any case, much more likely *prima facie* that Aeschylus knew Pindar's poetry than *vice versa*. The art of the tragedians is the legatee of choral lyric, without which it is inconceivable. Aeschylus with his lively and inquiring mind and his far-ranging interests will surely have known the work of the supreme practitioner of the choral art.[36] Pindar might well have found tragedy alien and mystifying. Tragedy, by bringing the people of history on stage in masks, presents imitations which invite, by their immediacy, disbelief that they can be faithfully recreated episodes of the past.[37] There is not even the presence of a Muse to guarantee, by her *autopsia*, that what we have before us is a faithful account of a bygone age. The tragic poet achieves a degree of detachment from the myth that the lyric poet does not contemplate.

If the Eleventh *Pythian* is earlier than the *Oresteia* of Aeschylus it may have been among the sources known to the tragic poet. But there are significant differences between the Pindaric and Aeschylean accounts.

First, the name of the nurse, Arsinoa in Pindar and Cilissa in Aeschylus (*Cho*. 732). Aeschylus has given a slave name to the nurse. This is very much in keeping with his dramatic purpose, which allows us to see how the fortunes of the great affect the humble (cf. the watchman and the herald in the *Agamemnon*). Pindar's nurse has an aristocratic name. The name means 'with the appropriate disposition' (from ἀραρίσκω and νόος)[38] and

---

36 On the possible indebtedness of the *Supplices*-trilogy (463) to the Ninth *Pythian* (474), see Winnington-Ingram 1969, esp. 13. The author of the *Prometheus Vinctus* appears to have borrowed from the Eighth *Isthmian* (478): see Farnell 1930–2: 2.380.
37 Cf. Snell 1955: chap. 6, esp. 145–6.
38 Fick 1874: 15.

well suits a faithful retainer who saves the life of a child. Certainly, Pindar frequently sees special significance in names.[39] The scholiast on *Cho.* 733 tells us that neither Pindar nor Aeschylus gives the nurse the name she had in Stesichorus (*PMG* 218). Perhaps both used names to fit their own purposes.

Second, the setting, Amyclae in Pindar, Argos in Aeschylus. Aeschylus has moved the action to Argos from the Mycenae of epic because of the importance of Argos in the mid-fifth century. A recent Athenian alliance with Argos is alluded to in the *Eumenides* (289 ff.). Pindar's setting, Amyclae, is close to the Stesichorean setting of Sparta (*PMG* 218). Bowra thought that Stesichorus had political reasons for making Sparta the scene of his *Oresteia*.[40] But both Pindar and Stesichorus may be drawing on an epic tradition that associates Agamemnon with Laconia.[41]

Third, the presence of Orestes at the time of his father's death in Pindar. In Aeschylus Orestes has been sent away by Clytemnestra before Agamemnon's return from Troy.

On the other hand, some of the similarities between Pindar and Sophocles are striking.

First, Orestes is snatched from death at Clytemnestra's hands. In Sophocles (*El.* 13) he is saved by Electra and given to a retainer; in Pindar he is saved by the nurse. The name of Orestes' nurse in Stesichorus was Laodameia (*PMG* 218). It seems possible that this name is a variant of Laodike of *Iliad* 9.145. We are told that Agamemnon's daughter Laodameia became Electra (*PMG* 700) after Clytemnestra's marriage to Aegisthus, presumably after Orestes has been removed. Certainly Laodike disappears as a sister. She may have left a trace of her passage in Stesichorus, becoming Laodameia the nurse. Pindar follows Stesichorus in keeping the nurse as saviour of Orestes and does not mention Electra. In Sophocles the sister Electra, once Laodike, saves Orestes and her role as a nurse is emphasized: ἐγὼ τροφός, / ἐγὼ δ'ἀδελφὴ σοὶ προσηυδώμην ἀεί (1147–8). In the case of Agamemnon's Ἰφι-daughters there is a similar instability in the second half of the name: we find variously Iphimede, Iphianassa, Iphigeneia for the same person.[42]

---

39 See my 'Jason and Cheiron: The Myth of Pindar's Fourth *Pythian*,' *Phoenix* 29 (1975) 211 and n18 [in this volume 198 and n18].
40 Bowra 1961: 114.
41 Lesky 1967: 12–14.
42 Iphigeneia is not in the *Iliad*. We have Iphimede sacrificed in the Hesiodic catalogue, Iphigeneia in the tragedians. Iphianassa (*Il.* 9.145) has not simply become Iphigeneia, for Sophocles (*El.* 157) tells us that Iphianassa is still living with Chrysothemis at Argos (and the scholiast *ad. loc.* claims that this was the case in the *Cypria*). Yet Lucretius

Second, the murder of Aegisthus is of secondary importance in both Pindar and Sophocles: in Sophocles it is not even within the play, in Pindar it is a detail added at the end of the narrative.

Third, Orestes' connection with Delphi may point to a curiously shared tradition. Ivan Linforth, commenting on the speech of the *paedagogus* which tells of Orestes' death in the games, wrote: 'it may be that in the legend of Orestes some part which did not concern the events of the play told of great athletic success at Delphi and that Sophocles introduced it because he liked it and knew his audience would like it.'[43] The story told by the *paedagogus* is false but gains in credibility by its plausibility, like the false stories which Hesiod's Muses can tell (*Theog.* 27). It has recently been argued that this tradition of Orestes as athlete stands behind the Eleventh *Pythian* and contributes to the parallel between the subject of the myth and the addressee of the poem.[44]

Pindar's 'Oresteia' and the tragedies of the later fifth century draw on common traditions. The epinician ode precedes the earliest surviving dramatic treatment, the *Oresteia* of Aeschylus. If the impressive list of parallels between Aeschylus' *Oresteia* and Pindar's Eleventh *Pythian* put together by Düring[45] shows dependence of one poet on the other, it must be, contrary to Düring's unargued assumption that Pindar knew the Aeschylean trilogy, the tragic poet who knew the work of his lyric predecessor.[46]

(1.85) makes Iphianassa the daughter sacrificed at Aulis. On the name see Lloyd-Jones 1983: 95.

43 Linforth 1963: 99.
44 Egan 1983: 196–8.
45 Düring 1943: 109–14.
46 Herington (1984: 145) claims that 'the possibility that Aeschylus might have structured his greatest masterpiece around a couple of totally uncharacteristic lines thrown out for some inexplicable reason by Pindar in or shortly after 474 BC seems ... remote.' But the argument advanced here is that (a) the Pindaric passage is not wholly uncharacteristic of him and hence does not bespeak indebtedness to tragedy; (b) Pindar's poetry was but one lyric source available to Aeschylus; the most important was undoubtedly Stesichorus.

NEREIDS WITH GOLDEN DISTAFFS: PINDAR, NEM. 5

In memoriam
J.M. Bell

Nowhere was Pindar so much at home as on Aegina. The poet's special feeling for the island is in part a strong sense of personal kinship, his native Thebes being the sister of Aegina (*Isth.* 8.15b–22). But the bond is also fruit of Aegina's pre-eminent place in heroic saga: for Pindar the island was truly 'this precious stone set in the silver sea, ... this teeming womb of royal kings,' as its most famous family numbered Aeacus, Peleus, Telamon, Achilles, Ajax, Teucer, and Neoptolemus, actors all in the great drama of Greece's involvement with Troy. And so it is not surprising to find eleven of the forty-four surviving epinician odes addressed to Aeginetan victors. These odes span almost four decades of Pindar's long career, the Eighth *Pythian* (446) being generally thought the final product of the poet's old age.

The Fifth *Nemean* is quite likely the earliest of the Aeginetan odes. 485 has been suggested as its date.[1] It is one of three poems for two brothers: *Nem.* 5 is for the elder of the two, named Pytheas, while *Isthmians* 5 and 6 are for the younger Phylacidas at a slightly later date. Bacchylides was commissioned to compose an ode for Pytheas' victory too; his contribution is one of his most memorable poems (number 13 in the Snell-Maehler collection).

Pytheas is the nominal addressee of the Fifth *Nemean* and in the first strophe we are given the necessary information about him in two perfunc-

---

First published in *QUCC* NS 25.1 (1987) 25–33.

The line numbers are in every case those of the Teubner text of Snell-Maehler[7]. I am grateful to Professors Bernardini and Gentili, and to Professors Anne Carson and Mark Golden, for helpful suggestions.

1 Wilamowitz 1922: 169; cf. Turyn 1952: 163–4. The Seventh *Nemean* may be slightly earlier, but a late date is now commonly accepted for this poem: see Finley 1951: 61–80.

tory lines (4–5): son of Lampon, he won in the pancratium at Nemea. His accomplishment is baldly stated and there is no extended praise, either at the beginning or later in the poem. Certainly there can be no question of a victory-list for a boy who has but one victory to his credit.[2] We are also told in the first strophe that Pytheas is without even the first traces of a beard. He was in all likelihood scarcely twelve years old when he won, at the very lower end of the age-range for competitors in boys' events, and he is quite possibly the youngest victor represented in our Pindaric corpus.[3] A victory-list in fact occupies the entire final triad of

---

[2] Gärtner 1978: 38 claims that the victory catalogue of Pytheas' uncle (lines 41 ff.) overlaps in part with an enumeration of the boy's victories. But the subject of ἀγάλλει (43) is Euthymenes. Virtually all modern editors adopt Mingarelli's emendation Πυθέα (vocative) in this line; the emendation derives its authority from a notice in the scholia and seems required since the nominative Πυθέας of the codices cannot stand in apposition to μάτρως (= maternal uncle), the subject of ἀγάλλει. Euthymenes is clearly the subject of ἐκράτει (45). It places, accordingly, a considerable strain on the understanding to see the intervening line (44) as referring to both uncle and nephew (Gärtner) when there is neither verb nor pronoun in the sentence to make this clear. The most natural construction is to take the entire passage as referring to Euthymenes, and this is what most commentators do.

[3] Maehler 1982: I.2 250–1 thinks that Pytheas belonged to a distinct class of ἀγένειοι, 17–20 year olds (he appears, in addition, to take the catalogue of the Fifth *Nemean* as mentioning once again Pytheas' Nemean victory, not that of Euthymenes). The inscription ΑΓΕΝΕΙΩΙ in the Teubner text is a supplement suggested by Schroeder and Blass (it is wrongly attributed to Boeckh in the apparatus of Snell-Maehler: Boeckh in fact proposed ΠΑΙΔΙ). Pindar does not, in any case, appear to make a distinction between παῖς and ἀγένειος: e.g., Melesias, the trainer of a παῖς ἐναγώνιος (*Nem.* 6.13), is said to derive his fame ἐξ ἀγενείων (*Ol.* 8.54 – this comprehensive designation must include both Alcimedon, the addressee of *Ol.* 8, and Alcimidas, the παῖς ἐναγώνιος of *Nem.* 6). Pytheas does not yet show the ὀπώρα (6) or beauty that awakens erotic interest (cf. *Isth.* 2.4–5). Such beauty is characteristic of many of the boys or young men for whom Pindar composes (cf. *Ol.* 8.19; 9.94; 10.103–4; *Pyth.* 10.58–9; *Nem.* 3.19–20; *Isth.* 7.22). There is a lapse of several years between the appearance of the first down (οἰνάνθα = ἴουλος, Σ) on the face and the growth of the full beard that indicates emergence from the classification as παῖς, and, with this, readiness for marriage (cf. Pelops at *Ol.* 1.68–9). Bury (1890: 84) says, correctly I think, that 'Pytheas is a strong-bodied boy not yet adolescent.'

There may be another indication of Pytheas' extreme youth at the time of *Nem.* 5 in the fact that he was his brother's trainer for the second of that brother's victories at the Isthmus (*Isth.* 5.59 ff.). Wilamowitz (*loc. cit.* above n1) implies that this means Pytheas had recently passed the upper limit for boys' events and was, thus, not competing himself. There appears to be a lapse of 5–7 years between Pytheas' own victory in *Nem.* 5 (485?) and the victory for which he trained his brother (480 Turyn, 478 Wilamowitz). Pytheas is not yet Phylacidas' trainer at the time of the latter's first Isthmian victory (484 Turyn, 480 Wilamowitz). The same Pytheas seems to have won an Isthmian

the ode, but it celebrates the victories of the maternal uncle, Euthymenes, and the maternal grandfather, Themistius (so the scholiast – the paternal grandfather was Cleonicus, named at *Isth.* 5.55). At line 37 we come with Poseidon to the Isthmus, where Euthymenes won two victories.[4] The first word in the third triad (γαμβρόν) is extraordinary. Zeus persuades Poseidon, who is not called Zeus' brother, as we might expect, but the Nereids' brother-in-law (Poseidon is married to the Nereid Amphitrite). This surely emphasizes Lampon's relationship to Euthymenes, who will be the victor of the catalogue. Αἰγινᾶθε δίς (41, an emendation accepted by virtually all modern editors) means 'from Aegina,' not 'at Aegina' (= Αἰγίνᾳ *Ol.* 7.86, *Pyth.* 9.90) and is meant to echo Αἰγᾶθεν (37). Euthymenes, like Poseidon, leaves home for the Isthmus, the place of his two victories. This is nicely corroborated by the Sixth *Isthmian*, where we hear (61–2) that the two boys and their uncle have 'carried off three victories in the pancratium from the Isthmus and others again from Nemea': the three Isthmian victories will be the two of Euthymenes and a third which is the occasion of the Sixth *Isthmian*. Poseidon and Euthymenes converge on the Isthmus in the first strophe of the third triad of the Fifth *Nemean*, and a victory list begins. It is not a catalogue of Pytheas' victories. There follows a mention of Nemea, where Euthymenes was victorious, and of local Aeginetan and Megarian contests where he also won. Then, after a short passage in praise of the general enthusiasm for athletics on Aegina and of Pytheas' Athenian trainer Menander (46–9), the poet devotes the final epode to Themistius, who twice won at Epidaurus. This virtual disappearance of the addressee and his replacement by his elders is unlike anything else in Pindar.[5] Equally

---

victory as an adult; it was mentioned after his death by Pindar (fr. 4). In the odes for the sons of Lampon there are four Isthmian victories mentioned, two of Euthymenes (*Nem.* 5.41), two of Phylacidas (*Isth.* 5.17); the number three (*Isth.* 6.61) represents, of course, the total before the second of Phylacidas' victories.

Εὐρυσθενής (4) suggests that Pytheas, for all his youth, was a strapping lad: Bernardini (1985: 125) rightly points out that such epithets may well be properly descriptive, not merely conventional.

4 At *Ol.* 8.48 ff. there is a very similar transitional passage that introduces a victory at the Isthmus: see von der Mühll 1964: 55.

5 Pindar has a variety of techniques for returning to the addressee, even if he is a boy who has no 'list' of victories to his credit. He may associate him closely, though plural verbs, with his father (*Pyth.* 11) or other relatives (*Isth.* 6); he may praise the boy's patrons and their interest in their protégé (*Pyth.* 10); he may show the boy's elders, dead and alive, rejoicing in his success (*Ol.* 8, 10, 14); or, quite simply, he may return to direct praise of the youth (*Nem.* 7). Pytheas does not totally disappear – he receives two further words of praise if we read μεταΐξαις σέ in 43 (the emended text printed by Snell and Maehler), but he is all but abandoned in the progress of the poem.

unparalleled and thus truly astonishing is the simultaneous presence of three successive generations of victors at one celebration.[6] The last lines of the poem say 'declare that he (Themistius) won double virtue at Epidaurus by his victory as a boxer and in the pancratium and bears his grassy garlands of flowers, accompanied by the fair-haired Graces, in the forecourts of Aeacus' shrine.' But there is general unwillingness to accept this. Some editors (e.g., Bowra, Snell-Maehler) print Wilamowitz's emendation φέρε for φέρειν in line 54 to produce a second imperative parallel to φθέγξαι (52). Themistius is thereby eliminated from the scene (he is not even necessarily alive) and others are told to carry garlands.[7] Bury retained the infinitive thinking that the reference must be to a statue of Themistius wearing a crown in the shrine of Aeacus.[8] But there is no reason to believe in a statue, and moreover 'wear' is a very doubtful meaning for φέρειν. Other commentators retain the infinitive but take it as imperfect and assume that the victories are in the distant past.[9] Farnell, characteristically, complains about Pindar's carelessness, but then appears to misread the scholium that he claims to be interpreting when he suggests that φέρειν may be an imperfect tense referring to a time 'long anterior to that of the main verb' (hence the difficulty, for it should refer to time simultaneous with φθέγξαι).[10] But the scholiast's paraphrase, φθέγξαι αὐτὸν νενικηκέναι ... καὶ κομίζειν αὐτὸν ... ἄνθη φθέγξαι,[11] says 'proclaim that he *has won*, and proclaim that he *brings* garlands.' This is simple and straightforward and is not contradicted by the following explanation in the scholia that garlands have already been placed (ἀνάκεινται) in the shrine of Aeacus. For the dedication of the garland is not the moment of the singing of the epinician ode.[12] At least one of the two victories of Themistius seems to have been

---

6 E.g., in *Ol.* 8 the addressee's grandfather is alive but his father and uncle are dead; in *Nem.* 4 the victor's grandfather may be alive, but the father and maternal uncle are dead. It is not necessary to make an exhaustive catalogue here. *Nem.* 5 is in any case unique in that all three generations are not only alive but victorious and that there is no mention of death.
7 I am uncertain whether those who print φέρε think of these garlands as for Pytheas or Themistius. Neither is satisfactory. It is hard to return to Pytheas immediately after mention of Themistius' victories, and if the garlands are for a Themistius who is not necessarily celebrating a triumph on this occasion the garlands must just be commemorative, again most unusual.
8 Bury 1890: 97.
9 Gärtner 1978: 39. Segal (1974: 408) speaks of 'remote' victories.
10 Farnell 1930-2: 2.280.
11 Drachmann *Scholia* 3.99-100.
12 E.g., in the Ninth *Olympian* the victor has dedicated his wreath in the shrine of Ajax (112) before the epinician ode is sung.

recent enough that this poem is a victory-celebration in his honour and in his presence. He need not have been old – he is maternal grandfather and his daughter, mother of a boy scarcely in his teens, may have been very young when Pytheas was born. It is certainly well within the bounds of possibility that Themistius is about forty-five years old, an age at which athletes, especially boxers, might still be competing.[13]

Given the unique circumstances of the ode's occasion, it is natural to expect to see some reflection of this in the mythical section of the poem. This narrative is remarkable too. Pindar begins (9) with a relative pronoun and ποτε, as so often, and gives us a picture of three sons of Aeacus – it is the two mothers, Endais and Psamatheia, who are named – praying at the altar of Zeus Hellanicus, their hands raised to heaven. But immediately an ominous note is sounded, and the poet alludes to the murder of Phocus by Telamon and Peleus without explicitly mentioning it, then tells us that they departed from Aegina but refuses to proceed further with the story. Thus the first triad ends. The second begins with a statement of the 'Bereitwilligkeits-Motiv'[14] and goes on to narrate the story of Peleus' rejection of Hippolyta's advances and his consequent winning of Thetis as reward for honouring Zeus Xenios. This story is a song within a song, so to speak, for it is sung by the Muses on Pelion, no doubt at Peleus' wedding (though we are not specifically told this). It is not easy to know exactly where the Muses' song ends and the poet resumes, but it would seem that at the beginning of the third triad, with the ὅς of line 37, we leave the world of myth and return to the present. The relative pronoun leads us out of the past as it led us in, and the overlapping γαμβρὸν Ποσειδάωνα πείσας, which unexpectedly prolongs the period that might have ended with the previous triad, is exquisitely placed, looking back to the myth and forward to the praise of the maternal family prowess that will fill the entire third triad.[15]

---

13 Philostratos (*Gym.* 43) says that athletes of olden times, in particular competitors in events that required strength, competed for eight or nine Olympiads. See also Ar. *Vesp.* 1383–1385.
   The only difficulty I see with the theory I advance here is that we must assume that Themistius has won only two victories in a fairly long career and that one at least is a recent victory. But even the theory that puts the victories in the past must limit the victories to two, for Pindar mentions but two, though it remains silent on the length of Themistius' career.
14 I take the term from Maehler 1982: 92.
15 Gärtner (1978: 36) thinks that the Muses' song ends with line 39. But it would be oddly anachronistic to have the Muses singing of the Isthmian games at the wedding of Peleus and Thetis. Θάμα νίσεται (37) is in the present, in any case: this Advent-Motif (my term) is common in Pindar, frequently with καί νυν (see, e.g., *Ol.* 3.34).

The most recent attempt to explain the significance of the poem's myth sees the Peleus story as directed at Lampon. The disparity of the Peleus-Thetis match — she is divine, he a mere mortal — mirrors the unequal relationship between Lampon and his wife, for she is carrier of their son's superiority.[16] This seems to me a dubious compliment at best. If Lampon is to see himself in Peleus the poet might well have concentrated on the one thing that would give him greatest pride, not his inferiority to his wife but his fathering of a splendid son. Yet there is no mention of Achilles in the myth. Pindar tells us of Peleus and Thetis in five other poems (*Ol.* 2, *Pyth.* 3, *Nem.* 3, *Nem.* 4, *Isth.* 8) but only here does he fail to speak of Achilles. One would have expected, if the point of the myth was to encourage Lampon's sense of identification with Peleus, at least a mention of Peleus' extraordinary boy.[17] It is silent about him, as the rest of the poem is about Pytheas. Bury thought that the myth bore on Euthymenes. Since Euthymenes is described as 'falling into the arms of victory' (42), Peleus' union with Thetis casts its light on him. This is a tenuous connection and makes too much of a single word (ἀγκώνεσσι, 42).[18] Pindar repeatedly uses language with sexual overtones to describe a victor's relation to victory[19] and his mythical narrative is everywhere filled with amorous encounters. It is easy, but not particularly illuminating, to find correlations of such nature — there must be more going on in the myth than this![20] That erotic language is used of Euthymenes points not so much to the myth of the poem as to his probable youth. The uncle may be but a few years older than Pytheas, the addressee.[21]

There is special emphasis in the poem as a whole on women,[22] on mothers in particular, as is appropriate on an occasion celebrating the repeated

16 Gärtner 1978: 39–40.
17 If the poet's purpose had been to honour Lampon, the myth of the Third *Nemean*, with its mention of Peleus' valour (not just his piety) and its loving recital of the prowess of the child Achilles, would have been ideal for the Fifth. The Sixth Isthmian *does* honour Lampon with its story (in prophecy) of the birth of a brave son (Ajax).
18 Bury (1890: 96) sees a continuation of the image in ἄραρεν (44). But this word does not carry erotic implications in Greek. The best explanation of the word is that advanced by Gärtner 1978: 37: the meaning is 'hat sich angereiht,' i.e., followed in close succession (examples from Homer).
19 See esp. Carne-Ross 1985: 26–30.
20 In *Ol.* 1 Pherenicus has wedded Hiero to victory (22), but this has not been used to support a theory of the import of the myth of the poem.
21 Carne-Ross (1985: 26) speaks of Euthymenes as a 'young athlete.' Though he belongs to the generation of Pytheas' elders, this is surely correct.
22 The contrast between good woman and bad woman is a favourite in Greek poetry: cf. e.g., *Od.* 11 (Penelope and Clytemnestra), Alcaeus 42 Lobel-Page (Thetis and Helen).

appearance of excellence in the maternal family. The πότμος ... συγγενής (40) that rules over every deed works on the mother's side and makes itself known in the performance of the μάτρως (43) and his nephew. The ὁμόσπορον ἔθνος of Peleus (= κείνου, 43) indicates that Pytheas' descent from the Aeacids is via the maternal family. Pytheas has glorified his ματρόπολιν (8). In the Fifth and Sixth Isthmians, for the other son of Lampon, the emphasis is, as usual in Pindar, on paternity and we hear of the πάτραν (clan) of the Psalychiadae (Isth. 6.63)[23] and of Aegina herself as πάτραν (Isth. 5.43). The poet's interest in maternity appears to influence his choice of language in a remarkable phrase at the beginning of the Fifth Nemean. In speaking of the earliest down on a young boy's face, not yet apparent on Pytheas' cheeks, Pindar speaks of the 'season of ripeness, mother of the tender grape-bloom' (6). Immediately thereupon the Aeacids are called the children of golden Nereids (7) – it is only here that Achilles enters the poem, however obliquely – and Peleus, Telamon, and Phocus are mentioned as the illustrious sons of Endais and Psamatheia (12–13).

Zeus, however, is central to the poem too. His presence is in order, for the Nemean games are in his honour and the Aeacids are his descendants (7).[24] His grandsons stand before his altar (10), the Muses begin their song with mention of him (25). Peleus acts out of respect for him in repelling Hippolyta (33), and he arranges the marriage of Peleus and Thetis (35). His interest in the family sprung from him is what guarantees its ultimate success and ensures the triumph of Themistius, Euthymenes, and Pytheas. I am certain that we should see Zeus or his representative[25] in the δαίμων (16) that drives the Aeacids from Aegina. This δαίμων is not evil[26] – δαίμων is never *per se* malign in Pindar but is always a force that works ultimately for the benefit of mortals.[27] Despite the shadow that

---

23 It is remarkable that in the Fifth Nemean there is no mention of the father's clan. Almost all the Aeginetan odes mention the paternal family: Blepsiadae (Ol. 8), Meidylidae (Pyth. 8), Theandridae (Nem. 4), Psalychiadae (Isth. 6), Bassidae (Nem. 6), Chariadae (Nem. 8), Euxenidae (Nem. 7). Nem. 3 is exceptional – there is no hint of any presence of family in the poem. Isth. 8 also mentions no earlier generation (a dead cousin is named at line 61). All poems, of course, give, as the genre requires, the name of the victor's father.
24 Cronus (7) is father of Zeus and grandfather of Endais (12), for she is a daughter of Cheiron.
25 Cf. Pyth. 5.122–3, Διός τοι νόος μέγας κυβερνᾷ / δαίμον' ἀνδρῶν φίλων.
26 Contra Stern 1971: 171. Segal (1974: 409) says that the voyage redounds to the island's shame. But it does so only apparently, and only initially.
27 Pyth. 3.34 is unique in specifying a δαίμων ἕτερος (i.e., κακός). But the δαίμων is normally, as this poem makes clear, the link between mortals and omniscient divinity (109) on whose behalf it acts, even when the gods πήματα ... δαίονται βρότοις (81).

falls on the house in the fratricide, Zeus directs its destiny.[28] The poet's *praeteritio* does not name the crime, but it makes explicit the divinely appointed diaspora, in a very real sense the answer to the prayer at Zeus' altar.

The diaspora was providential, for the Aeacids could not have been great had they remained on Aegina. Leaving was a precondition of their glory, which was won outside Aegina and now travels to the ends of the earth (*Isth.* 6.19–23). In parallel fashion the victors of the poem have left Aegina to compete in Panhellenic games: Αἰγίναθε, used of Euthymenes (41), recalls ἀπ' Οἰνώνας (16), of Peleus and Telamon. The poet's song also participates in this centrifugal movement ἀπ' Αἰγίνας (3) and αὐτόθεν (20): the ode will not be confined to the island.[29] Aegina is the matrix of greatness, but it is not the place where great deeds are performed or can get the attention they deserve. Line 21, καὶ πέραν πόντοιο πάλλοντ' αἰετοί, perhaps brings these ideas together, for the eagles are both the Αἰακίδαι (with a possible pun, as there is a pun on Αἴας / αἰετός in the Sixth *Isthmian*) and the poems (a possible pun with ἄειδ' in the following line and with the travelling ἀοιδά of line 2? – the eagle is, in any case, a common Pindaric figure for the poet himself or for his song).

There is in this a delicate counterpoint to the maternal inheritance. For the achievement of renown requires that the hero sever the umbilical cord. The desire of the Argonauts is, Pindar tells us, μή τινα λειπόμενον / τὰν ἀκίνδυνον παρὰ ματρὶ μένειν αἰῶνα πέσσοντ' (*Pyth.* 4.185–6) – a life at the mother's side is a life without distinction. A defeated athlete returns amidst derision to his mother (*Pyth.* 8.85).[30] Greatness must be won in the world of men, and Aegina will be great, as the young men standing at the altar of Zeus pray (9–10), only if they leave their mother-island. The one deed performed by the Aeacids at home is discreditable, ἐν δίκᾳ ... μὲ κεκινδυνευμένον (14). Hippolyta's attempt to ruin Peleus is, interestingly, an attempt to arrest him (πεδᾶσαι, 26): her destructive stratagems would

---

28 The departure of Tlepolemus from Argos after homicide in the Seventh *Olympian* is remarkably similar. Here too we see divine purpose at work behind mortal folly, leading a family to glory overseas.
29 The normal movement of a Pindaric ode is centripetal, with crowns, victor, chorus, poet, and song converging on the scene of celebration. Cf., e.g., *Ol.* 9.19–25, 83.
30 *Pyth.* 5.114, ἔν τε Μοίσαισι ποτανὸς ἀπὸ ματρὸς φίλος, belongs, I think, with these passages. Arcesilas has left his mother's side and risen to greatness. The poet is surely not saying that Arcesilas' greatness comes from his mother (an unprepared and unsupported compliment in a poem that emphasizes the succession of Cyrene's kings); nor can Arcesilas have come 'full-fledged from the womb' (these are the traditional interpretations): see Lefkowitz 1985: 53–4.

be immobilizing, as would a mother's enervating influence.[31] Thetis would have kept Achilles from greatness, hiding him on Scyros.[32] And it is worth remembering that the dreadful deed passed over in silence (but not denied) was done at the instigation of Endais, the mother of Peleus and Telamon.[33] This story must have been well known to Pindar's Aeginetan audience. The mothers of stalwart sons, even fair goddesses, do not assist them to their titles.

This is not stated outright in the poem. What we notice is, simply, an insistence on maternal inheritance on Aegina, for Aeacids and addressee alike, and, at the same time, a movement outward and away from the mother-island. It is odd that a canvas painted for an occasion so joyous – the concelebration of victory by three generations of the living – should place its figures against a background of treachery that twice threatens to undercut or invalidate heroism. There is one heinous crime of which Pindar will not speak and another shameful deed which he gives as the work of a woman. In both cases the outcome is happy because of the guiding or restraining presence of Zeus. The Nereids may have distaffs of gold (36), and gold is enduring value, intact from generation to generation like excellence in the mother's blood. But thread spun from the distaff must not hold back hero or athlete.[34] It is Zeus who will lead his progeny to greatness.

---

31 Ἀπανάνατο νύμφαν (33, in the second epode) recalls lines 17–18 in the first epode. There too Pindar uses wedding imagery: the truth not told is a bride not accepted – φαίνοισα πρόσωπον suggests a bride's unveiling at the ἀνακαλυπτήρια (cf. Cassandra at Aesch. Agam. 1178–1179).
32 Farnell 1930–2: 2.382–3, sees an allusion to this at Isth. 8.47b-48. The story of Thetis' concealment of Achilles on Scyros was certainly current in the fifth century: Polygnotus painted it at the entrance to the Acropolis (Paus. 1.22.6).
33 Cf. Paus. 2.29.9: ταῦτα δὲ ἐχαρίζοντο τῇ μητρί.
34 The Dantean punishment of Hippolyta, who attempted to bind a man, would be immobility, a perfect contrappasso: cf. Potiphar's wife, guilty of the same sin as Hippolyta, Inf. 30.91–7.

THE DIVINE TWINS IN EARLY GREEK POETRY

RONALD MORTON SMITH introduced me to the mysteries of Sandhi in Sanskrit when I was yet an undergraduate. Euphonic combination in Greek was a trivial matter by comparison! He also, and it changed my life, made me acquire Macdonell's *Vedic Reader* and *Vedic Grammar*. If I have never been able to do him proper credit in matters Vedic, he has always been able to show me, in his unassuming manner, his fine command of things classical. I offer this essay to him in esteem and gratitude and in the hope that it will appeal to some of his many interests.

1

Castor and Polydeuces (Latin *Pollux*) are two of the most appealing and memorable figures in Greek myth. Twins in myth and folklore are commonly hostile to each other. Examples that come to mind are Jacob and Esau, Romulus and Remus – Greek myth itself offers Proetus and Acrisius, Panopeus/Phanoteus and Crisus, who fought in the womb and ever thereafter, and Danaus and Egyptus, whose hostility extended even to their children. But Castor and Polydeuces stand out for their inseparability and mutual attachment, in life as in death. The unbreakable bond between them is one of the things that make them so like the twins of Vedic mythology, the Aśvins.

The complex of beliefs surrounding twins is enormous and, on the whole, reasonably consistent throughout the world. It is commonly be-

---

First published in Emmet I. Robbins and Stella Sandahl (eds) *Corolla Torontonensis: Studies in Honour of Ronald Morton Smith*. ISBN: 0920661222. Toronto 1994 29–45.

I would like to express my gratitude to Brian Blair for reading this article and offering helpful suggestions.

lieved that the foetus divides in the womb and that this is the beginning of later antagonism.[1] Or, even more common, it is believed that multiple birth is the result of multiple acts of copulation. Accordingly, the mother of twins is frequently thought to have been an unfaithful wife and is put to death along with her newborn children.[2] But it is also a persistent belief that the mother of twins has been visited by a divinity while she was carrying her husband's child or immediately before she mated with her husband.[3] This produces a great disparity in the infants who are born at the same time, one being divine, the other mortal. This disparity is a variation, perhaps, on the idea of hostility: twins, even when apparently alike, are in significant ways very different.

The double paternity is what we find in the case of Castor and Polydeuces. The common story is almost too famous to need re-telling: Zeus, taking the form of a swan,[4] visited Leda and the result was two sets of twins – a divine pair, Helen and Polydeuces, sired by Zeus, and a mortal pair, Clytemnestra and Castor, whose father was Leda's husband, Tyndareus, King of Sparta. There is a generally acknowledged doublet for this story in Greek myth, though there are also significant differences in the doublet. In the saga of the house of Thebes an episode, totally superfluous in the history of the reigning house of Cadmus and the Labdacidae, is found. This parenthesis deals with the twins Amphion and Zethus, sons of Antiope by Zeus. Both twins are in this case sons of a divine father in the usual form of the tale, and neither is immortal. Their personalities are also radically different, Amphion being a musician and Zethus a warrior. These two are seen as paradigms of different types of life, Amphion advocating the artistic and Zethus the practical. There are some reports of hostility between them (e.g., Horace *Epist.* 1.18.41–4), but for the most part there is remarkable unanimity of purpose, as in their rescuing and liberation of their mother. It is this rescue-motif that makes Amphion and Zethus like the Dioscuri, who retrieve their sister Helen when she is carried off by Theseus.

1 See Lévi-Strauss 1978: chapter 3.
2 Zeller 1990: §1.6, with extensive bibliography. Lévi-Strauss (1978) points out that the mother is sometimes seduced by a Trickster in the form of her husband and that, accordingly, one of the sons is a reprobate: twins have, from their conception, a connection with duplicity.
3 The most famous instance in Greek myth is Alcmena, who was visited by Zeus in the form of her husband Amphitryon the night before Amphitryon returned from the war with the Teleboans: see Apollodorus 2.4.8. The result was the birth of twins, Heracles and Iphicles.
4 The story of the swan is first found in Euripides *Helen* 16 ff.

Castor and Polydeuces, despite their different fathers, are regularly through their patronymics assimilated to a single father. They are called the Dioscuri (Διὸς κοῦροι), sons of Zeus, or the Tyndaridae (Τυνδαρίδαι / Τυνδαρίδαι), sons of Tyndareus. This seems to emphasize unity in diversity. There is little to suggest diversity in the Aśvins, who derive their names from their horses (Skt aśva, अश्व = Grk ἵππος, Lat. *equus*) and who are not strongly differentiated, though there is some indication that while both are 'Sons of God' (दिवो नपाता, *Ṛg Veda* 1.117.12) one is offspring of the sky and the other is son of the mortal Sumakha (*Ṛg Veda* 1.181.4). One of the effects of double parentage, divine and human, in a set of divinities is that the pair is regularly thought of as particularly close to humanity and solicitous of the needs of mankind: the dual divinities are dual in nature and ever mindful of their admixture of mortality. And indeed the protective function of both the Aśvins and the Dioscuri is very strong.

The similarities between Aśvins and Dioscuri, in particular the association of both pairs with horses and with light, is often thought to point to a common Indo-European heritage.[5] But the Greek twins exhibit many idiosyncrasies that are accountable, it would seem, specifically in terms of Greek religion. Theirs is a union not only of divine and human, but also of celestial and chthonic, at least in the iconography – poetry is more consistent in making them heavenly twins. Martin Nilsson, in fact, chose to emphasize the aspects of their cult that link them to the earth.[6] He sees in them survivors of the Minoan religion and points to the prominence of snakes in their worship – they belong with the Minoan snake goddess (a forerunner of Athena), and Zeus Meilichios, likewise associated with the snake. The snake was an auspicious creature, closely connected with the household. Just as the snake goddess, guardian of the Cretan palace, became the Athena who protected the Acropolis and the city (as well as the patron of βασιλῆες and individual warriors in Homer), so the two ἄνακ(τ)ες, as the twin gods are called in cult, are symbolized by snakes and become, at Sparta where they were held in especial honour, patrons of the dual kings and of the army. Nilsson sees the upright supports with crossbeam, so often iconographically associated with the two snakes or the two young lords, as a representation of the house which they protect.[7] Such a conflation of elements of sky-worship with elements of an earth-religion would make

---

5 See Burkert 1985: 212; West 1975: 8–9.
6 Nilsson 1967: 406–11.
7 Burkert, 1985: 212, on the other hand, sees this same structure as symbolizing a gateway or *rite de passage* in the initiation of young men.

the twins very characteristic of much else in developed Greek religion: it is a not infrequent phenomenon to find the gods and goddesses of the Olympian pantheon merging to a greater or lesser degree with earlier earth-bound figures native to Greece and antedating the arrival of the Greek-speaking peoples in the second millennium BC. It is perhaps the case that an Indo-European pair of twins associated with heaven and the sky-god (the Dioscuri) became assimilated to a native pair associated with the mother goddess, the Tyndarids.[8] Something of this sort would account very nicely for the most striking motif in the mythology of the twins, i.e., that these divinities in death strike a perfect balance between the darkness of the earth and the brightness of heaven, dividing their time equally between the world above and the world below.[9] The Dioscuri are the 'Chiaroscuri.'

In the well-known analysis of Indo-European society proposed by Georges Dumézil, there are three basic 'functions.' The first embraces sovereignty and shows a priestly stratum; characteristic gods are Varuna, Odin, or Jupiter. The second stratum is military and concerned with a warrior-class; its typical gods are Indra, Thor, or Mars. The third function is assigned to herder-cultivators and is connected with fertility. Though for all of Dumézil's functions the Indic, Germanic, and Latin evidence fits more neatly than the Greek, it is customary for those who subscribe to this tripartite division to assign to this third function the Indic Aśvins and the Greek Dioscuri – the important element in both cases is precisely twinship and association with horses.[10] There is some problem in that horses would seem to be most naturally associated with the warrior-function, but Jaan Puhvel has argued for the 'transfunctional' nature of the horse in this system.[11] It seems, in any case, that both the Dioscuri and the Aśvins are defenders or protectors rather than aggressive warriors and that a defensive military stance is quite compatible with the third function. It thus appears unnecessary to look for a separate function for the individual twins and to think of one as more aggressive and the other as

---

8 See Chapouthier 1935.
9 At the beginning of the century, probably because of the influence of the school of solar mythology associated with Max Müller, the divine twins were explained as representing the Morning and the Evening Stars. See, e.g., Harris 1906.
10 The most succinct statement of Dumézil's theories is Dumézil 1958. See more recently Mallory 1989: 130–2. There is also a shadowy pair of equine brothers, Horsa and Hengist, in Germanic mythology and a pair of divine brothers associated with horses in Baltic (Latvian) mythology who show many similarities to the Aśvins and the Dioscuri; see West 8–9.
11 Puhvel 1970: 159–72.

more peaceful.¹² The myths of early poetry overwhelmingly emphasize what the two members of each pair have in common rather than what divides them.¹³ And if a protective or nurturing aspect of the divine twins forms an essential part of their original personality, it becomes easier to understand how they were assimilated to guardian spirits of the home in Greek religion, which Nilsson insists they fundamentally were. In Greek ritual the Dioscuri regularly attend banquets or Theoxenies that mortals hold in their honour.¹⁴ In this respect they are singularly unlike the other gods, who may in an age long gone have shared the table of mortals, esp. at the weddings of Peleus and Thetis, Cadmus and Harmonia, but who have in more recent times withdrawn and no longer consort with mortals and share their tables.

In particular cases, perhaps, the two twins were 'untwinned' and became very different: most intriguing is the possibility that the divine twins stand behind the figures of the two best-known Trojans, the brothers Hector and Paris. They are not twins and they are radically differentiated in the *Iliad*. But both their names bespeak their third function. Ἕκτωρ, whose name means 'The Defender' and whose role, which corresponds to his name, is to protect his city, is in fact ἱππόδαμος 'breaker of horses'; and the puzzling and most frequent name for Paris in the *Iliad*, Ἀλέξανδρος 'Defender of Men,' becomes more intelligible if he is a third-function figure. We remember too that Paris was originally a shepherd on Mount Ida. If Dumézil is correct in thinking that the original Indo-European mythology contained a myth concerned with the conflict of the kingly and warrior classes against the third estate, this is possibly mirrored in the three principal figures of the *Iliad*: Agamemnon and Achilles form an (uneasy) alliance against Troy, personified in Hector. It is further worthy of note that Helen, sister of the Dioscuri, has become wife of Paris: the Aśvins are often associated

---

12 See, e.g., Ward 1970: 193–202.
13 A. Hermary, 'Dioskouroi,' *LIMC* III.1 567, maintains that 'La personnalité des deux frères apparaît sensiblement différente.' This is true inasmuch as Castor is called a tamer of horses while Polydeuces is a boxer, but both are athletes and if they sometimes have different qualifiers they do not have separate adventures before Hellenistic poetry: Polydeuces' fight with Amycus during the Argonautic expedition is first mentioned by Apollonius (2.1–153) and Theocritus (22.27–134).
14 The depth of this belief is revealed by an anecdote in Polyaenus (2.31.4; cf. Pausanias 4.27.1–3). During the Second Messenian War in the seventh century two Messenians dressed themselves in *pilos*, white *chiton*, and red *chlamys* and, carrying lances and mounted on white horses, went to Sparta where they were welcomed as the Dioscuri at a Theoxeny that was being celebrated. Admitted to the feast they massacred a large number of Spartans.

with Sūryā, who is their bride (*Ṛg Veda* 4.43.6, 1.116.17), just as the Dioscuri (notorious cattle-rustlers, which further associates them with the third function) are famous for their wooing.[15]

2

The Homeric poems know of Castor and Polydeuces as sons of Leda by Tyndareus; the parentage of Zeus is not mentioned. Helen, on the walls of Troy, points out to Priam the leaders of the Achaean host (*Iliad* 3.170 ff.). She knows them all individually, but is herself perplexed at the absence of her brothers:

> δοιὼ δ' οὐ δύναμαι ἰδέειν κοσμήτορε λαῶν,
> Κάστορά θ' ἱππόδαμον καὶ πὺξ ἀγαθὸν Πολυδεύκεα
> αὐτοκασιγνήτω, τώ μοι μία γείνατο μήτηρ. (236–8)

> But two I do not see, marshallers of the host,
> Castor breaker of horses and Polydeuces good at boxing,
> My own brothers, born to one and same mother as I was.

Helen's surprise, after ten years of fighting, at the absence of her brothers, has often been remarked upon. But similarly illogical is Priam's ignorance of his principal adversaries after this same lapse of time. The problem is solved if we consider the double perspective of the *Iliad*. Book 3 envisages the war as in its initial stages, not as ten years old (as does Book 2), since for the audience the battle *is just now* beginning. More surprising is the poet's personal comment after these lines that Castor and Polydeuces are not present because they are dead and buried in Lacedaemon. But this is necessary information too, for the twins have a history, during their lives on earth, of rescuing their sister Helen: they have already brought her back to Sparta once, after Theseus abducted her to Athens (that this story is implicit in the *Iliad* is certain, for Helen at Troy has with her Aethra, mother of Theseus, as her servant – her brothers brought Aethra back when they rescued Helen). Given the twins' record of rescuing their sister, some account must be given for their absence at Troy. The entire

---

15 Some of these points are made by Littleton 1970: 229–46. Littleton points out, drawing on Dumézil, that the Judgement of Paris is a clear example of the first two functions (Hera and Athena, representing sovereignty and war) set against earthly pleasure (Aphrodite, who, however, it must be pointed out, has little or nothing to do with fertility).

expedition would have been unnecessary had the Dioscuri been alive to perform their normal function of retrieving their sister.[16]

In the *Odyssey*, Odysseus sees Leda in the Underworld (11.298–304). It is made very clear there that both Castor and Polydeuces are her children by Tyndareus. But Odysseus also tells the Phaeacians (he is the narrator at this point) that

οἳ καὶ νέρθεν γῆς τιμὴν πρὸς Ζηνὸς ἔχοντες
ἄλλοτε μὲν ζώουσ' ἑτερήμεροι, ἄλλοτε δ' αὖτε
τεθνᾶσιν· τιμὴν δὲ λελόγχασιν ἶσα θεοῖσι. (302–4)

They dwell beneath the earth, having honour from Zeus.
Alive and dead on alternate days, they have honour
Equal to the gods'.

The same story appears to have been told in the cyclical epic, the *Cypria*. This poem, which recounted the events leading up to the Trojan War, is known from a prose summary by Proclus; the account includes the information that the poem told the story of the last exploit of the earthly life of Castor and Polydeuces, their battle with Idas and Lynceus, whose cattle they had stolen. Castor was killed by Idas; Polydeuces killed both Lynceus and Idas. Zeus granted the twins immortality on alternate days.[17] The *Cypria* was composed after the *Iliad* and the *Odyssey* and attempts to fill in details not recounted in the *Iliad*. We have here an obvious attempt to account for the *Iliad*'s mention that the twins are dead and not at Troy, while acknowledging, as the *Odyssey* does, that they play a part in the religious life of the Greeks.

It is significant that the Homeric sources, while they mention Zeus' having accorded immortality to the twins, never mention his having sired them. The first attested appearance of the term Dioscuri (Διὸς κοῦροι) is on an inscription from Thera (*Inscriptiones Graecae* XII.3 359). This inscription, in Ionic dialect, is not far from Homer in time and place —it is to be dated to the end of the eighth or beginning of the seventh century.[18]

---

16 Similarly some reason must be found for detaching Heracles from the Argonautic expedition, as he would upstage Jason, whose story it is, though Heracles cannot be excluded from a crew of all the noblest heroes of Greece. Heracles is thus accidentally left behind in Mysia when he wanders off to look for his missing page Hylas.
17 Text and translation of the epic cycle can be found in the Loeb edition of Hesiod and the Homeric Hymns (Evelyn-White 1914).
18 The exact date of Homer is, of course, still a matter of dispute, though a consensus now puts him at ca. 730 BC. Most recently, Taplin (1992: 33) argues for a date after 700.

The first use in poetry of the term Dioscuri is in the second Homeric Hymn to these divinities (no. 33 in the collection), probably from the beginning of the sixth century. In this Hymn the twins, both of them, are born to Leda and to Zeus, but they are also called Tyndaridae.[19] They are horsemen, and they are invoked as the patrons of mariners, something which may suggest an astral connection (cf. Euripides *Helen* 1495–1505).[20]

The Hymn points to their birth under Mount Taygetus (i.e., in Sparta) as does the appellation Tyndaridae. And indeed the twins seem to have had special prominence in the work of the choral writer Alcman, who, whatever his exact dates, produced his poetry in the Sparta of the middle or late seventh century. The evidence is very fragmentary, coming as it does mostly from tattered papyri, but the glimpse into a world of song, dance, and piety is especially tantalizing.[21] Fragment 2 is a citation of less than two full lines by an ancient rhetorician who was interested in a figure, the so-called *schema Alcmanicum*, which derives its name from the poet. The device consists in the placing of modifiers for a plurality of nouns or names after the first, in anticipation of the plural. It would be hard to find a rhetorical device that more clearly emphasizes that we have identical twins:

> Κάστωρ τε πώλων ὠκέων δματῆρες ἱππόται σοφοὶ
> καὶ Πωλυδεύκης κυδρός.
>
> Castor and, subduers of swift foals, skilled horsemen,
> glorious Polydeuces.

Two papyrus fragments which are commentaries on this line (2 [iii] [iv]) seem to indicate that the context is a reference to a dwelling place of the twins. It must be a centre of their cult and, presumably, the place where they reside for half of their shared lives; it may in fact be a subterranean dwelling. Another piece of papyrus (fragment 7), also a commentary, seems to refer to the Dioscuri and their cult and to include a citation from Alcman in the words κῶμα σιῶν, the 'entranced sleep of the gods.' Interesting in the fragment quoted above is the emphatic association of *both* twins with horses. The Laconian dialect of Alcman writes Πωλυ- rather than the normal Πολυ- as the first part of the

---

19 Hesiod is also said to have made both Castor and Polydeuces sons of Zeus, according to the scholiast on Pindar (*Nem.* 10.80); but the text does not survive.
20 An astral, i.e., celestial, aspect is more likely Indo-European than a maritime connection would be, for the Proto-Indo-European pantheon does not appear to have had sea-gods.
21 All references are to Davies *PMGF*.

name of Polydeuces, and this has exercised critics.[22] But it seems almost obvious from the juxtaposition of the name in the form Πωλυδεύκης with the word πώλων that a play on words is intended – perhaps the name of the god was believed to contain the word for 'foal' (an English equivalent).[23]

Our longest piece of Alcman is the Louvre *Partheneion* (fragment 1), 101 lines of choral poetry discovered, along with broken bits of scholia, in 1855 by Mariette in a tomb near the Great Pyramids. 67 of these lines are almost intact; they are a song by a choir of maidens, apparently to the Goddess of the Dawn. Two of the maidens, Agido and Hagesichora, appear to have special prominence in the ceremony. No piece of Greek lyric is more difficult, partly because of our lack of knowledge of the occasion of performance. But a few things are certain. The part of the poem that is mutilated or lost contained a myth, and Castor and Polydeuces were prominent in the myth: the first surviving word of the poem is]Πωλυδεύκης, Polydeuces. It seems, moreover, likely that the myth was told at some length, occupying 70 lines at the beginning of the poem, with the subsequent 70 of a total of 140 lines being the self-description by the chorus that we possess.

What was the story told in the myth?[24] Since lines 2–12 of what we have contain a badly broken list of names of the sons of Hippocoon, cousins of Castor and Polydeuces, it is reasonable to suppose that the story told was a battle between the Tyndaridae and the Hippocoontidae. A scholiast on Clement of Alexandria (*Protr.* 36) tells us that the Hippocoontidae were rival suitors of Castor and Polydeuces: this is the only clue to what their quarrel might have been. The twins are often pitted against the Apharetidae, Idas and Lynceus, for their cattle, as in the epic *Cypria* (mentioned above) and in the Tenth *Nemean* of Pindar (see below); or alternatively the quarrel is for their fiancées, Phoebe and Hilaeira, whom Castor and Pollux

---

22 See, e.g., Page 1951a.
23 The name of Polydeuces is certainly native Greek (as is that of Castor) and therefore probably Indo-European. But neither element of the name is very clear. δευκ- appears in a variety of words the etymology of which is irrecoverable; most probably δευκ- means 'to care for' (see Chantraine 1970 vol. 2 *s.v.* ἀδευκής). If this sense was alive for Alcman he may have thought of the name Polydeuces as meaning 'caring for foals.' The (now unpopular) derivation of δευκ- from an Indo-European root that yields *dūco* in Latin could, if operative for Alcman, give a meaning 'leader of horses,' very like the name Hipparchus. See Frisk 1973 *s.v.* ἀδευκής.
24 I have addressed this question in an article, 'Alcman's Louvre *Partheneion*: Legend and Choral Ceremony' (forthcoming in *Classical Quarterly*) [in this volume 88–100].

carried off.[25] And indeed these maidens appear to have been mentioned by Alcman at some point, for their names appear in a papyrus commentary on the poet (fragment 8). It seems, then, that Alcman in the poem in question here transferred the fiancées of Idas and Lynceus to the sons of Hippocoon and put the two sets of cousins in competition for these maidens.

The point is important for our purposes, for Phoebe ('The Bright One') is very possibly the Goddess of the Dawn mentioned in the ceremony ('Αῶτι, line 87, a Laconian form containing the more usual 'Hώς) and provides an important link between the two parts of the poem, myth and occasion. Fragment 5(c), yet another papyrus commentary on the poet, in fact appears to refer to a Spartan festival associated with Phoebe. If there is anything to all this we have an intriguing connection with the Aśvins in this Laconian ritual, for the Aśvins are regularly associated with the Dawn, उषस् (= Grk 'Hώς), e.g., Ṛg Veda 7.72.1–5. The prominence of horses in Alcman's poem becomes more interesting too – the girls in the choir seem to envisage themselves as in friendly competition with a pair of virtual twins (their leaders Agido and Hagesichora) who are repeatedly compared to horses in similes; they are perhaps the counterpart, in the friendly competition of the ritual, to the twin horsemen Castor and Polydeuces in the deadly fight of the legend, with in both cases a divine Phoebe the object of general attention. This poem, then, seems to me the place in early Greek poetry where the Indic and Greek mythologies of the horsemen come closest together.

From Dorian Sparta we move to Lesbos in the eastern Aegean and the poet Alcaeus, a generation or two after Alcman. There survives of his work three stanzas of a hymn to the Dioscuri (the entire poem appears to have contained six strophes, but no sense can be made of the last three, so little remains):[26]

δεῦτέ μοι νᾶσ]ον Πέλοπος λίποντες
παῖδες ἴφθ]ιμοι Δ[ίος] ἠδὲ Λήδας,

---

25 It is hard to tell which story, the carrying off of brides or of cattle, is the older. The rape of the Leucippides, Phoebe and Hilaeira, was pictured on the Amyclaean throne at Sparta (ca. 550 BC), where it was seen by Pausanias (3.18.11). It was also painted by Polygnotus at Athens about a century later (Pausanias 1.18.1). Late sources, like Apollodorus (3.11.1–2) and various scholia, lead one to believe that the rape of the maidens is the traditional story, with the cattle-rustling a variant.

26 Text is that of Page 1973b: 34.1–12, with Page's supplements; the Sapphics of the translation are my own. All other references to Sappho and Alcaeus are to the larger edition of Lobel-Page.

.....ω]ι θύ[μ]ωι προ[φά]νητε, Κάστορ
καὶ Πολύδε[υ]κες,

οἲ κὰτ εὔρηαν χ[θόνα] καὶ θάλασσαν
παῖσαν ἔρχεσθ᾽ ὠ[κπό]δων ἐπ᾽ ἴππων,
ῥῆα δ᾽ ἀνθρώποι[ς] θα[ν]άτω ῥύεσθε
ζακρυόεντος

εὐσδ[ύγ]ων θρωίσκοντ[ες ἐπ᾽] ἄκρα νάων
π]ήλοθεν λάμπροι πρό[τον᾽ ὀν]τρ[έχο]ντες,
ἀργαλέαι δ᾽ ἐν νύκτι φ[άος φέ]ροντες
νᾶϊ μ[ε]λαίναι

Come now[27] hither, leaving the isle of Pelops,
Stalwart brothers, children of Zeus and Leda.
Show yourselves in kindness of spirit, Castor
And Polydeuces.

You who range o'er all the broad earth and ocean
Mounted on your swift-footed chargers, present
Help you bring to mortals and save the lost from
Death's icy clutches.

Leaping to the mastheads of ships well-fashioned,
From afar you run up the forestays gleaming,
Bringing light, the woes of the night relieving
For the black vessel.

We are in a world here very similar to that of the Homeric Hymn. The twins are again the sons of Zeus, they are associated with Sparta, or at least with the Peloponnese, they are horsemen, and they are a light to mariners in distress. This is not surprising, since Aeolic, the dialect of Alcaeus, is very close to Ionic (indeed the Ionic of epic contains a noticeable admixture of Aeolic). The poem is in many ways an adaptation to Sapphics of the hexameters of the Homeric Hymn. But the important difference is that whereas the hexameter Hymn is a simple address to the god the stanzas of Alcaeus are a 'cletic' hymn, actually invoking the gods to appear.

What sort of occasion is appropriate? The detailed description of the role of the Dioscuri as saviours in a tempest at sea may be but a digression

---

[27] I translate 'come now,' where Page writes 'come *to me.*' But the word μοι is a supplement and thus not certain; I do not think that this is a personal prayer. Sappho 128, for instance, begins δεῦτέ νυν rather than δεῦτέ μοι, and that is what I translate here.

before a return to the situation 'now,' elaborated in the three lost stanzas. But even so the current situation must be one in which the traditional role will have some significance, and that significance is clearly their ability to bring help in a storm at sea. There are in fact several poems in which Alcaeus describes such a storm. Fragments 6 and 326 give us a good idea of his poetry in this vein; they were quoted by Heraclitus in a work on allegory and he states that these poems are allegorical, with the storm-tossed vessel representing (perhaps for the first time in European literature) the Ship of State. This, the traditional understanding, is most appealing, for the poetry then fits well into the turbulent life and times of the poet, three times an exile and forever, it would seem, losing the struggle against the detested rulers of his maladministered city of Mytilene. But the idea of allegory has been challenged, by those who see the storm-poetry as poetry for an audience of fellow-symposiasts, describing as present what was past in a sort of chamber theatre,[28] and by those who think of the storm-tossed ship as an extended metaphor for a drinking-party that has got out of hand.[29] I would suggest that the Hymn to the Dioscuri fits in very well with an understanding of the storm-poetry as concerned with the Ship of State and its persistent troubles. Further, it is to be noted that several of the hymns of Alcaeus are to young male gods – there are hymns to Hermes and to Apollo as well as to the Dioscuri. These are all most appropriate divinities to be invoked by the young men, exiles or not, of Alcaeus' political club or ἑταιρεία. Very relevant here is Burkert's observation that 'the Dioskouroi are to a large extent a reflection of the body of young men capable of bearing arms.'[30] As supporters of political order they were patrons of the Spartan kings.

If the Dioscuri are powerful presences in the epinician odes of Pindar, the reasons are not far to seek. The victory ode for athletes in the games of the great Panhellenic venues is an innovative and precarious form. For the ode is in some sense a hymn, but it celebrates a mortal, not a god, and so must not forget that god and man alike look with disfavour on the man who forgets his human station in the moment of triumph. For Pindar Heracles and the Dioscuri are mythical types of supreme human accomplishment. The former is the pre-eminent exemplar, for he is the supreme athlete (ἀθλητής): his labours are ἆθλοι and his prize (ἆθλον) apotheosis, a permanent enhancement of the moment of glory that the victor is allowed. The Dioscuri are similarly athletes,

---

28 Bowie 1986a: 13–35, esp. 15–18.
29 Slater 1976: 161–70.
30 Burkert 1985: 212.

in particular horsemen (the equestrian games were unquestionably the most important), and their beatitude, if not unalloyed, is nonetheless continuing. It would seem, in fact, that the epinician or victory ode grew out of a hymn in honour of Castor, for it is called, by Pindar himself, a Καστόρειον or Castor-song (*Pyth.* 2.69, *Isth.* 1.16). Moreover, Pindar not only knows the traditional story that Heracles founded the Olympic games (*Ol.* 10), but reveals a detail, not attested elsewhere in poetry, art, or cult, that Heracles, when he went to Olympus, left the twins in charge of the Olympic contests (*Ol.* 3.35-8). The reason for Pindar's surprising revelation in the Third *Olympian* of 472 BC is in all likelihood the particular devotion of the addressee, Theron of Acragas, and his brother Xenocrates, to the Dioscuri. Theron and Xenocrates, themselves inseparable and both highly successful competitors in the equestrian contests, are typified by the twins, who in addition grant them victory because they are repeatedly honoured with Theoxenies or banquets in Acragas.[31]

Pindar's presentation of the twins naturally varies with his purpose in individual poems. The First *Pythian*, composed in 470 for Hieron of Syracuse, celebrates even more than his chariot victory at Delphi his military conquests and his foundation of a new city on Mt Aetna. To this Dorian city he accorded an ultra-Dorian constitution, praised by the poet in lines 61 ff. Precious pieces of information about the entry of the Dorians into Greece are found here: we are told that the descendants of Heracles, Dorians, came from the Pindus mountains of Thessaly, whence they entered the Peloponnese, to dwell there under Mt Taygetus (i.e., in Sparta) according to the ordinances of Aegimius, one of their kings. They are blessed in their possession of the Lacedaemonian land where they are (65)

> λευκοπώλων Τυνδαριδᾶν βαθύδοξοι γείτονες.
>
> glory-laden neighbours of the sons of Tyndareus
> with their white foals,

Hieron, the founder of the new Dorian city of Aetna in Sicily, is assured of the pedigree of his colony: it extends back to Heracles and to the Dioscuri in their Spartan home.

---

31 See Robbins 1985: 219-28 [in this volume 157-66]. I point out there that the most beautiful of the archaic Greek temples in that city was in the Middle Ages a church of Saints Peter and Paul; given the continuity of cult and the frequent connection of the Dioscuri in Christian art with Peter and Paul, it is reasonable to assume that this 'Temple of Concord' was originally a temple of the Dioscuri.

In writing for King Arcesilaus of Cyrene, in the Fourth *Pythian* of 462, Pindar tells his most ambitious myth, the tale of the voyage of the Argonauts (for Arcesilaus was descended from an Argonaut, and the Argonauts came to Cyrene on their return voyage). A catalogue (170 ff.) sets out the names and parentage of all the children of gods who sailed on the Argo; only demigods are named in order to paint the expedition in its most brilliant colours. Castor and Polydeuces lead the list along with Heracles, forming a trio (υἱοὶ τρεῖς) of sons of Zeus. The Dioscuri are in fact among the most important members of the Argonautic expedition in all versions (cf. n13) of the saga. In late authors (e.g., Ovid *Met.* 8.298–317) they are also companions of Meleager in the hunt of the Calydonian Boar, though they are not found associated with this enterprise in any early source.

Theaeus of Argos is another victor whose success was due to the honour given the Dioscuri in his city. An ancestor of his named Pamphaës (the name is interesting – it means 'all-shining' and could itself be applied to a solar or celestial divinity) set out tables in their honour and offered them hospitality (*Nem.* 10.49). Pindar, accordingly, tells a tale of the Dioscuri as the myth of the poem. It is the story of their last fight, and possibly Pindar's own swan-song.[32] Quite extraordinarily for Pindar, who usually returns to the occasion of celebration and to the poet's work of praise after telling the myth, the narrative of the Tenth *Nemean* ends that poem.[33] We are given, in the last third of the poem, without further commentary on the victor or moralizing on the meaning of events, a narrative which is a paradigm of dedication, of suffering, and of transfiguration. It is the quintessence of Pindar's poetry, and it is the finest presentation of the Dioscuri in Greek literature. Pindar describes the battle between the Dioscuri and the sons of Aphareus, Idas and Lynceus. His inspiration seems to have been the *Cypria*, as that of Alcaeus was the Hymn to the Dioscuri. The penultimate triad tells of the mortal wounding of Castor by Idas, the intervention of Zeus, and the destruction of Idas by Zeus and of Lynceus by Polydeuces, who until the moment of his brother's death is unaware of the circumstance of his own birth. I give the final triad in full:

---

32 Wilamowitz thought so: see 1922: 423–9. His date of 444 BC continues to be entertained by the editor of the Teubner text, Herwig Maehler.

33 The Eleventh *Pythian* ends with a mention of Castor and Polydeuces and their dwelling alternately on Olympus and in Therapne. But this does form part of the myth of the poem, which comes earlier and is concerned with the House of Atreus. The First *Nemean* provides the best parallel to the Tenth – the myth there ends with the reception of Heracles on Olympus, and Pindar fails to return to the addressee of the poem.

στρ.
 ταχέως δ' ἐπ' ἀδελφεοῦ βίαν πάλιν χώρησεν ὁ Τυνδαρίδας,
 καί νιν οὔπω τεθναότ᾽, ἄσθματι δὲ φρίσσοντα πνοὰς ἔκιχεν.
75 θερμὰ δὴ τέγγων δάκρυα στοναχαῖς
 ὄρθιον φώνασε· 'Πάτερ Κρονίων, τίς δὴ λύσις
 ἔσσεται πενθέων; καὶ ἐμοὶ θάνατον σὺν τῷδ᾽ ἐπίτειλον, ἄναξ.
 οἴχεται τιμὰ φίλων τατωμένῳ φωτί· παῦροι δ᾽ ἐν πόνῳ πιστοὶ βροτῶν

ἀντ.
 καμάτου μεταλαμβάνειν.' ὣς ἤνεπε· Ζεὺς δ᾽ ἀντίος ἤλυθέ οἱ,
80 καὶ τόδ᾽ ἐξαύδασ᾽ ἔπος· "Ἐσσί μοι υἱός· τόνδε δ᾽ ἔπειτα πόσις
 σπέρμα θνατὸν ματρὶ τεᾷ πελάσαις
 στάξεν ἥρως, ἀλλ᾽ ἄγε τῷδέ τοι ἔμπαν αἵρεσιν
 παρδίδωμ'· εἰ μὲν θάνατόν τε φυγὼν καὶ γῆρας ἀπεχθόμενον
 αὐτὸς Οὔλυμπον θέλεις <ναίειν ἐμοὶ> συν τ᾽ Ἀθαναίᾳ κελαινεγχεῖ τ᾽ Ἄρει,

ἐπ.
85 ἔστι σοι τούτων λάχος· εἰ δὲ κασιγνήτου πέρι
 μάρνασαι, πάντων δὲ νοεῖς ἀποδάσσασθαι ἴσον,
 ἥμισυ μέν κε πνέοις γαίας ὑπένερθεν ἐών,
 ἥμισυ δ᾽ οὐρανοῦ ἐν χρυσέοις δόμοισιν.'
 ὣς ἄρ᾽ αὐδάσαντος οὐ γνώμᾳ διπλόαν θέτο βουλάν,
90 ἀνὰ δ᾽ ἔλυσεν μὲν ὀφθαλμόν, ἔπειτα δὲ φωνὰν χαλκομίτρα Κάστορος.

Strophe
Polydeukes ran to his brother's side
  and found him still alive
    but gasping in death's throes.
  The warm tears fell amid his groans
as Polydeukes cried aloud:
                  'Father Kronion,
what relief from pain
             will there be now?
On me too, lord,
         together with him,
pass sentence of death.
             A man deprived of those he loves
has seen his honour go,
  though in times of suffering few
    among mortal men can be trusted   (73–8)

Antistrophe
to share the burden.' He spoke,

and Zeus appeared before him, face to face,
   saying: 'You are my son.
Your mother's husband
came to her after I did
                  and left in her womb
the mortal seed
         that is your brother there.
But hear me:
      I grant you a choice
of two alternatives:
            if you yourself, avoiding
death and loathsome old age,
   would dwell on Olympos with me,
      with Athenaia, and Ares of the dark spear – (79–84)

Epode
you may, such is your inheritance.
                  But if you strive
in your brother's behalf, intending
to share in all things equally with him,
                     then you may live
beneath the earth half the time,
               the other half
together in the golden halls of Olympos.'
So Zeus spoke, and Polydeukes felt
no hesitation in his mind, but opened the eyes
and restored the voice of Kastor clad in bronze.[34] (85–90)

---

34 Nisetich 1980: 286 (with one change: the original reads 'after me' in line 80).

FAMOUS
ORPHEUS

Orpheus. Few names from Greek myth are so evocative. Few figures have so appealed to later ages. For us the name has immediate and automatic associations. We think first of the lover who harrowed hell to win back his beloved, second of the minstrel whose sweet music enchanted all nature. We may, if we have made particular study of antiquity, be able to add a third role to the first two. Not only lover and musician but priest: the name of Orpheus is regularly linked in antiquity with mystery religion and special illumination, with initiation into knowledge of the secret workings of the universe. These three facets of this astonishing character account for the universality of his appeal, for in them myth, folklore, and legend come together.[1] Myth, folklore, and legend are not mutually exclusive categories and definitions of each might be disputed. But it would probably be reasonable to claim that Orpheus the revealer of the mysteries is the most truly mythical figure: myth, if it is to be separated from folklore and legend, may most easily be recognized as distinct by its more speculative nature and by the seriousness of its preoccupations.[2] Orpheus the lover is the folklore figure: the motif of the lover who braves the powers of darkness to find his loved one is common to many parts of the world, as is the taboo against looking back or speaking to her which the lover must observe if he is to be successful in his quest.[3] Orpheus the musician is the figure of legend, for legend comes closer to history than do myth and folklore, and the story of the gentle singer whose gift makes

---

First published in *Orpheus. The Metamorphosis of a Myth* edited by John Warden. ISBN: 0802065937. Toronto (1982) 3–24.

1 Cf. Lee 1965: 402–12.
2 There is a good discussion of these matters in Kirk 1974: 30–8.
3 See, e.g., Thompson 1935: F 81.1 and C 331.

savage nature tame is certainly none other, on one level, than the story of the advance of civilization and the arts. The Roman poet Horace knew this:

> When men lived wild, a spokesman of the gods
> The sacred Orpheus, scared them from their foul
> And murderous ways; and so the legend says:
> *Ravening lions and tigers Orpheus tamed.*[4]

The triple personality which European art and literature inherited from antiquity is a complicated amalgam which took centuries to emerge. Most of Greek tradition, we shall see, knew or cared little about Orpheus the lover. Of Orpheus the religious teacher there was certainly much talk among the Greeks, but it has proved notoriously difficult to establish anything definite regarding the beliefs and traditions that accompanied his name. Orpheus the musician is the best attested of all – early art and poetry know this figure well. The final product was the patient work of centuries, perhaps of more than a millennium. And the centuries that followed the end of classical civilization were left in possession of a composite personality they could in turn dismember, faithful to the Greek tradition of Orpheus' end, selecting whatever aspect best suited the purposes of different ages and different artists. In the succeeding chapters of this book we shall see what various periods of European history made of Orpheus. In the Middle Ages he became a type of Christ, overcoming death, a psalmist or a troubadour, courtly lover and singer of pretty lyrics.[5] From the Renaissance on, Orpheus is the very incarnation of the power of music, an art in which scientific and mathematical precision creates a language intelligible on a plane that transcends reason: since the voice of Orpheus is the voice of Music, he presides over the transformations and interaction of poetry and science in the period 1600–1800.[6] In the very same period he becomes the patron of the newly emergent art of opera, from the time of Monteverdi to that of Gluck, again in his role as Music Incarnate.[7] To the Romantics and to our own century he has been the eternal seeker beyond the threshold: different Eurydices summon, new hells yawn.[8]

4 *The Art of Poetry* 391–3 tr. J.G. Hawthorne in Lind 1957: 140.
5 See Friedman 1970.
6 See Sewell 1960, esp. Part II.
7 See Kerman 1956: 25–50.
8 See Strauss 1971.

Priest, lover, musician – a figure of myth, folk-tale, and legend. Does a real person stand behind this great name or is Orpheus simply the product of the imagination of a nation that has bequeathed to us other names equally evocative but almost certainly fictitious? To some the matter is of no consequence, for the real value of many great names – Oedipus, Odysseus, Hamlet, Don Quixote, Robinson Crusoe, to list but a few – is undiminished even if there is no historical personality that can be disinterred for our scrutiny. Orpheus, however, is somewhat different, for he is not only a figure whose exploits have furnished substance to poets and artists. The Greeks persisted in regarding him as a great poet and one of the spiritual founders of their nation. Aristophanes, writing in the late fifth century BC, accords Orpheus a place with Homer and Hesiod.[9] Socrates, a few years later, could, as he faced death, put Orpheus on a par with Homer and Hesiod as someone he looked forward to meeting in the realm beyond the grave provided life did not end with bodily death.[10] And Orpheus, in both cases, is mentioned before Homer and Hesiod. It appears highly likely that he was regarded as more ancient and more venerable than the two poets whose works are our first surviving monuments of Greek literature. No Greek of any period, certainly, ever questioned the existence of Homer or Hesiod. As poets and teachers they enjoyed an honour that no hero we might describe as purely mythical could ever claim.

And so one is inevitably tempted to look for a historical reality behind the great name, inclined to suspect that there was, once, a real Orpheus whose memory lived on, first in the hearts of his countrymen. When and where, if at all, can he be located?

Our first literary mention of the name of Orpheus occurs in the midsixth-century poet Ibycus. A brief mention in a lyric fragment is all we have: 'famous Orpheus.' The name is, thus, celebrated one hundred and fifty years before Aristophanes and Socrates mention him, though we are given no indication why. More intriguing yet is the first representation of Orpheus in art. It antedates the first poetic reference by perhaps a quarter of a century and is thus the first certain appearance of Orpheus we know. It allows us to make some fascinating, if cautious, surmises.

About the end of the first quarter of the sixth century BC, the people of Sicyon, a town in the northwestern Peloponnese, dedicated, under their tyrant Cleisthenes, a 'treasury' or small temple at Apollo's famous shrine at Delphi. On one of the metopes or relief sculptures from the frieze, surviving in badly damaged state and visible today in the museum at

---

9 Aristophanes *Frogs* 1032 ff.
10 Plato *Apology* 412.

Delphi, are the mutilated outlines of a ship, shown in profile and flanked by two mounted horsemen. Two lute players are standing on the ship, one of them with his name, Orpheus, clearly visible beside him. The ship has been plausibly identified as the Argo, the two horsemen as the twins Castor and Pollux. The tradition is well-established, certainly, that Orpheus formed part of the crew of the illustrious expedition that set out to bring back the Golden Fleece. Pindar, in 462 BC, gives us the first detailed account of the voyage of the Argo and he lists Orpheus, as well as Castor and Pollux, among the heroes who sailed from Greece on the great venture.[11] All later accounts give special prominence to Orpheus too. Notable among later versions is a fourth-century BC epic by Apollonius of Rhodes, a work which we still possess in its entirety. So long as classical civilization lasted Orpheus was linked with the Argo. An account of the voyage of the Argo, difficult to date but most probably from the early centuries of the Christian era, is put into the mouth of the singer Orpheus. The poem is regularly called the *Orphic Argonautica*. The association of Orpheus with the Argo is secure from the very beginning. Another lyric fragment, by the poet Simonides (556–468 BC), is our first definite literary reference to Orpheus after that by Ibycus and it is most easily understood if taken as presupposing his presence on board the Argo:

> Over his head flew innumerable birds and to
> his beautiful song fish leapt straight out of
> the blue sea.[12]

Orpheus' link with the fabulous Argonautic expedition is both early and certain. It is, in fact, the earliest incident in his biography for which we have evidence and it would seem reasonable to look more closely at this myth and to attempt to understand its import.

No other Greek myth is so venerable in its antiquity. The voyage of the Argo was already famous when Odysseus met Circe and received navigational advice from her on his way home from Troy:

> One of two courses you may take,
> and you yourself must weigh them. I shall not
> plan the whole action for you now, but only
> tell you of both.
>   Ahead are beetling rocks

---

11 Pindar *Pythian* 4.171–7.
12 Simonides fr. 62 in *PMG* tr. Bowra 1961: 364.

> and dark blue glancing Amphitritê, surging,
> roars around them. Prowling Rocks, or Drifters,
> the gods in bliss have named them – named them well.
> Not even birds can pass them by, not even
> the timorous doves that bear ambrosia
> to Father Zeus: caught by downdrafts, they die
> on rockwall smooth as ice.
>   Each time, the Father
> wafts a new courier to make up his crew.
> Still less can ships get searoom of these Drifters,
> whose boiling surf, under high fiery winds,
> carries tossing wreckage of ship and men.
> Only one ocean-going craft, the far-famed
> Argo, made it, sailing from Aiêta;
> but she, too, would have crashed on the big rocks
> if Hêra had not pulled her through, for love
> of Iêson [Jason], her captain.[13]

It has long been understood that Odysseus' men are Argonauts in disguise, that many of the episodes in the wanderings of Odysseus were taken by the poet we call Homer from an earlier epic, no longer surviving, about the Quest for the Golden Fleece and transferred to Odysseus.[14] That the borrowing occurred is no longer doubted, though there must necessarily be some uncertainty regarding the exact nature of the original poem. It is probable that the poem known to the poet of the *Odyssey* supplies him with a good deal of geographical information about the Propontis, the Black Sea, and the land of Helios the Sun (the father of Circe and the grandfather of Medea) – in a word, about the eastern extremities of the world known to the Greeks. This information may well have been, in the pre-Odyssean *Argonautica*, the record of information brought back to the shores of Ionia by explorers and colonizers and thus current in the land where the *Odyssey* seems to have taken, at a date somewhere around 700 BC, the form in which we know it. But even if there were details of mariners' travels to the Black Sea area embedded in the *Argonautica* in question, and thus in the later *Odyssey*, there is no necessity to believe that the story of the voyage to Colchis and of the Argonauts' return with the grand-daughter of the Sun was primarily the story of an actual voyage of exploration to the Caucasus. There are too many archetypal elements

---

13 *Odyssey* 12.57–72 tr. Fitzgerald 1961.
14 See Meuli 1921; Page 1973a: chapters 2 and 4.

in the story to permit us to reduce it to a simple record of historical fact. We have, in the myth of the Argonautic expedition, too much that seems to jump the confines of possible history and land us in the realm of pure imagination: the evil king (Pelias) who deprives a young hero of his throne and sends him on an impossible mission; the never-never land at the end of the world, complete with beautiful princess, golden treasure, fire-breathing dragon; the perilous voyage, especially the passage through the Clashing Rocks that threaten to pulverize the traveller and his crew.

Something in all this suggests experience psychological more than historical. It has been argued that the myth of the Quest for the Golden Fleece is the oldest and most significant of all Greek myths, that it is essentially the account of the voyage out and return of the shaman, that figure familiar to so many cultures, who mediates between this world and the beyond and whose most extraordinary characteristic is his ability to bring souls back from the realm of the dead.[15] Jason is such a figure, his mission to rescue and repatriate a lost soul. Pindar's King Pelias sends Jason forth with the following words:

> You have the power to lay the wrath of those in earth.
> Phrixos is calling, that someone redeem his ghost,
> And, going to the hall of Aietas, fetch
> The thick-piled Fleece
> Of the Ram, by whom he was saved of old
> From the sea.[16]

'Redeem his ghost' (the Greek for 'ghost' here is *psychê*). And so Jason is a psychopomp, the voyage of the Argo a voyage through the narrow passage to the furthermost bourne in search of a wraith.

The presence of Orpheus on the Argo becomes, thus, of particular interest. For he, par excellence, was remembered as an intermediary between this world and the next; he more than any other was famous for his descent to the underworld and his mission to redeem a ghost. The Greeks remembered Orpheus as the first of their great poets and spiritual teachers. They remembered him as an Argonaut and placed him on a boat the commander of whose crew curiously resembles him as psychopomp. Argonautic poetry stands behind Homeric poetry just as the Argonautic myth is well known to the author of the *Odyssey*. It would not, it seems, be rash to believe

---

15 Lindsay 1965.
16 Pindar *Pythian* 4.158–61 tr. Bowra 1969. The passage is discussed by W. Burkert (1962: 36–55) in his article on Greek shamanism.

that there was once an Orpheus, a shaman and poet, himself a traveller to the other side and expounder of its secrets to those to whom he returned. His teaching may have been contained in poetry – the attribution to him of musical gifts is ubiquitous – and one of his works may, in all likelihood, have been a poem about the Argo, the skipper of whose crew is so like himself. His 'signature' survives, even if the original poem does not, in his continuing association with the Argonautic myth in the art and literature available to us.

To return to the metope of the Sicyonian treasury at Delphi. The Argo is there flanked by the twins Castor and Pollux, two of the most haunting figures of Greek myth. Theirs is a union which holds life and death, this world and the next, in eternal, fixed conjunction. The mortal twin Castor was redeemed from death by his brother who sacrificed, in part, his immortality that he might live. The twins, as a result, either live together, one day on Olympus alternating with one day in Hades, or they take turns to die, one replacing the other with regularity in the underworld. The association of these figures with the voyage of the Argo is surely no more gratuitous than the inclusion of Orpheus in its crew. They are the patrons of mariners to whom they appear 'bearing light in the grievous night.'[17] These figures link the nether world with the upper air, the dark land of the dead with the bright land of the living. Life and death are not so much opposites as the complementary halves of a single whole, the twins holding in their embrace knowledge of both sides of the tomb. They represent, symbolically, the two terms of the shaman's voyage, this world and the beyond. Orpheus, like Jason, is privy to their knowledge and, like them, straddles the grave.

The Greeks of the classical period have been much admired by some for their 'direct and unequivocal acceptance of man's mortality.'[18] There is not much in the Greek myths, we are told, that probes the boundaries between mortal and immortal as does the Mesopotamian *Epic of Gilgamesh*. Shamanic figures, who exist to explore and to initiate into a world beyond the grave, are exceptional, the established Olympian religion being hostile to any attempt on man's part to overcome death. One suspects, in the admiration, a reading of contemporary religious feelings into the distant past: in an age when belief in an afterlife has, for the most part, considerably weakened, we are reassured to find that the Greeks demanded in their myths what we demand today – acceptance of the finality of death.[19] But

---

17 Alcaeus fr. 34.11 in Voigt 1971.
18 Kirk 1970: 231–2.
19 One example among many possibilities might be cited: N.O. Brown's influential book (1959).

if this 'freedom from illusion' is 'most often admired,'[20] it has been criticized too.[21] The Olympian religion, the product of an invading patriarchal society, superseded and suppressed an earlier Aegean religion, dominated by the figure of a Mother Goddess who generously shared her deathlessness with her devotees. The sky gods of the Indo-Europeans were jealous of their prerogatives, most important of which was their immortality, and demanded that man should recognize his limits. His limits were fixed in this life and he was forbidden to seek knowledge beyond it. Value judgments apart, it is accurate enough to explain the relative absence of immortal longings in the Greek myth we find in classical literature as the product of a historical process in which Olympian dynastic gods replaced powerful female deities as Indo-European assumed a parallel dominance, in the second millennium BC, over native Aegean stock.

This consideration may help us in establishing an approximate period for Orpheus. Every attempt to resurrect this shadowy figure must be, to a considerable degree, speculative. But if we believe, as Greeks of the classical period were wont to do, that an actual Orpheus preceded the poets Homer and Hesiod and if we are inclined to see in him a shaman who could penetrate the world beyond the grave, we shall also be tempted to place him in the Bronze Age, in the second millennium BC, and to see in him a shaman-priest connected with the cult of the Mother Goddess.

A particularly tantalizing fresco from the Throne Room of the Late Bronze Age Palace of Nestor at Pylos in the southwestern Peloponnese shows a seated bard, attired in a long garment, playing a five-stringed instrument and appearing to charm a large, winged creature. The excavator of this site, C.W. Blegen, himself suggested that this might be Orpheus.[22] The invading Indo-Europeans, or Mycenaeans as they are generally called, took many mythical and religious motifs from the people they subdued. One of the most prominent of recurring themes in Greek myth is the story of the recovery of an abducted princess: examples are Persephone, Helen, Eurydice. The leading twentieth-century scholar of Greek religion has, in fact, suggested that the myth of a Maiden snatched from the embrace of Death is one that the Mycenaeans took over from the older religion.[23] They found in the area they occupied a religion not haunted by thoughts of the finality of death: its central divinity was the Mother Goddess who ever grants continuing life, just as the earth, with which

---

20 Kirk 1970: 231–2.
21 Campbell 1964, Part One 'The Age of the Goddess'.
22 Blegen 1956: 95.
23 Nilsson 1963: 74–6, 171–4

she is always associated, is both tomb and womb, restoring the life it takes. The Indo-Europeans, a warrior people, secularized at least one of the myths that tell of the recovery of a stolen princess and transferred it from the divine to the heroic level. Helen is not, for those of us familiar with the *Iliad*, a divinity. But divine she undoubtedly was in her origins, and there survive in Greek myth stories of her abduction by Theseus – that same Theseus who carried off the Cretan princess Ariadne and who, in some versions, attempted to carry off Persephone. In the story of Theseus' attempted abduction of Persephone it was the new religion, which insisted on maintaining the distinction between this world and the next, which would not allow Persephone to come to the shores of light but forced Theseus to remain among the dead. Orpheus may well be another figure, taken from the Throne Room at Pylos from the repertory of the pre-Greek natives. Orpheus is, after all, a successful *revenant* from the beyond. The earliest versions of the Eurydice story known to us tell of his recovery of her, as we shall see.

The case for a Mycenaean origin for Orpheus has been extensively argued in the most recent contribution to Orphic studies, R. Böhme's *Orpheus: Der Sänger und seine Zeit* ('Orpheus: The Singer and His Age'). Response to the book has been guarded, the prevailing opinion on the topic being sceptical, but Böhme's ideas have received favourable notice from W.K.C. Guthrie, who refuses to accept the minimalist position and whose own book, *Orpheus and Greek Religion*, remains the most widely read work on the subject in the English language.[24] Guthrie, in his book on Orpheus (1935) and in a chapter of his later work *The Greeks and Their Gods* (1950), is also disposed to believe that there was a historical Orpheus even though he would not place him so far back in time as would the more recent writer on the subject. The most impressive part of Böhme's treatment, Guthrie feels, is his minute analysis of remarkably similar, often virtually identical, passages in Homer and Hesiod and other early poets which argue a common archetype rather than mutual borrowing. One example among many might be cited.

In Hesiod's *Theogony* we read of:

> ... the place where Night and Day
> Approach and greet each other as they cross
> The great bronze threshold.[25]

---

24 Böhme 1970. An earlier book, Böhme 1953, is reviewed by Guthrie in *Gnomon* 26 (1954) 303–7.
25 Hesiod *Theogony* 748–50 tr. D. Wender (Harmondsworth 1973).

In the eighth book of the *Iliad* there are 'gates of iron and a brazen doorstone'[26] before the entrance to Tartarus while in the *Odyssey* the Laestrygonians of Book Nine, living at the extreme end of the known world, are placed where 'the courses of Night and Day lie close together.'[27] Another parallel is provided by the poem of the pre-Socratic poet-philosopher Parmenides. He describes his voyage from the House of Night into the presence of a goddess who reveals to him the truth. The way lies through 'the gates of the paths of Night and Day.'[28] All four passages speak of a threshold. If they have a common source could it be in the songs of Orpheus, the figure on the threshold between this world and the next?

The past century has seen an enormous amount of controversy over the possibility of believing in a historical Orpheus. Guthrie and Böhme, convinced by circumstantial evidence, have held for an actual historical figure who gave rise to the stories associated with his name. An important work written in the period between the books of Guthrie and Böhme, I.M. Linforth's *The Arts of Orpheus* (1941), sifts all the available evidence and arrives at absolutely minimal conclusions: no justification for believing in a historical Orpheus; so little uniformity in the information to be gleaned from studying the texts, mostly of late antiquity, that claim Orphic inspiration, that it is impossible to construct a coherent doctrine recognizable as the product of a single religious teacher. There is a bewildering miscellany of religious writings, conveniently collected for those who have the Greek to read it, in Kern's *Orphicorum fragmenta* (1922). Guthrie and Linforth deal with the same evidence but reach different conclusions, the latter arriving at the position that we have no right to believe in any religious institution founded by a historical figure, the former unable to avoid the conclusion that a sect did exist in historical times and that the impulse behind it was an actual religious teacher.

Linforth finds the term 'Orphic' completely vague and virtually meaningless. It has no utility as a label and is better avoided. We know that the mythical figure was a fabulous musician and an Argonaut, that stories were told of his descent to the underworld, that a host of philosophic and religious doctrines were promulgated with his name attached to them. None of this warrants the assumption that the mythical figure was more than a convenient referent for mystical, ritual, eschatological, and philosophic doctrine and we simply cannot know how early he was popular in the Greek imagination. The argument does not lend itself to summary, for Linforth's

26 *Iliad* 8.15 tr. Lattimore 1951.
27 *Odyssey* 9.86.
28 Parmenides fr. B 1.11 in Diels-Kranz[11] 1964.

book is essentially a detailed examination of individual items of evidence, avoiding all but negative conclusions. The reader who tackles it will find it stringent and difficult, tough-minded and chary of broad generalizations. Its effect has been considerable, as one example will suffice to demonstrate.

E.R. Dodds, in his epoch-making book *The Greeks and the Irrational*, admits that Linforth was largely responsible for disabusing him of almost everything he once thought he knew about Orphism. Dodds is quite willing to believe that there once was an Orpheus. He thinks too that this Orpheus was a shaman, but he is quite unwilling to attach to him the fantastic theogonical speculation that went on for a thousand years in the ancient world and he finds himself quite lacking the tools necessary to separate the wheat from the chaff in the vast amount of 'Orphic' material.[29] The trouble with most of the evidence is its lateness. Some, of course, is comparatively early, but Linforth has detected, even in the earliest material, nothing more than a desire to foist upon an august name the most disparate doctrine. Orpheus was associated with the mysteries from an early date, hence anything liturgical, ritualistic, or speculative was loosely called Orphic. But there is nowhere in antiquity a clearly discernible Orphic sect, generally acknowledged and admitted and identifiable by a characteristic body of doctrine.

Guthrie, in contrast, does not see a nebulous mass of popular tradition and loose speculation that disintegrates upon close examination but is impressed by a core of belief evinced in many writers, some of whom ascribe the teaching to Orpheus, others of whom do not. Most prominent are a belief in transmigration and in an afterlife in which good is rewarded and evil punished, and a belief in the necessity of catharsis or purification to free our immortal soul from the fleshly tomb in which it is incarcerated. Abstention from eating flesh and reliance on the efficacy of scrupulously performed ritual were likely to go along with these beliefs. Multifariousness or lack of doctrinal coherence and absence of canonical scripture is, for him, the hallmark of practically all of Greek religion outside Orphism, and Orphism was the direct antithesis of the common attitudes. It was structured, dogmatic, authoritative, based on holy writings that were inspired by the teaching of a great religious reformer, if not his own composition, and ever peripheral or esoteric, the property of a sect whose ideas never filtered very far down into the general consciousness of a nation whose religious life was not characterized by holy books, a priestly caste, personal piety, and moral injunctions, in other words, the very things which those of us reared in a

---

29 Fragment 1 B 11 in Diels-Kranz[11] 1964. Dodds 1951: 147 ff.

Judaeo-Christian tradition expect of religion and which Orphism alone in the classical period of Greek culture provided.

Guthrie is convinced that a historical figure spawned the myths, legends, and teachings associated with his name. But rather than place him at a point remote in time from the writers of classical Greece, in the Bronze Age hundreds of years before our first explicit mention of him, he places him, or at least the most important incident in his biography, at a point geographically remote from the life of the civilized Hellenes. Orpheus is, for Guthrie, a Greek missionary preaching his Apolline religion of catharsis and asceticism among the wild barbarians of Thrace, the orgiastic devotees of the un-Greek Dionysus. He came to grief at the hands of the women votaries of the god of ecstasy. An Alexandrian author of a treatise of the constellations, one Eratosthenes, tells us the story of Orpheus' end and in so doing mentions a lost play of Aeschylus, the *Bassarids*, probably written early in the fifth century BC and taking its name from the chorus of women in the tragedy. He writes as follows:

> He [Orpheus] paid no honour to Dionysus but considered Helios to be the greatest of the gods and addressed him as Apollo. Hastening through the night he reached the summit of Mount Pangaeus and waited there to see the rising sun. Dionysus in his anger set the Bassarids against him, as the poet Aeschylus says, and they tore him to pieces and scattered his limbs broadcast. The Muses gathered his remains and buried them in what is called Leibethra [a mountain district of Thrace]. Having no one to whom to give his lyre they asked Zeus to set it among the stars as a memorial to him and to themselves.[30]

Fifth-century vase paintings show both Orpheus playing his lyre among the Thracians and Orpheus being attacked by hostile women.[31] The reason for the hostility of the women is difficult to understand, but it is a well-attested part of his story; Plato alludes to it, a century after Aeschylus, in the famous Vision of Er with which the *Republic* ends. Er, witnessing the souls of the departed preparing to return to this world after a long period of purification, sees among them the soul of Orpheus choosing the life of a swan for his next incarnation because of his refusal to be born of the sex that had been responsible for his death (10.620A). Guthrie assumes that there was something profoundly misogynistic[32] about the religion that

---

30 Kern 1963: Test. 113 (my translation).
31 Guthrie 1966: figures 4 and 5, plates 4 and 6.
32 *Ibid.* 49.

Orpheus preached. He offended not only Dionysus, the mighty antagonist of Apollo, but along with him the entire female sex which the god admitted enthusiastically to his following but which the ascetic preacher outraged by his anti-feminism as he ensorcelled their husbands through his music and his summons to a celibate community.

How to reconcile the view that Orpheus was a Bronze-Age shaman (Böhme) and the view that he was a missionary among the Thracians (Guthrie)? The Mycenaean figure appears to have a reality more psychological than historical, as we have seen. And no doubt the story pattern and the ritual experience are older than the name we attach to them. At some point – it is difficult to say when – the stories became attached to a name, as did poetry and a body of religious doctrine. It is interesting to note a possibly similar pattern in the case of Heracles. First, a shamanic figure and Master of Animals whose origins may go back even beyond the Bronze to the Stone Age;[33] then, perhaps, a real man who became the focal point of the tradition and who contributed the name by which the character, partly historical and partly mythical, was to be known.[34] Scholars are unlikely to come to complete agreement regarding who the historical Orpheus was and when he lived. But Homer is a vague figure too, though the Greeks never doubted that there had been such a man, even if modern scholars have. So it is in the case of Orpheus.

Whatever truth there may be in Guthrie's interpretation, it is interesting to note that the Romans, who inherited a much impoverished Orpheus, concentrating as they did almost exclusively on the love story of Orpheus and Eurydice, made much of the hostility of the female sex towards poor Orpheus. Virgil, in the *Fourth Georgic*, the first and still the most beautiful account of the unsuccessful attempt of Orpheus to bring Eurydice back from the nether world, describes the antagonism of the women of Thrace. For Virgil the hatred of the women is simply the result of the singer's undying attachment to the woman he has lost, his death at the hands of the Thracian women a motif directly subservient to a romantic story:

> No thought of love
> Or wedding rites could bend his inflexible will.
> He wandered lonely through the icy North,
> Past the snow-encrusted Don, through mountain fields
> Of unadulterated frost, conveyed the grief

---

33 See Burkert 1979: chapter 4.
34 Rose 1958: 205.

> At Hell's ironic offerings, and rapt
> Eurydice. By such unwavering faith
> The Thracian women felt themselves outraged,
> And at their sacred exercise, nocturnal
> Bacchanals, they tore the youth apart,
> And scattered his limbs around the spacious fields.
> But even then his voice, within the head
> Torn from its marble neck, and spinning down
> The tide of his paternal River Hebrus,
> The cold-tongued voice itself, as life fled away,
> Called out 'Oh, my forlorn Eurydice!
> Eurydice!' and the shoreline answered back
> Along the river's breadth, 'Eurydice!'[35]

Ovid, at the beginning of the eleventh book of the *Metamorphoses*, tells in lurid detail the story of the dismemberment of Orpheus by the spurned women – the motif here too grows out of the romantic story – and adds the detail that Orpheus' head was washed up on the island of Lesbos. The story of Orpheus' extreme devotion to his wife was what the Romans best liked, and they combined it with the mysterious story, at least as old as Aeschylus, of his being rent asunder by the Thracian women. The detail of the severed head floating down the river Hebrus and being washed ashore on Lesbos is in all likelihood an old one too. The head of Orpheus was buried in a temple at Antissa on Lesbos, where it continued to give oracles, and his lyre was preserved in a temple of Apollo. These illustrious relics were widely held to have inspired the flowering of poetry on the remarkable island that produced Terpander, Sappho, and Alcaeus, the first lyric monodists of the Greek world (late seventh and early sixth centuries BC). A fragment of Alcaeus, frustratingly incomplete, mentions the river Hebrus:

> Most beautiful of rivers, Hebrus, are you, as you pour forth beside Aenus into the purple sea surging through the land of Thrace ... And many maidens visit you, with delicate hands [? to bathe] their beautiful thighs; they are beguiled ... wondrous water like unguent ...[36]

The invocation of the river would in all probability suggest the story of Orpheus, and the poem may well have gone on to tell it. A singing

---

35 Virgil *Georgics* 4.516–27 tr. Bovie 1956.
36 Alcaeus fr. 45 (tr. Page); see Page 1955: 285–8

head endowed with oracular powers is something which points towards shamanism again. In all parts of the world, in addition to having the ability to travel to the Beyond and recover lost souls and a not infrequent power to summon birds and beasts to listen to his music, the shaman lives on after death as a magical head which gives oracles that are but a continuation of the incantations he practised while alive.[37]

The love story of Orpheus and Eurydice, so important to the Romans and to us, seems quite clearly the tail-end of a centuries-old tradition that knew Orpheus, shaman and Argonaut, as traveller to the world beyond and master of its mysteries. Romantic love was of little interest to the early Greeks. It was essentially a creation of the Alexandrian Age and forms part of its legacy to Rome. The first truly romantic narrative in European literature is, in fact, the love story of Jason and Medea in the *Argonautica* of Apollonius of Rhodes. Nowhere before do we find the intimate analytical handling of a love theme which makes the third book of this poem so much more interesting than the story of the voyage within which the love story is contained. The Romans inherited the Alexandrian interest and turned it to account, no one more splendidly than Virgil, who could use Apollonius' handling of Jason and Medea as model for his own story of Dido and Aeneas and who has given us the classical account of Orpheus' tragic love for Eurydice. The unhappy ending has been, since Virgil, an essential ingredient of the great love story: passion and death are indissolubly linked. But if the Virgilian story has the unhappy ending which we have come to regard as the regular one when we think of Orpheus and Eurydice, it is likely Virgil's own invention or something he took from a lost Alexandrian source. Ideas of taboo, so prominent in folk-tales, are rare in Greek myth and are not likely early ingredients of stories in which they are found at a late date.[38] The Greeks, in a period before interest in romantic love demanded the unhappy ending, seem to have known Orpheus – and this is what we would expect – as one who was successful in bringing his wife back from the underworld.[39] The name Eurydice, which means 'Wide-Ruler,' may well be late. It is used for the first time in literature in the *Lament for Bion*, probably of the first century BC. Earlier she had been called Agriope, 'Savage Watcher,' by the poet Hermesianax in the third

---

37 Eliade 1964: 391; Dodds 1951: 147.
38 Nilsson 1964: 52–7.
39 The tradition of the unsuccessful return of Orpheus is discussed by Dronke 1962: 198–215. Dronke is primarily interested in the use of the myth in medieval poetry where Orpheus is a type of Christ. He argues that the dominant tradition remained strong and was never eclipsed by the Virgilian version.

century. The names are rough equivalents, both being obviously names of the Queen of the Night, Persephone. The Bronze Age archetype discussed earlier would suggest that the lost princess was released and recovered, that the earth gives back life, that the shaman is not defeated in the House of Death. Both in the *Lament for Bion* and in Hermesianax Orpheus is successful in bringing back Eurydice/Agriope. And so it is not surprising to learn that the first passing reference to Orpheus' descent for his own bride is a reference to a successful recovery. In Euripides' play, the *Alcestis* (438 BC), the poet puts into the mouth of Admetus, the husband of the doomed Alcestis, the following words:

> Had I the lips of Orpheus and his melody
> to charm the maiden daughter of Demeter and
> her lord, and by my singing win you back from death,
> I would have gone beneath the earth, and not the hound
> of Pluto could have stayed me, not the ferryman
> of ghosts, Charon at his oar. I would have brought you back
> to life.[40]

There can be no doubt that Euripides is referring to a story, already well known, in which Orpheus was successful in bringing back his wife. If the commonly known story had been one in which he had failed, reference to it on the part of Admetus would have been totally inappropriate at this moment.

Almost contemporary with the reference in Euripides' *Alcestis* is a late fifth-century Attic relief extant in three copies, the finest of which is in the National Museum in Naples. The three figures in the relief are identified by inscriptions above their heads as Hermes, Eurydice, and Orpheus, though it is likely that the inscriptions were not on the original. In any case the figures are clearly identifiable. Orpheus is holding his lyre in his left hand. Hermes looks on as Orpheus, with his right hand, touches Eurydice's left, apparently lifting the veil from her face. Interpretation of this famous piece of sculpture is uncertain. Is Orpheus here portrayed in the act of breaking the taboo which causes him to lose Eurydice a second time? Is he simply taking his first farewell at her death? Or are we shown the moment of his triumph in the underworld? The most natural interpretation would seem to be the last: the lyre suggests that Orpheus has just finished singing, the veil brushed aside that he has learned the secrets of the afterlife and is united to Eurydice, whom he is to escort

---

40 Euripides *Alcestis* 357–62 tr. Lattimore 1955.

back.[41] A remarkably similar scene, clearly a scene of union rather than of separation, is visible on one of the reliefs from the frieze of a temple at Selinus in Sicily. This metope, today in the National Museum in Palermo, shows the Holy Marriage of Zeus and Hera. Zeus, like Orpheus, touches the veil and the left wrist of his bride with his right hand. The pieces in Naples and Palermo both date from approximately the middle of the fifth century BC.

Plato speaks in the *Symposium* of the failure of Orpheus, but not in the manner familiar to us from Virgil. In this dialogue the speaker, Phaedrus, contrasts Alcestis, who was brave enough to die for Admetus, with Orpheus, who was sent back from Hades 'without accomplishing his mission' (*atelê* 179D). The underworld gods show him a phantom rather than give him his wife since they found him a poor-spirited fellow, as lyre players are wont to be. The story in the *Symposium* is probably Plato's own invention: it would be hazardous to regard it simply as something taken over intact from the current stock of myth. Plato may be influenced here by the well-known story, mentioned by the poet Stesichorus (ca 630–ca 555 BC) and repeated by Plato himself in the *Republic* (9.586C), that the war at Troy was fought over a phantom, Helen never having been at Ilium. The Orpheus story in the *Symposium* relies for its effect on the shock value of the word *atelê* ('unsuccessful') at the beginning of the passage in which it is told. It presupposes, surely, an accepted version in which Orpheus was successful, stands the known story on its head, and surprises us by informing us that what Orpheus found was a phantom, not his real wife. In other words, the tale of the phantom explains the word 'unsuccessful.'

Of especial interest in this version is the notice that the gods found Orpheus reprehensible as being insufficiently heroic. Something in this seems to pick up a preoccupation older than Plato. A commentator, or scholiast, on the *Argonautica* of Apollonius of Rhodes[42] has a fascinating discussion of authors who mentioned Orpheus' connection with the Argo long before Apollonius. It appears to have been of major concern to explain just how Orpheus, generally so unlike most Greek heroes, could have sailed

---

41 Rilke's account of the second loss of Eurydice by Orpheus in the poem 'Orpheus. Eurydike. Hermes' is probably inspired by the sculpture discussed here: see Strauss 1971: 172. Rilke clearly interprets the sculpture in accordance with the tradition of the unsuccessful attempt to restore Eurydice to life. But the bas-relief is not explicit: much of its fascination comes precisely from the fact that it must be interpreted in accordance with a view of the myth formed by literary versions. Rilke accepts the Virgilian version.

42 Wendel 1958: 8–9.

with the Argonauts. One fifth-century writer, Pherecydes, had, according to the commentator, been quite unwilling to believe that Orpheus was in the company of the stalwart crew that sailed with Jason and had, accordingly, made the striking statement that Orpheus had never really been on the Argo. There is, without any doubt, something about Orpheus that sets him apart from all the other great figures of Greek myth. Greek myth is pre-eminently heroic myth, myth that enshrines martial values: courage, killing, blood-lust. Not surprising in the legacy of a male-dominated warrior society that produced, in the *Iliad*, the world's supreme battle epic and whose agonistic, competitive impulse never faltered for a moment. The finest products of classical Greek poetry, a thousand years after the Indo-European invasion of the peninsula, are plays, produced at competitive festivals, and victory odes for triumphant athletes. The contest dominated Greek life in all its aspects, from the gymnasium and the law-courts to dialectic. A modern theologian points out that there is even an intimate connection between the characteristic competitive impulse of the Greeks and their concept of love, always seen as a striving or an *agôn*.[43] Orpheus clearly belongs to another world, as has been suggested above. All the other great figures of Greek myth, whatever else they may be, are great killers: Achilles, Heracles, Jason, Perseus, Oedipus, Odysseus, Agamemnon – the list could be extended indefinitely and would show not a single figure of note who is not blood-stained. Orpheus is unique and he seems to have puzzled the Greeks. He did not particularly interest the poets of the classical period and he seems not to have escaped the charge of cowardice when compared with his fellows. Prometheus is not a killer, certainly, but he is undeniably aggressive and his hands reek of the blood of sacrifice: the two most important items in the myth concerning him are his contest of wits with Zeus and his establishment of the laws of sacrifice. A recent book by W. Burkert, *Homo necans*[44] ('Man the Slaughterer'), is an intriguing study of the Greek obsession with animal sacrifice and its relation to aggressive

---

43 Scheler 1972: 84–6.
44 Burkert 1972. A rather different position is taken by J. Huizinga (1955) in his famous book *Homo Ludens: A Study of the Play-Element in Culture*. Huizinga thinks that the Greeks were no more competitive or aggressive than other peoples and criticizes scholars who have maintained that they were (pp. 71 ff): for him war, contests, sacrifice are but manifestations of a play-impulse that is ubiquitous in world culture. But when Huizinga posits the superiority of Greek civilization to others (e.g., pp. 174) he does so on the grounds that the play-element in Greek culture was more lively and imaginative than it was elsewhere. It appears to be chiefly a question of the value-judgment attached to the agonistic habit; Burkert's 'necans' is less complimentary than Huizinga's 'ludens,' but both authors find special evidence among the Greeks for what they are seeking.

biological drives found in animals and in primitive hunters. And certainly there is no honest way of minimizing the role of blood-letting either in Greek heroic myth or in Greek religious practice. Every hero fleshes his sword. Altars were steeped in the blood of animals of all sorts. Priests were butchers, temples slaughterhouses. The Greeks were fortunate in having these outlets for their murderous instincts. On the ritual level animals could be slaughtered instead of human beings; in myth the same impulse was discharged in fantasy, in stories of war and of dragon-slaying. Both these channels were innocent and socially beneficial.

But Orpheus cuts a strange figure among the heroes. He seems tame if not weak in comparison, as the Greeks themselves noticed. He restores to life instead of killing; he is surrounded by the fiercest of animals which, far from slaying, he leads from savagery to docility and meekness by his music. Claude Lévi-Strauss and his followers in the structuralist school of anthropology have asserted that mental and social processes are fundamentally binary, coded in mythical examples which, when deciphered, reveal simple polarities. The psychic life of a people sends up directly contradictory impulses that will crystallize in antithetical figures. If there is any truth in this, it may be reasonable to see in Orpheus the necessary and precious counterpiece to his numerous more ferocious brethren. One of Lévi-Strauss's disciples has written a fascinating essay on this very theme, comparing Orpheus, the unnaturally gentle – his subjugation of wild animals through the power of music is contrary to expectation and all normal experience – with Orion, the excessively savage, whose thirst for blood knows no bounds.[45] On this interpretation the musician is, as he appears to be judged in the *Symposium*, a cowardly creature, though as inevitable a product of the mythical imagination of antiquity as is his equally extreme opposite number. The mean would lie somewhere between

---

45 Detienne 1971: 7–23. Perhaps the tradition of Orpheus' death at the hands of women is no more than a further proof of his untypical, unheroic nature. Normal heroes (e.g., Achilles, Heracles, Bellerophon, Theseus) are superior even to Amazons: only a weakling could fall to female assailants. In the *Odyssey* it is Aegisthus who kills Agamemnon. In Aeschylus, where Clytemnaestra commits the murder, there is a reversal of normal roles, Clytemnaestra being masculine, Agamemnon effeminate. And the Pentheus of Euripides' *Bacchae*, before his murder by the women, has himself been virtually turned into a woman by Dionysus.

Of interest in this respect, perhaps, is the possible existence of a tradition that sees Jason as weak and unheroic; see Hadas 1936: 166–8. This may provide another link between Jason and Orpheus. It is noteworthy, certainly, that these two Argonauts became the two Greek 'heroes' most famous for their loves. Something in their very nature seems to have lent itself especially well to romantic exploitation by Apollonius and Virgil.

the extremes, the mythopoeic imagination creating the embodiments of opposite and discordant qualities and inviting that reconciliation or repose which is created by the presence of balance and stress.

It is, of course, not necessary to view the matter this way. If Orpheus is viewed as a culpable extreme by a speaker in a Platonic dialogue or by a modern structuralist, he may be, and most often is, received without any pejorative value-judgment clinging to him. When George Steiner describes Lévi-Strauss himself as 'Orpheus with his myths'[46] he is being highly complimentary: Lévi-Strauss is Orpheus in his traditional and time-honoured role, both musician (and the various parts of Lévi-Strauss's work correspond to musical forms and the author continually turns to music to provide the best analogy for myth as he understands it) and prophet who reveals, in difficult and enigmatic language, a vision which ranges beyond that of the generality of men. The *Mythologiques* of Lévi-Strauss are, for Steiner, Orphic in the best possible sense of the word, advancing the cause of harmony where there is silence (death) or discord (savagery). One is tempted to add another Orphic point to all this. The closing paragraph of the third volume of the *Mythologiques* shows its author's urgent concern to turn European civilization back from the hell ('enfer') in which it has become imprisoned by self-centredness.[47] Who better than Orpheus to perform such a task?

The Orpheus that the ancients know was priest, lover, musician. Most times one or two of the three, rarely all in combination. There is one avatar of Orpheus in European art who is quintessentially all three, the perfect amalgam that is nowhere else so fully present, even on the stage of antiquity. Since his name is not Orpheus and since he will, thus, not appear in the succeeding pages of this book, he must not be passed over here. There can be little doubt that his creators had the ancient myths in mind when they designed him. He is the perfect Orpheus, lacking only the traditional name.

Mozart's opera *The Magic Flute* was written in 1791, in the last months of the composer's life. The author of the libretto, Emmanuel Schikaneder, worked closely under the composer's supervision, the result being an opera in which Mozart was able to exercise the greatest degree of control over the text he set to music. One of the composer's closest friends at this time was the master of the Masonic Lodge to which he belonged. This remarkable person, Ignaz von Born, was learned in countless fields and had a knowledge of ancient myth and ritual that was unmatched in the Austria of his time.

46 Steiner 1967: 239–50.
47 Lévi-Strauss 1968: 422.

He influenced Mozart as Mozart influenced his librettist, and the result is the most profoundly felt of all the composer's great works.

In the First Act, Tamino, the hero of the opera, charms, by the power of his music, the beasts of the wild wood; in the Second Act he quells, by the same magic, the hostile forces, here fire and water, that threaten to engulf him. Further, he gains his beloved princess Pamina through his steadfastness in refusing to break the taboo imposed on him if he is to win her. Through a succession of trials he moves from the Realm of Night – Pamina is the daughter of the Queen of the Night – to membership in the brotherhood of the Temple of Light. His progress is transparently a successful emergence from the underworld, successful because he observes the prohibition enjoined on him. Pamina pleads with him but he is adamant. Only thirty years earlier (1762) Viennese audiences had seen a Virgilian Orpheus, the Orfeo of Gluck's opera *Orfeo ed Euridice*, lose his princess because he was unable to persist in observing the taboo. The audience that saw Pamina pleading with Tamino to speak to her will certainly have remembered Euridice pleading with Orfeo in Gluck's opera. Most important of all, Tamino, in Mozart's work, moves through his self-mastery and asceticism into possession of the mystic secrets of an esoteric sect (much influenced by Masonry, a society in many ways comparable to the Orphic sect for the existence of which in ancient Greece scholars like Guthrie have, as we have seen, argued). Goethe wrote a dramatic sequel to Mozart's opera. In it he elevated Tamino to the role of High Priest and mediator of salvation for humanity. Nothing could correspond more closely than this to the role assigned to Orpheus by those who have seen in him an authentic religious teacher of the Greeks, revealing truth and instituting ritual. In Tamino all the attributes of Orpheus have been blended in fairly equal proportions.

Orpheus entire or Orpheus dismembered. The figure is fascinating however we take him. We have seen what he was to the Greeks. Let us now see in some detail what he has been since.

TO BE REDEEMED FROM FIRE BY FIRE: THE DEATHS OF HERACLES AND SIEGFRIED

> *The only hope, or else despair*
> *Lies in the choice of pyre or pyre –*
> *To be redeemed from fire by fire.*
>   T.S. Eliot, Little Gidding

Wagner openly professed admiration for Aeschylus, and certainly his vast *Ring of the Nibelung* has inevitably invited comparison with the *Oresteia*, the only trilogy to have survived from antiquity.[1] Though both the *Ring* and the *Oresteia* end on the same note of optimism, Aeschylean optimism is nonetheless the very antithesis of Wagner's. In the Aeschylean trilogies – and the *Oresteia* enables us to form some ideas of the design of the others – human action and suffering are directed by the gods to a beneficial end: violence may be the way of divinity, but this violence is grace (*Agamemnon* 182). In Wagner's great tetralogy the cruelty and selfishness of the gods precipitate their fall. One of the dramatist's most strikingly original adaptations of his source material was to combine the Eddic concept of Ragnarök, the doom or twilight of the gods, with the *Volsunga Saga*, in which the transgressions of the gods of Valhalla are expiated not by the gods themselves but solely by their descendants on earth. Wagner established a moral link between the sins of the gods and their downfall. The corrupt pantheon passes away in cataclysm and hope is born for mankind through the elimination of the divine government of the universe.

Wagner is in reality closer to the Sophoclean than the Aeschylean vision. It is Nietzsche who implicitly reveals this. In *The Birth of Tragedy* Nietzsche attempts to show that Greek tragedy is the supreme art form, one in which the hero manifests his will in the face of a universe that overwhelms

---

First published in Hans de Groot and Alexander Leggatt (eds) *Craft and Tradition: Essays in Honour of William F. Blissett*. ISBN: 0919813747. Calgary 1990 147–56.

I am grateful to Rev. M. Owen Lee, C.S.B., for valuable comments and suggestions.
1 See, for example, Ewans 1982.

him, confirming his stature at the moment of his fall. Tragedy does not purge the emotions of the audience (whatever Aristotle may have meant by this), but strips away our illusions and brings us face to face with the fundamental truths of existence: the apprehension of these truths gives heroism its validation. This insight is arguably the most significant one in the essay. Nietzsche elaborates his intuition in terms of the now famous opposition between Apolline and Dionysiac principles, but recognition of the value of the insight does not require acceptance of Nietzsche's symbols and the names he gives them. The essential point is the conflict between an inexorable individual and an inexorable universe.

It would be hard to deny that the Nietzschean description fits Sophoclean tragedy far better than that of either of the other tragedians.[2] The very idea of 'tragic hero' ubiquitous in Nietzsche, is a Sophoclean legacy.[3] In Sophocles' tragic universe self-assertion, suffering, and glory are one. Violence does not bring grace, for there is no insistent theodicy as in Aeschylus. But neither is there mere despair as in Euripides. Nietzsche applies his analysis of Greek tragedy to the work of Wagner too, finding the Hellenic ideal fully realized in *Tristan and Isolde*. But Siegmund and Sieglinde, Siegfried and Brünnhilde of the *Ring* (not completed when Nietzsche published *The Birth of Tragedy*) also meet Nietzschean criteria. Victims of transhuman powers, they find victory in defeat and the final impression communicated is one of exhilaration. They are tragic heroes of stature, human actors who suffer and in that suffering reveal the measure of their greatness.[4]

We do not have, as far as I know, any statement by Wagner that admits a direct debt to Sophocles. Even if we did, though, it would be of questionable utility. Wagner's own claim that Hans Sachs's speech at the end of *Die Meistersinger* is indebted to the close of the *Eumenides* is not particularly illuminating: one could scarcely have divined the connection, and even with the composer's statement the comparison cannot be pushed very far. The process by which Wagner's energetic mind worked on the material he so omnivorously devoured is not necessarily to be discovered by listening to his own proclamations. In *Opera and Drama* Wagner mentions,

---

2 The two figures discussed at greatest length by Nietzsche are Oedipus and Prometheus. Few contemporary scholars believe in the Aeschylean authorship of the *Prometheus Bound*. One of the (many) reasons for rejecting the traditional attribution is the 'Sophoclean' nature of the hero of the play: see esp. Knox 1964: 45–50. Lloyd-Jones (1982: 132–4) shows the importance of *Prometheus Bound* and the fragmentary *Prometheus Unbound* for the *Ring*.
3 Knox 1964: Chapter 1.
4 The fully anthropomorphized Wotan is a Sophoclean figure too – proud, isolated, magnificent, doomed: see Nietzsche 1876.

in any case, three Sophoclean heroes – Ajax, Philoctetes, and Oedipus – as commendable examples of individuality expressed in a propensity for self-annihilation. They are images of the eternal truth of myth which it is the job of dramatists in every age to expound. In the same work he analyzes Sophocles' so-called Theban trilogy (*Oedipus The King, Oedipus at Colonus, Antigone*) and its political significance. There are certainly remarkable points of similarity between the Siegfried legend in the Wagnerian version and the Oedipus legend. Both heroes are exposed at birth. The one kills his father (Laius) and marries his mother (Jocasta), the other overcomes his grandfather (Wotan as the Wanderer) to be united with his aunt (Brünnhilde, whom Siegfried at first sight takes to be his mother). The issue of incest is, of course, paramount both in *Oedipus The King* and in *Die Walküre*.[5] There are, in addition, striking parallels between *Parsifal* and *Philoctetes*. In both we have the drama of a young man,[6] little more than a boy, who grows before our eyes when he learns pity for an older man who, because of an incurable wound, is estranged from a society (the Knights of the Grail, the Greek army before Troy) that needs him desperately. In both cases the wound must be healed and a weapon restored to its crucial place in the life of the imperilled community.

Most impressive of all is the fact that Sophocles and Wagner dramatized the deaths of the supreme heroes of their national mythologies, both sent to their funeral pyres by the women who best loved them. In the *Trachiniae* Heracles, the *pantōn ariston andra tōn epi chthoni* (811) is killed by Deianira in unwitting collaboration with the hero's enemy Nessus. In *Götterdämmerung* (originally entitled *Siegfrieds Tod*) Brünnhilde, openly plotting with Hagen, Siegfried's enemy, compasses the death of *den hehrsten Helden der Welt*.

The dramatists have proceeded in similar fashion. Each has reworked a mass of epic material and focused on the dramatic reaction of a jealous woman confronted with her husband's new bride. Secondary or background material necessary to understanding the situation before us is conveyed in long speeches that recapitulate the action that precedes the confines of the drama. This technique is used throughout the *Ring*; the dialogue of the Norns and Waltraute's long report to Brünnhilde (a sort of messenger

---

5 See the fascinating analysis in Rather 1979, esp. 47–63. Rather finds Siegfried, born of incest and destroyer of an unjust political order (Valhalla), parallel to Antigone, likewise born of incest and overthrower of the state (Creon).

6 The young Neoptolemus was introduced into the story by Sophocles. The epic tradition and the (lost) dramas of Aeschylus and Euripides associated Diomedes with Odysseus in the bringing of Philoctetes from Lemnos. It was Sophocles who was interested in the young man who learns pity.

speech) are not the most notable instances in *Götterdämmerung*. In the *Trachiniae* about one-quarter of the play, an abnormally large proportion even by standards of Greek tragedy, consists of narrative background material. Further, the density and consistency of the imagery are striking even for Sophocles: there is no finer example of drama with recurring leitmotifs than this play.[7] And it occupies a unique position among the remains of Greek tragedy in another respect: no other play contains a similar amalgam of myth, fairy-tale magic, oracles, battles between beasts and human beings, the quintessentially human element of passion linked with the primordial and the divine – precisely that blend which gives the *Ring* its unique position among the great works that hold the lyric stage.

Sophocles reshaped an epic legacy largely lost to us. There were Heracles epics by Pisander of Rhodes, Panyassis of Halicarnassus, and in particular by Creophylus of Samos. Of the 'Capture of Oechalia' by the last named (it is sometimes attributed to Homer himself, attesting both to its antiquity and to the esteem in which it was held) we have only a single line. But this poem was in all probability Sophocles' most important epic source, for it told of Heracles' capture and the sack of a city in order to win the beautiful Iole. It is reasonable to assume that this maiden played an important role in the poem – the one line we possess appears to be addressed to her. Sophocles' play dramatizes Deianira's reaction to Heracles' bringing home his captured bride, the sexual jealousy of the woman who in desperation turns to magic (the Nessus shirt) with disastrous consequences. Uncertain as must be hypotheses that are based on lost sources, it can be said with reasonable certainty that Sophocles' distinctive treatment is to be seen in his presentation of the confrontation of the two women. At the same time, however, he made Iole a silent figure in this play, one with no dramatic personality whatsoever.[8]

Wagner had done much the same. The formidable adversary of Brynhilde in the epic sources, Gudrun of the *Volsunga Saga*, Kriemhilde of the *Nibelungenlied*, becomes the pathetic and almost totally inconsequential Gutrune of *Götterdämmerung*. She is present for little other purpose than to enkindle Brünnhilde's anger by her betrothal to Siegfried. She is there, in other words, as Iole is in the *Trachiniae*. Sexual jealousy is not entirely absent from the Saga. But there Brynhilde does not seem to

---

7 I list a few: night, Deianira's fear, fire, Zeus, Cypris (Aphrodite), release from toils, the poison, the centaur, learning, hope. Others will wish to extend this list. Many of these poetic motifs cry out for translation into music, for it is through music that their interrelation could most clearly be shown (in the best Wagnerian manner.)
8 On Sophocles' adaptation of his source see the sensitive treatment of Beck 1953: 10–21.

be especially troubled by Sigurd's marriage to Gudrun (which Brynhilde in fact prophesied!) and she has herself lived comfortably with Gunnar for some time before the angry exchange between the two queens on a question of honour and precedence precipitates the disaster. Brynhilde's wound in the Saga is primarily an affront to her self-esteem. It comes from her realization that her husband Gunnar is not who she boasted he was, since it was Sigurd who rode through the barrier of flame in Gunnar's form. And so her oath to marry none but the very noblest has come to nothing. This it is that makes her take revenge, seek Sigurd's death despite his readiness to renounce Gudrun and return to her. Wagner's Brünnhilde, immediately upon seeing a Siegfried who has forgotten her and become betrothed to another, plots his death. Similarly Deianira meets Iole who has replaced her in her husband's affections and in seeking to win him back brings about his death. Both Sophocles and Wagner have given a new emphasis in refashioning an epic patrimony and have produced tragedies of eros.

The 'world's greatest hero' (for so he is styled in both dramas) is in neither presentation a very attractive figure. Siegfried has always been an embarrassment to lovers of Wagner – there is something coarse and over-robust about the Siegfried of the drama that bears his name though he is somewhat more attractive in *Götterdämmerung*. It is his music that ultimately gives him stature, a stature which his words and actions do not convey. In like manner the Heracles of the *Trachiniae* has been seen as simply repellent by many readers, as a near tasteless creation in his ferocity and blustering self-absorption. But the greatness of this Sophoclean hero is not something communicated by the words of the tragedy. His special, extra-dramatic importance must be taken into account. The aura of Heracles was, for a Greek audience, part of the air they breathed, a living part of the environment in which the actors' words were heard. All the figures of Attic tragedy come trailing clouds of myth, that of Heracles perhaps more than any other. Apart from the epics one can point to his importance with vase painters and sculptors, his paradigmatic place in Pindar's odes. That he was a favourite figure of the comic stage does not militate against this, for the Greeks from Homer onwards could treat even their gods with good humour. Siegfried and Heracles do not rise from the texts of their dramas as sympathetic.[9] It is the accompanying music that gives the one

---

9 It might be argued that this is beside the point – that we need not be expected to like Heracles and Siegfried: a world of 'nice' people is no place for a tragic poet. The fact remains that Heracles and Siegfried are the most unappealing heroes of their respective creators.

his appeal, circumambient myth that ennobles the other. Many writers have described for us, none more eloquently than Nietzsche, the kindred capacities of myth and music to convince us at a level inaccessible to the words of a text.

The women, Deianira and Brünnhilde, are as different as the men are similar, though both, as has been noted, act largely for the same reason – sexual jealousy. It is curious to note that the timid Deianira may have begun life as a sort of Greek Valkyrie. Her name means 'slayer of men' – the Amazons themselves are described by the epithet *antianeirai* 'opponents of men.' Apollodorus mentions that Deianira rode a chariot and practised martial arts (1.8.1). It was only after her story became linked to that of Heracles that her name was interpreted to mean 'destroyer of a husband.' Perhaps like the Brynhilde of the Saga she originally resisted marriage and preferred to ride into battle. There is nothing of this left in Sophocles' Deianira, who has been seen to embody the quiet virtues admired in fifth-century Athens.[10] Whether this is so or not, she certainly embodies the virtues admired in Victorian England. Sir Richard Jebb, the greatest of modern Sophoclean scholars, writes of her:

> The heroine of the *Trachiniae* has been recognized by general consent as one of the most delicately beautiful creations in literature; and many who feel this charm will also feel that it can no more be described than the perfume of a flower ... She, indeed, is a perfect type of gentle womanhood; her whole life has been in her home; a winning influence is felt by all who approach her; ... a high and noble courage is the very spring of her gentleness ... This Deianeira is a creation of the Hellenic spirit, refined by the sweetness, the restrained strength of Athens at her best.[11]

One hundred years later Deianira does not appear quite the glistening Pentelic marble she seemed to Jebb. Today we find her pathetic, a middle-aged woman overcome by an emotion she cannot control, in her desperation ready to clutch at anything with little or no reflection. It is fascinating to look at the poetry Sophocles puts into her mouth: the entire, rich Greek vocabulary of fear-words settles on her speech. She lives in a world haunted by images of fear and night. Faced with a rival she turns to magic. This problem does not seem to me to be satisfactorily resolved, as it is for many critics, by the simple observation that in fifth-century Athens no stigma

10 Segal 1977.
11 Jebb 1892: xxxi–ii, xliv.

attached to the use of love charms. For this is no ordinary love charm. Deianira has kept an ointment of the envenomed blood of her husband's enemy Nessus, taken as he lay dying, and she has chosen to act on the enemy's word. She uses the poisoned blood knowing what it is[12] because she cannot tolerate the presence of Iole. And she acts in secrecy. This pusillanimity and clutching at straws are hardly Jebb's 'high and noble courage.'

Early in the *Trachiniae* Deianira delivers a lecture on honesty to the herald Lichas, who has deceived her (436–69). We have here, it seems, the key to a curious feature of the play's construction, the duplication of the traditional messenger scene announcing Heracles' return by Lichas' appearance, which does essentially the same thing though it also deceives Deianira on the critical point, the identity and role of the concubine Iole. Critics like to point to the dramatic excitement generated by having Deianira's hopes raised to a pitch of false joy, only to be dashed when the messenger reveals the full truth. But the duplication is shabby drama if it serves no other purpose than to prolong Deianira's ignorance and intensify a brutal shock.[13] An important effect of this deception scene is to point the contrast between the principles proclaimed by Deianira and her inability to act in accordance with these principles. The famous Sophoclean irony is at work here, for the deceived woman deceives in turn. Deianira gives Lichas, the herald who lied to her, a garment to carry to Heracles without telling him what it is that he is carrying. This has fatal consequences for Lichas. Heracles, in his first agony, murders the man who brought him the gift. This is normally seen as an instance of Heracles' brutality, and so it certainly is. But it must be remembered that it is Deianira's deception that has sent Lichas to his death.

Jebb, who so admired Sophocles' Deianira, makes the further statement in his introduction to the play:

> It was difficult for the Latin races to imagine a woman, supplanted in her husband's love, who did not wish to kill somebody, – her rival, or her husband, or both.[14]

12 There can be no doubt about this. Deianira herself says (574) that the magic will be effective only if it includes the poison. This startling admission seems to be glossed over by the critics.
13 Sophocles elsewhere portrays the deliberate deception of women – Tecmessa by Ajax, Electra by Orestes. But he does not revel in the psychological torture of his women as, it seems to me, Puccini does.
14 Jebb 1892: xliv.

This astonishing statement, which doubtless issues from a conviction of the profound sympathy between Hellenic purity and Northern virtue, was written at approximately the same time that Wagner was creating his Brünnhilde.

Wagner might have been more than a little surprised at the suggestion that he was Latin in his creation of a woman who kills because she is supplanted in her husband's love.[15] His Brünnhilde is, in any case, one of the great women of any stage, any age. She is fearless, ever a creature of light, from her sleep on the fire-encircled crag to her final immolation. There cannot be two more different exits in all of dramatic literature than those of Deianira and Brünnhilde. The former leaves the stage silently in one of Greek tragedy's most moving exits. Other Sophoclean women (Jocasta in *Oedipus The King*, Eurydice in *Antigone*) leave the stage to commit suicide, but they leave precipitately and comment is made only after their departure, hence their exits are not important in the stage action. Deianira must leave slowly. There is much discussion of her exit but she does not say a word to the questions that are put to her. Brünnhilde holds our attention alone for one of the longest and most thrilling scenes in Wagner. Her exit too is one of the drama's great moments. Whereas Deianira never confronts the unfaithful Heracles directly (it is a sobering thought that Deianira and Heracles would have been played by the same actor), Brünnhilde openly and vehemently taxes Siegfried with his infidelity. Frustrated by his apparent inability to recall anything except what suits him at the moment,[16] she openly allies herself with Hagen, who kills him. Deianira's alliance with Heracles' dead enemy is unwitting, but Nessus is, as Dante emphasizes, very much the murderer of Heracles.[17] Both women expiate their offences by their own deaths. Neither is allowed to come face to face with her dying husband and so neither can ask for the forgiveness she wants.

Brünnhilde's death is atonement. It is also redemptive, for the fire she ignites brings about the end of the whole corrupt order whose self-centredness has caused the sufferings of these mortals. The piled lumber

---

15 Medea is proof enough (if proof is needed) that the Greeks, like all other races, found it possible to imagine a woman, supplanted in her husband's love, who wished to kill.

16 The magic potion has obliterated Siegfried's memory of what preceded his meeting with Gutrune. But he can forget events subsequent to the drinking of the potion too, as when he tells Brünnhilde that he took the Ring from Fafner, not from her (II.iv). On Siegfried's amnesia, see the interesting essay 'Siegfried-Idyll' in Hillard 1966.

17   Quelli è Nesso
che morì per la bella Deianira
e fè di sè la vendetta elli stesso? (*Inf.* XII.67–9)

of Wotan's shattered spear and of the withered World Ash, set ablaze by Brünnhilde's torch, sets Valhalla alight. The fire is also the purifying fire of love:

> Fühl meine Brust auch,
> wie sie entbrennt;
> helles Feuer
> das Herz mir erfasst. (III.iii)

The final conflagration redeems from the earlier fires of jealousy and anger (cf. 'Ratet nun Rache ... Zündet mir Zorn,' II.iv).

The end of *Götterdämmerung* is an optimistic vision and, as such, has been described as antithetical to tragedy.[18] But is this fair? Aeschylean tragedy is, as we noted, optimistic too. If optimism is basically the belief that something is won through human suffering, optimism is surely consonant with tragic vision. We cannot be willing to award the title tragedy only where we find despair and damnation. Wagner's vision is, however, humanistic. Man is the measure of all things. He arraigns the gods at the bar of his own understanding, burns them for their misdemeanours, and looks with confidence to a brave new world.[19]

It is more difficult to determine the tone of the end of the *Trachiniae*. We may state with confidence that Sophocles would have used, did use, the full force of his genius to combat the Protagorean dictum that man is the measure. It was a contemporary heresy and he met it head on. We must consider the final scene of the *Trachiniae* closely.

Heracles will die offstage on a funeral pyre on Mount Oeta. His cortège assembles and prepares to move away. Hyllus remarks on the great cruelty of the gods. It would be patently absurd, however, to think of toppling these divinities. Olympus will know no twilight. The universe is what it is and there is no hope of a better one, though there is every hope that we may continue in the flawed one we know, especially if we learn the lesson of pity, a lesson to which all gods and most heroes are deaf. The gods are cruel and they abide.

---

18 Steiner 1961: 127–8.
19 Brünnhilde remains to the end the incarnation of Wotan's will. In ending his world as he wants she accomplishes that will. But despite this strain of Schopenhauerian pessimism in the *Ring*, the final impression is one of humanism and optimism: the gods, who are not fit to rule mankind, are overthrown. The new world will have no gods.

And yet ... I have mentioned the mythical baggage that a fifth-century Athenian carried with him into the theatre. The audience that watched the funeral procession carrying the tortured Heracles to his pyre knew full well that Heracles, alone of mortals, came through suffering to a place on Olympus. It is but a slight exaggeration to say that the spectators could look up from their place in the Theatre of Dionysus to the pedimental structures of the Parthenon and see Heracles reclining among the Olympians.[20] The reception of Heracles on Olympus is a standard item in the repertory of the vase painters of the time. Would the audience necessarily have connected apotheosis with the funeral pyre?[21] The earliest instances in art of the apotheosis of Heracles from his pyre are perhaps twenty years later than the *Trachiniae*.[22] Is it implicit in the play? If it is, we are present at the birth of the motif that finds its final splendid flowering more than two thousand years later in the art of Tiepolo, the master so beloved of the honorand of this volume. Above the misery of this world, the clouds open to receive a martyr into the courts of heaven. This may be what Hyllus glances at, albeit unknowingly, when he says, immediately following his comment on the cruelty of the gods, that no one foresees the future. Whatever the case, Eliot's lines are as applicable to Heracles' death as to Siegfried's, in this sense at least: the fires of the hero's funeral pyre bring redemption from the fires of human passion.

---

20 The reclining figure referred to here is thought by some to be Heracles, by others Dionysus. It is usually dated to the decade preceding the outbreak of the Peloponnesian War. The exact date of the *Trachiniae* is unknown, though most critics today would incline to a date in the third quarter of the fifth century.
21 In several plays Sophocles seems to allude in the closing lines to events subsequent to the drama, but in all the other cases the references cast a pall over an apparently 'happy' ending: the further sufferings of Orestes are hinted at in the *Electra*, the later transformation of the gentle Neoptolemus in the *Philoctetes*, and the death of Antigone in *Oedipus at Colonos*.
22 Assuming, that is, an early date for the play. The vases in question are from the last quarter of the fifth century. See Easterling 1982: 17–18.

Bibliography

Abbreviations

Allen = Monro and Allen 1912
Collected Writings = Brown, C.G.; Fowler, R.L.; Robbins, E.I.; and Wallace Matheson, P.M. (eds) 1991. *Leonard E. Woodbury: Collected Writings*. Atlanta, GA.
Daux, G. 1960. 'Chronique des fouilles 1959' *BCH* 84, pp. 618–868.
Diels-Kranz = H. Diels, with additions by W. Kranz, 1951, 1954, 1964 *Die Fragmente der Vorsokratiker: griechisch und deutsch* 1–3. 5th–7th eds, 11th ed. Berlin. (The 6th and 7th eds are photographic reprints, 1951 and 1954, of the 5th ed., with Nachträge by Kranz.)
Drachmann *Scholia* 1–3 = Drachmann, A.B. (ed.) 1964. *Scholia vetera in Pindari carmina* 1–3. Leipzig. (repr. from 1903–1927 originals)
Entretiens Hardt 31 = Gerber, D.E. and Hurst, A. 1985. *Pindare: entretiens sur l'Antiquité classique, Vandoeuvres-Genève, 21–26 août 1984*. Fondation Hardt. Entretiens sur l'Antiquité classique 31. Geneva.
How and Wells = How, W.W. and Wells, J. 1961–1964. *A Commentary on Herodotus* with introduction and appendices, vols 1–3. Oxford. (repr. with corrections from ed. of 1912)
IEG² = W = West 1989
Leaf and Bayfield = Leaf, W.L. and Bayfield, M.A. (eds) 1895. *The Iliad* ed. with general and grammatical introductions, notes, and appendices. London.
LIMC = Ackermann, H.C. and Gisler, J.-R. (eds) 1981–1997. *Lexicon Iconographicum Mythologiae Classicae*. Zurich.
Lobel-Page = Lobel, E. and Page, D. (eds) 1955. *Poetarum Lesbiorum Fragmenta*.
M.-W. = Merkelbach and West 1967.

PG = Migne, J.P. 1857–91. *Patrologiae cursus completus ... series graeca.* Paris.
Pf = Pfeiffer, R. (ed.) 1949–53. *Callimachus.* Oxford.
PMG = Page 1962.
PMGF = Davies 1991.
RE = Pauly, A.F. von; Wissowa, G. et al. 1894–1963. *Paulys Realencyclopädie der classischen Altertumswissenschaft: neue Bearbeitung.* Munich.
SLG = Page 1974.
Snell[3] = Snell, B.; T.G. Rosenmeyer (tr.). 1953. *The Discovery of the Mind. The Greek Origins of European Thought.* Oxford.
Snell-Maehler 1971. = Snell, B. and Maehler, H. (eds) 1971. *Pindari Carmina cum fragmentis* Leipzig. (*post Brunonem Snell edidit Hervicus Maehler*)
TrGF = Snell, B. (ed.) 1964. *Tragicorum Graecorum Fragmenta.* Hildesheim. (based on N. Nauck [ed.] 1889. *Tragicorum Graecorum Fragmenta.* Leipzig.)
V = Voigt 1971
W = *IEG*[2] = West 1989
Wilamowitz = von Wilamowitz-Moellendorff, U.

Works Cited

Ahrens, L. 1860. 'Coniecturae Pindaricae,' *Philologus* 16, pp. 52–9.
Alzinger, W. 1974. 'Raps, Eber und der Concordiatempel in Akragas,' *ZPE* 14, pp. 295–9.
Arrighetti, G. 1981. 'Mito e Realtà nell' Olimpica II di Pindaro' in M. Fusillo *et al.* (eds) 1981. *Studi di letteratura greca*, pp. 77–96. Biblioteca di studi antichi 34. Ricerche di filologia classica 1. Pisa.
Ashmole, B. and Yalouris, N. 1967. *Olympia: The Sculptures of the Temple of Zeus.* London.

Bagg, R. 1964. 'Love, Ceremony and Daydream in Sappho's Lyrics,' *Arion* 3.3, pp. 44–82.
Barrett, W.S. (ed.) 1964. *Euripides. Hippolytus*, with introduction and commentary. Oxford.
Bassett, S.E. 1938. *The Poetry of Homer.* Berkeley.
Beattie, A.J. 1955. 'Pindar, *Ol.* 8. 45–6,' *CR* n.s. 5, pp. 1–3.
— 1956. 'Sappho Fr. 31,' *Mnemosyne* 4.9, pp. 103–11.
Beazley, J.D. 1963. *Attic Red-figure Vase-painters.*[2] Oxford.

Beck, A. 1953. 'Der Empfand Ioles zur Technikund Menschengestaltung in ersten Teile der Trachinierinnen,' *Hermes* 81, pp. 10–21.
Beck, F.A.G. 1975. *Album of Greek Education: The Greeks at School and at Play*. Sydney.
Bell, J.M. 1978. '*Kimbix kai Sophos*: Simonides in the Anecdotal Tradition,' *QUCC* 28, pp. 29–86.
Berard, C. et al. 1989. *A City of Images: Iconography and Society in Ancient Greece*. Princeton.
Bernabé, A. 1987. *Poetae Epicorum Graecorum: Testimonia et Fragmenta* I. Leipzig.
Bernardini, P.A. 1983. *Mito e attualità nelle odi di Pindaro. La Nemea 4, l'Olimpica 9, l'Olimpica 7*. Filologia e Critica 47. Rome.
— 1985. 'L'attualità agonistica negli epinici di Pindaro,' in Entretiens Hardt 31, pp. 117–49.
Blegen, C.W. 1956. 'The Palace of Nestor Excavations of 1955' *AJA* 60, pp. 95–101.
Blundell, M.W. 1989. *Helping Friends and Harming Enemies: A Study in Sophocles and Greek Ethics*. Cambridge.
Boeckh, A. 1821. *Pindari opera quae supersunt* 2.2. Leipzig.
Boedeker, D. 1995. 'Simonides on Plataea: Narrative Elegy, Mythodic History,' *ZPE* 107, pp. 217–29.
Böhme, R. 1953. *Orpheus: Das Alter der Kitharoden*. Berlin.
— 1970. *Orpheus: Der Sänger und seine Zeit*. Berlin and Munich.
Bolling, G.M. 1961. 'Textual Notes on the Lesbian Poets,' *AJP* 82, pp. 151–63.
Bolton, J.D.P. 1962. *Aristeas of Proconnesus*. Oxford.
Bonelli, G. 1977. 'Saffo, 2 Diehl = 31 Lobel-Page,' *AC* 46, pp. 453–94.
Bovie, S.P. (tr.) 1956. *Virgil Georgics*. Chicago.
Bowie, E. 1986a. 'Early Greek Elegy, Symposium and Public Festival,' *JHS* 106, pp. 13–35.
— 1986b. 'Lyric and Elegiac Poetry' in J. Boardman, J. Griffin, and O. Murray (eds), *The Oxford History of the Classical World*, pp. 93–106. Oxford.
Bowra, C.M. 1936. *Greek Lyric Poetry from Alcman to Simonides*. Oxford.
— 1961. *Greek Lyric Poetry from Alcman to Simonides*.[2] Oxford.
— 1962. 'Composition' in Wace and Stubbings 1962, pp. 38–74. London.
— 1964. *Pindar*. Oxford.
— 1969. *The Odes of Pindar*. Harmondsworth.
Braswell, B.K. 1971. 'Mythological Innovation in the *Iliad*,' *CQ* 21.1, pp. 16–26.

Brelich, A. 1958. *Gli eroi greci: un problema storico-religioso*. Rome.
Bremer, J.M. 1987. 'Stesichorus: "The Lille Papyrus,"' in J.M. Bremer, A. Maria van Erp Taalman Kip, and S.R. Slings, *Some Recently Discovered Greek Poems*, pp. 128–74. *Mnemosyne* Supplement 99. Leiden.
Bremmer, J. 1983. 'The Importance of the Maternal Uncle and Grandfather in Archaic and Classical Greece and Early Byzantium,' *ZPE* 50, pp. 175–86.
Brillante, C. 1991. 'Crescita e apprendimento: l'educazione del giovane eroe,' *QUCC* n.s. 37.1, pp. 7–28.
Brize, P. 1980. *Die Geryoneis des Stesichoros und die frühe griechische Kunst*. Beiträge zur Archäologie 12. Würzburg.
Brommer, F. 1942. 'Herakles und die Hesperides auf Vasenbildern,' *JDAI* 57, pp. 105–23.
— 1972. *Herakles: Die Zwolf Taten des Helden in Antiker Kunst und Literatur*. Cologne.
Brown, N.O. 1951. 'Pindar, Sophocles, and the Thirty Years Peace' *TAPhA* 82, pp. 1–28.
— 1959. *Life against Death: The Psychoanalytic Meaning of History*. New York.
Bundy, E.L. 1962a. 'The Eleventh Olympian Ode,' *Studia Pindarica* 1, pp. 1–34. Publications in Classical Philology 18.1. Berkeley, CA.
— 1962b. 'The First Isthmian Ode,' *Studia Pindarica* 2, pp. 35–92. Publications in Classical Philology 18.2. Berkeley, CA.
Buongiovanni, A.M. 1985. 'Sulla composizione della III Pitica,' *Athenaeum* n.s. 63.3–4, pp. 327–36.
Burkert, W. 1962. 'ΤΟΗΣ. Zum griechischen Schamanismus,' *RhM* 105, pp. 36–55.
— 1972. *Homo necans: Interpretationen altgriechischer Opferriten und Mythen*. Berlin and New York. (= 1983. P. Bing (tr.), *Homo Necans: The Anthropology of Ancient Greek Sacrificial Ritual and Myth* Berkeley.)
— 1975. 'Apellai und Apollo,' *RhM* 118, pp. 1–21.
— 1977. *Griechischer Religion der Archaischen und Klassischen Epoche*. Stuttgart.
— 1979. *Structure and History in Greek Mythology and Ritual*. Berkeley.
— 1985. *Greek Religion* (tr. J. Raffan). Cambridge, MA.
— 1987. 'The Making of Homer in the Sixth Century BC: Rhapsodes versus Stesichoros,' in J. Paul Getty Museum, *Papers on the Amasis Painter and His World*, pp. 35–92. Malibu, CA.
Burnett, A.P. 1964. 'The Race with the Pleiades' *CP* 59, pp. 30–4.
— 1979. 'Desire and Memory (Sappho Frag. 94)' *CP* 74, pp. 16–27.

— 1983. *Three Archaic Poets: Archilochus, Alcaeus, Sappho.* Cambridge, MA.
— 1989. 'Performing Pindar's Odes,' *CP* 84.4, pp. 283–93.
Burton, R.W.B. 1962. *Pindar's Pythian Odes: Essays in Interpretation.* Oxford.
Bury, J.B. (ed.) 1890. *The Nemean Odes of Pindar*, with introductions and commentary. London/New York.

Cairns, F. 1972. *Generic Composition in Greek and Roman Poetry.* Edinburgh.
Calame, C. 1977a. *Les choeurs de jeunes filles en Grèce archaïque 1. Morphologie, fonction religieuse et sociale.* Rome.
— 1977b. *Les choeurs de jeunes filles en Grèce archaïque 2. Alcman.* Rome.
— 1983. *Alcman. Fragmenta.* Rome.
Calder, W.M. III and Stern, J. (eds) 1970. *Pindaros und Bakchylides.* Darmstadt.
Campbell, D.A. 1967. *Greek Lyric Poetry. A Selection of Early Greek Lyric, Elegiac and Iambic Poetry.* London.
— 1982–1993. *Greek Lyric* 1–5. Loeb Classical Library. Cambridge, MA.
— 1983. *The Golden Lyre: The Themes of the Greek Lyric Poets.* London.
— 1987. 'Three Notes on Alcman 1P (= 3 Calame)', *QUCC* n.s. 26.2, pp. 67–72.
— 1991. *Greek Lyric* 3. Loeb Classical Library. Cambridge, MA.
— 1992. *Greek Lyric* 4. Loeb Classical Library. Cambridge, MA.
— 1993. *Greek Lyric* 5. Loeb Classical Library. Cambridge, MA.
Campbell, J. 1964. *The Masks of God: Occidental Mythology.* New York.
Campbell, R. (tr.) 1960. *St. John of the Cross. Poems.* Harmondsworth.
Cannatà Fera, M. 1986. 'Pindaro interprete di Omero in "Pyth." 3, 81–2,' *Giornale italiano di filologia* 38, pp. 85–9.
Carey, C. 1981. *A Commentary on Five Odes of Pindar.* Salem, NH.
— 1989. 'The Performance of the Victory Ode,' *AJP* 110.4, pp. 545–65.
— 1991. 'The Victory Ode in Performance: The Case for the Chorus,' *CP* 86, pp. 192–200.
Carne-Ross, D.S. 1975. 'Three Preludes for Pindar,' *Arion* n.s. 2.2, pp. 160–93.
— 1985. *Pindar.* New Haven/London.
Carson, A. 1981. *Odi et amo ergo sum.* Diss. Toronto.
— 1992. 'How Not to Read a Poem: Unmixing Simonides from *Protagoras*,' *CP* 87, pp. 110–30.

Cataudella, Q. 1940. 'Saffo fr. 5(4)–6(5) Diehl,' *Atene e Roma* ser. 3.8, pp. 199–201.
Cazzaniga, I. 1968. 'Il dio e la cerva nella monetazione di Caulonia e la tradizione ecistica Cauloniate,' *PP* 23, pp. 371–90.
Chamoux, F. 1953. *Cyrène sous la Monarchie des Battiades*. Paris.
— 1955. *L'Aurige de Delphes*. Fouilles de Delphes 4.5. Paris.
Chapouthier, G. 1935. *Les Dioscures au Service d'une Déesse. Etude d'Iconographie Religieuse*. Bibliothèque des Écoles Françaises d'Athènes et de Rome 137. Paris.
Clark, G. 1962. *World Prehistory: An Outline*. Cambridge.
Clay, D. 1991. 'Alcman's Partheneion,' *QUCC* n.s. 39.3, pp. 47–67.
Cole, T. 1992. *Pindar's Feasts or the Music of Power*. Rome.
Contiades-Tsitsoni, E. 1990. *Hymenaios und Epithalamion: Das Hochzeitslied in der frühgriechischen Lyrik*. Stuttgart.

Dale, A.M. (ed.) 1954. *Euripides. Alcestis*, with introduction and commentary. Oxford.
D'Alessio, G.B. 1994. 'First-Person Problems in Pindar,' *BICS* 39, pp. 117–39.
Davies, M. 1982. 'The Paroemiographers on τὰ τρία τῶν Στησιχόρου,' *JHS* 102, pp. 206–10.
— 1988. 'Monody, Choral Lyric, and the Tyranny of the Hand-book,' *CQ* 38.1, pp. 52–64.
— 1991. (ed.) *Poetarum Melicorum Graecorum Fragmenta*. Oxford.
Davies, M.I. 1960. 'Thoughts on the *Oresteia* before Aeschylus,' *BCH* 93, pp. 214–60.
DeJean, J. 1989. *Fictions of Sappho 1546–1937*. Chicago/London.
de Jong, I.J.F. 1985. 'Iliad 1. 366–92: A Mirror Story,' *Arethusa* 18.1, pp. 5–22.
Demand, N. 1975. 'Pindar's *Olympian* 2, Theron's Faith and Empedocles' Katharmoi,' *GRBS* 16.4, pp. 347–57.
Denniston, J.D. (ed.) 1939. *Euripides Electra*. Oxford.
— 1959. *The Greek Particles*.[2] Oxford.
Detienne, M. 1971. 'Orphée au miel,' *QUCC* 12, pp. 7–23.
Devereux, G. 1966. 'The Exploitation of Ambiguity in Pindaros *O*. 3.27,' *RhM* 109, pp. 289–98.
— 1970. 'The Nature of Sappho's Seizure in Fr. 31 LP as Evidence of her Inversion,' *CQ* n.s. 20, pp. 17–31.
Dissen, L. 1830. *Pindari carmina quae supersunt cum deperditorum fragmentis selectis*. Gotha.
Dodd, C.H. 1961. *The Parables of the Kingdom*.[2] London/Glasgow.

Dodds, E.R. 1951. *The Greeks and the Irrational.* Sather Classical Lectures 25. Berkeley, CA.
Dornseiff, F. 1921. *Pindars Stil.* Berlin.
— 1933. *Die archaïsche Mythenerzählung: Folgerungen aus dem homerischen Apollonhymnos.* Berlin.
Dover, K.J. (ed.) 1968. *Aristophanes. Clouds.* Oxford.
— 1978. *Greek Homosexuality.* London.
— 1988. 'Expurgation of Greek Literature' in K.J. Dover, *The Greeks and their Legacy. Collected Papers* 2, pp. 270–91. Oxford. (repr. from Willem den Boer et al., *Les études classiques aux XIXe et XXe siècles: leur place dans l'histoire des idées,* pp. 55–62. Entretiens Hardt 26. 1980. Geneva.)
Drexler, H. 1931. 'Nachträge zur Kyrenesage,' *Hermes* 66, pp. 455–64.
Dronke, P. 1962. 'The Return of Eurydice,' *C&M* 23, pp. 198–215.
Duchemin, J. 1955. *Pindare: Poète et Prophète.* Paris.
— (ed.) 1967. *Pindare: Pythiques (III, IX, IV, V)* with introduction and commentary. Paris.
— 1970. 'Pindare et la Sicile; réflexions sur quelques themes mythiques,' in M. Delcourt, *Hommages à Marie Delcourt,* pp. 78–91. Collection Latomus 114. Brussels.
Dumézil, G. 1958. *L'Idéologie tripartite des Indo-européens.* Brussels.
Düring, I. 1943. 'Klutaimestra – νηλὴς γυνά,' *Eranos* 41, pp. 91–123.

Easterling, P. 1974. 'Alcman 58 and Simonides 37,' *PCPhS* 20, 37–43.
— (ed.) 1982. *Sophocles Trachiniae.* Cambridge.
Edmonds, J.M. 1922a. 'Sappho's Book as depicted on an Attic Vase,' *CQ* 16, pp. 1–14.
— 1922b. *Lyra Graeca* 1 and 2. London/New York.
— 1928. *Lyra Graeca* 1.² London/New York.
Edwards, M.W. 1987. *Homer. Poet of the Iliad.* Baltimore/London.
Egan, R.B. 1983. 'On the Relevance of Orestes in Pindar's Eleventh Pythian,' *Phoenix* 37, pp. 189–200.
Eliade, M. 1964. W.R. Trask (tr.) *Shamanism: Archaic Techniques of Ecstasy.* New York.
Erbse, H. 1960. 'Beiträge zum Pindartext,' *Hermes* 88, pp. 23–33.
— 1983. *Scholia Vetera in Homeri Iliadem* 6. Berlin.
Escher, J. 1899. *RE* 3, s.v. 'Chiron.'
Evelyn-White, H.G. 1914. *Hesiod, The Homeric Hymns and Homerica.* Loeb Classical Library. Cambridge, MA/London.
Ewans, M. 1982. *Wagner and Aeschylus: The Ring and the Oresteia.* London.

Farnell, L.R. 1896. *The Cults of the Greek States* 2. Oxford.
— 1907. *The Cults of the Greek States* 4. Oxford.
— 1915. 'Pindar, Athens and Thebes: Pyth. IX.151–70,' *CQ* 9, pp. 193–200.
— 1930–2. *The Works of Pindar* 1–3. London.
Fehr, K. 1936. *Die Mythen bei Pindar*. Zurich.
Fennell, C.A.M. 1879. *Pindar: The Olympian and Pythian Odes*. Cambridge.
Fernández-Galiano, M. (ed.) 1956. *Pindaro: Olimpicas*. Madrid.
Festugière, A.-J. 1960. *Personal Religion Among the Greeks*. Berkeley.
Fick, A. 1874. *Die griechischen Personennamen*. Göttingen.
Figueira, T.J. 1991. *Athens and Aegina in the Age of Imperial Colonization*. Baltimore/London.
Finley, J.H. 1951. 'The Date of *Paean* 6 and *Nemean* 7,' *HSCP* 60, pp. 61–80.
Fitzgerald, R. (tr.) 1961. *Homer. The Odyssey*. New York.
Floyd, E.D. 1965. 'The Performance of Pindar, *Pythian* 8.55–70,' *GRBS* 6, pp. 187–200.
Fowler, R.L. 1987. *The Nature of Early Greek Lyric: Three Preliminary Studies*. Phoenix Supplement 21. Toronto/Buffalo/London.
— 1988. ΑΙΓ- in Early Greek Language and Myth,' *Phoenix* 42.2, pp. 95–113.
Fraccaroli, G. 1894. *Le Odi di Pindaro*. Verona.
— 1903. *L'Irrazionale nella Letteratura*. Turin.
Fränkel, H. 1924. 'Eine Stileigenheit der frühgriechischen Literatur,' in *Nachrichten von der Gesellschaft der Wissenschaften zu Göttingen. Philologisch-historische Klasse*, pp. 63–127 = Fränkel 1960: 40–96.
— 1960. *Wege und Formen frühgriechischen Denkens: Literarische und philosophiegeschichtliche Studien*.[2] Munich.
— 1961. 'Schrullen in den Scholien zu Pindars Nemeen 7 und Olympien 3,' *Hermes* 89, pp. 385–97.
— 1962. *Dichtung und Philosophie des frühen Griechentums. Eine Geschichte der griechischen Epik, Lyrik und Prosa bis zur Mitte des fünften Jahrhunderts*.[2] Munich.
— 1969. *Dichtung und Philosophie des frühen Griechentums. Eine Geschichte der griechischen Epik, Lyrik und Prosa bis zur Mitte des fünften Jahrhunderts*[3]. Munich
— 1975. M. Hadas and J. Willis (trs) *Early Greek Poetry and Philosophy: A History of Greek Epic, Lyric and Prose to the Middle of the Fifth Century*. New York.
Frazer, J.G. 1921. *Apollodorus. The Library* 2. London and Cambridge MA.

Friedländer, P. 1907. *Herakles. Sagengeschichtliche Untersuchungen.* Philologisches Untersuchungen 19. Berlin.
Friedman, J.B. 1970. *Orpheus in the Middle Ages.* Cambridge, MA.
Friis Johansen, H. 1939. 'Achill bei Chiron,' in *Dragma. Martino P. Nilsson, A.D. 4 id. Iul. anno 1939 dedicatum*, pp. 181–205. Lund.
Friis Johansen, H. and Whittle, E.W. (eds) 1980. *Aeschylus The Suppliants* 3. Copenhagen.
Frisk, H. 1970. *Griechisches etymologisches Wörterbuch* 2. Heidelberg.
— 1973. *Griechisches etymologisches Wörterbuch* 1.² Heidelberg.
Führer, R. 1967. *Formproblem-Untersuchungen zu den Reden in der frühgriechischen Lyrik.* Zetemata 44. Munich.
Furtwängler, A. 1885. *Beschreibung der Vasensammlung im Antiquarium.* Berlin.

Gallavotti, C. 1942. 'Esegesi e testo dell' Ode fr. 2 di Saffo,' *RFIC* 70, pp. 113–24.
— 1966. 'Per il testo di Saffo,' *RFIC* 94, pp. 257–67.
Gärtner, H.A. 1978. 'Die Siegeslieder Pindars für die Söhne des Lampon,' *Würz. Jahrb. Altertums* n.f. 4, pp. 27–46.
Garvie, A.F. 1965. 'A Note on the Deity of Alcman's Partheneion,' *CQ* 15, pp. 185–7.
— 1969. (ed.) *Aeschylus' Supplices: Play and Trilogy.* Cambridge.
Garzya, A. 1954. *Alcman: I Frammenti. Testo Critico, Traduzione, Commentario.* Naples.
Gendler, O. 1995. 'Les Dioscures et les Apharétides dans le *Parthénée, (frgt. 3 Calame)*,' *LEC* 63, pp. 3–21.
Gentili, B. 1958. *Anacreon.* Rome.
— 1966. 'La veneranda Saffo,' *QUCC* 2, pp. 37–62.
— 1970. 'Polemica antitirannica,' *QUCC* n.s. 1, pp. 153–4.
— 1988. A.T. Cole (tr.) *Poetry and its Public in Ancient Greece: From Homer to the Fifth Century,* with introduction. Baltimore.
— and Bernardini, P.A.; Cingano, E.; Giannini, P. 1995. *Pindaro: le Pitiche.* Milan.
Gerber, D.E. 1969. *A Bibliography of Pindar 1513–1966.* Cleveland.
— 1970. *Euterpe. An Anthology of Early Greek Lyric, Elegiac and Iambic Poetry.* Amsterdam.
— 1976. 'Studies in Greek Lyric Poetry: 1967–1975,' *CW* 70.2, pp. 65–157.
— 1982. *Pindar's Olympian One. A Commentary. Phoenix* Supplement 15. Toronto/Buffalo/London.

— 1987. 'Pindar's *Olympian* Four: A Commentary,' *QUCC* n.s. 25.1, pp. 7–24.
— 1989. 'Pindar and Bacchylides 1934–1987,' *Lustrum* 31, pp. 97–269.
— 1990. 'Pindar and Bacchylides 1934–1987 (Continuation),' *Lustrum* 32, pp. 7–292.
— 1994. 'Greek Lyric Poetry Since 1920. II. From Alcman to Fragmenta Adespota,' *Lustrum* 36, pp. 7–188, 285–97.
Giacomelli, A. 1980. 'The Justice of Aphrodite in Fr. 1,' *TAPhA* 110, pp. 135–42.
Giangrande, G. 1977. 'On Alcman's Partheneion,' *Museum Philologum Londiniense* 2, pp. 151–64.
Giannini, P. 1995. 'Note esegetiche alle *Pitiche* 6 e 8 di Pindaro,' *QUCC* 49, pp. 45–53.
Gildersleeve, B.L. 1885, 1890. *Pindar. The Olympian and Pythian Odes.* New York.
Gill, SJ, D. 1974. '*Trapezomata*: A Neglected Aspect of Greek Sacrifice,' *HTR* 67, pp. 117–37.
Gomme, A.W. 1957. 'Interpretations of Some Poems of Alkaios and Sappho,' *JHS* 77.2, pp. 255–66.
Gould, J.P. 1973. 'Hiketeia,' *JHS* 93, pp. 74–103.
Gow, A.S.F. 1952. *Bucolici Graeci.* Oxford.
— 1965. *Theocritus.*² Cambridge.
Graf, F. 1979. 'Das Götterbild aus dem Taurerland,' *Antike Welt* 10.4, pp. 33–41.
Gransden, K.W. 1976. *Virgil. Aeneid VIII.* Cambridge.
Grant, M. and Hazel, J. 1973. *Who's Who in Classical Mythology.* London.
Greengard, C. 1980. *The Structure of Pindar's Epinician Odes.* Amsterdam.
Griffin, J. 1980. *Homer.* Oxford.
Griffith, R.D. 1989. 'Pelops and Sicily: The Myth of Pindar *Ol.* I,' *JHS* 109, pp. 171–3.
Gronewald, M. 1974. 'Fragmente aus einem Sapphokommentar: Pap. Col. Inv. 5860,' *ZPE* 14, pp. 114–18.
Gruben, G. 1976. *Die Tempel der Griechen.*² Munich.
Gruppe, O. 1918. *RE* Supp. 3, s.v. 'Herakles.'
Guerrini, L. 1958–9. 'L'Infanzia di Achille e sua educazione presso Chirone,' *Stud. Misc.* 1, pp. 43–53 with Tavv. XIII–XVIII.
Guido, M. 1967. *Sicily: An Archaeological Guide.* New York.
Guthrie, W.K.C. 1950. *The Greeks and their Gods.* London.
— 1935, 1966. *Orpheus and Greek Religion.* 1st ed. 1935; 2nd ed. rev. 1952., repr. 1966. New York.

Hadas, M. 1936. 'The Tradition of a Feeble Jason,' *CP* 31, pp. 166–8.
Hamilton, R. 1974. *Epinikion. General Form in the Odes of Pindar*. The Hague and Paris.
Harris, J.R. 1906. *The Cult of the Heavenly Twins*. Cambridge.
Hansen, O. 1993. 'Alcman's Louvre-Partheneion vv. 58–9 again,' *Hermes* 121.1, pp. 118–19.
Heath, M. 1986. 'The Origins of Modern Pindaric Criticism,' *JHS* 106, pp. 85–98.
— 1988. '"Receiving the κῶμος": The Context and Performance of Epinician,' *AJP* 109.2, pp. 180–95.
— and Lefkowitz, M. 1991. 'Epinician Performance,' *CP* 86, pp. 173–91.
Heimsoeth, F. 1847. 'Erklärungen zu Pindar,' *RhM* 5, pp. 1–32.
Heinimann, F. 1945. *Nomos und Physis: Herkunft und Bedeutung einer Antithese im griechischen Denken des 5. Jahrhunderts*. Basel.
Henrichs, A. 1981. 'Human Sacrifice in Greek Religion: Three Case Studies,' in J.-P. Vernant et al. (eds) *Le Sacrifice dans l'antiquité*, pp. 195–235. Entretiens Hardt 27. Geneva.
Herington, C.J. 1984. 'Pindar's Eleventh Pythian Ode and Aeschylus' Agamemnon,' in D. Gerber (ed.) *Greek Poetry and Philosophy: Studies in Honour of Leonard Woodbury*, pp. 37–46. Chico, CA.
— 1985. *Poetry into Drama: Early Tragedy and the Greek Poetic Tradition*. Berkeley/Los Angeles/London.
Heubeck, A. 1949. 'Homerica III. Τιμή,' *Gymnasium* 56, pp. 252–4 (= 1984. *Kleine Schriften zur griechischen Sprache und Literatur*, pp. 203–7. Erlangen.)
— 1979. *Schrift*. Göttingen. (= F. Matz and H.-G. Buchholz [eds] *Archaeologia Homerica. Die Denkmäler und das frühgriechische Epos* 3.10), pp. 109–16.
Heyne, C.G. 1798. *Pindari carmina ex interpretatione Latina emendatiore*. Göttingen.
— 1807. *Pindari carmina et fragmenta* 1. Oxford.
Hill, D.E. 1963. 'Pindar, *Olympian* 8. 37–46,' *CR* n.s. 13.1, pp. 2–4.
Hillard, G. 1966. *Recht auf Vergangenheit: Essays, Aphorismen, Glossen*. Hamburg.
Hubbard, T.K. 1985. *The Pindaric Mind: A Study of Logical Structure in Early Greek Poetry*. Mnemosyne Supplement 85. London.
— 1992. 'Remaking Myth and Rewriting History: Cult Tradition in Pindar's *Ninth Nemean*,' *HSCP* 94, pp. 77–112.
— 1993. 'The Theban Amphiaraion and Pindar's Vision on the Road to Delphi,' *MH* 50, pp. 193–203.

— 1995. 'On Implied Wishes for Olympic Victory in Pindar,' *ICS* 20, pp. 35–56.
Huizinga, J. 1955. R.F.C. Hull (tr.) *Homo Ludens: A Study of the Play-Element in Culture*. Boston.
Hummel, P. 1993. *La syntaxe de Pindare*. Paris.
Huxley, G.L. 1969. *Greek Epic Poetry from Eumelos to Panyassis*. London.
— 1975. *Pindar's Vision of the Past*. Belfast.

Illig, L. 1932. *Zur Form der Pindarischen Erzählung. Interpretationen und Untersuchungen*. Berlin.
Immerwahr, H.R. 1964. 'Book Rolls on Attic Vases,' in C. Henderson (ed.) *Classical, Mediaeval and Renaissance Studies in Honor of Berthold Louis Ullman* 1, pp. 18–48. Rome.

Jachmann, G. 1964. 'Sappho und Catull,' *RhM* 107, pp. 1–33.
Jaeger, W. 1945. G. Highet (tr.) *Paideia. The Ideals of Greek Culture*² 1–3. Oxford. (from the 2nd German ed.)
Janko, R. 1982a. *Homer, Hesiod and the Hymns: Diachronic Development in Epic Diction*. Cambridge.
— 1982b. 'P. Oxy. 2513: Hexameters on the Sacrifice of Iphigeneia?,' *ZPE* 49, pp. 25–9.
— 1984. 'P. Oxy. 2509: Hesiod's Catalogue on the Death of Actaeon,' *Phoenix* 38.4, pp. 299–307.
Jaufmann, A. 1977–8. 'Interpretation einer Pindarode (Olympie III),' *Jahresber. des Bismarck-Gymnasiums Karlsrühe*, pp. 34–41.
Jones, P.V. 1989. 'Iliad 24.649: Another Solution,' *CQ* 39.1, pp. 247–50.
Jebb, R.C. 1892. *Sophocles. The Plays and Fragments Part V: The Trachiniae*. Cambridge.
— 1905. *Bacchylides. The Poems and Fragments*. London
Jeffery, L.H. 1961. *The Local Scripts of Ancient Greece: A Study of the Origin of the Greek Alphabet and its Development from the Eighth to the Fifth Centuries B.C.* Oxford.
Jessen, O. 1916. *RE* 9, s.v. 'Iason.'
Jurenka, H. 1894. *Pindars erste und dritte olympische Ode: Proben einer exegetisch-kritischen Ausgabe*. Vienna.
— 1903. 'Die neuen Bruchstücke der Sappho und des Alkaios,' *Zeitschrift für Österreiches Gymnasien* 53, pp. 290–8.

Kakridis, J.T. 1930. 'Die Pelopssage bei Pindar,' *Philologus* 86, pp. 463–77. (= Calder and Stern 1970, pp. 175–90.)
Kannicht, R. 1969. *Euripides. Helena* 1 and 2. Heidelberg.

Kemp-Lindemann, D. 1975. *Darstellungen des Achilleus in griechischer und römischer Kunst.* Archäologische Studien 3. Bern/Frankfurt.
Kern, O. 1922, repr. 1963. *Orphicorum fragmenta.* Berlin.
Kenyon, F.G. 1987. *The Poems of Bacchylides.* London.
Kirk, G.S. 1970. *Myth: Its Meaning and Functions in Ancient and Other Cultures.* Cambridge, Berkeley/Los Angeles.
— 1974. *The Nature of Greek Myths.* Harmondsworth.
— and Raven, J.E.; Schofield, M. 1983. *The Presocratic Philosophers.*² Cambridge.
— 1985. *The Iliad. A Commentary* 1: *Books I–IV.* Cambridge.
Kirkwood, G.M. 1974. *Early Greek Monody. The History of a Poetic Type.* Cornell Studies in Classical Philology 37. Ithaca/London.
— 1984. 'Blame and Envy in the Pindaric Epinician,' in D.E. Gerber (ed.) *Greek Poetry and Philosophy: Studies in Honour of Leonard Woodbury,* pp. 169–84. Chico, CA.
Knox. B.M.W. 1956. 'The Date of the *Oedipus Tyrannus* of Sophocles,' *AJP* 77, pp. 133–47.
— 1964. *The Heroic Temper: Studies in Sophoclean Tragedy.* Berkeley, CA.
Köhnken, A. 1971. *Die Funktion des Mythos bei Pindar: Interpretationen zu sechs Pindargedichten.* Berlin.
— 1983a. 'Time and Event in Pindar O. 1.25–53,' *Classical Antiquity* 2, pp. 66–76.
— 1983b. 'Mythological Chronology and Thematic Coherence in Pindar's Third Olympian Ode,' *HSCP* 87, pp. 49–63.
— 1985. '"Meilichos Orga." Liebesthematik und aktueller Sieg in der neunten pythischen Ode Pindars' in Entretiens Hardt 31, pp. 71–111.
Koniaris, G.L. 1968. 'On Sappho, fr.31 (L.-P.),' *Philologus* 112, pp. 173–86.
Kraay, C.M. 1976. *Archaic and Classical Greek Coins.* London.
Krappe, A.H. 1942. 'Ἀπόλλων κύκνος,' *CP* 37.4, pp. 353–70.
Kretschmer, P. 1919. 'Mythische Namen,' *Glotta* 10, pp. 38–62.
Krischer, T. 1985. 'Pindars achte Pythische Ode in ihrem Verhältnis zur ersten,' *WS* 19, pp. 115–24.
Kullmann, W. 1960. *Die Quellen der Ilias. Hermes* Einzelschrift 14. Wiesbaden.
Kurke, L. 1990. 'Pindar's Sixth *Pythian* and the Tradition of Advice Poetry,' *TAPhA* 120, pp. 85–107.
— 1991. *The Traffic in Praise: Pindar and the Poetics of Social Economy.* Ithaca/London.

Lanata, G. 1960. 'L'Ostrakon fiorentino con versi di Saffo,' *SIFS* 32, 64–90.

Laroche, E. 1949. *Histoire de la racine NEM- en grec ancien*. Paris.
Latacz, J. 1985. 'Realität und Imagination: Eine neue Lyrik-Theorie und Sapphos φαίνεταί μοι κῆνος-Lied,' *MH* 42, 67–94.
Lattimore, R. 1947. (tr.) *The Odes of Pindar*. Chicago.
— 1948. 'Pindar's Fourth Pythian Ode,' *CW* 42.2, pp. 19–25.
— 1951. (tr.) *Iliad*. Chicago.
— 1955. (tr.) *Euripides. Alcestis*. Chicago.
Lawall, G. 1961. 'The Cup, the Rose, and the Winds in Pindar's *Seventh Olympian*,' *RFIC* 89, pp. 33–47.
Leaf, W. 1912. *Troy: A Study in Homeric Geography*. London.
Lee, M.O. 1965. 'Orpheus and Eurydice: Myth, Legend, Folklore,' *C&M* 26, pp. 403–12.
Lefkowitz, M.R. 1963. 'ΤΩ ΚΑΙ ΕΓΩ: The First Person in Pindar,' *HSCP* 67, pp. 177–253.
— 1973. 'Critical Stereotypes and the Poetry of Sappho,' *GRBS* 14.2, pp. 113–23.
— 1976. *The Victory Ode: An Introduction*. Park Ridge, NJ.
— 1981. *The Lives of the Greek Poets*. Baltimore.
— 1985. 'Pindar's *Pythian* V,' in Entretiens Hardt 31, pp. 33–69.
— 1988. 'Who Sang Pindar's Victory Odes?' *AJP* 109.1, pp. 1–11.
— 1991. *First-Person Fictions: Pindar's Poetic 'I.'* Oxford.
— 1995. 'The First Person in Pindar Reconsidered – Again,' *BICS* 40, pp. 139–50.
Lehnus, L. 1981. *Olimpiche/Pindaro; traduzione, commento, note e lettura critica*. Milan.
Lerza, P. 1982. *Stesicoro: tre studi*. Genoa.
Lesky, A. 1963. *Geschichte der griechischen Literatur*.² Bern/Munich.
Lesky, A. 1966. J. Willis and C. de Heer (trs) *A History of Greek Literature*. New York. (translation of Lesky 1963)
— 1967. 'Die Schuld der Klytaimestra,' *WS* 80, pp. 5–21.
Lévi-Strauss, C. 1963. C. Jacobson and B.G. Schoepf (tr.) *Structural Anthropology*. New York.
— 1968. *Mythologiques III: L'origine des manières de table*. Paris.
— 1978. *Myth and Meaning*. Toronto/Buffalo.
Lind, L.R. 1957. (ed.) *Latin Poetry in Verse Translation*. Boston.
Lindsay, J. 1965. *The Clashing Rocks: A Study of Early Greek Religion and Culture and the Origins of Drama*. London.
Linforth, I.M. 1941. *The Arts of Orpheus*. New York.
— 1963. *Electra's Day in the Tragedy of Sophocles*. Publications in Classical Philology 19.2, pp. 89–125. Berkeley, CA.
Littleton, C.S. 1970. 'Some Possible Indo-European Themes in the *Iliad*' in J. Puhvel (ed.) *Myth and Law Among the Indo-Europeans: Studies*

in Indo-European Comparative Mythology, pp. 229–46. Berkeley/Los Angeles/London.
Livrea, E. 1973. *Apollonii Rhodii Argonauticon: Liber IV: Introduzione, testo critico, traduzione e commento*. Florence.
Lloyd-Jones, H. 1967. 'Heracles at Eleusis,' *Maia* n.s. 19, pp. 209–29 (= *Greek Epic, Lyric, and Tragedy: The Academic Papers of Sir Hugh Lloyd-Jones*, pp. 167–87. Oxford 1990.)
— 1971. *The Justice of Zeus*. Berkeley/Los Angeles.
— 1972. 'Pindar *Fr.* 169,' *HSCP* 76, pp. 45–56.
— 1973. 'Modern interpretations of Pindar: The Second Pythian and Seventh Nemean Odes,' *JHS* 93, pp. 109–37.
— 1982. 'Wagner,' in *Blood for the Ghosts: Classical Influences in the Nineteenth and Twentieth Centuries*, pp. 126–42. Baltimore.
— 1983. 'Artemis and Iphigeneia,' *JHS* 103, pp. 87–102.
— 1985. 'Pindar and the After-Life,' in Entretiens Hardt 31, pp. 245–84.
Lohmann, D. 1970. *Die Komposition der Reden in der* Ilias. Untersuchungen zur antiken Literatur und Geschichte 6. Berlin.
Lowrie, W. 1947. *Art in the Early Church*. New York.

MacLachlan, B. 1989. 'What's Crawling in Sappho,' *Phoenix* 43, pp. 95–9.
Macleod, C.W. 1974. 'Two Comparisons in Sappho,' *ZPE* 15, pp. 217–20.
— 1982. (ed.) *Homer. Iliad Book XXIV*. Cambridge.
Maehler, H. 1982. *Die Lieder des Bakchylides* 1.I and 1.II. *Mnemosyne* Supplement 62. Leiden.
— 1989. *Pindarus* 2. Leipzig.
Mallory, J.P. 1989. *In Search of the Indo-Europeans*. London.
Malten, L. 1911. *Kyrene. Sagengeschichtliche und historische Untersuchungen*. Philologische Untersuchungen 20. Berlin.
March, J.R. 1987. *The Creative Poet: Studies on the Treatment of Myths in Greek Poetry*. BICS Supplement 49. London.
Marcovich, M. 1972. 'Sappho Fr. 31: Anxiety Attack or Love Declaration?' *CQ* 22, pp. 19–32.
Mattusch, C.C. 1988. *Greek Bronze Statuary: From the Beginnings through the Fifth Century B.C*. Ithaca, NY/London.
McEvilley, T. 1971. 'Sappho, Fragment Ninety-Four,' *Phoenix* 25.1, pp. 1–11.
— 1972. 'Sappho, Fragment Two,' *Phoenix* 26, pp. 323–33.
— 1978. 'Sappho, Fragment Thirty-One: The Face Behind the Mask,' *Phoenix* 32.1, pp. 1–18.
McLeod, W. 1987. Review of Kirk 1985. *EMC/CV* 31, n.s. 6.3, pp. 360–5.
Méautis, G. 1962. *Pindare le dorien*. Neuchatel.
Merkelbach, R. 1957. 'Sappho und ihr Kreis,' *Philologus* 101, pp. 1–29.

— and West, M.L. 1967. (eds) *Fragmenta Hesiodea*. Oxford.
Mette, H.-J. 1963. *Der verlorene Aischylos*. Berlin.
Meuli, K. 1921. *Odyssee und Argonautika*. Basel.
— 1960. 'Scythica Vergiliana. Ethnographisches, Archäologisches und Mythologisches zu Vergils Georgica 3, 367 ff.' in *Schweitzer Archiv für Volkskunde* 56, pp. 88–200. (= 1975. *Gesammelte Schriften* 2. Basel.)
Mezger, F. 1880. *Pindars Siegeslieder erklärt*. Leipzig.
Molyneux, J.H. 1992. *Simonides: A Historical Study*. Wauconda, Ill.
Mommsen, T. 1852. (tr.) *Des Pindaros Werke in die Versmasse des Originals*.² Leipzig.
Monro, D.B. and Allen, T.W. 1912. (eds) *Homeri Opera* 5. Oxford.
Morgan, K.A. 1993. 'Pindar the Professional and the Rhetoric of the κῶμος,' *CP* 88, pp. 1–15.
Most, G.W. 1981. 'Sappho Fr. 16.6–7 L-P,' *CQ* n.s. 31, pp. 11–17.
— 1985. *The Measures of Praise: Structure and Function in Pindar's Second Pythian and Seventh Nemean Odes*. Hypomnemata 83. Göttingen.
— 1987. 'Alcman's "Cosmogonic" Fragment (fr. 5 Page, 81 Calame),' *CQ* 37, pp. 1–19.
— 1994. 'Simonides' Ode to Scopas in Contexts,' in I.J.F. de Jong and J.P. Sullivan (eds) *Modern Critical Theory and Classical Literature*, pp. 127–52. *Mnemosyne* Supplement 130. Leiden.
Moyne, J. and Barks, C. 1984. (tr.) *Open Secret: Versions of Rumi*. Putney, VT.
Mullen, W. 1982. *Choreia: Pindar and Dance*. Princeton.
Müller, C.W. 1984. *Zur Datierung des sophokleischen Ödipos*. Mainz: Akademie der Wissenschaften und der Literatur. Wiesbaden.

Nagy, G. 1990. *Pindar's Homer: the Lyric Possession of an Epic Past*. Baltimore/London.
Newman, J.K. 1979. 'The Relevance of the Myth in Pindar's Eleventh Pythian,' *Hellenika* 31, pp. 44–64.
— 1982. 'Pindar, Solon and Jealousy: Political Vocabulary in the Eleventh Pythian,' *ICS* 7.2, pp. 189–95.
Nietzsche, F.W. 1876. *Richard Wagner in Bayreuth*. Schloss-Chemnitz.
Nilsson, M.P. 1906. *Griechische Feste von religiöser Bedeutung*. Leipzig. (repr. Darmstadt 1957)
— 1955, 1967. *Geschichte der Griechische Religion*. 2nd ed. 1955; 3rd ed. 1967. Munich.
— 1949, 1964. F.J. Fielden (tr.) *A History of Greek Religion*.² Oxford. (repr. 1964 New York)
— 1963. *The Mycenean Origins of Greek Mythology*. New York.

Nisetich, F.J. 1980. *Pindar's Victory Songs: Translation, Introduction, Prefaces.* Baltimore/London.
— 1989. *Pindar and Homer.* AJP monographs in Classical philology 4. Baltimore/London.
Norsa, M. 1937. 'Dai papyri della Società Italiana: Versi di Saffo in un ostrakon del sec. ii a. C.,' *Annali della Scuola Normale Superiore di Pisa* ser. 2.6, pp. 8–15.
Norwood, G. 1945. *Pindar.* Sather Classical Lectures 19. Berkeley, CA.

Oates, W.J. 1932. *The Influence of Simonides of Ceos upon Horace.* Princeton.
Oldenburg, H. 1923. *Die Religion des Veda.*[4] Stuttgart/Berlin.
Onians, R.B. 1954. *The Origins of European Thought.*[2] Cambridge.
Ostwald, M. 1965. 'Pindar, *Nomos*, and Heracles (Pindar, frg. 169 [Snell[2]] + POxy. No. 2450, frg. 1),' *HSCP* 69, pp. 109–38.
Owen, E.T. 1946. *The Story of the Iliad, as Told in the Iliad.* Toronto.

Page, D.L. 1951a. (ed.) *Alcman: The Partheneion.* Oxford.
— 1951b. 'Simonidea,' *JHS* 71, pp. 133–42.
— 1955. *Sappho and Alcaeus: An Introduction to the Study of Ancient Lesbian Poetry.* Oxford.
— 1962. (ed.) *Poetae Melici Graeci.* Oxford.
— 1973a. *Folktales in Homer's Odyssey.* Cambridge, MA.
— 1973b. (ed.) *Lyrica Graeca Selecta.* Oxford.
— 1973c. 'Stesichorus: *The Geryoneïs*,' *JHS* 93, pp. 138–54.
— 1973d. 'Stesichorus: The "Sack of Troy" and "The Wooden Horse" (P. Oxy. 2619 and 2803),' *PCPhS* 19, pp. 46–65.
— 1974. *Supplementum Lyricis Graecis.* Oxford.
— 1975. (ed.) *Epigrammata Graeca.* Oxford.
— 1981. (ed.) *Further Greek Epigrams: Epigrams before A.D. 50 from the Greek Anthology and other Sources, not included in "Hellenistic Epigrams" or "The Garland of Philip."* Revised and prepared for publication by R.E. Dawe and J. Diggle. Cambridge/New York.
Palmer, L.R. 1962. 'The Language of Homer,' in Wace and Stubbings 1962, pp. 75–178.
Parker, H.N. 1993. 'Sappho Schoolmistress,' *TAPhA* 123, pp. 309–51.
Parry, A. 1971. (ed.) *The Making of Homeric Verse: The Collected Papers of Milman Parry.* Oxford.
Parsons, P.J. 1977. 'The Lille "Stesichorus,"' *ZPE* 26, pp. 7–36.
Pavese, C.O. 1975. 'La decima e undecima Pitica di Pindaro,' in *Studi Triestini di antichità in onore di Luigia Achillea Stella*, pp. 235–53. Trieste.

— 1992. *Il Grande Partenio di Alcmane*. Amsterdam.
Pedrick, V. 1982. 'Supplication in the *Iliad* and *Odyssey*,' *TAPhA* 112, pp. 125–40.
Pelliccia, H. 1987. 'Pindarus Homericus: *Pythian* 3.1–80,' *HSCP* 91, pp. 39–63.
Péron, J. 1976. 'Pindare et la victoire de Télésicrate dans la IXe Pythique (v. 76–96),' *RPh* 50, pp. 58–78.
— 1987. 'Demi-choeurs chez Alcman: *Parth*. I, v. 39–59,' *Grazer Beiträge* 14, pp. 35–53.
Perrotta, G. 1935. *Saffo e Pindaro: due saggi critici*. Bari.
Perry, B.E. 1937. 'The Early Greek Capacity for Viewing Things Separately,' *TAPhA* 68, pp. 403–27.
Pfeijffer, I.L. 1995. 'Pindar's Eighth Pythian: The Relevance of the Historical Setting,' *Hermes* 123, pp. 156–65.
Pinsent, J. 1969. *Greek Mythology*. London.
Podlecki, A.J. 1984. *The Early Greek Poets and their Times*. Vancouver.
Powell, J.U. 1925. (ed.) *Collectanea Alexandrina: reliquae minores poetarum graecorum aetatis ptolemaicae 323–146 A.C., epicorum, elegiacorum, lyricorum, ethicorum. Cum epimetris et indice nominum.* Oxford.
Privitera, G.A. 1969. 'Ambiguità antitesi analogia nel fr. 31 L.P. di Saffo,' *QUCC* 8, pp. 37–80.
Pschmadt, C. 1911. *Die Sage von der verfolgten Hinde*. Diss. Greifswald.
Puech, A. 1930, 1931. (ed.) *Pindare 1 Olympiques*.² Paris. (2nd ed. rev. from original of 1922.)
Puelma, M. 1977. 'Die Selbstbeschreibung des Chores in Alkmans grossem Partheneion-Fragment (fr. 1P. = 23B, 1D, v. 36–105),' *Museum Helveticum* 34, pp. 1–55.
Puhvel, J. 1970. 'Aspects of Equine Functionality,' in J. Puhvel (ed.) *Myth and Law Among the Indo-Europeans: Studies in Indo-European Comparative Mythology*, pp. 159–72. Berkeley/Los Angeles/London.

Rabel, R.J. 1988. 'Chryses and the Opening of the *Iliad*,' *AJP* 109.4, pp. 473–81.
Rather, L.J. 1979. *The Dream of Self-Destruction: Wagner's Ring and the Modern World*. Baton Rouge, LA.
Rauk, J. 1989. 'Erinna's *Distaff* and Sappho Fr. 94,' *GRBS* 30.1, pp. 101–16.
Reinach, T. and Puech, A. 1937. (eds) *Alcée, Sapho*. Paris.
Ridgeway, W. 1894. 'First Meeting,' *PCPhS* 39, pp. 14–15.
Rilke, R.M. 1930. R. Sieber-Rilke and C. Sieber (eds), *Briefe aus den Jahren 1906 bis 1907*. Leipzig.

Rimmon-Kenan, S. 1983. *Narrative Fiction: Contemporary Poetics*. London.
Robert, C. 1881. *Bild und Lied*. Berlin.
— 1921. (ed.) *Die griechische Heldensage*.⁴ *Griechische Mythologie* von Ludwig Preller Bd. 2. Berlin.
Robertson, D.S. 1940. 'The Food of Achilles,' *CR* 54.4, pp. 177–80.
Rohde, E. 1925. W.B. Hillis (tr.) *Psyche: the Cult of Souls and Belief in Immortality Among the Greeks*. London/New York. (tr. from 8th ed.)
Rose, H.J. 1931. 'Iolaos and the Ninth Pythian Ode,' with note by L.R Farnell, *CQ* 25.3–4, pp. 156–61, and 162–4.
— 1958. *A Handbook of Greek Mythology*⁶. London.
Ruck, C.A.P. and Matheson, W.H. 1968. (tr.) *Pindar: Selected Odes*. Ann Arbor.
Rumpel, J. 1883. *Lexicon Pindaricum*. Stuttgart.

Saake, H. 1971. *Zur Kunst Sapphos*. Paderborn.
— 1972. *Sapphostudien*. Paderborn.
Sandgren, F. 1972. 'Funktion der Reden in Pindars *Pythia* IV,' *Eranos* 70, pp. 12–22.
Sandys, J. 1919. (tr.) *The Odes of Pindar*. Cambridge, MA/London.
Schadewaldt, W. 1928, 1966. *Der Aufbau des Pindarischen Epinikion*. 1st ed. 1928 Halle; 2nd ed. 1966 Tübingen.
— 1950. *Sappho: Welt und Dichtung: Dasein in der Liebe*. Potsdam.
Schefold, K. 1966. *Myth and Legend in Early Greek Art*. London.
— 1978. *Götter- und Heldensagen der Griechen in der spätarchaïscher Kunst*. Munich.
Scheler, M. 1972. (ed.), W.W. Holdheim (tr.) *Ressentiment*.² New York.
Schroeder, O. 1922. *Pindars Pythien*. Leipzig/Berlin.
Schubart, W. 1902. 'Neue Bruchstücke der Sappho und des Alkaios,' *SBBerl*, pp. 195 ff.
— 1907. *Griechische Dichterfragmente. 2 Lyrische und dramatische Fragmente*. Berliner Klassikertexte 5.2. Berlin.
— 1938. 'Bemerkungen zu Sappho,' *Hermes* 73, pp. 297–306.
Schwenn, K. 1940. *Der junge Pindar*. Berlin.
Scodel, R. 1984. 'The Irony of Fate in Bacchylides 17,' *Hermes* 112, pp. 137–43.
Séchan, L. 1926. *Études sur la tragédie grecque*. Paris.
Segal, C.P. 1964. 'God and Man in Pindar's First and Third Olympian Odes,' *HSCP* 68, pp. 211–67.
— 1974. 'Arrest and Movement: Pindar's Fifth Nemean,' *Hermes* 102, pp. 397–411.

— 1976. 'Bacchylides Reconsidered: Epithets and the Dynamics of Lyric Narrative,' *QUCC* 22, pp. 99–130.
— 1977. 'Sophocles' *Trachiniae*: Myth, Poetry, and Heroic Values,' *YClS* 25, pp. 99–158.
— 1983. 'Sirius and the Pleiades in Alcman's Louvre Partheneion,' *Mnemosyne* 36, pp. 260–75.
— 1989. 'Stesichorus' in P.E. Easterling and B.M.W. Knox (eds), *The Cambridge History of Classical Literature* 1: *Greek Literature*, Part 1: 'Early Greek Literature,' pp. 186–201.
Seifert, A. 1982–3. 'Die Rheinhymne und ihr Pindarisches Modell: Struktur und Konzeption von Pythien 3 in Hölderlins Aneignung,' *Hölderlin-Jahrbuch* 23, pp. 79–133.
Seltman, C. 1948. 'The Engravers of the Akragantine Decadrachms,' *NumChron* Ser. 6.8, pp. 1–10.
Setti, A. 1939. 'Sul fr. 2 di Saffo,' *SIFC* n.s. 16, pp. 195–221.
Severyns, A. 1933. *Bacchylide, essai biographique*. Liège.
Sewell, E. 1960. *The Orphic Voice: Poetry and Natural History*. New Haven, CT.
Shorey, P. 1930. 'On Pindar Pyth. IV 96 ff.' *CP* 25, pp. 280–1.
Siegmann, E. 1941. 'Anmerkungen zum Sappho-Ostrakon,' *Hermes* 76, pp. 417–22.
Slater, P.E. 1968. *The Glory of Hera*. Boston.
Slater, W.J. 1969a. *Lexicon to Pindar*. Berlin.
— 1969b. 'Futures in Pindar,' *CQ* n.s. 19, pp. 86–94.
— 1976. 'Symposium at Sea,' *HSCP* 80, pp. 161–70.
— 1977. 'Doubts about Pindaric Interpretation,' *CJ* 72, pp. 193–208.
— 1979. 'Pindar's Myths: Two Pragmatic Explanations,' in G. Bowersock, W. Burkert, M.C.J. Putnam (eds) *Arktouros: Hellenic Studies Presented to Bernard M.W. Knox*, pp. 63–70. Berlin.
— 1983. 'Lyric Narrative: Structure and Principle,' *CA* 2, pp. 117–32.
— 1988. 'Pindar's *Pythian* 3: Structure and Purpose,' *QUCC* n.s. 29.2, pp. 51–61.
Snell, B. 1931. 'Sapphos Gedicht 'Φαίνεταί μοι κῆνος,'' *Hermes* 66, pp. 71–90 = Snell 1966: 82–97.
— 1955. 'Mythos und Wirklichkeit in der griechischen Tragödie,' in *Die Entdeckung des Geistes*³, pp. 95–110. Hamburg.
— 1966. *Gesammelte Schriften*. Göttingen.
— and Maehler, H. (eds) 1970. *Bacchylides. Carmina cum Fragmentis*. Leipzig.
— 1976. *Frühgriechische Lyriker* Vol. 3: *Sappho, Alkaios, Anakreon*. Schriften und Quellen der alten Welt 24.3. Berlin.

— 1987. H. Maehler (ed. with revisions) *Pindarus*[8] vol. 1 Leipzig.
Snyder, J.M. 1989. *The Woman and the Lyre: Women Writers in Classical Greece and Rome.* Carbondale, IL.
Solmsen, F. 1981. 'The Sacrifice of Agamemnon's Daughter in Hesiod's *Ehoeae*,' *AJP* 102, pp. 353–8.
Stanford, W.B. 1974. 'Ulysses in Later Greek Literature and Art,' in W.B. Stanford and J.V. Luce (eds), *The Quest for Ulysses*, pp. 139–59. London.
Stéfos, A. 1975a. *Apollon dans Pindare*. Athens.
— 1975b. 'Les amours d'Apollon dans l'oeuvre de Pindare,' *Platon* 27, pp. 162–81.
Stehle, E. 1996. *Performance and Gender in Ancient Greece. Nondramatic Poetry in its Setting*. Princeton.
Steiner, G. 1961. *The Death of Tragedy*. New York.
— 1967. *Language and Silence: Essays on Language, Literature and the Inhuman*. New York.
Stella, L.A. 1946. 'Studi Simonidei I. Per la cronologia,' *RFIC* n.s. 24, pp. 1–24.
Stern, J. 1971. 'The Structure of Pindar's *Nemean* 5,' *CP* 66, pp. 169–73.
Strauss, W.A. 1971. *Descent and Return: The Orphic Theme in Modern Literature*. Cambridge, MA.
Studniczka, F. 1890. *Kyrene: Eine altgriechische Göttin*. Leipzig.

Taplin, O. 1992. *Homeric Soundings*. Oxford.
Theander, C. 1934. 'Studia Sapphica,' *Eranos* 32, pp. 57–85.
Thompson, S. 1935. *Motif-Index of Folk-Literature*. Bloomington, IA.
Toohey, P. 1987. 'Shades of Meaning in Pindar, *Pythian* 8, 95–7,' *QUCC* 26, pp. 73–87.
Torraca, F. 1926. *Commento alla 'Divina Commedia.'*[6] Rome/Milan.
Treu, M. 1954, 1968. *Sappho* 2nd and 4th eds. Munich.
Turner, E.G. 1968. *Greek Papyri: An Introduction*. Oxford.
Turyn, A. 1929. *Studia Sapphica*. *Eos* Supplement 6. Leopoli.
— 1942. 'The Sapphic Ostracon,' *TAPhA* 73, pp. 308–18.
— 1948. (ed.) *Pindari Epinicia*. Cracow.
— 1952. *Pindari carmina cum fragmentis*.[2] Oxford.
Tsagarakis, O. 1979. 'Some Neglected Aspects of Love in Sappho's fr. 31 LP,' *RhM* 122, pp. 97–118.
Tzedakis, J. 1971. 'Λάρνακες Ὑστερομινωικοῦ Νεκροταφείου Αρμένων Ρεθύμνης,' *AAA* 4, pp. 216–22.

Vallet, G. 1985. 'Pindare et la Sicile,' in Entretiens Hardt 31, pp. 285–320. Geneva.

van Compernolle, R. 1959. *Étude de chronologie et d'historiographie siciliotes*. Brussels/Rome.
van der Kolf, M.C. 1923. *Quaeritur quomodo Pindarus fabulas tractaverit quidque in eis mutarit*. Rotterdam.
van Groningen, B.A. 1960. *La composition littéraire archaïque grecque*. Amsterdam.
Verdenius, W.I. 1972. *Pindar's Seventh Olympian Ode*. Amsterdam.
Vermeule, E. 1966. 'The Boston Oresteia Krater,' *AJA* 70, pp. 1–22.
— 1979. *Aspects of Death in Early Greek Poetry and Art*. Berkeley CA.
— and S. Chapman, 1971. 'A Protoattic Human Sacrifice?' *AJA* 75, pp. 285–93.
Vetta, M. 1982. 'Studi recenti sul primo *Partenio* di Alcman,' *QUCC* n.s. 10, pp. 127–36.
Vidal-Naquet, P. 1968. 'The black hunter and the origin of the Athenian ephebeia,' *PCPhS* n.s. 14, pp. 49–64.
Voigt, E.-M. 1971. *Sappho et Alcaeus*. Amsterdam.
von Kamptz, H. 1982. *Homerische Personennamen*. Göttingen.
von der Mühll, P. 1954. 'Kleine Bermerkungen zu Pindars Olympien,' *MH* 11, pp. 52–6.
— 1964. 'Weitere pindarische Notizien,' *MH* 21, pp. 50–7.
von Wilamowitz-Moellendorff, U. 1900. *Die Textgeschichte der griechischen Lyriker*. Abhand. der Königl. Gesellschaft der Wissenschaften zu Göttingen, Phil.-Hist. Klasse. n.f. 4.3. Berlin.
— 1913. *Sappho und Simonides*. Berlin.
— 1922. *Pindaros*. Berlin.
— 1931. *Der Glaube der Hellenen* 1. Berlin.
Vürtheim, J. 1919. *Stesichoros' Fragmente und Biographie*. Leiden.

Wace, A.J.B. 1929. 'The Lead Figurines' in Dawkins, R.M. (ed.) *The Sanctuary of Artemis Orthia at Sparta*. *JHS* Supplement 5, pp. 249–84.
Wace, A.J.B. and Stubbings, F.H. (eds) 1962. *A Companion to Homer*. London.
Wade-Gery, H.T. and C.M. Bowra, 1928. *Pindar: Pythian Odes*. London.
Wade-Gery, H.T. 1952. *The Poet of the Iliad*. Cambridge.
— 1958. 'Thucydides Son of Melesias,' in *Essays in Greek History*, pp. 239–70. Oxford.
Ward, D.J. 1970. 'The Separate Functions of the Indo-European Divine Twins' in J. Puhvel 1970, pp. 193–202.
Waters, W.K. 1974. 'The Rise and Decline of Some Greek Colonies in Sicily,' *AncSoc* 5, pp. 1–19.

Welcker, F.G. 1845. *Sappho von einem herrschenden Vorurtheil befreit* = *Kleine Schriften* 2. Bonn.
Weinreich, O. 1909. *Antike Heilingswunder: Untersuchungen zum Wunderglauben der Griechen und Römer*. Religionsgeschichtliche Versuche und Vorarbeiten 8.1. Giessen.
Wendel, C. 1958. *Scholia in Apollonium Rhodium Vetera*.[2] Berlin.
— 1914, 1967. *Scholia in Theocritum vetera*. Stuttgart. (repr. 1967)
West, M.L. 1965. 'Alcmanica,' *CQ* 15, pp. 188–202.
— 1966. *Hesiod: Theogony*. Oxford.
— 1970. 'Burning Sappho,' *Maia* 22, pp. 307–30.
— 1971. 'Stesichorus,' *CQ* 21, pp. 302–14.
— 1974. *Studies in Greek Elegy and Iambus*. Untersuchungen zur antiken Literatur und Geschichte 14. Berlin/New York.
— 1975. *Immortal Helen*. London.
— 1978. *Hesiod. Works and Days*. Oxford.
— 1980. *Delectus ex iambis et elegis Graecis*. Oxford.
— 1989. *Iambi et Elegi Graeci ante Alexandrum Cantati* 1.[2] Oxford.
Whitman, C.H. 1958. *Homer and the Heroic Tradition*. Cambridge, MA.
Wiesmann, P. 1972. 'Was heißt κῶμα? Zur Interpretation von Sapphos "Gedicht auf der Scherbe,"' *MH* 29, pp. 1–11.
Willcock, M.M. 1978. *The Iliad of Homer Books I–XII* vol. 1. Oxford.
Williams, F. 1978. *Callimachus: Hymn to Apollo*. Oxford.
Wills, G. 1967. 'Sappho 31 and Catullus 51,' *GRBS* 8, pp. 167–97.
Winkler, J.J. 1990. *The Constraints of Desire*. New York.
Winnington-Ingram, R.P. 1969. 'Pindar's Ninth Pythian Ode,' *BICS* 16, pp. 9–15.
Woodbury, L.E. 1966. 'Equinox at Acragas: Pindar, *Ol.* 2.61–2,' *TAPhA* 97, pp. 598–616 (= *Collected Writings*, 1991, pp. 151–67).
— 1968. 'Pindar and the Mercenary Muse,' *TAPhA* 99, pp. 527–42 (= *Collected Writings* 1991, pp. 188–200).
— 1972. 'Apollo's First Love: Pindar, *Nem.* 7.30 ff.,' *TAPhA* 103, pp. 561–73 (= *Collected Writings*, 1991, pp. 233–43).
— 1982. 'Cyrene and the τελευτά of Marriage in Pindar's Ninth Pythian Ode,' *TAPhA* 112, pp. 245–58 (= *Collected Writings* 1991, pp. 396–409).
— 1985. 'Ibycus and Polycrates,' *Phoenix* 39, pp. 193–220 (= *Collected Writings* 1991, pp. 410–38).
Woodford, S. 1986. *An Introduction to Greek Art*. Ithaca, NY.

Young, D.C. 1964, 1970. 'Pindaric Criticism,' *The Minnesota Review* 4, pp. 584–641 = Calder and Stern 1970, pp. 1–95.

— 1968. *Three Odes of Pindar: A Literary Study of Pythian 11, Pythian 3, and Olympian 7*. *Mnemosyne* Supplement 9. Leiden.
— 1983. 'Pindar *Pythians* 2 and 3: Inscriptional ποτέ and the "Poetic Epistle,"' *HSCP* 87, pp. 31–42.

Zarker, J.W. 1978. 'King Eëtion and Thebe as Symbols in the *Iliad*' in K. Atchity, R. Hogart, and D. Price (eds), *Critical Essays on Homer*, pp. 146–52. Boston.

Zeller, G. 1990. *Die Vedischen Zwillingsgötter. Untersuchungen zur Genese ihres Kultes*. Freiburger Beiträge zur Indologie 24. Wiesbaden.

General Index

Where a note number is given in the indexes the reference is to the note only; page numbers may include references to the notes as well as to the text.

Achilles xvii, 16, 25, 33, 58–71 *passim*, 72–87 *passim*, 168, 172, 184, 185, 186, 187, 197, 198, 205, 207, 222, 229, 234, 235, 237, 242; afterlife of 55, 165n34, 187; and Agamemnon 51, 73–4, 77, 80, 82–4, 85–7, 126, 242; and Ajax 50n171, 51, 168, 170n12; and Apollo 70–1; 73nn3 and 4, 74, 76, 78–80; and Cheiron 35n108, 58–71 *passim*, 172, 197–8, 205, 207, 209; and Chryses 73–5, 78–9, 81–3; on cup (Oltos) 59, 67n34, 68, 182; death of 25, 185, 186; hands of 63–70, 172; and Hector 51, 66, 69, 73n3, 77, 81n26, 82, 84, 87; on kylix (Sosias) 198; medical skill of 61n15, 62, 198n15; and Patroclus 25, 61–2, 67n30, 68, 70, 75, 76, 83, 198n15; and Peleus 58–63, 69n37; and Phoenix 59–61; in Pindar 65–6; and Priam 69–70, 76–7, 79, 84–5, 132, 184; in Simonides 25; spear of 61, 62, 63, 69, 91, 199, 209; and Thetis 58–61 *passim*, 68, 72–87 *passim*, 116n23, 234, 237; in Vergil 69n39

Acragas 66, 153, 154–6, 157–66 *passim*, 179, 183, 189n45, 190, 225n35, 250

Adonis 125, 160n17

Aeacus 167–73, 229, 232, 233

Aegina xvii, 31, 33, 38–49 *passim*, 50, 52, 167, 168n6, 172, 174n23, 229, 231, 233, 235, 236, 237

Agido 4, 5, 89–91 *passim*, 97, 246, 247

Alcaeus viii, 12n37, 103n9, 234n22, 247, 248, 249, 251, 260n17, 267; and Sappho 125, 126, 131, 267. *See also* Index Locorum: Alcaeus

Alcman 1–9 *passim*; and Sappho 128, 132. *See also* Index Locorum: Alcman

Anaxagoras 21

Anacreon 7, 21n66, 133, 141n66, 173, 222n21. *See also* Index Locorum: Anacreon

Aphareus, sons of/Apharetidae xx, 4, 96, 246–7, 251. *See also* Hippocoontidae

Aphrodite vii, 4, 77n15, 91n13, 116, 121–44 *passim*, 202, 243n15, 278n7

GENERAL INDEX

Apollo viii, xvi, xix, 47, 48, 76, 167–71, 173, 197, 199n21, 200, 203–4, 210–19, 225n35; and Bacchylides 56; and Cheiron 202–16 *passim*; and Chryses 73–5, 78; and Cyrene 33, 64–5, 202–16 *passim*; and Delphi 55, 56; god of destruction and healing 70, 71, 78, 211, 212; and music 70; and Orestes 16; and Patroclus 76n13, 79n19; prophetic powers of 17, 18, 76, 169, 171, 173, 212

Arcesilas/Arcesilaus/Arkesilas, king of Cyrene 34, 64, 170, 193–6 *passim*, 199–201 *passim*, 202, 236n30, 251

Archilochus 7, 10, 20, 23, 30, 117n28, 132, 137n53, 200n24. *See also* Index Locorum: Archilochus

Argonauts 34, 170, 193, 194, 201n29, 236, 244n16, 251, 258–60 *passim*, 271, 272n45

Aristeas *Arimaspea* 163

Aristaeus xvi, 203–4, 212–13

Aristarchus 9n24, 58, 59, 75, 90n7, 158, 161

Aristophanes 256. *See also* Index Locorum: Aristophanes

Aristotle 6, 26, 141, 276. *See also* Index Locorum: Aristotle

Artemis 52, 79, 91n13, 128, 134n40, 149n13, 150, 152–3, 162, 185, 220n14

Asclepius xix, 35n108, 60n10, 61, 63n20, 64, 70n42, 173n20, 179–80, 181, 184, 186, 187, 188n42, 197, 198, 201, 205, 209

Aśvins xix, 98, 159n11, 238–53 *passim*

Bacchylides xvi, 2, 18, 19, 20, 24, 27, 29, 30, 33, 47, 49–57 *passim*, 229; paeans 56; and Pindar 24, 49, 50, 52–3, 54, 55, 57; and Simonides 19, 29, 33, 49; and Stesichorus 51, 54, 56. *See also* Index Locorum: Bacchylides

Baudelaire, C. 122, 139n59

Beattie, A.J. 104n12, 168n3, 170n12

Beck, A. 59nn4 and 6, 125n14, 278n8

Bell, J. 229

Bellerophon 222, 272n45

Bernardini, P. 179n13, 229, 231n3

Blegen, C.W. 261

Boeckh, A. 36, 38n123, 145, 145n2, 146n3, 160n16, 168n5, 187, 193nn3 and 6, 194, 195n9, 218n6, 225, 230n3

Böhme, R. 262–3, 266

Bolton, J.D.P. 162–3n27, 163n29

Bowie, E. 25n78, 110, 113, 249n28

Bowra, M. 75n8, 76, 92n18, 101n1, 105n16, 136n50, 150n17, 162n24, 170n12, 193n3, 195n10, 199n20, 222n20, 223, 225, 227, 232, 257n12, 259n16

Brown, C.G. 58, 118, 121, 136n48, 156n40, 165n34

Brown, N.O. 38n122, 260n19

Bundy, E.L. 36, 37, 41, 160, 214n37, 215n38, 225n31

Burkert, W. 10, 11, 70n41, 71n44, 97n37, 98n41, 151n20, 153n27, 159n11, 164n33, 208n21, 240nn5 and 7, 249, 259n16, 266n33, 271

Burnett, A.P. 91n13, 108n1, 109n3, 110, 113, 114n17, 116, 117, 118n30, 123, 131, 134n39, 138, 139n58, 180n17

Burton R.W.B. 157nn1 and 4, 163n29, 180n17, 194n7, 195n10, 196n12, 203, 203n6, 210n24, 221n19

Bury, J.B. 64n23, 199n19, 230n3, 232, 234

GENERAL INDEX 311

Cadmus 239, 242; and Peleus 55, 184, 185, 186, 188n42; daughters of xix, 185, 186, 188n42
Cairns, F. 134
Calchas 74, 80, 84, 167–9, 220
Callimachus 57, 145. *See also* Index Locorum: Callimachus
Campbell, D.A. 1, 5n12, 15n50, 89n2, 90n6, 91n12, 97n36, 109n3, 118, 121n2, 125, 126n18, 134, 136n50, 261n21
Cannatà Fera, M. 184n32
Carey, C. 37n116, 41n136, 180n17
Carne-Ross, D.S. 38n120, 210n25, 234nn19 and 21
Carson, A. vii–ix, 22n69, 118n31, 219n12, 229
Castor 250, 1. *See* Dioscuri
Cazzaniga, I. 150
Chamoux, F. 68n35, 190, 193nn3 and 4, 196n11, 200, 210n24, 215n37
charis 45, 218
Charites. *See* Graces
Cheiron 56, 172, 180, 181, 186n37, 235n24; and Achilles 58–71 *passim*; and Apollo 202–16 *passim*; and Cyrene 202–16 *passim*; as healer xix, 61, 64, 68n35, 69, 70, 180, 198, 199–201, 204, 205, 211n27; and Jason 192–201 *passim*, 205; and Peleus 206; precepts of 66, 197n14; as prophet xvi, 204, 205, 211, 212, 213, 214n37; role in Pindaric odes xvi, xvii, 186n37, 203–4; semi-feral 67, 70, 207–10, 213–15; as teacher viii, xvi, xvii, 35, 58–71 *passim*, 172, 186n37, 192–201 *passim*, 205, 211n27
chorus of maidens 3–6, 7, 27, 89–94, 97, 99, 246, 265. *See also* partheneia
Clytemnestra xvii, 16, 219, 221, 222, 225, 227, 234n22, 239

Coronis xix, 54n178, 99, 171, 175, 179, 181, 184, 185–7, 188, 197, 202
Crete 1, 56, 133, 134n43, 138, 139n58, 166n36
Croesus 21, 54, 55, 163, 196
Cypria 61, 63, 75n10, 82n28, 96, 219, 220n13, 227n42, 244, 246, 251. *See also* Index Locorum: *Cypria*
Cyrene, city 31, 33, 34, 41, 64, 157, 170, 183n27, 193–6, 200, 201, 210n24, 212, 213, 215n37, 216n42, 225n35, 236n30, 250, 251
Cyrene, nymph xvi, 33, 64, 199n21, 202–16 *passim*; Pindaric odes for 202

Damophilos 193–4, 195n10, 200
Danae 23–4
Dante (Durante degli Alighieri) 129, 178, 237n34, 282
Davies, M. 16, 30n89, 89n5, 91n12, 92nn20 and 22, 180n17, 218n8, 245n21
Dawn Goddess xx, 4, 91, 93, 98, 99, 247
Deaneira/Deianira xviii, 54, 277–82
Debussy, C. xv, 122
Denniston, J.D. 119, 219
Detienne, M. 213n31, 272n45
Devereux, G. 101n1, 106n19, 131n30, 146n3, 151, 152n22
Diagoras of Rhodes 52n174, 154
Dionysus 9, 55, 126, 265–6, 272n45, 284n20
Dioscuri xix–xx, 3, 4, 20–1, 95–9, 149n13, 157–9, 160–2, 164, 165, 166, 223n35, 238–53 *passim*, 257, 260. *See also* Index Locorum: Alcman, *Partheneion* 1
Dissen, L. 36, 145n2, 167n2, 169n10, 187, 216n39, 218n5

Dodds E.R. 79n19, 80n22, 146n5, 264, 268n37
Dover, K.J. 101n1, 107n24, 122n3, 223n25
Drachmann, A.B. 28–9n86, 41nn131 and 133, 146n7, 149n13, 150, 151n20, 153n28, 154, 158, 167n1, 168n8, 172n19, 176nn5 and 7, 182n24, 184n31, 185n33, 186n37, 189n45, 192n1, 193n3, 197n13, 198n17, 206n13, 214n37, 217n2, 223n23, 232n11
Drexler, H. 203n3, 210n24
Dronke, P. 268n39
Duchemin, J. 146n3, 155, 196n11, 200n28
Dumézil, G. 241, 242, 243n15
Düring, I. 228

Egan, R.B. 221n19, 223n28, 228n44
Eliot, T.S. 275, 284
Empedocles 153n31, 159n11
epithalamium/epithalamia vii, 123, 125, 130
Eratosthenes 164n29, 265
eros/Eros 7, 132, 133, 279
Escher, J. 206n14
Eurydice 255, 261, 262, 266–70 *passim*, 282
Euripides 24, 85n34, 178n10, 276, 277n6. *See also* Index Locorum: Euripides
Euthymenes 230nn2 and 3, 231, 234, 235, 236

Farnell, L.R. xvii, 38n123, 145n2, 153n28, 159n12, 167n2, 168n5, 173n21, 195n10, 177, 214n37, 217, 220, 221, 226n36, 232, 237n32
Fernández-Galiano, M. 146n2, 169n10
Finley, J.H. 229n1

Fowler, R.L. 74n6, 110n8, 118n31, 119
Fraccaroli, G. 75n10, 76, 78, 110, 145n2, 199n22
Fränkel, H. 123, 158, 159, 160, 199n21, 204n7, 209n23
Franyó, Z. 109n3, 115n20

Gärtner, H.A. 230n2, 232n9, 234n16
Gela 154, 176, 190
Gelon 32n97, 162, 176, 189–90
Gentili, B. xxii, 101n1, 102n6, 105n20, 225, 229
Gerber, D.E. 1, 9n22, 19n56, 27n82, 49n162, 101n1, 156n40, 157, 181n21, 185n33, 200n24, 221n18
Gildersleeve, B.L. 145n2, 153n29, 157n2, 159n12, 168, 170n13, 185, 193nn3 and 5, 194n8, 197, 205n8, 210n25, 215nn37 and 38, 216n41
Gilgamesh, Epic of 260
Gluck, W. 255, 274
Goethe, J.W. 274
Golden, M. 229
Graces 100, 127, 140, 157, 161, 206, 232
Gregory of Nazianus, St viii, xxi, 137–9
Guthrie, W.K.C. 146n3, 205n9, 262–6, 274

Hadas, M. 272n45
Hagesichora 4, 5, 89–94 *passim*, 97, 246, 247
Hardy, T. 140
Heath, M. 30n89, 32n91, 36n111, 37n119, 180n17, 181n21, 188n42
Hector 83n30, 178; and Ajax 177; and Andromache vii, 81, 82, 116, 130, 178n10; and Patroclus 61, 70n40, 76, 77. *See also* Achilles, and Hector
Heimsoeth, F. 150

GENERAL INDEX

Helen as abducted princess 261-2; in Alcaeus 234n22; in the *Cypria* 75n10, 82n28; as goddess 4, 91n13; in Herodotus 16n51; in the *Iliad* 75n10, 77n15, 85, 116, 242; in Sappho 116, 129-30, 139; sister of Castor and Pollux 3n5, 97, 149, 158, 165, 239, 243; in Stesichorus 15-16, 270; at Troy 168n4
Henrichs A. 153n29, 220nn13 and 14
Heracles apotheosis of xviii, xix, 134, 166n36, 275-84 *passim*; in Alcman 3, 95; in Bacchylides 51, 53-4, 56; as hero xix, 67, 163, 214n37, 244n16, 271, 272n45; in Pindar 145-56 *passim*, 157-66 *passim*, 214n37, 249, 250, 251, 279; as shaman 266; in Simonides 20; in Stesichorus 12-15, 18; at Troy 168n4, 169n10; as twin 239n3
Hermary, A. 242n13
Herington, J. 228n46
Hesiod/Hesiodic 12, 16, 24n73, 66, 149n13 197n14, 204, 206n11, 211, 212, 227n42, 245n19, 256, 261, 262. *See also* Index Locorum: Hesiod
Hesperides, garden of 151, 162, 163n27
Heyne, C.G. 146nn3 and 6, 158
Himera 11, 155n39, 162, 179, 189n45
Hilaeira 98, 246; and Phoebe *see* Leucippides
Hippocoontidae xx, 3, 94-9 *passim*, 244, 246-7. *See also* Aphareus, sons of
Hippolyta 233, 235, 237 and n34
Hippolytus 128, 134n40
Hoffmannsthal, H.A.P. von 88
Hölderlin, F. 189n44
Homer xvi, xix, 2, 24nn73 and 75, 58, 77, 81n27, 240, 243, 244, 258, 259, and Alcman 8, 90; and Bacchylides 51, 56; and Hesiod 12, 256, 261, 262; and Pindar 32nn92 and 93, 36n109, 50n171, 60, 66, 67, 71, 169, 173, 177, 178n10, 184, 187, 188n42, 218n7, 221, 222, 234n18; and Sappho 106n22, 114, 116n25, 117, 119, 120, 132; and Stesichorus 10, 11, 14, 16, 17, 18; and Simonides 25. *See also* Index Locorum: Homer
Huizinga, J. 271n44
Hyperboreans xviii, xix, 55, 145-56 *passim*, 159, 162-5

Ibycus 10n26, 12, 29, 106, 256, 257. *See also* Index Locorum: Ibycus
Idas (and Lynceus). *See* Hippocoontidae
Illig, L. 146, 163n29
Indo-European tradition i, 98, 141, 159n11, 240, 241, 242, 245n20, 261, 262, 271
Iphigeneia 16, 153, 220, 227
Ixion 54n178, 175, 202, 206, 218, 223n28

Janko, R. 61n13, 186n36, 220n13
Jason xvi, 222, 192-201 *passim*; as Argonaut 34, 244, 258-60; and Cheiron xvii, 35n108, 64, 172-3, 192-201 *passim*, 205; as hero 222, 271, 272n45; and Medea 268; and Pelias 18, 170; as shaman 259, 260
Jebb, R. 280-1
Jessen, O. 198n16
John of the Cross, St viii, xv, xxi, 136-7
Jurenka, H. 110, 112, 145n2, 150n17

Kakridis, J.T. 145n2, 147
Kirk, G. xvii, 6n15, 67n33, 72n1, 81nn26 and 27, 85n34, 198n16, 208,

27, 208, 214nn34 and 37, 254n2, 260n18, 261n20
Kirkwood, G.M. 118n31, 139n58
Köhnken, A. 34n102, 150, 159n13, 163n28, 162–3n29, 179n13, 221n17

Lee, M.O. xxii–xxiii, 121n2, 254n1, 275
Lampon 230, 231, 234, 235
Lattimore, R. 195n10, 222n20, 263n26, 29n40
Lefkowitz, M. xxi, 28n83, 30n89, 101n1, 103n10, 176n4, 178n10, 179, 180n17, 236n30
Lehnus, L. 146n2, 148, 152n25, 159n13, 169n10, 171n16
Lesky, A. 22n69, 219n9, 227n41
Leucippides 96–8, 246, 247n25
Lévy-Strauss, C. 208, 214, 239nn1 and 2, 271, 272, 273
Libya 199–200, 204, 210, 211, 212, 213, 215nn37 and 38
Linforth, I. 228, 263–4
Lloyd-Jones, H. 33, 54n180, 63n21, 198n18, 204n7, 213n30
Louÿs, P. xv, 122–3
Lynceus (and Idas). *See* Hippocoontidae

Macleod, C.W. 77, 86n37, 130n27, 184n31
McLeod, W.E. 72, 85n34
Maehler, H. 182n25, 230n3, 233n14, 251n32. *See also* Snell, B. and Maehler, H.
Matthews, V.J. 223n27
Maximus of Tyre 141n63
Medea 198, 258 and Jason 268, 282n15; as healer 201n29; prophetic powers of 170, 194, 200n23, 208n19
Merkelbach, R. 101n1, 102n4, 123, 197n14

Mezger, F. 145n2, 146n6, 160, 187n39, 195nn9 and 10
Melesias 33n101, 172–4, 230n3
Mimnermus 14, 23, 116n23. *See also* Index Locorum: Mimnermus
Molyneux, J.H. 19n57, 20n62, 21n64, 25n76, 49n164, 53n175
Mommsen, T. 146n3, 153
Most, G. xxii, 6, 7, 22n69, 33n99, 45n151, 53n176, 130n25, 182n23
Mozart, W.A. xv, xx, xxiii, 118, 203n2, 273–4
Mullen, W. 187n41
Müller, M. 241n9
Muse(s) 6, 25, 34, 36, 42n141, 70, 121–44 *passim*, 226, 228, 233, 235, 265

Neoptolemus 63, 168, 170, 172, 173, 216n42, 229, 277n6, 284n21
Nereids 229–37 *passim*
Newman, J.K. 218n5, 225n34
Nietzsche, F.W. xvii, 122, 275–6, 280
Nilsson, M.P. 61n12, 159n11, 164n32, 240, 242, 261n23, 268n38
Nisetich, F.J. 29n88, 66n28, 146n2, 217n3, 218n5, 253n34
Norsa, M. 133n36, 134n43, 141
Norwood, G. 195n10, 198n18, 200n28, 202n1, 207, 208n17, 214n36, 216n39

Odysseus 59n3, 63, 73n3, 75n10, 77, 80n23, 85n35, 87n37, 218n7, 244, 256, 257, 258, 271, 277n6
Olympia 146, 147, 150, 151n20, 159, 160–6 *passim*, 171, 176, 177, 179, 181n21, 182, 183, 206, 210n24, 219, 223
Orestes 16, 153, 218–28 *passim*, 281n13, 284n21
Orpheus xx, 56, 213n31, 254–74 *passim*

GENERAL INDEX

Orphic/Orphism 262, 263, 264–5, 273, 274
Orthosia 148, 152

Page, D.L. 4n10, 5, 10n27, 12n39, 13, 15nn48 and 49, 19nn56 and 58, 20n63, 24, 26, 27n81, 89nn4 and 5, 91, 92n22, 94, 96n30, 101n1, 102, 104, 106n18, 110n3, 112n14, 113n15, 123, 124n8, 126n17, 133n36, 137n51, 207n16, 246n22, 247n26, 248n27, 258n14, 267n36
Palatine Anthology 26
Paris 78n15, 85, 116n23, 242, 243n15
Parker, H.N. 141n66
partheneion/partheneia 2, 3, 6–8, 27, 28, 50, 88–100 *passim*, 89n2, 128. *See also* chorus of maidens
Pavese, C.O. 5n11, 89nn4 and 5, 91n12, 94n26 and 28, 220n16
Peleiades 5, 91–2
Peleus xix, 7, 33, 50n171, 51, 55, 58–63 *passim*, 69n37, 74n5, 168n4, 170n12, 184, 185, 186, 188n42, 205, 206, 209, 229, 233–7 *passim*, 242
Pelias 12, 18, 170, 193n3, 194, 195, 196, 198n18, 259
Pelops 36n109, 54, 160, 221, 222, 223n28, 230n3, 248
Persephone 15n48, 54, 261, 262, 269
Perseus 24, 106n22, 163, 219, 222, 271
Philoctetes 55, 100n49, 179, 277
Phoebe 4, 99, 246, 247; and Hilaeira *see* Leucippides
Phylacidas 229, 230n3
Pindar xv, xvi, xix, xx, xxi, xxii, 27–49 *passim*, 51, 62, 64, 66, 67, 71, 132, 147, 148, 152, 154, 156, 157, 159, 160, 162, 165, 171, 172, 173, 174n23, 180n15, 195, 196, 202n2, 207, 213n30, 214, 216n39, 222, 224, 225, 226, 231n5, 233, 236n29; and Aeschylus 217–28 *passim*; and Alcman 89n2, 90, 95, 96, 97, 99; and Bacchylides *see* Bacchylides, and Pindar; dialect of 29; epinicians, performed 29–31; and Hieron xviii, xix, 29, 30, 32–3, 40n130, 42n140, 48, 52–5, 154n32, 162, 175–91 *passim*, 197, 226, 250; and Homer 167, 184, 187; paeans 28, 150n15; patrons of 31–4, 175; poetry as choral/monodic xxi, 27, 30–1, 41–3, 180, 183, 236n29; and Simonides 53; and Sophocles 227–8; and Stesichorus 10, 29, 30, 54, 57, 227, 228n46; unity in poems of 36, 43–4, 47–9, 188n42, 204n7, 218n5. *See also* Index Locorum: Pindar
Pinsent, J. 198n16
Plutarch: 1, 49. *See also* Index Locorum: Plutarch
Pollux/Polydeuces/Polydeukes xx, 3, 93, 94, 98, 99, 252–3. *See also* Dioscuri
Proust, M. 129n24
Puech, A. 101nn1 and 2, 146n2, 172n18
Puhvel, J. 241
Pytheas 50, 52, 229–31, 232n7, 233, 234, 235

Rather, L.J. 277n5
Rauk J. 117n28, 118n31
Rhodes 31, 52, 148–9, 154–6, 200
Rilke, R.M. viii, xv, xxi, 131, 270n41
Robert, C. 147n9, 199nn20 and 21, 219n9
Rose, H.J. 148, 268n34
Rumi, J. viii, xxi, 136

Salamis 19, 25, 31, 125
Sandgren, F. 195n10, 198n18
Sandys, J. 145n2, 222n20
Sappho vii–viii, xv, xx–xxi, xxii, 7, 81n26, 101–7, 108–18 *passim*, 119–20, 121–4, 160n17, 267; and Alcaeus *see* Alcaeus, and Sappho; and Alcman *see* Alcman, and Sappho; and Anacreon 141n66; and Aphrodite 121, 123–4, 125, 127–41 *passim*; and Aristotle 121; and Archilochus 117n28; companions of 124–7, 141n66; and Helen *see* Helen, and Sappho; homosexuality in 122, 131; and Ibycus 106; and the Muses 140–1; and Phaon 123; poetry of, publicly performed 127; and Stesichorus 12n37; as teacher 123, 125–8; *thiasos* of 105n20, 110n4, 123–4, 126, 141n66; *See also* Index Locorum: Sappho
Séchan, L. 220n13
Schubart, W. 109–10, 111n10, 139n58, 143
Segal, C.P. 9n25, 17n53, 18n55, 57n186, 91nn14 and 16, 92n17, 146n3, 154n32, 232n9, 235n26, 280n10
Semele 185–6, 187
shaman xx, 259–61, 264, 266, 268, 269
Shorey, P. 196n12
Siegfried 275–84 *passim*
Semonides 23n71. *See also* Index Locorum: Semonides
Simonides 2, 11, 18–27 *passim*, 52–3, 55, 57, 257; and Bacchylides *see* Bacchylides, and Simonides; and elegiac poetry 19, 26–7; and epinicians 19–21; and payment 20–2
Slater, P.E. 41n134, 90n11, 156n40, 160n16, 163nn28 and 29, 176n3,
180n16, 204n7, 205n8, 207n15, 215n38, 222nn20 and 22, 224n29, 249n29
Smith, R.M. 238
Snell, B. 101n2, 102n4, 104n15, 109n3, 115n20, 123, 150n15, 226n37
Snell, B., and Maehler, H. 27n82, 49nn162 and 163, 65, 102n4, 199n20, 230n3, 231n5, 232
Socrates 22, 141n63, 256
Solmsen, F. 220n14
Sophocles xviii, 16, 18, 54, 79n20, 80n24, 100n49, 111n11, 162n27, 173n22, 227, 228, 275–9, 280, 281, 283, 284n21. *See also* Index Locorum: Sophocles
Sparta 1–3, 7, 10, 11, 25, 26, 27, 31, 38, 42, 91, 94, 95, 97, 128, 149, 152, 153, 227, 239, 240, 242n14, 243, 245, 247–50 *passim*
Stesichorus 2, 9–18 *passim*, 29, 30, 51, 54, 56, 85n34, 163n27, 195, 227, 228n46, 270. *See also* Index Locorum: Stesichorus

Tantalus 31, 54n178, 175, 202, 221n18, 223n28
Taplin, O. 244n18
Taygete 148–9, 151n20, 152
Telamon 33, 50n171, 51, 168, 169n10, 170, 174n23, 229, 233, 235–7 *passim*
Telesikrates 33, 171, 202, 210nn24 and 25, 215
Terpander xxi, 10, 11, 267
Thales/Thaletas 1, 21
theoxeny 154, 157–60, 162, 165, 225n35, 242n14
Theron xix, 21n66, 32n97, 33, 55, 153, 154–6, 157, 161, 162, 164–6, 179, 187, 189n45, 190, 208n17, 223, 250

GENERAL INDEX 317

Theseus 24, 56, 63n19, 149n13, 243, 262, 272n45
Thetis xvii, 6, 14, 58, 59, 60–1, 68, 72–87 *passim*, 185, 186n37, 205, 215n37, 233, 234, 235, 237, 242. *See also* Achilles, and Thetis
Thrasybulus 66, 161, 189, 224n28
Thrasydaios/Thrasydaeus 157, 179, 218, 221, 222–3, 224n29, 226
Tlepolemus 148, 154, 156, 236n28
Tsagarakis, O. 101n1, 104nn11 and 12
Tyndareus 3, 95, 96n35, 149n13, 239, 240, 243, 244, 250
Tyndaridae. *See* Dioscuri
Turyn, A. 101n1, 105n19, 138n55, 199n20, 202n1, 215n37, 229n1, 230n3
Typho/Typhoeus 38, 48, 54n178, 169, 175, 202

Valéry, P. 189n44
Vermeule, E. 162n27, 166n36, 218nn8 and 10, 220n13
Vidal-Naquet, P. 210n25
Visser, M. xxiii–xxiv
von Platen, A. 101

Wilamowitz-Moellendorff, U. von 2n3, 8n18, 36, 44n147, 45n152, 47, 71n44, 101n1, 102n4, 104, 105, 109, 110, 122–5, 129n22, 131, 132, 134, 146n3, 150, 157n3, 159n12, 160, 163nn27 and 29, 167n2, 170n13, 175, 182n23, 190, 192, 193n3, 195n10, 208n17, 221, 224, 225, 229n1, 230n3, 232, 251n32
Wagner, R. xviii, xxi, xxiii, 63n21, 275–84 *passim*
West, M.L. 9n23, 11, 19, 25n77, 93n25, 98nn40 and 41, 101n1, 117n28, 126n18, 127n19, 134, 135, 139, 184n30, 197n14, 199n20, 200n24, 240n5, 241n10
Winkler, J.J. 131, 135
Winnington-Ingram, R.P. 215, 216nn39 and 40, 226n36
Woodbury, L.E. xxiii, 10n26, 42n141, 65n26, 156n40, 164n31, 167, 199n21, 210n26, 216n41

Xanthus 16n52
Xenocrates xix, 32n97, 154, 161, 162, 189n45, 223n26, 224n28, 250

Young, D.C. 36, 155n35, 160n18, 175n1, 176n3, 177, 178nn10 and 11, 179n14, 180n18, 188n42, 200n28, 204n7, 216n39, 218, 224, 225

Index Locorum

Entries for the authors listed in this index may also be found in the General Index.

Aeschylus
- *Agamemnon*: 220, 226, 227n31, 250, 275
- *Bassarids*: 265
- *Choephorae*: 226, 227
- Danaid trilogy: 216
- *Eumenides*: 171, 227, 276
- *Oresteia*: 217–28 passim
- *Persae*: 106n22
- *Prometheus Bound / PV*: 63n20, 226n36, 276n2
- *Prometheus Unbound*: 276n2
- *Supplices*: 226n36
- fragment 125 (Mette): 216n40

Alcaeus fragments 6 (V): 249; 34 (Page): 247–8; 34 (V): 260n17; 42 (Lobel-Page): 234n22; 45 (Lobel-Page): 267; 129 (V): 126; 130b: 126; 326 (V): 249; 344.1 (V): 103n9; 384 (Lobel-Page): 131

Alcman fragments 1 (*Partheneion* 1 Page = 3 Calame): xx, 1n1, 3–6, 8n19, 88–99 passim, 246; 2: 245; 3 (*Partheneion* 3 Page = 26 Calame): 6; 5 col. iii (= 81 Calame): 6–7, 247; 5c: 247; 7: 245; 8: 247; 16 (= 8 Calame): 2; 27: 3; 41 (= 143 Calame): 2; 56 (= 125 Calame): 9; 58 (= 147 Calame): 7; 59 (= 148–9 Calame): 7; 89 (= 159 Calame): 8; 145 (= 225 Calame): 1

Anacreon fragments (*PMG*) 358: 7; 376: 133; 391: 173; 398: 133; 413: 7, 133; 419: 222n21

Anthologia Palatina 2.393 ff: 44n148; 7.75: 18; 9.184: 18; 9.189: 126. See also Plato

Apollodorus *Library*
- 1.7.3: 149n13; 1.8.1: 280; 1.9.5: 96n35, 149n13
- 2.4.8: 239n3; 2.5.3: 145n1; 2.5.4: 209n23; 2.5.10: 13n41; 2.5.11: 151n21, 215n37; 2.5.12: 13n42; 2.7.2: 146n6
- 3.9.2: 209n23; 3.10.1: 151n20; 3.10.4: 96n35; 3.10.5: 95; 3.11.1–2: 247n25; 3.11.2: 96; 3.12.6–7: 62n17; 3.13.6: 209; 3.13.7: 198n17

Apollonius of Rhodes *Argonautica*
- 2.1–153: 242n13; 2.498–527a: 206n11; 2.507: 212
- 3.9.2: 209n23; 3.744 ff.: 8n20
- 4.282–7: 163n27; 4.816: 58n2

INDEX LOCORUM

Archilochus fragments 11 (W): 200n24; 13.8 (W): 200n24; 19 (W): 137n53; 91 (W): 7; 168–71: 10; 191: 10; 196 (= Cologne Epode): 117n28
Aristophanes
- *Clouds*: 223n25
- *Frogs*: 256n9
- *Peace*: 16, 21n65
- *Wasps*: 233n13

Aristotle: 26, 141, 276
- *Athenaion Politeia*: 21n66
- *Ethica Nichomachea*: 21n65
- *Poetics*: 56
- *Rhetoric*: 21n65, 121n2

Athenaeus *Deipnosophists*: 7, 124, 143, 21n65

Bacchylides
- *Odes*
  3: 33n99, 52, 54–5, 163, 182n24
  5: 18, 52–4, 176, 179
  11: 52, 149n12
  13: 50, 229
  17: 56, 63n19
- *Dithyrambs* fragments 10: 24; 15–20: 55; 16: 54; 17: 56; 18: 56

Callimachus *Hymns*: 2: 210n24; 3: 145; 5: 185
Catullus *Poem 38*: 24
Clement of Alexandria *Protreptikon* 2.36.2 (Stählin): 95
Cypria
- fragments 3 (Bernabé): 61n16; 4: 126, 127; 5 (Allen): 154, 164n33; 24 (Allen = 32 Bernabé = 26 Davies): 14n44
- *fragmenta dubia*: 58n1

Diodorus Siculus *Historical Library*
- 11.38.7: 176, 189; 11.46: 21n66;

  11.48.3–5: 189; 11.48.8: 155n39; 11.49.1: 178
- 49.3–4: 155n39
- 68.5–7: 189

Eumelus fragment 696 (PMG): 1
Euripides
- *Alcestis*: 269
- *Andromache*: 168n4, 222n21
- *Bacchae*: 9, 272n45
- *Electra*: 219
- *Helen*: 16, 158, 178n10, 239n4, 245
- *Heracles Furens*: 145n1
- *Hippolytus*: 128
- *Iphigeneia at Aulis*: 153
- *Orestes*: 16
- *Phoenissae*: 17–18
- *Troades*: 178n10

Herodotus *Histories*
- 1.23: 1
- 2.113–17: 16n51
- 3.131: 200
- 4.34.2: 150; 4.87.2: 152; 4.103.1: 153; 4.145–67: 34n103
- 7.153: 154; 7.188 ff.: 25; 7.228: 26
- 8.134: 44
- 9.36: 25

Hesiod
- *Aigimos* (attributed to): 58n2
- *Eoiae, Ehoiai*: 179n13, 203, 205–6, 209n23, 227n42
- *Precepts of Cheiron* (attributed to): 197n14
- *Theogony*: 25–7: 70; 27: 228; 201: 106, 133; 748–50: 262; 902: 163n27, 213n33, 228, 262–3
- *Works and Days* 289 ff.: 23
- fragments (M.-W.) 23a: 219, 220; 60: 171n17 220; 209: 206n13; 216 and 217: 212n28; 300: 58n2

Homer
– *Iliad*
  1: 51; 1.1: 70; 1.9: 74; 1.10: 79; 1.13: 83; 1.14: 21; 1.22–3: 79; 1.26–33: 83n32; 1.37: 81; 1.39–41: 73; 1.44: 74; 1.44–7: 79; 1.46: 74; 1.54–6: 79; 1.59–60: 80; 1.64: 74, 78, 79n21; 1.67: 79n20; 1.74: 73; 1.75: 70, 74; 1.97: 79n20; 1.99: 84; 1.100: 81; 1.107: 80; 1.165–6: 67; 1.175: 73; 1.177: 80; 1.178: 77; 1.186: 77; 1.268: 61; 1.353–4: 73; 1.365–92: 73; 1.365–412: 72–87 *passim*; 1.393–412: 73; 1.366–7: 81; 1.371: 83; 1.380: 74; 1.380–2: 73; 1.390: 81; 1.395–6: 58; 1.396: 83n31; 1.404: 74 n6; 1.414–16: 14; 1.473: 70; 1.586 ff.: 74; 1.603: 70
  2.1 ff.: 8; 2.229–31: 84; 2.308–29: 167; 2.323–9: 80n24; 2.354–6: 85n34; 2.489 ff.: 92; 2.690–1: 81; 2.731–2: 60n10; 2.743: 61
  3:39: 77; 3.40: 116n23; 3.56–7: 116n23; 3.159–60: 75n10; 3.170 ff.: 243; 3.173 ff.: 116; 3.174: 85n34; 3.204–24: 75n10; 3.236–8: 243; 3.288–90: 84n33; 3.399: 77; 3.428: 116n23; 3.451–4: 116n23
  4.218: 63; 4.218–19: 60n10, 61, 198
  5.31: 79n20; 5.123: 76; 5.349: 77; 5.432: 69n36; 5.440–2: 76; 5.899 ff.: 70
  6.37 ff.: 85; 6.247: 83; 6.281–2: 116n23; 6.345 ff 116; 6.358: 116n25; 6.407 ff.: 82; 6.414 ff.: 81; 6.423: 83n30; 6.428: 83n31; 6.433–4: 167
  7.270: 99n44; 7.390: 116n23; 7.452–3: 167
  8.15: 263n26; 8.102: 100

  9:117–18: 73; 9.120: 84; 9.129–30: 82n30; 9.145: 227; 9.160: 77; 9.182: 60n11; 9.186: 70; 9.188: 81n27, 83n30; 9.189: 60; 9.194: 70; 9.313: 80; 9.391: 77; 9.419: 69n36; 9.427–30: 80n23; 9.438–45: 59; 9.478–95: 60; 9.485: 60; 9.485–95: 59; 9.496: 60; 9.524: 60; 9.608: 73; 9.650 ff.: 80n23
  10.380: 85n35; 10.383: 86n35
  11.101–10: 85; 11.123 ff.: 85; 11.134: 85; 11.221: 63; 11.765–9: 59n3; 11.769 ff.: 74n5; 11.831–2: 70; 11.832: 59, 61, 198, 208
  12.128–30: 206n12; 12.161: 99n44; 12.322 ff.: 14; 12.438: 76
  13:361–84: 76; 13.769: 77
  14: 126–7
  15.395: 76
  16.54: 77; 16.94: 76; 16.140–4: 61; 16.143–4: 208; 16.153: 83n30; 16:222–4: 74n5; 16.558: 76; 16.570–6: 59, 60; 16.685: 76; 16.700–9: 76; 16.844–50: 76
  17.127: 77; 17.241: 76; 17.575: 83n30; 17.577: 83n30; 17.590: 83n30
  18.23: 68; 18.27: 68; 18.33: 68; 18.55: 59; 18.55–60: 58, 73n5; 18.71: 69; 18.82–5: 61; 18.98: 116n23; 18.317: 68; 18.569: 70n43; 18.604–6: 9n24, 70n43
  19.138: 84; 19.291–4: 81; 19.326 ff.: 63; 19.386 ff.: 69; 19.388–91: 61
  20.92: 81; 20.193–4: 82; 20.371–2: 69; 20.463 ff.: 85n35; 20.468: 85
  21.42–3: 83n30; 21.86–7: 82n29; 21.99–102: 84; 21.475: 83n31
  22.83 ff.: 14; 22.127–8: 69n37; 22.338–54: 84; 22.346: 66; 22.359–60: 71; 22.368: 82; 22.481: 116n23

23.18: 68; 23.144–51: 71; 23.641–2: 69n38; 23.827: 83n30
24.63: 70; 24.133–7: 84; 24.203–5: 77; 24.276: 84; 24.478–9: 69–70; 24.502: 84; 24.506: 69; 24.527–8: 184; 24.560: 83n32; 24.579: 84; 24.605–6: 79; 24.654–5: 87; 24.687: 87; 24.707: 81n26; 24.724: 69; 24.759: 79; 24.764: 116
– *Odyssey*
1: 221; 1.22: 234n20; 1.35–41: 219; 1.168: 63n20
2.312: 114
3.111: 170n13; 3.193–200: 219; 3.310: 219
4.96: 114; 4.663–7: 111n11, 115n21
8: 54; 8.153: 86n37; 8.256–60: 9
9.86: 263; 9.394: 63; 9.414: 63; 9.418 ff.: 63; 9.566: 222n21
11: 234n22; 11.271–80: 17; 11.298–304: 244; 11.603: 134
12.57–72: 257–8; 12.347: 114
17.501: 75
– *Homeric Hymns*
Aphrodite 5: 140n61; 10.2: 129
Apollo 3: 171
Hermes 4: 171
Dioscuri 33: 245, 251
Horace
– *The Art of Poetry* 391–3: 255
– *Epistle* 1.18: 239
– *Odes* 3.27: 24

Ibycus fragments 266 (*PMG*): 106; 267 (*PMG*): 106; 286 (*PMG*): 9, 30, 133; 287 (*PMG*): 7, 8; 166–219 (*SLG*)(= *P. Oxy.* 2735): 12n37

Lucretius *De Rerum Natura* xxi, xxiii
– 1.1 138n56; 1.85: 227n42
– 4.1133–4: 130

Mimnermus fragments (W) 1.2: 116n23; 2: 23n71
Moschus *Lament for Bion*: 268–9

Orphic Argonautica: 257
Orphicorum fragmenta: 263, 265
Ovid *Metamorphoses*
– 3.138: 185
– 8.298–317: 251
– 11.1 ff.: 267
– 13.669 ff.: 24n75

Parmenides fragment B 1.11 (D-K) 263
Pausanias *Description of Greece*
– 1.18.1: 96n34, 247n25; 1.22.6: 237n32
– 2.29.4: 168n6, 174n23; 2.29.9: 62n17, 237n33
– 3.15.3: 95; 3.17.3: 96n34, 147n9; 3.18.11: 96n34, 247n25
– 4.27.1–3: 242n14; 4.31.9: 96n34
– 5.14.2: 164n29
– 8.42.9: 182n24
Philostratus *Gymnasticus*: 233n13
Pindar
– *Isthmians*
1: 250
2: 32n95, 161, 170n13, 182n22, 223n26, 230n3
3: 176n6; 3/4: 28n85, 151, 215n37
4: 225n34
5: 50, 229, 230n3, 231, 235
6: 50, 168, 229, 231, 234n17, 235, 236
7: 230n3
8: 29, 225n34, 226n36, 229, 234, 235n23, 237n32
– *Nemeans*
1: 32, 54, 215n37, 251n33
2: 29, 31

(Pindar *Nemeans* cont'd)
  3: 64, 65, 66, 168, 172–3, 182n22, 186n37, 197, 199, 205, 207, 209, 210, 230n3, 234, 235n23
  4: 7, 29, 33n101, 47, 168, 172, 205, 232n6, 234, 235n23
  5: 33n101, 50, 51, 160, 168n6, 172, 183, 186n37, 229–37 *passim*
  6: 33n101, 172, 173, 230n3, 235n23
  7: 41, 147, 154, 186, 218n7, 229n1, 231n5, 235n23
  8: 35, 235n23
  9: 29, 32, 159, 162, 182n22
  10: 96, 99, 159n11, 162, 163, 164, 216n42, 245n19, 246, 251
  11: 159
– *Olympians*
  1: 29n87, 30, 32, 35n107, 36n109, 52, 54, 135, 156, 160, 161n22, 162, 175, 176, 179, 182n24, 183, 185n33, 186, 187, 188, 202, 221, 222, 223n28, 224, 230n3, 234n20
  2: xix, 30, 32n97, 33, 46, 53, 55, 153, 154–5, 156, 157, 161, 162, 164, 165, 187, 189n45, 208, 222, 224, 234
  3: xvii, xviii, xix, xx, 20, 30, 32n97, 98, 145–56 *passim*, 157–66 *passim*, 170n13, 224, 225n35, 233n15, 250
  4: 30, 157, 181n21
  5: 30, 157, 159
  6: 39n124, 42nn138 and 139, 44, 147n8, 159, 176n6, 198n18
  7: 31, 36n109, 46, 52, 148, 149, 154–5, 156, 160, 200, 214n37, 216n42, 231, 236n28
  8: 32n96, 33n101, 45n154, 167–74 *passim*, 230n3, 231nn4 and 5, 232n6, 235n23
  9: 20, 151, 157, 230n3, 232n12, 236n29
  10: 30, 159, 160, 182n22, 215n38, 230n3, 231n5, 250
  11: 30
  12: 35
  13: 29, 213n33, 222
  14: 29, 35, 157, 181n21, 231n5
– *Paeans*
  4: 49
– *Pythians*
  1: xx, 29, 30, 31, 32 (*PMG*), 39, 40n130, 48, 52, 54n178, 55, 98, 138n56, 159n11, 162, 169, 171, 175, 176, 178, 179, 189n45, 190, 196, 202, 250
  2: 20, 29, 32, 33, 53, 54n178, 175, 176n6, 183n27, 185n27, 202, 206, 217, 218, 223n28, 226, 250
  3: xviii, 29, 32, 33, 35n108, 41n137, 47, 52, 54n178, 64, 99, 149, 171, 173n20, 175–91 *passim*, 197, 202, 205, 207, 209, 234, 235n27
  4: xvi, xx, 18, 29, 30, 31, 34, 35n108, 64, 114, 149, 157, 160n17, 169, 185n35, 192–201 *passim*, 202, 203, 205, 208n19, 222, 236, 251, 257n11, 259
  5: 27, 30, 31, 34, 41, 42, 157, 183n27, 185n27, 193, 200, 202, 211, 213, 225n35, 235n25, 236n30
  6: 29, 32n97, 35n108, 66, 161, 197, 222
  7: 31, 229n1
  8: 28, 32n96, 35, 38–49 *passim*, 159, 183n27, 185n27, 222, 229, 235n23, 236
  9: xvi, 31, 33, 35n108, 64, 171, 179n13, 199n21, 200n23, 202–16 *passim*, 222–3, 226n36, 231
  10: 6, 22n70, 27, 31, 44n149, 150, 153n31, 163, 165, 210n25, 222, 224, 230n3, 231n5

INDEX LOCORUM 323

11: xvii, 31, 157, 160, 163, 164, 217–28 *passim*, 223n28, 231n5, 251n33
12: 29
– fragments
  4: 231n3; 94c: 27; 105: 198n18; 119: 155; 169: 149, 151, 208n19, 215n37; 175: 149; 188: 1; 190: 40; 193: 159; 199: 2; 209: 206n13; 216: 212n28; 217: 212n28; 283: 197n283; 329: 153
Plato
– in *Anthologia Palatina* 9.506: 141
– *Apology*: 256n10
– *Phaedrus*: 15
– *Protagoras*: 22
– *Republic*: 16, 184, 265, 270
– *Symposium*: 270, 272
pseudo-Plato *Hipparchus*: 21n66
Plutarch *Moralia*: 24A–B, 105C, 369C, 473B, and 600D: 184–5n32; 1136B: 150n15
Polyaenus *Stratagems in War* 242n14

Ṛg Veda 1.116.17: 243; 4.43.6: 243; 7.72.1–5: 247

Sappho poems and fragments (Voigt)
– 1: 129, 131, 132, 134, 135-6, 143, 160n17
– 2: 124, 133–44 *passim*
– 5: 140
– 16: 112, 116n24, 127, 129, 130, 132
– 17: 126
– 22: 126
– 29: 126
– 30: 125, 143n73
– 31: xx–xxi, 101–7 *passim*, 112, 132, 135
– 33: 129
– 39: 126
– 44: 111, 127, 130–1

– 47: 7, 132
– 49: 112, 125
– 55: 116n25, 139
– 57: 126
– 58: 140
– 60: 129
– 86: 129
– 92: 126
– 94: 108–18 *passim*, 119–20, 127, 130, 132
– 95: 109, 137
– 96: 109, 117n27, 127, 130, 132, 134n41, 135, 137
– 98: 126
– 101: 126
– 103: 127
– 128: 127, 248n27
– 130: 7, 127, 132
– 134: 129
– 140a: 125
– 147: 116n25
– 150: 140, 141
– 151: 140
– 155: 127
– 159: 133
– 160: 143
– 172: 132
– 193: 140
– 194: 125, 136
– 198: 133
– 201: 106, 133n35
– 208: 127
– 214B (= *P. Colon.* 5860): 125–6
– [3 additional poems from papyrus: 144]
Semonides fragment 1.4 (W): 91n15
Servius (*ad* Virgil *Georgics* 1.14): 212
Simonides fragments: 18–27 *passim*
– 62 (*PMG*): 257; 564 (*PMG*): 11n36; 570 (*PMG*): 163; Hibeh Papyrus 17: 23

Sophocles
- *Antigone*: 277
- *Electra*: 227–8, 284n21
- *Oedipus at Colonus*: 277, 284n21
- *Oedipus the King*: 79 and n20; 277
- *Philoctetes*: 277, 284n21
- *Trachiniae*: 277–81 *passim*, 283, 284
- fragment 956 (Radt): 162n27
Stesichorus fragments: 12–18 *passim*
- 7 (*SLG*): 163n27; 218 (*PMG*): 227; 236 (*PMG*): 186; 507 (*PMG*): 20n63; 509 (*PMG*): 20; 510 (*PMG*): 20; 519 (*PMG*): 20n63; 700 (*PMG*): 227; Lille Papyrus: 9n22, 14, 17 and n53

Stobaeus *Eclogues* 3.10.38: 21

Theocritus *Idylls* 2.38 ff.: 8n20; 2.115: 223n27; 7: 181; 15.143–4: 160n17; 16: 21n68; 22.27–134: 242n13
Theognis *Elegies* 1287–94: 199n21; 1288–91: 209n23
Thucydides *History of the Peloponnesian War*: 3.62–3: 225–6

Virgil
- *Aeneid* 268; 1.487: 69; 4.522: 8n20; 8.276: 164n29
- *Georgics* 1.14: 212; 4.516–27: 266–7

PHOENIX SUPPLEMENTARY VOLUMES

1 *Studies in Honour of Gilbert Norwood*   edited by Mary E. White

2 *Arbiter of Elegance: A Study of the Life and Works of C. Petronius*   Gilbert Bagnani

3 *Sophocles the Playwright*   S.M. Adams

4 *A Greek Critic: Demetrius on Style*   G.M.A. Grube

5 *Coastal Demes of Attika: A Study of the Policy of Kleisthenes*   C.W.J. Eliot

6 *Eros and Psyche: Studies in Plato, Plotinus, and Origen*   John M. Rist

7 *Pythagoras and Early Pythagoreanism*   J.A. Philip

8 *Plato's Psychology*   T.M. Robinson

9 *Greek Fortifications*   F.E. Winter

10 *Comparative Studies in Republican Latin Imagery*   Elaine Fantham

11 *The Orators in Cicero's* Brutus: *Prosopography and Chronology*   G.V. Sumner

12 *Caput and Colonate: Towards a History of Late Roman Taxation*   Walter Goffart

13 *A Concordance to the Works of Ammianus Marcellinus*   Geoffrey Archbold

14 *Fallax opus: Poet and Reader in the Elegies of Propertius*   John Warden

15 *Pindar's* Olympian One: *A Commentary*   Douglas E. Gerber

16 *Greek and Roman Mechanical Water-Lifting Devices: The History of a Technology*   John Peter Oleson

17 *The Manuscript Tradition of Propertius*   James L. Butrica

18 Parmenides of Elea *Fragments: A Text and Translation with an Introduction* edited by David Gallop

19 *The Phonological Interpretation of Ancient Greek: A Pandialectal Analysis*   Vít Bubeník

20 *Studies in the Textual Tradition of Terence*   John N. Grant

21 *The Nature of Early Greek Lyric: Three Preliminary Studies*   R.L. Fowler

22 Heraclitus *Fragments: A Text and Translation with a Commentary*   edited by T.M. Robinson

23 *The Historical Method of Herodotus*   Donald Lateiner

24 *Near Eastern Royalty and Rome, 100–30 BC*   Richard D. Sullivan

25 *The Mind of Aristotle: A Study in Philosophical Growth*   John M. Rist

26 *Trials in the Late Roman Republic, 149 BC to 50 BC*   Michael Alexander

27 *Monumental Tombs of the Hellenistic Age: A Study of Selected Tombs from the Pre-Classical to the Early Imperial Era*   Janos Fedak

28 *The Local Magistrates of Roman Spain*   Leonard A. Curchin

29 Empedocles *The Poem of Empedocles: A Text and Translation with an Introduction*   edited by Brad Inwood

30 Xenophanes of Colophon *Fragments: A Text and Translation with a Commentary*   edited by J.H. Lesher

31 *Festivals and Legends: The Formation of Greek Cities in the Light of Public Ritual*   Noel Robertson

32 *Reading and Variant in Petronius: Studies in the French Humanists and Their Manuscript Sources*   Wade Richardson

33 *The Excavations of San Giovanni di Ruoti, Volume I: The Villas and Their Environment*   Alastair Small and Robert J. Buck

34 *Catullus Edited with a Textual and Interpretative Commentary*   D.F.S. Thomson

35 *The Excavations of San Giovanni di Ruoti, Volume 2: The Small Finds*   C.J. Simpson, with contributions by R. Reece and J.J. Rossiter

36 The Atomists: Leucippus and Democritus *Fragments: A Text and Translation with a Commentary*   C.C.W. Taylor

37 *Imagination of a Monarchy: Studies in Ptolemaic Propaganda*   R.A. Hazzard

38 *Aristotle's Theory of the Unity of Science*   Malcolm Wilson

39 Empedocles *The Poem of Empedocles: A Text and Translation with an Introduction, Revised Edition*   edited by Brad Inwood

40 *The Excavations of San Giovanni di Ruoti, Volume 3: The Faunal and Plant Remains*   M.R. McKinnon, with contributions by A. Eastham, S.G. Monckton, D.S. Reese, and D.G. Steele

41 *Justin and Pompeius Trogus: A Study of the Language of Justin's* Epitome *of Trogus*   J.C. Yardley

42 *Studies in Hellenistic Architecture*   F.E. Winter

43 *Mortuary Landscapes of North Africa*   edited by David L. Stone and Lea M. Stirling

44 Anaxagoras of Clazomenae *Fragments and Testimonia: A Text and Translation with Notes and Essays*   by Patricia Curd

45 *Virginity Revisited: Configurations of the Unpossessed Body*   edited by Bonnie MacLachlan and Judith Fletcher

46 *Roman Dress and the Fabrics of Roman Culture*   edited by Jonathan Edmondson and Alison Keith

47 *Epigraphy and the Greek Historian*   edited by Craig Cooper

48 *In the Image of the Ancestors: Narratives of Kinship in Flavian Epic*   Neil W. Bernstein

49 *Perceptions of the Second Sophistic and Its Times—Regards sur la Seconde Sophistique et son époque*   edited by Thomas Schmidt and Pascale Fleury

50 *Apuleius and Antonine Rome: Historical Essays*   Keith Bradley

51 *Belonging and Isolation in the Hellenistic World*   edited by Sheila L. Ager and Riemer A. Faber

52 *Roman Slavery and Roman Material Culture*   edited by Michele George

53 *Thalia Delighting in Song: Essays on Ancient Greek Poetry*   Emmet I. Robbins, edited by Bonnie MacLachlan